420. MER

D0505595

Learning English
development and diversity

The English Language: past, present and future *course team*

The Open University
Sally Baker (liaison librarian)
Pam Berry (compositor)
Helen Boyce (course manager)
Martin Brazier (cover designer)
David Calderwood (assistant project controller)
Joan Carty (liaison librarian)
Lene Connolly (print buying controller)
Christine Considine (editor)
Anne Diack (BBC producer)
Margaret Dickens (print buying co-ordinator)
Sue Glover (editor)
Sharon Goodman (author/book co-ordinator)
David Graddol (author/book co-ordinator)
Martin Kenward (assistant project controller)
Julie Laing (BBC production assistant)
Avis Lexton (secretary)
Rob Lyon (designer)
Paul Manners (BBC producer)
Gill Marshall (editor)
Janet Maybin (author/book co-ordinator)
Barbara Mayor (author and course manager)
Neil Mercer (author/book co-ordinator)
Ray Munns (cartographer/graphic artist)
Kay Pole (developmental testing co-ordinator)
Pam Powter (course secretary)
Cathy Rosario (editor)
Lynne Slocombe (editor/editorial co-ordinator)
Gill Smith (editor)
Linda Smith (assistant project controller)
Joan Swann (course team chair)
Nikki Tolcher (main compositor)
Iva Williams (BBC production assistant)

External assessor
Professor Peter Trudgill, University of Lausanne

Assessors for this book
Professor Suzanne Romaine, Merton College, University of Oxford
Professor Michael Stubbs, University of Trier, Germany

Developmental testers and critical readers
Kim Beckley
Nigel Blake
Susan Gander
Gilberto Giron
Anthea Fraser Gupta
Lindsay Hewitt
Diana Honeybone
Karen Hovey
Mike Hughes

The four volumes of the series form part of the second level Open University course U210 *The English Language: past, present and future*. If you wish to study this or any other Open University course, details can be obtained from the Central Enquiry Service, PO Box 200, The Open University, Milton Keynes MK7 6YZ.

For availability of the video and audiocassette materials, contact Open University Educational Enterprises Ltd (OUEE), 12 Cofferidge Close, Stony Stratford, Milton Keynes MK11 1BY.

Learning English

development and diversity

Edited by
Neil Mercer and Joan Swann

The Open
University

ROUTLEDGE

LONDON AND NEW YORK

First published 1996
by Routledge
11 New Fetter Lane
London EC4P 4EE

Simultaneously published in the USA and Canada
by Routledge
a division of Routledge, Chapman and Hall, Inc.
29 West 35th Street, New York, NY 10001

Published in association with The Open University

Edited, designed and typeset by The Open University

Printed in Great Britain by Bath Press Colourbooks, Glasgow

A catalogue record for this book is available from the British Library

Library of Congress Cataloguing-in-Publication Data applied for

ISBN 0 415 13122 7 (paper)
ISBN 0 415 13121 9 (hardbound)

Book editors

Neil Mercer is Reader and Director of the Centre for Language and Communications at the Open University School of Education. He is a psychologist with special interests in language use and the process of teaching and learning. He is co-author, with Derek Edwards, of *Common Knowledge: the development of understanding in the classroom* (Methuen/Routledge, 1987) and author of *The Guided Construction of Knowledge: talk amongst teachers and learners* (Multilingual Matters, 1995).

Joan Swann is a lecturer in the Centre for Language and Communications at the Open University School of Education. She has a particular interest in language and gender, and language and educational policy making. She is co-author with David Graddol of *Gender Voices* (Blackwell, 1989), and author of *Girls, Boys and Language* (Blackwell, 1992). She is production chair of the Open University course U210 *The English Language: past, present and future*.

Other original contributors

Dennis Bancroft is a lecturer in psychology in the School of Education at the Open University. For the School's Centre for Human Development and Learning, he has written on children's cognitive and language development and edited a book on some of the implications of work in developmental psychology for the lives of children. His current research investigates the development of children's ability to reason about the temporal concepts of order and duration.

Douglas Barnes was a Reader in Education at the University of Leeds until 1989. His central research interest has been the role played by language in school learning. His books include *From Communication to Curriculum* (1992, 2nd edn, Boynton-Cook, Heinemann, Portsmouth, New Hampshire), and (as co-author) *Language, the Learner and the School* (Penguin, 1971), *Communication and Learning in Small Groups* (Routledge & Kegan Paul, 1977), *Versions of English* (Heinemann, 1984), *School Writing: discovering the ground rules* (Open University Press, 1991) and (most recently) *Communication and Learning Revisited* (Boynton-Cook, Heinemann, Portsmouth, New Hampshire, 1995). Since retirement he has maintained his interest in spoken language in schools through an advisory role in the National Oracy Project and by contributing to publications such as *Thinking Voices* (Norman) and (in the USA) *Cycles of Meaning* (Pierce, Gilles and Barnes).

Tony Bex is senior lecturer in English Language and Linguistics at the University of Kent, Canterbury. Prior to this he was a lecturer at the Universities of Papua New Guinea, Khartoum and Algiers. His main research interests are in genre study and stylistics and he is an assistant editor of the journal *Language and Literature*.

Jill Bourne is a senior lecturer in the Centre for Language and Communications at the Open University School of Education. She has been involved in research, teaching and teacher training in a number of programmes on applied linguistics and the teaching of English to speakers of other languages around the world. She is author of *Moving into the Mainstream: LEA provision for bilingual pupils* (NFER-Nelson, 1989) and co-author of *Partnership Teaching* (HMSO, 1991).

Sue Brindley was a lecturer in education at the Open University, and contributed to the secondary English line of the Open University's PGCE. She has a particular interest in policy and practice in education. She edited *Teaching English* (Routledge, 1994) and is presently researching international perspectives in English teaching. She is currently working as a government officer in education and English.

Christopher Brumfit is a Professor of Education with reference to Language and Linguistics, and Director of the Centre for Language in Education, at the University of Southampton, UK. He is a former Chair of the British Association for Applied Linguistics, and has published many books and papers on language teaching, literature teaching, and language in education. In recent years he has concentrated on the role of explicit knowledge in language teaching, on language policy, and on literature in education. His most recent books include (as coauthor) *Applied Linguistics and English Language Teaching* (Macmillan, 1991), *Teaching Literature: a world perspective* (Macmillan, 1993) and *Language Education in the National Curriculum* (Blackwell, 1995).

Pam Czerniewska was an Open University lecturer in the School of Education. From 1985–1989 she was Director of the National Writing Project and is the author of *Learning About Writing* (Blackwell, 1992). She is now a freelance writer.

Lorraine Dawes is Advisory Teacher for English in the London Borough of Redbridge. Her work focuses on the language and literacy development of primary children, and her publications include *Writing: the drafting process* (NATE, 1995). She chairs an age-range committee of the National Association for the Teaching of English.

Hugh Drummond grew up in England then trained teachers of English as a second language in Mexico for several years. He is currently Professor of Behavioral Ecology in the Centro de Ecologia of the Universidad Nacional Autónoma de Mexico.

Neville Grant is an educational writer specializing in syllabus design and materials development. He has worked in many parts of Africa, the Caribbean, China and the Pacific Basin. He is the author or co-author of many English language textbooks, and is the General Editor of Longman's *Keys to Language Teaching* series.

Anthea Fraser Gupta is senior lecturer in the Department of English Language and Literature at the National University of Singapore. She is primarily a sociolinguist with a particular interest in the acquisition of Singapore English, and in its historical development, an area explored in her book *The Step-Tongue: children's English in Singapore* (Multilingual Matters, 1994).

Elizabeth Hoadley-Maidment is senior lecturer in the School of Health and Social Welfare at the Open University where she is developing English language materials for students preparing to enter the University. Before joining the Open University she worked in adult and further education where she had a particular interest in teaching English as a second language to adults. Her current research interests are in the acquisition of academic writing skills by students on open and distance learning courses.

G.D. Jayalakshmi was brought up in India but came to Britain to undertake research for a PhD on the use of video in the English curriculum of an Indian secondary school. She has maintained an interest in English teaching, and the role of English in education in India. She now works as a BBC producer at the Open University Production Centre, where she produces programmes for the Arts faculty.

Yamuna Kachru is Professor of Linguistics at the University of Illinois at Urbana-Champaign, USA. Her research areas include syntax, semantics and pragmatics of South Asian languages, cross-cultural pragmatics, and contrastive rhetoric. Currently she is working on a book on writing styles across languages and cultures, and co-authoring a book on crosscultural communication in world Englishes.

Barbara Mayor is project officer (English language teaching) in the Centre for Language and Communications at the Open University. She has a particular interest in bilingualism and bilingual education, and has contributed to a variety of courses concerned with both language and equality issues. She is currently researching the possibility of the Open University entering the field of English language teaching to speakers of other languages.

Stuart Middleton, Principal of Aorere College (a co-educational school in which 80 per cent of the 1,200 students are Maori and Pacific Islanders), is President of the New Zealand Association for the Teaching of English. His work has included teaching English in secondary schools, training teachers of English, acting as English teaching consultant to Pacific countries, and being chief examiner for major public examinations in New Zealand. He has spoken and published widely on the relationship between English as a mother tongue and English as a second language, on the education of linguistically diverse groups of students, and on the role of language in learning.

Tony Pugh is on the full-time staff of the Open University School of Education. He is responsible for courses in Yorkshire and is a member of the Centre for Human Development and Learning. He has contributed to several Open University courses on language and chaired *Language in Use* (E263). His research is mainly in reading, from historical and from experimental standpoints. Publications include *Silent Reading* (Heinemann, 1978) as well as several other co-authored and edited books. Much of his recent research has been into eye-movements in reading, in collaboration with researchers in France where, in 1990, he was Visiting Professor at the University of Toulouse le Mirail.

Sylvia Rojas-Drummond was born in Mexico City, Mexico. She studied for her PhD in the USA and is Professor of Psychology at the Universidad Nacional Autónoma de Mexico, where her current research is on the process of teaching and learning in the classroom.

CONTENTS

INTRODUCTION

Joan Swann

The most casual observer cannot fail to be impressed by the rapidity, and apparent facility, with which young children learn language. The topic has also fascinated academic researchers from a range of disciplines, shedding light both on learning processes and on the nature of language itself – how language works and how it is used. In this book our focus in on the acquisition of English, tracing its development from the earliest years, through its formal teaching in schools, to its use as a language of higher education.

At least until recently, much academic knowledge about language learning, and particularly about young children's language, has come from fairly restricted contexts: primarily from the experiences of children growing up in middle-class, monolingual households, often in the USA or the UK. In this book we do consider evidence from such sources, but we also try to represent something of the diverse contexts in which English is learned.

People learn English in different parts of the world, under very different conditions and for different purposes. Many learn English as their 'mother tongue', or first language: somewhere between 320 and 377 million internationally, according to Crystal (1995), depending on whether English-related creoles are included in the total. However, most people who speak English have learned this alongside another language – either as a second language (about 150–300 million) or as a foreign language (a much looser estimate of between 100 and 1,000 million). Commentators such as Kachru (1992) argue that it is these two groups of speakers, with English as their 'other tongue', who have given English its current status as an international language.

> These figures give an indication of the balance between different types of learner, but need to be interpreted with caution. Figures are often based on estimates, they depend on what language varieties are included as 'English', and on what degree of competence you need to have to be regarded as a speaker of English. Chapter 7 of this book contains further discussion of different types of learners in educational contexts. The first book in this series, *English: history, diversity and change* (Graddol et al. (eds), 1996) discusses some of the problems involved in deciding who speaks English.

Distinguishing different types of learner in this way is by no means unproblematical, but because such distinctions are routinely made (in terms of research traditions, as well as teacher training and educational provision) we retain them, to some extent, in the organization of this book. The earlier chapters focus on learning English in the home and community, in 'mother-tongue' and bi- or multilingual contexts; later chapters look at the formal teaching of English, both as a mother tongue (or assumed mother tongue) and as a second or subsequent language.

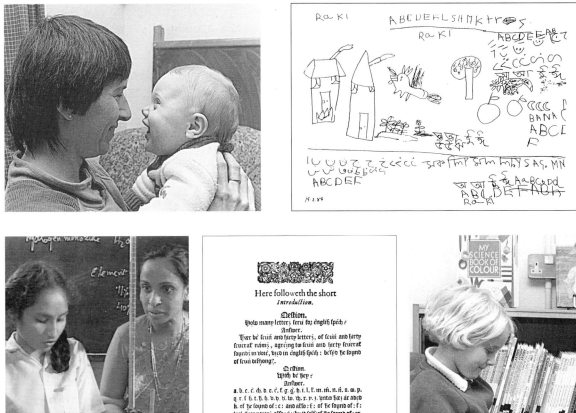

- Chapter 1 considers how young children learn English as their first language. It sees such learning primarily as a collaborative, social activity, in which children learn to use the linguistic forms and structures of English to achieve certain ends.

- Chapter 2 discusses how bi- and multilingual children learn English alongside other languages; and how all children acquire different varieties of English. Children, in effect, acquire a 'repertoire' of language varieties to express different personal and social identities.

- In Chapter 3, the focus is on children's reading and writing. The chapter suggests that literacy, from the earliest years, involves much more than an understanding of the English writing system: children are actively engaged in working out the meaning of literacy in social contexts.

- Chapter 4 is about the use of English as a classroom language, a role in which it can have a powerful influence on older children's language development. The chapter considers the language of different subjects, and the use of English and other languages in the classroom.

- Chapter 5 gives a historical account of English teaching: it is concerned with the changing content of English, and with changing aims and methods of English teaching. It suggests how these may be related to differing social and political events.

- Chapter 6 discusses some recent controversies in English teaching – what varieties of English children should learn, and how early reading and writing should be taught. The chapter focuses both on pedagogical debates and the social and cultural values that underlie them.

- Chapter 7 discusses the teaching of English to speakers of other languages: how English is taught in different contexts, what social positions students are invited to take up through their learning of English, and the effects of English teaching on other languages and cultures.

- Chapter 8 turns to the increasing use of English as a language of higher education: it looks at what students are required to learn under the guise of 'academic English'; and at different approaches to teaching academic genres and discourses.

Although the chapters cover different topics, and the authors themselves have differing academic backgrounds and interests, there are some common threads that run through the book as a whole. Children in the home, and pupils and students in formal education, are all seen as active learners, making hypotheses about the structures of English and how the language is used. Viewing learners in this way suggests that we may need to reinterpret what have traditionally been regarded as 'mistakes' in language use. Such language learning errors can be seen as creative attempts to make sense of English: they also provide vital clues about developing 'learner grammars' of the language.

Throughout the book as a whole we also take a broadly functional approach to language learning; this sees the roots of young children's language development in their pre-verbal behaviour, and suggests that learners at all stages of development are not simply acquiring linguistic structures, but also an ability to use these to perform social acts: to quote Barbara Mayor's discussion in Chapter 2, people learn 'rules of social behaviour and then grammatical rules through which these are realized'. This has implications for the teaching of English: debates about the English curriculum often revolve around the extent to which students should be taught linguistic forms independently of their use in social situations.

Two further points derive from this functional perspective. First, language learning is seen not as an individual matter but as a collaborative enterprise, involving interaction between the learner and parents, family members, friends, teachers and others. And second, children and adults necessarily learn how to behave as a certain kind of person (a child, a girl or a boy, a student, etc.) through their acquisition of English: they take on a set of identities as they learn different aspects of the language.

This link between language and identity lies behind many of the more controversial aspects of the English curriculum. English teaching is not a neutral activity. It can be seen as potentially empowering, giving learners access to powerful language varieties or ways of using language. But it is viewed also as a mechanism for keeping learners firmly in their social place. In characterizing different approaches to English teaching in Chapter 6, Sue Brindley argues 'their advocates often suggest that a version of a future adult (and a future society) is being shaped by the decisions made by the English teacher'.

The book is designed for anyone with a general interest in the learning of English, as well as those with a more specialist interest (such as students, parents or teachers). It can be read independently but it is also one of a series of four books (listed on the back cover) designed for an Open University undergraduate course: U210 *The English Language: past, present and future*. We occasionally refer interested readers to these books, as well as another course book, *Describing Language* (Graddol et al., 1994), for further discussion of topics touched on here.

Most of the core team who have contributed to *Learning English* live and work in Britain: this undoubtedly affects the research we draw on and the aspects of language learning, and educational policies and practices, that we discuss. Through the readings attached to each chapter, however, we have tried to introduce different voices and different perspectives into the debate. We have also tried to make the book accessible to readers from different linguistic and cultural backgrounds. We hope that, whatever interests and experiences readers bring to the book, they will feel able to enter into a critical debate with all of the contributors.

Features of each chapter include:

- *activities*: these provide guidance on the readings or suggestions for tasks to stimulate further understanding or analysis of the material:

- *boxed text*: boxes contain illustrative material or definitions or alternative viewpoints;

- *marginal notes*: these usually refer the reader to further discussion in other parts of the book, or to other books in the series, or to *Describing Language*; where necessary, they are also added to explain conventions used in the text;

- *key terms*: key terms in each chapter are set in bold type at the point where they are explained; the terms also appear in bold in the index so that they are easy to find in the chapters.

1 ENGLISH AS A FIRST LANGUAGE

Dennis Bancroft

1.1 INTRODUCTION

What does it mean to learn a language such as English? The task is such an ordinary one that it's easy to forget it's also quite a remarkable achievement. David Crystal (1995) outlines the knowledge that young language learners need to acquire in order to speak English:

- The 20 or so vowels and 24 or so consonants of a spoken dialect of the language, and over 300 ways of combining these sounds into sequences (such as /s+k+r/ into *scream*, and /m+p+s/ into *jumps*).

- A vocabulary which can evidently reach 50,000 or more active words, and a passive ability to understand about half as many again.

- At least a thousand aspects of grammatical construction, dealing with all the rules – some very general, some very specific – governing sentence and word information.

- Several hundred ways of using the prosodic features of pitch, loudness, speed, and rhythm, along with other tones of voice, to convey meaning: 'it's not what you say, it's the way that you say it'.

- An uncertain (but large) number of rules governing the ways in which sentences can be combined into spoken discourse, both in monologue and dialogue.

- An uncertain (but very large) number of conventions governing the ways in which varieties of the language differ, so that the linguistic consequences of region, gender, class, occupation, and other such factors can be assimilated.

- An uncertain (but even larger) number of strategies governing the ways in which all the above rules can be bent or broken in order to achieve special effects, such as in jokes and poems.

(Crystal, 1995, p. 426)

What is all the more remarkable is the speed with which such knowledge is acquired. Crystal comments that by the time they attend their first school 'most children … give the impression of having assimilated at least three-quarters of all the grammar there is to learn' (1995, p. 428).

This chapter describes the development of young children's ability to speak English and considers how this development is influenced by specific linguistic and cultural factors. The particular perspective on language development that I take in this chapter is this: when young children acquire English, or any other language, they are acquiring a tool for social action. They learn language in social situations where they, and other people, are trying to get things done. Consider, for example, the case of Susie, recorded at the age of 4 years 7 months talking to her babysitter (quoted in Crystal, 1986, pp. 9–10). What does Susie seem to have learned about English?

Susie	Oh, look, a crab. We seen – we were been to the seaside.
Baby-sitter	Have you?
Susie	We saw cr – fishes and crabs. And we saw a jellyfish, and we had to bury it. And we – we did holding crabs, and we – we holded him in by the spade.
Baby-sitter	Did you?
Susie	Yes, to kill them, so they won't bite our feet.
Baby-sitter	Oh.
Susie	If you stand on them, they hurt you, won't they.
Baby-sitter	They would do. They'd pinch you.
Susie	You'd have to – and we put them under the sand, where the sea was. And they were going to the sea.
Baby-sitter	Mhm.
Susie	And we saw some shells. And we picked them up, and we heard the sea in them. And we saw a crab on a lid. And we saw lots of crabs on the sea side. And I picked the – fishes up – no, the shells, and the feathers from the birds. – And I saw a pig.
Baby-sitter	Gosh, that was fun.
Susie	Yes, and I know a story about pigs.
Baby-sitter	Are you going to tell it to me?
Susie	One – one day they went out to build their houses. One built it of straw, one built it of sticks, and one built it of bricks. And he – the little busy brother knowed that in the woods there lived a big bad wolf, he need nothing else but to catch little pigs. So, you know what, one day they went out – and – the wolf went slip slosh slip slosh went his feet on the ground. Then – let me see, er – now I think – he said let me come in, you house of straw. And he said, no no by my hair of my chinny-chin-chin, I will not let you come in. Then I'll huff, and I'll puff, and I'll puff, and I'll blow your house down. So he huffed, and he puffed, and he puffed, and he puffed, and he blew the little straw house all to pieces. Then away went the little brother to his brother's house of sticks …

'–' indicates a pause.

Susie is clearly a competent conversationalist, able to take turns, involve her interlocutor, respond to prompts and questions, etc. Crystal comments on her retelling of 'The three little pigs':

> The story-line … comes from one of her favourite bed-time sagas, and she has evidently been a keen listener. She reproduces several of its phrases very accurately – not only the wolf's words, but some of the story-teller's style, such as 'Away went … ' She also dramatizes the narrative – though you can't tell from the above transcription: 'big bad wolf' is said with long, drawn-out vowels; and the huffing and puffing is accompanied by a great puffing out of the cheeks, and an increased presence, as Susie draws herself up to her full height – all 42 inches of it. You can easily tell, from her version, how her parents must have acted out the story.
>
> On the other hand, this is definitely Susie's story, not the book's. If you compare her words with those of the original, there are all kinds of partial correspondences, but hardly anything is repeated exactly as it was.

For instance, the book does not begin with that opening line; the phrase *the little busy brother* isn't used there; and she puffs far more than the wolf does. Susie may have learned the events of the story off by heart, and several of its words and phrases, but it is largely her own grammar which is stringing them together. It is also very much her style: at the time, the use of the *you know what* and *let me see* were definite 'Susie-isms'.

As you can tell from the pauses and the rephrasings, Susie's speech isn't perfectly fluent. It's rather jerky at times, and sometimes it comes out in such a rush that it's difficult to follow. Her pronunciation, too, is somewhat immature – she says [kwab] for *crab*, for instance, and [bwʌə] for *brother*. And she has the child-like preference for joining sentences using *and* – the commonest linking word among children, from around age 3 onwards. She is also still sorting out some points of grammar, especially in relation to the way verbs are used: she says *knowed* instead of *knew*, *we seen* alongside *we saw*, *we did hold[ing]* instead of *we held*, and there is the interesting *we were been*, with its confusion of tenses.

But the overwhelming impression we receive from the story, as from the whole dialogue, is one of great competence and confidence.

(Crystal, 1986, pp. 10–11)

The linguist Michael Halliday (1973) was one of the first to develop an understanding of language development based on analysis of the functions of utterances. In particular he introduced the valuable, but difficult, notion that a *functional* approach to the development of meanings (i.e. looking at what children learn to do with language) implies a *social foundation* for the development of language. This perspective is very influential among developmental psycholinguists and it has informed the selection of materials in this chapter.

This seems to me to be a plausible start to our journey since it does not constrain us to an investigation of children from the moment they begin to speak, but allows us to explore the possibility that the basis of later language development rests in children's early, preverbal, efforts to make their wishes known.

The chapter has four main sections, dealing in turn with the development of the sounds of language, a child's first words, the beginnings of grammar and finally, as examples of sophisticated usage, the development of humour and narrative skills. Each of these four sections includes some description, some analysis and, where possible, some comparison with children learning a language other than English. The discussion of these four areas is illustrated by examples. Where there are competing explanations, evidence is deployed to identify the most consistent interpretation.

A great deal of research interest in language development in general, and English language development in particular, has come from British and US psychologists. The participants in this research have often been children and families whose first language is a (standard) variety of US English or British English. And when this field of research was developing rapidly during the 1960s and 1970s, it was often the case that the participants in research studies came from a rather restricted range of social and cultural backgrounds (for example, the children studied were often those of researchers or other university personnel). The consequence is that care is needed in making broad generalizations based on these findings, because they may be characteristic only of how English is acquired by the children of particular social groups. You will see, however, that there are some (generally more recent) studies which help overcome this problem, and allow us to identify those aspects of language development that are specifically related to English and those that perhaps characterize early language development more generally.

Children's acquisition of different varieties of English (including standard and nonstandard varieties) and bilingual children's learning of English alongside other languages are explored in the next chapter. Chapter 3 focuses on children learning to read and write in English.

1.2   SOUNDS, EXCHANGES AND GAMES

English makes use of a wide range of sounds. Each of these sounds may be stressed or unstressed and delivered in one of a range of intonations according to the conventions of the particular variety of English being learned. A flexible vocal system over which one has control seems to be an essential attribute of all spoken language users. During the first year of life, infants produce a range of sounds and begin to indulge in vocal play. These sounds will become closer and closer to the distinctive sounds, or **phonemes**, of their language community. Accordingly, this section of the chapter describes how infants play with sound. I also discuss the utility of **intonation** as a device which allows a considerable range of expression even with a limited (one-word) vocabulary.

> Phonemes are the distinctive sounds of a language. The number of phonemes varies from one language to another, and between different varieties of a language. For instance, Scots has a phoneme, the sound at the end of the word *loch*, that is not found in most varieties of English. Children need to learn the set of phonemes that make up their own language variety, as well as how these are pronounced.

For further discussion of the sounds of language, see Describing Language (Graddol et al., 1994).

The section focuses on two questions about children's early production of speech sounds.

1   Are the early sounds made by human infants universally the same? Or do the sounds produced vary with the language community that the child is born into?

2   At what point in this early speech development is there a constructive role for the **caregiver** – the person (or people) who cares for the infant and who therefore provides most of the child's early social and linguistic contact?

The term 'caregiver' is widely used in the literature; the practice is therefore followed in this chapter.

Before we address these questions we need to have some idea of the development of sound production by human infants. Several, rather similar, descriptions have been made; the box below summarizes one by Rachel Stark (1986).

Stages of vocal development

Stage 1: Reflexive crying and vegetative sounds
This is the first stage of sound production and occurs between birth and 8 weeks of age.

Stage 2: Cooing and laughter
From 8 to 20 weeks. Stark reports that these sounds are produced in comfortable states and in response to smiling and talking by the caregiver.

Stage 3: Vocal play
From 16 to 30 weeks. Longer segments of sound are produced which contain variations in pitch and stress as well as other aspects of sound control.

Stage 4: Reduplicated babbling
From 25 to 50 weeks. This is defined as a series of consonant–vowel syllables in which the consonant is the same in every syllable – for example, *dadadada* or *nahnahnah*. Reduplicated babbling does not seem to be used in communication with adults although it may be a part of imitation games towards the end of the first year.

Stage 5: Non-reduplicated babbling
From around the end of the first year infants may produce vowel–consonant–vowel combinations or consonant–vowel–consonant combinations. Within each series the components may vary. Towards the end of this stage, stress and intonation patterns can be imposed on the babbling which can give the babbling a language-like 'feel'.

(Adapted from Stark, 1986, pp. 156–62)

There are several points to note about this description. First, it is offered as a description of the development of *all* children, regardless of language or culture. One might ask whether or not there is evidence from research on infants in a wide variety of language communities to support this description. My own view is that such evidence as is available does support it. Secondly, the list is a description of progressively increasing control by the infant over the sound-making system. Such control is essential for a person to be able to make, consistently, the recognizable sounds of a language. Thirdly, while each 'stage' corresponds to the appearance of a new form of vocalizing, the previous form does not immediately disappear. Fourthly, the last stage in Stark's description occurs just before the infants' early word production. Finally, the fact that the vocal development of infants invariably follows this pattern is evidence that physiological maturation has an important role in speech development.

❖ ❖ ❖ ❖ ❖

Activity 1.1   Playing with sound   *(Allow 5–10 minutes)*

If you are able to enlist the aid of friends and family, do so; but this demonstration works quite well as a solo effort. Choose one word, such as *coffee* or *milk* or *cabbage*, and try saying it to convey the following:

- pleasure;
- disgust;
- resignation;
- request.

Listen carefully to yourself or your friends while you do this task.

Comment

Here is an example of how it is possible to have a one-word vocabulary and yet be capable of a range of different expressions. When infants acquire control over their sound-making equipment in the first months of life they are taking control of a system which may be later used in just the way demonstrated here.

❖ ❖ ❖ ❖ ❖

Are the early sounds made by children universally the same?

It is now time to return to the first of our questions, which was to ask whether the sounds made by human infants are the same for all. That is, even if all children go through the stages of babbling as described by Stark (see box above), do the particular sounds produced vary with the language community that the child is born into (in which English, say, and/or any other language is spoken)? Any review of the research literature on early language development will show that, despite the considerable effort which has been put into research in this field, there is no clear agreement among researchers about the answer to this question.

Some researchers take a 'universalist' line and state that infants start life able to make all the possible speech sounds that a human can make and then cease to make those sounds not found in the particular linguistic environment. In complete contrast, others claim that infants begin with no ability to make sounds other than cries and rely on the environment to provide sounds to learn and copy.

There are also some researchers who support neither of these views, and instead claim that the production of speech sounds depends on a genetically determined programme which is the same for all human children, and that this takes place independently of the linguistic environment provided by their own language community. And yet others uphold what is sometimes called the 'attunement' theory which states that infants start with a basic set of sounds common to all but then build up a repertoire of other sounds found in their own particular environment.

In principle, the validity of each of these conflicting views ought to be testable through observational and experimental research – that is, if suitable data of the sounds infants make were collected from children across a range of different language communities it would be possible to evaluate the competing theoretical positions. But one of the reasons why there is continuing disagreement is that various methods are used to analyse speech data from young children. David Ingram (1989) has identified three methods.

First, researchers may use the International Phonetic Alphabet (IPA) to transcribe children's speech. The IPA consists of a set of standard symbols into which the sounds of any language can be translated. This method works well for describing the sounds of adult languages, but many of the sounds produced in the early months of life do not fit easily into the IPA system, and so subtle differences between the sounds made by children may not be transcribed. Much of the early theorizing about infant sound productions was based on phonetic transcriptions of this problematical kind.

A second, more recently developed, analytic method uses spectrographic analysis. A spectrograph takes a sound signal as its input and translates this to a visual image, termed a spectrogram. This method of representing sounds is more sensitive to subtle differences. Some researchers have used spectrographs to investigate particular sounds, such as vowels, with infants as young as 4 months of age. However, as Ingram notes, spectrograms can be difficult to interpret, especially those representing the sounds produced by very young infants. Researchers relying on spectrographic analysis may also fail to see subtle differences between children from different language backgrounds.

A third method, often used to compare children from different linguistic communities, has been to ask listeners to make global judgements about the similarity of the sounds made by infants after listening to a series of tape recordings (e.g. Atkinsen et al., 1970). In this case, however, great reliance is being placed on the subjective judgements of listeners (often untrained listeners, such as parents).

In conclusion, then, it is difficult to answer the first of our questions with any confidence. Analysing and comparing the sounds produced by young infants is difficult, and interpretations of the evidence differ.

It may help you to understand the nature of this kind of research if I describe one study in more detail. Andrea Levitt and Jennifer Aydelot Utman (1992) conducted a longitudinal study (i.e. a study over a period of time) which compared the sounds produced by one US English-speaking child and one French-speaking child. This study was intended to identify some of the differences between the two languages. Recordings were made of these children at 5 months, 8 months, 11 months and 14 months. Levitt and Utman used both phonetic transcription and the spectrograph in analysing their results.

The reason for comparing a child from a French-speaking community and a child from an English-speaking community was that there are specific and known phonemic differences between the two languages, as well as differences in terms of **prosody** (rhythm and intonation). For example, of the 21 vowel sounds in these varieties of English and French, 8 are shared, 5 occur in English but not in French, and 8 occur in French but not in English. These differences suggest that if the

For a fuller discussion of phonetic description of speech sounds, see *Describing Language* (Graddol et al., 1994).

language environment has an influence on infant babbling then this influence might become apparent in the sounds infants make. Alternatively, if children's physical development is the main influence on the types of sounds produced, then the sounds made by the two infants should be quite similar to each other.

The detailed findings of this study are quite complex; in summary, the analyses show evidence of similar developmental patterns *and* of the influence of adult language.

The sounds produced by the infants were similar in terms of the range of consonants and vowel sounds they produced and in terms of the kinds of consonant sounds they preferred. This similarity is consistent with the idea that infants from different language communities pass through the same stages of phonological development.

But Levitt and Utman also report that effects specific to the language environment began to be identifiable within the recordings made at 11 months. They observe:

> Each infant's phonetic inventory began to resemble that of the adult language both in composition and frequency, so that over the course of time, the two infants' phonetic inventories, in particular their consonantal inventories, diverged.
>
> (Levitt and Utman, 1992, pp. 46–7)

This finding, consistent with other evidence, points to language-specific influences becoming identifiable towards the end of the first year of life – though the acquisition of the full set of phonemes of any variety of English takes very much longer. On the basis of such research, then, a tentative answer to our first question would be that there *is* a relationship between the language environment and a child's early sound-making.

What is the role of a caregiver in early speech development?

We can now move on to consider our second question, which concerns the role of a child's caregivers in influencing the sounds made by the child. It has been the practice in much research in this area to focus on the pair, often termed a **dyad**, consisting of the child and the child's usual caregiver. A great deal of this research has been done in western societies (e.g. the USA and UK) and in middle-class communities where the caregiver is usually the child's mother. In some English-speaking communities, children may also be cared for by other relatives; in fact it seems that any motivated adult could fill the linguistic role assigned to the caregiver.

The sort of evidence described above points to a clear role for the other people with whom the infant has contact. They provide, in speech addressed to the child and in speech to others, the language environment that the infant is able to sample.

Providing experience of the sounds of a language is not the only service rendered to the infant. Many caregiving routines like feeding and bathing give opportunities for predictable exchanges involving language. Even though infants of this age cannot reply, adults and others speak to them as though they can and, by this means, introduce them to a world in which language accompanies and complements most of our doings. One particular kind of exchange between caregiver and child merits more detailed discussion. This is a very common game (sometimes called 'peek-a-boo') played between infant and caregiver in western cultures. The game has many variants but will often involve an adult

Note: in line with the
conventions used elsewhere
in this book, we show
phonemes between slashes,
/p/ etc. This varies from
the original article's
convention.

Learning English phonemes

To master English phonology the child must acquire many different sounds (henceforth phonemes), and one salient characteristic of child phonology is that different phonemes are acquired at different rates. By the age of three children tend to have mastered the vowels, and certain consonants such as plosives (e.g. /p, b/) and nasals (e.g. /m, n/), but they may be in their seventh year before a few troublesome consonants such as the 'th' (/θ/) in *thing* and 'ch' (/tʃ/) in *church* are acquired. Children vary greatly with regard to the rate of acquisition of the different phonemes. [Table 1.1] shows the progress of acquisition, and while the order and particular time schedules may vary, it's unlikely that you will find a child who (for example) masters *sh* (/ʃ/) before *p* (/p/).

Table 1.1   Acquisition of English phonemes

Phonemes	Median age
p, b, m, h, n, w	1;6 (years;months)
k, g, d, t, ŋ	2;0
f, y	2;6
r, l, s	3;0
tʃ, ʃ	3;6
z, dʒ	4;0
θ	4;6
ð	5;0
ʒ	6;0

(Aldridge, 1991, p. 15; adapted from Sanders, 1961, p. 62)

A variety of factors determine the rate at which phonemes are mastered. Visibility is one such factor: sounds produced by visible movement such as front labial sounds like /p/ (where the lips are brought tightly together) are acquired before invisible sounds produced at the back of the mouth like /k/. Another factor is complexity: some sounds are harder to pronounce than others. For example, /t/ is a relatively easy phoneme to articulate since it involves only one movement of the tongue with the alveolar ridge [just behind the top front teeth]; in contrast *ch* (tʃ) is a complex phoneme involving two movements, where the tongue must come into contact with the alveolar ridge but there must also be simultaneous contact of the tongue with the hard palate. Children are therefore likely to acquire /t/ before /tʃ/. Similarly, single consonants will be mastered before consonant clusters, so we would anticipate that the child will correctly articulate /r/ in *red* before /r/ in *street*.

(Aldridge, 1991, p. 15)

attracting the infant's attention and then 'hiding' their eyes behind a book or a hand or something similar. Then follows a sort of dialogue in which the adult may say 'Are you ready?' to which the infant's movements or vocalizations are interpreted as a reply. The question-and-reply sequence is repeated several times until, with the tension becoming almost unbearable, the adult removes the book or hand and says 'Boo!'.

I imagine this kind of interaction (if not exactly this form) will be familiar to most readers. There are several ways in which the interaction is like many other kinds of conversation.

- It involves turn taking. It is not clear in the early months that infants *intend* to make a contribution but adults interpret their behaviour as though they did.
- It is contingent – in other words, each person's turn depends on the prior contribution of the partner.
- The partners share the same purpose and understand the sequence.
- It is pleasurable.

This sort of interaction therefore introduces young children to many of the formal characteristics of conversations a long time before they are able to take part in conversations involving language. Of course, in the exchange I have described it is clear that the caregiver is taking the major part and is interpreting the child's behaviour. Psychologists have studied how the responsibility for initiating the interaction develops over the first year or so; some findings of that research are represented in Figure 1.1.

❖ ❖ ❖ ❖ ❖

Activity 1.2 Interpretation *(Allow 10 minutes)*

Look carefully at Figure 1.1. Make notes to describe the main features of the changes over the first year of life that the graph records. What does this imply for our understanding of the role of the child in development?

Comment

As you can see from Figure 1.1, until the child is about ten months old control over the game rests with the adult. Then, after a brief period of child dominance, the responsibility becomes equally shared between caregiver and child. It is tempting to think that this sort of 'training' makes a considerable contribution to the child's understanding of what it means to be a participant in a conversation.

❖ ❖ ❖ ❖ ❖

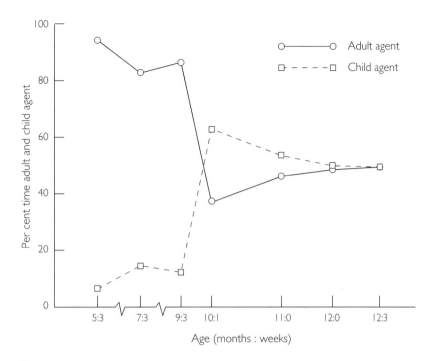

Figure 1.1
Change of control with age over the first twelve months of a particular infant's life
(Adapted from Bruner, 1978, p. 78)

But how universal is this kind of experience, for infants across the world? Remember that psychologists have often collected data from children in their own and related communities (which, as I have said, are usually middle-class communities in countries such as the UK and the USA). Reasoning that 'children are children wherever they are' the psychologists have then commonly made an assumption that the processes they observe are a universal feature of early language experience.

One of the common observations about the sort of speech addressed to children by adults, sometimes termed **child directed speech (CDS)**, is that it is different from the kind of speech addressed to other adults. Caregivers modify their speech in various ways – for example, by giving it a higher pitch, exaggerated intonation and a slower delivery. In fact, it sounds rather like the adult is speaking to a budgerigar! It has also been noted that older children modify their speech to younger children in a roughly similar way. Observations of this kind are so common in western literature that it has been suggested that this 'motherese' speech style plays an essential role in language acquisition. However, if it could be shown that there are cultures where children develop their language successfully and where these western observations do not hold true, then it could not be claimed that 'motherese' is *essential* for language development. Relevant here is the work of Clifton Pye (1986), who describes some of the cultural practices of the Quiché people of central America, who speak one of the indigenous Mayan languages. Pye found that the Quiché caregivers do not modify their speech in the way that western caregivers do, and notes other differences in the amount and kind of vocal interaction:

The mothers are quick to interpret any movement or vocalisation as a signal to feed their babies, which they accomplish without interrupting their own activities. Vocal interaction between infants and parents is minimal, although there is some variation between parents in this regard. They certainly lack any concept of talking with their children for the sake of stimulating their linguistic development. ...

I did not observe Quiché parents engaged in any special games with their children. When I asked them if they knew of any games similar to nursery rhymes or finger games, they said they did not. Children five and over had a large repertoire of games (marbles, string figures, football), but these were not played with younger children.

(Pye, 1986, pp. 86, 91)

Despite this cultural variation in parent–child interaction, Quiché children grow up to be perfectly fluent speakers of their mother tongue.

Research by Shirley Brice Heath (1983), who has observed the language practices of parents and children in different English-speaking communities in south-west USA, is also relevant here. She found that adults in black working-class communities were less likely to use 'baby talk' in their interactions with young children.

It seems, then, that the exchanges often described as characteristic of caregivers and infants and the distinct vocal style that the caregivers adopt are not a universal, or a necessary, feature of early language experience. However, it is still possible that such language practices can *contribute* to language development without being *essential* to it.

❖ ❖ ❖ ❖ ❖

Activity 1.3   *(Reading A)*

Now read 'Language addressed to children: linguistic and cultural variations' by Elena Lieven (Reading A). As you do, note

- questions she finds of interest, and

- the way her questions relate to those which we have been addressing in this chapter.

In Reading A Lieven uses the terms 'dyadic' and 'polyadic' to refer to different types of interaction between people. As before, 'dyadic' refers to interactions or relationships involving two people; 'polyadic', by analogy, refers to more than two people.

Comment

Lieven extends our discussion by describing some of the methodological and other issues which face those interested in this area. In particular, the reading outlines the contrasting poles of the theoretical debate concerning the importance or otherwise of child directed speech. In addition, she refers to the wide range of environments in which language is learned and reinforces the point that much of the research effort has occurred in a relatively small number of cultures. One reason for an interest in the existence and role of 'motherese' or CDS is that if the language addressed to young children can be shown to be structured in a consistent and helpful way *and* infants can be shown to make use of this language, then we will have moved closer to understanding an aspect of the context of language development. To the extent that cultural practices can be shown to vary, the argument for the importance of CDS is challenged.

❖ ❖ ❖ ❖ ❖

In this section I have suggested the following:

- The sounds made by infants have cross-cultural similarities to begin with, but by the end of the first year differences that depend on the specific language environment can be found.

- Infants are clearly sensitive to the language environment provided for them by their caregivers. However, from cross-cultural data, much of caregiver activity may complement development without being essential to it.

- Much preverbal behaviour has conversation-like structure; well before language appears, children know about and have experienced contingent turn taking and a shared focus of attention.

- Some language-related skills are developed very early in life, and can be used for communication in advance of the development of other language skills. A good example here is intonation. Through the use of intonation, children can greatly extend the range of meanings that can be conveyed using only a limited vocabulary.

1.3   WORDS AND THINGS

Our story so far takes us to the point at which an infant has control over a range of sounds and may be using this control selectively – that is, meaningfully. The infant may also have some experience of being a partner in social, communicative interactions. The scene is set for the appearance of a child's first word. But this raises the question of what counts as a word. The first word produced by a child may resemble a word to be found in that child's language environment but, equally, it may not.

Children's early words

At one level, a word is a sound or set of sounds produced consistently and with a consistent meaning. These sounds must be recognized as having significance by at least one other person. In these circumstances, any sound produced by an infant on

Children's early vocabulary development

We can say quite confidently that initially vocabulary development is slow, with children producing about 50 words in the first eighteen months (they may understand five times as many). But from around 21 months a vocabulary growth spurt occurs and during that period the child may acquire about 10 new words per week making the task of word counting increasingly difficult. Thus, rather than talking about the rate of vocabulary growth, it is perhaps more interesting to examine the type of words that are first acquired.

[Listed below are] all the utterances produced by Dewi (19 months) in a twenty-minute recording of his spontaneous speech.

> Blue, book, that, see this, what that, look, blow, bubble, want, quack, drum, in there, down, here bubble, boot, no, big, yeah, car, baby, dog, slide, coat.

These utterances are typically one-word structures, and the lexical items produced are short and concrete, that is to say they denote physical objects (*book, car*), actions (*look, blow*), spatial relations (*in, down*), and attributes (*blue, big*), whereas grammatical words such as determiners (*the, a*), pronouns (*I, he*) and modal verbs (*can, may*) are systematically absent. Clearly, children's early vocabularies contain words that pertain to things and actions that are of immediate relevance to their lives. Why are these concrete words first acquired? Among the many explanations which have been proposed, two points are of particular importance. Firstly, in the speech children hear it is these concrete words which carry the stress, thus perhaps the acoustic salience of these items helps the child to acquire them early. Secondly, the child's main aim is to communicate, and it is precisely these concrete words which carry meaning. For example, we can all understand the meaning of the word 'dog' or 'run' but what does 'can' or 'a' mean? Another example is the use of pronouns. Names are stable: 'Jane' is 'Jane' whoever is talking; in contrast, the meaning of pronouns changes from speaker to speaker: 'a person who is you when I speak, becomes I when he speaks!' Thus the child's early vocabulary consists of concrete words, and it is only gradually, from around the age of two years onwards, that abstract, grammatical words emerge.

(Aldridge, 1991, pp. 16, 17)

Linguists commonly distinguish between lexical (or 'content') items and grammatical items. This distinction is discussed further in the second book of this series, *Using English: from conversation to canon* (Maybin and Mercer (eds), 1996).

a regular and consistent basis and recognized by the child's caregiver could be considered a word. These 'words' may be unrecognizable as words outside of the specific contexts created by a child and caregivers. Establishing the idea of sound-to-meaning correspondence is an important breakthrough in developing language. This development may have its roots in the development of sound control that I have already described. Once a child has started to produce words a repertoire is accumulated, slowly at first but with increasing speed as the child grows.

Developmental psychologists, particularly those from English-speaking countries, have been very interested in children's accumulation of vocabulary and have used language records, among other things, to investigate aspects of children's understanding of language itself; to investigate children's understanding of the meanings of the words they use; and to study some of the factors which may contribute to language development. In this section I will look at two issues. The first is the need to establish a description of early verbal development in terms of

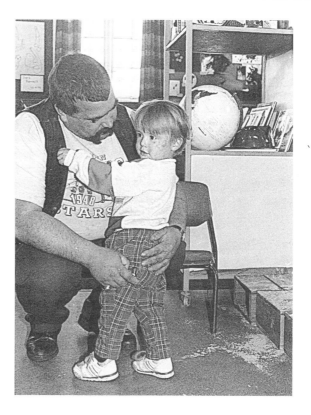

rate of acquisition and age of acquisition. The second issue concerns the role, if any, that caregivers have in the development of vocabulary.

In what follows my focus will be on the role of the *primary* caregiver although of course it is the case that many people may enjoy communicative exchanges with young children. The variety of these exchanges may have useful consequences for a child's language development by increasing the range of talk to which the child is exposed. For example, Barton and Tomasello (1994) have described evidence which shows that (in US English-speaking families) fathers' speech to children, while structurally similar to that of mothers, is characterized by a different range of pragmatic functions.

There have been many descriptive accounts of the acquisition of vocabulary, dating back to the work on the acquisition of German by Otto Preyer in 1882 (an English translation appeared in 1889). The great majority of these accounts, however, are based on studies of language acquisition in English-speaking communities. Except on points of detail the accounts tally quite well, so here we consider the more recent account by Benedict (1979) which traces the vocabulary development of eight children over a six-month period. This might seem a small number of children to study, but the amount of data which an observational study of this kind can gather from just one child is extremely large (Preyer's account was of the development of a single child, his son Axel). Benedict chose a number of children large enough to allow for individual variation and yet small enough to avoid being swamped by large amounts of language data. Table 1.2 summarizes what Benedict found, regarding the children's apparent ability to *comprehend* words and to *produce* words, from when they were aged about 10 months until they were aged about 1 year 9 months.

Table 1.2
Mean age of acquisition (comprehension and production) of 20th, 30th, 40th and 50th words

Comprehension (no. of words)	Mean age (years; months, days)	Production (no. of words)
0	0;10,14	
20	0;11,15	
30	1;0,3	
40	1;0,19	
50	1;1,5	
	1;1,21	0
	1;3,6	20
	1;4,14	30
	1;5,16	40
	1;9,15	50

(Ingram, 1989, p. 142, Table 6.1; adapted from Benedict, 1979)

The last entry in the central column – 1;9,15 – indicates that the average age at which the children had a production vocabulary of 50 words was at 1 year 9 months and 15 days.

❖ ❖ ❖ ❖ ❖

Activity 1.4 Interpreting the data *(Allow 10–15 minutes)*

Look carefully at the information provided in Table 1.2. What is the relation between comprehension and production indicated by these data? Is there a difference in the rate of acquisition between comprehension vocabulary and production vocabulary?

Comment

One obvious interpretation is that the onset of comprehension is about four months in advance of production on these figures. This is consistent with the general developmental phenomenon that perception advances before production and the widely held parental view that infants understand more than they can say. The second point is that, in this early stage of development, it takes longer to acquire words in production than it does in comprehension. Before we leave these data we should note that averaging the data from eight children in the way presented here can disguise individual differences between the children. Although there was a gap between comprehension and production for all the children, the size of this gap varied considerably between individual children.

❖ ❖ ❖ ❖ ❖

Words in use

Having established something of the time and rate of vocabulary development, the next issue concerns the uses to which these words are put. Katherine Nelson (1973) devised a set of semantic categories which has proved useful to students of child language. She identified five categories of words.

1   *Specific nominals.* These words refer to one specific person or thing, e.g. 'Daddy'.
2   *General nominals.* These are words which refer to all members of a category as well as pronouns, e.g. 'doggy', 'ball'.
3   *Action words.* These words accompany or elicit actions, e.g. 'eat', 'give'.

Overextensions and underextensions

A striking aspect of many children's early vocabulary development is the way they overextend a word to refer to objects that lie outside its normal range of application for adults. For example, a child might use the word *doggy* to refer not only to all dogs but also to cows, horses, sheep and cats. The overextension of a particular word may last for some months, but often it occurs only briefly before the child learns the correct names of the objects. Furthermore, the child may overextend only some of his words; others will be used appropriately from the beginning.

The list of overextensions reproduced here is taken from early diary studies in which linguists kept a record of children's words and the first referents of those words.

Child's word	First referent	Extensions	Possible common property
bird	sparrows	cows, dogs, cats, any moving animal	movement
mooi	moon	cakes, round marks on window, round shapes in books, tooling on leather book covers, postmarks, letter O	shape
fly	fly	specks of dirt, dust, all small insects, his own toes, crumbs, small toad	size
koko	cockerel crowing	tunes played on violin, piano, accordion, phonograph, all music, merry-go-round	sound
wau-wau	dogs	all animals, toy dog, soft slippers, picture of old man in furs	texture

In many cases it seems that the child has identified the meaning of the word with only one property of the object: its shape or sound or size. He then uses the word to refer to all objects sharing that property. As the child learns more words, he adds other defining properties to his word meanings to distinguish them from one another. When a child who overextends *doggy* to all four-legged creatures comes to learn the word *cow*, he may add to the property of four-leggedness the requirement that things called *cow* be relatively large and things called *doggy* relatively small. ...

Whereas the overextensions of words are most noticeable in early language, children also underextend some words. The word *animal* is typically applied only to mammals at first. Two-year-olds will deny that some birds, fish and insects are animals or that people can also be called animals. In this sense the range of application of some early words needs to be narrowed down, but the meaning of other words needs to be expanded in the child's vocabulary development.

(de Villiers and de Villiers, 1979, pp. 35–7, 40)

4   *Modifiers.* These words refer to properties or qualities, e.g. 'hot', 'sticky'.
5   *Personal social.* These words express personal states and social relationships, e.g. 'no' and 'bye, bye'.

Nelson's study concerned an analysis of the parental diary records of eighteen children. This began when the children were about 1 year old and continued until the 50th word had been produced. Nelson sorted the words produced by the children into the five categories (plus a spare category for those words which did not fit into the system). In this way she was able to quantify the children's use of each of the five semantic categories of words.

Nelson found that there were two 'styles' of acquisition. The children were either what she termed 'expressive', in that they used few general nominals but a considerable number of personal-social words; or 'referential', in that they used large numbers of general nominals but few personal-social words. The explanations that might account for this difference include the possibility that some children are naturally disposed to focus on naming rather than self-expression; or, alternatively, that it is a matter of variation of parental input, with some parents concentrating on naming and others focusing on self-expression. Nelson took the view that the former possibility was more likely since she found that some children had a 'style' which was different in this respect from that of their parents.

I noted earlier that research has found that, in many (but not all) language communities, caregivers' speech to young children has some particular characteristics (a higher pitch, slower delivery etc.) which make it different from the speech addressed to older children and to adults. Even though the use of such 'baby talk' is not universal, we can ask if there is some relation between the speech style and content addressed to children and their language development. We know that individual children vary in the rate at which they develop vocabularies. We know too that children's language and development appear to vary in a way which Nelson (1973) describes in terms of expressive and referential styles of acquisition, and that this does not appear to be entirely determined by the language style of a caregiver.

To conclude this section I turn to a couple of recent research studies which have addressed the question of the role of (in these cases) maternal speech in early language development. The first of these reports considers the impact of maternal speech on the *rate and style* of development while the second report looks at the relation between maternal speech and children's *use* of words.

June Hampson and Katherine Nelson (1993) have reported a study of 45 US English-speaking mothers and their children. There were 24 female and 21 male children. Each family was visited when the children were aged 13 and 20 months; during these visits video recordings of the children and their mothers were made. The group of children was divided in two ways. One of these was in terms of an expressive/referential distinction very similar to the one I described in relation to Nelson's earlier work. In addition, 36 of the children were placed into two groups of 18 on the basis of their being 'early' or 'late' talkers. The basis for this separation was that 'early' talkers had a vocabulary of at least 15 words on the first visit while the 'late' talkers had a maximum of 7 words. By making these divisions, Hampson and Nelson were able to compare maternal speech to each group in order to identify any aspects of it which assisted either the style (by comparing 'expressive' with 'referential' groups) or rate (by comparing early with late talkers) of the children's language development.

The recordings and other investigations made on each visit were analysed by the researchers who noted, among other things, the number and kind of nouns produced by the children as well as the range of things that the mothers referred to. In addition, the researchers noted the various functions of maternal speech, such as 'requests for information', 'requests for action' and 'statements'. Once this kind of data had been abstracted from the recordings, Hampson and Nelson were able to make some comparison between the mothers of the various groups of children. For example, when the children were 13 months old, they compared the talk of the mothers of the early talkers with that of the mothers of the late talkers during play activities. They found that:

> mothers of linguistically advanced children provided a higher percentage of descriptions and referential repetitions than mothers of the later talkers. In contrast, mothers of the later talkers provided ... more conversational devices and a higher percentage of requests for action than mothers of earlier talkers ... [The] earlier talkers were exposed to a significantly higher percentage of nouns, object references and object nouns than the later talkers.
>
> (Hampson and Nelson, 1993, p. 327)

When the children's performance at 20 months was considered the researchers found that there were some aspects of maternal speech that would predict the amount of speech a child had developed. However, one difficulty with this study and many others is that we are not able to identify cause and effect. It may be that the speech of the mothers of early talkers helped this development *or* it might be the case that these mothers adopted their speech patterns as a result of having a child who was a rapid language learner. There is no evidence currently available which would help us to choose between these two explanations.

The same problem of interpretation exists when we look at the relation between maternal speech and the speech style (expressive vs. referential) adopted by the children. Hampson and Nelson did find that there were some differences between the mothers of these two groups – for example in their use of nouns – although there were many measures on which the mothers of the two groups were similar.

Hampson and Nelson's study was valuable because it identified some of the different characteristics of maternal speech and suggested possible links between those characteristics and the rate of children's language development.

I want to conclude this section with a brief consideration of the uses that children make of words and the impact of maternal speech on this usage. Here I am drawing on research by Barrett et al. (1991), who were working in the UK. They looked at the first ten words produced by each of four children growing up in English-speaking families, and tried to determine the uses to which these words were put. This use was compared to the most frequent maternal use of the same term. There are two points to make. First, there was a very close relationship between the child's first use and the child's mother's use of the words.

> This finding suggests that linguistic input may play an important role in early lexical development, with children deriving their initial use of a word from the most frequently occurring use which is modelled for them in their environment.
>
> (Barrett et al., 1991, p. 22)

Having pointed to this relationship between maternal and child speech these researchers went on to look at the children's subsequent usage of the same words. Here they found an interesting change. The children's *first* use was linked to the maternal example in the great majority of cases (92.5 per cent). In subsequent use this link was greatly weakened, dropping to 58.6 per cent. This suggests that children rapidly move on from the support provided by maternal speech and begin to deploy their new linguistic resources on the basis of their own understanding.

As with taking control of the turn-taking games described earlier, the phenomena described by Barrett et al. point to the active nature of children in taking control of language. This active involvement in language will become more apparent as we move on to consider children's ability to assemble words into grammatical utterances.

I have made the following points in this section:

- First, I have suggested that infants' first words in English may not be recognizable as words of the language, but to count as 'first words' (rather than merely sounds) they must involve the systematic use of a sound (or sounds) to convey meaning.

- Secondly, research has shown that in vocabulary development the ability to understand words precedes the ability to produce words, although there is considerable variation between children in this respect.

- I noted that although much psychological research has assumed that infants are invariably looked after by a mother who talks to them in 'motherese', this is not a universal condition of learning to speak English. However, research has shown that maternal speech to children is related to the speed and style of acquisition of English, although children rapidly begin to deploy words to express their own meanings rather than those modelled for them.

1.4   STRINGING IT TOGETHER

In this section, I first describe the early stages of grammatical development; and then I discuss some of the factors which contribute to that development. Some of what I say is relevant to children's acquisition of any language; but I also deal with the particular consequences of learning English rather than any other language.

I am using **grammar** in this section in the sense of **descriptive grammar** – that is, an attempt to describe the structure and organization in a child's speech which may or may not coincide with grammatical structures used by adults. It follows from this that it is possible to write a grammar (that is, to describe the system) for any stage of a child's language development. We are not concerned here with much of the detail of such grammars, although the term is used in what follows. The important point is that identifying and understanding a system that is being used by a child can be very revealing about what that child understands.

Researchers studying children's grammar have attempted to distinguish a series of developmental stages. Crystal, for instance, identifies several stages running from infancy through to the teenage years (see box). Over the next few pages I discuss children's acquisition of **grammatical items** such as verb inflections (I eat, she eats); plural markers (one cat, two cats); use of the possessive 's' (Anne's book); tense markers (I played); and auxiliary verbs (is, do). I focus here on just two stages of early grammatical development which correspond closely to the *second* and *third* of the stages in the box: a stage in which children use short utterances of two to three words containing no grammatical markers; and the next stage, when children start to add these markers to the words they produce.

A point I made in section 1.1 is again relevant here: research evidence on language acquisition tends to come from a restricted range of social and cultural backgrounds. Evidence of early grammatical development in English has come mainly from speakers learning a standard variety of the language, in which all these markers are present. Other varieties may mark plurality, possession, etc., differently, and children will have a different set of distinctions to learn.

Descriptive grammars simply describe what is there. They have nothing to say about how people *should* speak, or about what counts as 'correct' English. For a discussion of different types of grammar, see *Describing Language* (Graddol et al., 1994).

The first book in this series, *English: history, diversity and change* (Graddol et al. (eds), 1996), discusses variation in English grammar. Chapter 2 in the present book discusses children's development of a 'repertoire' of different varieties and styles of English.

Grammatical development

Grammar learning is a continuous process, but it is possible to spot certain types of development taking place at certain stages, as children grow up in English.

- The earliest stage is hardly like grammar at all, as it consists of utterances which are just one word long, such as *Gone, Dada, Teddy,* and *Hi.* About 60 per cent of these words have a naming function, and about 20 per cent express an action. Most children go through this stage from about 12 to 18 months. It is often called a *holophrastic* stage, because the children put the equivalent of a whole sentence into a single word.

- The next stage looks more like 'real' grammar, because two words are put together to make primitive sentence structures. *Cat jump* or *Cat jumping* seem to express a Subject + Verb construction. *Shut door* seems to express a Verb + Object construction. Other sequences might be more difficult to interpret ([for instance], what could *mummy off* mean … ?), but on the whole we are left with the impression that, by the end of this stage (which typically lasts from around 18 months until 2), children have learned several basic lessons about English word order.

- The next step is the 'filling out' of these simple sentence patterns – adding extra elements of clause structure … and making the elements themselves more complex. The 3-element *Daddy got car* and the 4-element *You go bed now* show this progress, as does (at a more advanced level) *My Daddy put that car in the garage.* To get to this point, and to be able to ring the changes on it (such as by asking a question – *Where daddy put the car?*) takes up much of the third year.

- At around 3 years, sentences become much longer, as children start stringing their clauses together to express more complex thoughts and to tell simple stories. *And* is the word to listen out for at this stage … Other common linking words at this stage are *because* (*'cos*), *so, then, when, if,* and *before.* This stage takes six months or so for the basic patterns of clause sequence to be established.

- This takes us towards the age of 4, when children typically do a great deal of 'sorting out' in their grammar. A child aged $3\frac{1}{2}$ might say *Him gived the cheese to the mouses.* By $4\frac{1}{2}$ most children can say *He gave the cheese to the mice.* What they have done is learn the adult forms of the irregular noun and verb, and of the pronoun. As there are several dozen irregular nouns and several hundred irregular verbs, and all kinds of other grammatical irregularities to be sorted out, it is not surprising that it takes children the best part of a year to produce a level of English where these 'cute' errors are conspicuous by their absence. …

- And after $4\frac{1}{2}$? There are still features of grammar to be learned, such as the use of sentence-connecting features … and complex patterns of subordination … The process will continue until the early teens, especially in acquiring confident control over the grammar of the written language – at which point, the learning of grammar becomes indistinguishable from the more general task of developing an adult personal style.

(Crystal, 1995, pp. 428–9)

Plurality in English

Within any variety of English, aspects of grammar such as plurality and tense are marked in different ways. The notion of **morpheme** is useful here. Morphemes may be defined as the minimal units of analysis of sentence and word structure. A morphemic analysis would divide the word 'cats', for instance, into two morphemes: *cat* (a 'free morpheme', which can stand alone); and *s* (the plural morpheme; this cannot stand alone, it needs to be 'bound' to other morphemes: cats, dogs, horses, etc.).

We often think that, to make a word plural we 'add an s'. But this applies only in the written language. The plural morpheme takes different forms in spoken English: /s/ in *cats*; /z/ in *dogs*; and /ɪz/ in *horses*. Children need to learn such differences. They also need to learn that plurality may sometimes be signalled by a change of form (*mouse* becomes *mice*); or by no change at all (*sheep* stays as *sheep*). Young children often overextend their use of the plural *s*, giving rise to terms such as *sheeps*.

See *Describing Language* (Graddol et al., 1994) for further discussion of morphemes.

At Crystal's second stage, children will not be using grammatical markers. Children at this stage will use nouns, verbs and adjectives and also temporal adverbs (words like *now, soon*, etc.). The expression **telegraphic speech** is often used to describe the language of children in this stage. All the detail and nicety are stripped away, leaving the essential bones. It is also reported that children's imitation of adult speech has this telegraphic character; for example, asking a child to repeat 'I am playing with the dogs' is likely to be met with 'I play dog'.

This example of selective imitation is more than just an instance of tele-graphic speech. The sentence 'I am playing with the dogs' contains six words and includes the plural 's' marker (after *dog*) and the progressive 'ing' ending (to the main verb *play*). All these refinements are stripped away in the child's imitation. There is also the intriguing question of why these three particular words appear in the child's reply, apart from the fact that only one of them – *I* – appears in the adult's sentence. Perhaps you might argue that a child of this age has some memory limit that means only three words can be retained. If this is the case, why does the child not remember just the first three words? – or the last three? The child's answer supports the view that the child is able to scan the whole sentence and to abstract the crucial elements. The child evidently has this ability even though unable to duplicate the production of the sentence.

A conversation

Naomi (N) at $22\frac{1}{2}$ months is in discussion with her mother about a storybook that they have just been reading. Notice here that, as often happens in such conversations, Naomi's mother (M) expands her daughter's telegraphic utterances. (Although the examples here are of a child at stage 2, in fact Naomi was already using the progressive 'ing' form and the plural 's' and so was moving into stage 3.)

M	I go fast asleep
N	Fast asleep
M	Yes he's fast asleep isn't he? What's he got in his bed with him?
N	Elephant
M	An elephant yes and what's this here?
N	Teddy bear

Any record of children in the second of Crystal's stages is likely to contain examples of the following kind:

Allgone sticky; baby drink; look elephant; a more water

The point to note about these examples is that they do not appear to be the kind of utterances that the children will have heard an adult say. If this is so, then these utterances cannot be said to be 'imitations'. The meaning of such examples will be clear enough in context, so they can be described as novel and successful utterances.

The evidence I have discussed is consistent with a view that, even at this early stage of language development, children are being creative. Does this mean that there is no role for imitation as a means whereby children gain access to language? The answer has to be a guarded 'no'. Almost all parents will have heard their children use parental expressions complete with intonation – for example, *Shall we go upstairs?* (This can be embarrassing when the expression imitated reveals an aspect of one's verbal style that one might wish to hide!) Clearly children do imitate and equally clearly adults often think that this imitation is a primary route into language. The evidence from children's creative use of language allows us to see imitation as only part of the process.

There have been attempts to map formal grammatical structures on to children's early two-word utterances. However, a purely structural analysis of decontextualized utterances may not do justice to children's linguistic sophistica-tion. There is a much used example in the literature which comes from the work of Lois Bloom (1973). The child that Bloom describes used the expression 'mommy sock' on two separate occasions. On one of these occasions the utterance was produced as the child's mother was putting a sock on the child. On the other occasion, the child had picked up one of her mother's socks. The child used the same simple construction on each occasion, but for rather different purposes. The uses seem to have been, first, to indicate both the mother's role as the person fitting the sock to the child and, secondly, to indicate the ownership of her mother's sock. This shows us that to understand the extent of a child's communicative competence we need to have access to the contexts in which utterances are used.

Some meanings attributed to telegraphic speech

English-speaking children express a limited range of meanings in their first sentences. They talk about actions, what happened to what and who does what:

> Me fall.
> Bump table.
> Car go vroom!

They are concerned, not to say obsessed, with the relationship of possession:

> My teddy.
> Mommy hat.
> Daddy hair.

Equally prevalent is the relationship of location:

> Cup in box.
> Car garage.
> Mommy outside.

Among other early meanings that find frequent expression at this stage are recurrence:

> More milk.
> Tickle again.

nomination, or labelling:

> That Teddy.
> This steamroller.

and nonexistence:

> Beads all gone.
> No more soup.

Comparatively rare in the earliest word combinations, but still occasionally expressed, are relations involving experiences that are not actions:

> See that.
> Listen clock.

and relations involving states:

> Have coat.
> Daddy [is a] policeman.

Children learning many different languages, among them Samoan, German, French, Hebrew, Luo (in Kenya), and Russian, seem to encode the same limited set of meanings in their first sentences. This lends credence to the notion that the meanings depend on, and are restricted by, the two-year-old's understanding of the world.

(de Villiers and de Villiers, 1979, pp. 48–50)

The English tense and aspect systems are closely related. *Tense* refers to the location of an event in time with respect to the moment of speech – contrast the 'present tense' *I eat* and the 'past tense' *I ate*. *Aspect* refers to the duration or type of temporal activity denoted – e.g. *I run* vs. *I am running*. The first book in this series, *English: history, diversity and change* (Graddol et al. (eds), 1996), discusses variation in English tense and aspect systems.

The rate of language development varies from child to child, but we can say that a new stage has arrived when the child begins to use any of the grammatical items that were so obviously absent before. The appearance of **tense** and **aspect markers** in English has been a rich source of material for those interested in the development of children's understanding of concepts of time and, more importantly, for those interested in language development itself.

The sequence of development of the Standard English tense and aspect systems, which seems consistent over a range of longitudinal studies, is as follows:

1   At first there are no tense or aspect inflections, such as the progressive 'ing' suffix (e.g. *he's playing*), past tense inflections on regular verbs (e.g. *she played*) or the use of irregular past tense forms (e.g. *she slept*).

2   First to appear on the scene are the past tense forms of irregular verbs. For example, one might find both *sleep* and *slept* in a child's language. Both of these forms will appear to be used appropriately.

3   At some later point in development the past tense forms of regular verbs appear.

4   From this moment on, it is reported that *all* references to the past will use verbs with a past tense inflection, even those irregular verbs which had been in the child's vocabulary before this time. So, for example, *slept* becomes *sleeped*.

Actually the picture seems to be more complex than this, with appropriate and inappropriate usage coexisting for some time before adult usage is established. In any case there is some evidence from my own work (Bancroft, 1985) that children are able to locate events in time using language well before they use the Standard English system of verb inflections. There are, in fact, several means available to a speaker of English to refer to the temporal location of an event, including temporal adverbs like *before, after* and *soon*. Some of these alternative means are used by children among their earliest vocabularies. It seems that temporal reference is achieved by locating the event referred to and, then, having established that this knowledge is shared, the use of the 'present tense' becomes adequate.

An explanation consistent with the description of the development of the grammatical tense and aspect systems is that when children begin to use, for instance, irregular past tense forms, these are treated as though they were new words and not particularly related to the present tense form. When children begin to use regular past tense inflections, they have discovered that it is possible to make a great number of past tense forms by this simple addition. The children, however, do not realize the existence of exceptions to the rule and thus we see the use of inflections after irregular verbs as well. This gives rise to the widely noted child creations such as *comed*, *goed* and *holded*.

The crucial point is that this language behaviour is consistent with the idea that children are trying to discover the *rules* of language. The rule systems they try out are sensible and plausible but they are not the rule systems of adult English. The business of discovering or generating rules is a much more sophisticated activity than the rote learning of new words and expressions. Children who produce *comed* and *goed* are making creative use of the rules they have learned, rather than copying what they hear adults saying.

There are languages unrelated to English, for example Mandarin Chinese and British Sign Language, as well as English-related creoles, and nonstandard varieties of English, which do not use verb inflections in the way that Standard English does to signal the temporal location of an event. In some cases, locating an event in time seems to be achieved in a manner similar to that found in the language of children *learning* English. There are other languages, for example French and Russian – and, in fact, Old English – which have a more elaborate inflectional system. In short, there are various solutions to the problem of locating an event in time using language. These alternatives may have some impact on speakers' concepts of time although this is not established. Perhaps it is more likely that the various grammatical solutions to the problems of such things as temporal reference or plurality may differ in complexity as far as the learner is concerned. This, in turn, may affect the length of time needed to acquire particular aspects of language.

I have covered the following points in this section:

- When children first begin to assemble words to make more complex utterances, the structure of these utterances can tell us something about their developing understanding of the English language.

- It is possible to divide language development into (approximate) stages. Using examples of early language development in speakers of Standard English I distinguished between a stage in which children produce utterances that use no grammatical markers, and the next stage in which they begin to do so.

- An important characteristic of children's early grammatical development is its creativity. Children produce, in a systematic way, utterances they have not heard in their environment. They must, therefore, be active agents in the development of language.

- Different languages and language varieties may use different linguistic solutions to the various problems of reference. These different solutions can pose problems for learners, with some taking longer to acquire than others. In some cases the English solution seems the simpler; in other cases it is the more complex.

1.5   LATER LANGUAGE, NARRATIVES AND JOKES

Much of the psycholinguistic research effort investigating language development has concentrated upon the, admittedly interesting, early stages. Indeed, it is sometimes thought to be the case that nearly all the problems facing the language learner have been solved by the time the child is four or five years old. While my own focus so far in this chapter has been on early development, I have also indicated ways in which language development continues in older children.

It is obviously the case that children's vocabulary greatly increases during their school years; indeed, this development is part of a process that never really stops. Adults can have the experience of learning new words, although the rate at which this happens is very much slower than for children in school. Similarly, children develop their grammatical skills, producing more complex constructions as they hear them used by others or come across them in books, magazines, etc.

In addition to these developments, children have to learn more of the skills needed to maintain a conversation, to be aware of their partner's progress in understanding the communication, and to be able to repair it if it breaks down. In other words, to be an effective communicator a person needs to know much about language but also much about other people and the things that they know and understand. In this section we look at some of the other skills children need to develop in order to become effective communicators beyond the skills of being able to take turns in conversations (as described earlier).

In the next reading, Barton and Tomasello describe research on the social context of language development. The reading is a short extract from a chapter in which they develop the theme that children need to expand their range of conversational partners in order to become more effective communicators.

❖ ❖ ❖ ❖ ❖

Activity 1.5   *(Reading B)*

Now read 'The child's expanding social world' by Michelle G. Barton and Michael Tomasello (Reading B). As you do so, consider the following questions.

- What skills beyond those of producing language do children need to acquire in order to take part in conversations?
- What reasons do Barton and Tomasello give to support their view that some family members are typically better than others at engaging children in conversations?

❖ ❖ ❖ ❖ ❖

In order to explore further some of the issues raised by Barton and Tomasello, I focus next on research which has investigated the development of the skills needed to maintain a dialogue and to tell stories. I conclude with a brief look at some work on the nature and development of children's ability to make jokes.

Introducing new information

Anne Anderson and her colleagues, working in Glasgow, have investigated one particular aspect of communicative skill, that of introducing new information into a dialogue (Anderson et al., 1991). This is illustrative of the kind of skill we are discussing. In their study 85 pairs of children aged between 7 and 13 years were given a map-reading task. Pairs of children sat at a desk with a small screen between them, each having a map. The maps were quite similar but not identical, and one of them had a 'safe' route through various dangers while the other did not. The child whose map had the safe route on it had to pass this information to their partner. Giving all the children the same task in this way allowed a more direct comparison between their dialogue styles on this particular task than would have been possible through informal observation. The conversations of the children were recorded and transcribed and then analysed in terms of the ways in which new information was introduced.

The researchers' major interest was in the extent to which new information was introduced in a question form as opposed to a statement. The use of the question form (e.g. *Have you got a palm beach?*) checks up on what the listener knows in a way which the statement version (e.g. *It's by the palm beach*) does not.

There were two major outcomes from this study, one concerning the speakers and one concerning the listeners. This last is important since we should not forget that effective listening is itself a conversational skill. In the study, the younger children used question introductions much less than did the older children.

> It seems as if children only become fully aware of the INTERACTIONAL aspects of successful communication as they grow older. Young speakers behave as if the prime responsibility for introducing entities in the dialogue is theirs, with the listener's task being to interpret their messages. They rather infrequently directly seek their listener's involvement by checking on his or her knowledge state and hence on his or her ability to interpret what is being said.
>
> (Anderson et al., 1991, p. 682)

With respect to listener behaviour, Anderson and her colleagues found that the introduction of new information by using a question form was the most effective means of eliciting useful listener response with children of all the ages studied. Introducing information in the form of a statement resulted in effective responses only from children of 12 years and older. Although rather beyond the scope of this chapter, we should note that these findings have implications for both educationalists and parents.

Telling a good story

Studies like that of Anderson et al. allow us a glimpse of the development of conversational strategies and the development of increasing sensitivity to the needs of listeners. Rather different skills are needed to tell a good story in addition to those involved in making sure your listener is following you. To tell a good story one needs to be able to organize material in such a way as to preserve a sequence, explain motives and purposes, and maintain the interest of the listener. Children developing storytelling and narrative skills will need to learn a set of conventions, which may differ between different English-speaking communities.

The ways narrative in English is used in various cultures is dealt with in the second book of this series, *Using English: from conversation to canon* (Maybin and Mercer (eds), 1996).

❖ ❖ ❖ ❖ ❖

Activity 1.7 Just joking? *(Allow about 10–15 minutes)*

This joke was told to a friend by my daughter Anna, who was 12 years old at the time.

> A man was running to catch a moving bus but when he got there the conductor refused him entrance and he was … he fell off the bus and was run over by a car. The conductor was taken to court on trial for murder and was sentenced to be electrocuted. And the day when he was electrocuted his last request was a bowl of mashed bananas and milk … and he sa … and he had this bowl of mashed bananas and milk and then they switched the current on and it didn't work, so they tried again and again the last request was a bowl of mashed bananas and milk. And they put a

higher current on that time but it still didn't work and the third time …
after the third time it's meant to be you have to free the prisoner. And so
they tried again and the last request was again a bowl of bananas and
milk. And it still didn't work even though they switched the power up.
And the con … and they asked the conductor how he did it and the
conductor said maybe it's just because I'm a bad conductor!

What is the crucial item of information about the English language that Anna was
relying on her listener to know, in order for the joke to be successful?

Comment

The joke is constructed so that listeners are likely to think that the condemned
man's choice of food was related to the malfunctioning of the electric chair. But
for the punchline to be effective, it is of course crucial that listeners are aware of
the alternative uses in English for the term 'conductor', so that they would
recognize they have been misled. (You might also need to know that your
friendship was strong enough to survive after inflicting this grievous 'joke' upon
your friend!)

❖   ❖   ❖   ❖   ❖

We can use Anna's joke to consider some aspects of effective communication, in
relation to specific audiences. When we tell jokes we are often intending to amuse
or surprise by manipulating our listener's expectations in a way which makes the
punchline a violation of those expectations. Jokes are a special case involving an
element of misleading information. More often in dialogues and in narratives,
speakers are at pains to ensure that their listeners *do not* misunderstand or get lost.
In order to do this speakers need to be aware of what their listeners know on the
basis of the story so far, and what they can be expected to know on the basis of their
sharing the same cultural knowledge as the speaker. As well as this knowledge,
speakers need to be able to use a range of linguistic devices for developing stories
and dialogues in a way that ensures their listeners' continued understanding.

The ability to tell jokes is an extremely sophisticated form of verbal behaviour
requiring, as we have seen, both knowledge of language and the ability to identify
and manipulate the mental state of another person. Joke making, as with other
aspects of language that we have considered, seems to have its roots in very early
exchanges between child and caregiver. Dianne Horgan (1981) has reported a
study of the development of joke making by her own daughter Kelly. Playing with
language demonstrates both developing language skills and the development of
metalinguistic ability, which refers to the ability to think about and reflect on
language itself. The ability to reflect on language is a more sophisticated one than
the ability to produce language.

Horgan's original article
is reprinted in *Child
Language: a reader* (Franklin
and Barten (eds), 1988).
The page references given
here are from this reprint.

Horgan describes Kelly's joking in terms of a four-stage progression. As each
new stage appeared it was added to the preceding stage and did not replace it. The
first stage involved the deliberate violation of semantic categories. For example,
when Kelly was 16 months and had a vocabulary of about 20 words she added the
word *shoe* to her list. Horgan reports: 'Several days later, she put her foot through
the armhole of a nightgown, saying *Shoe*, accompanied by shrieks of laughter'
(1981, pp. 343–4). In Horgan's view semantic violations of this kind can be a very
useful device for a language learner to explore the boundaries of the concept
represented by the word.

Horgan's second category of joking consists of games based on phonetic
patterns. For example, at 20 months, Kelly said, '*Cow go moo. Mommy go mamoo.
Daddy go dadoo. Ha ha.*' (p. 344). In Horgan's view, the child must have begun to

treat the sounds of a word as 'arbitrary symbols for the objects and not as essential properties of the objects' (p. 346) in order that she is able to 'bend' the sounds to make a rhyme or fit into a regular pattern. You may recall an aspect of my earlier discussion at this point: in the early stages of development children seem to be developing a mastery of their ability to make sounds which are recognizable parts of their language.

The third kind of joke described by Horgan appeared in her daughter's speech early in the third year. Kelly produced a more sophisticated version of the earlier humour by introducing new words into established sequences. The new words were related in some way to the words that had been replaced. For example, Kelly produced '*Little Bo People had lost her steeple*' (p. 344). In this case the syntax is preserved and the introduced words are real words and make (a sort of) sense.

Rather later in the third year, Kelly began to produce jokes which had a regular discourse format. This form was something like that of a riddle although her parents reported that Kelly had never heard a riddle. For example:

K   How do aspirins make?
M   Huh?
K   How do aspirins make?
M   I dunno, how do aspirins make?
K   They make you feel better.

(Horgan, 1981, pp. 345–6)

By the end of the third year Kelly was able to make up jokes which still retained this format although they were also used to set up a linguistically misleading context. For example:

K   Mommy, do you love me?
M   Yes.
K   Do you love me to HIT you? Ha, ha!

and

K   Do we kick Mary?
M   No, we don't kick Mary!
K   Do we kick Jennifer?
M   No, we don't kick Jennifer!
K   Do we kick the swimming pool?
M   No, we don't kick the swimming pool!
K   We kick IN the swimming pool. Ha, ha!

(Horgan, 1981, p. 346)

The purpose of describing these jokes is first to illustrate how children become able to manipulate the English language in order to achieve surprise and amusement, and secondly to show how learning to use English creatively in this way depends in part on the learning of certain conventional discourse structures or formats.

When children begin to go to school they already know something of the potential of language to amuse – however, there is still much to learn. Young children may know the purpose and structure of a joke form without a complete understanding of its semantics. For example:

Knock knock
Who's there?
James.

James who?
James Bond.

In this case the form of the joke is known (as is the expectation of mirth) but it does not have any of the manipulation of sound or semantic similarities which are needed in the joke proper.

As children become a little more aware of jokes the humour becomes more apparent although the joker may feel the need to explain the joke, not being sure that the listener has understood. For example, the following was collected by a colleague of mine:

What do you get if you cross a kangaroo and a sheep?
I don't know.
A woolly jumper!
[*Pause*] the because the sheep gives the wool and the kangaroo is the jumper.

In summary, the development of joking is an area where the development of linguistic skill and social awareness are very closely entwined. In order to be amusing, children deploy their knowledge of language, of its sounds and meanings, in concert with their understanding of other people. In a rather similar way, dialogue and narrative skills depend on an awareness of what listeners know or can be expected to deduce.

I have covered the following points in this section:

- There is more to becoming an effective communicator in English (or any other language) than learning how to produce the language. For example, an essential requirement is the development of a sensitivity to what a listener knows.

- Sensitivity to the needs of listeners affects how new information should be introduced within a dialogue. Some ways of doing this are more effective than others. By the time they are about 13 years, children can deploy these more effective means.

- The developing ability to make jokes is particularly revealing of children's ability to manipulate language and of their awareness of the communicative needs of their audience.

1.6 CONCLUSION

In this chapter I have traced something of the developmental history of children learning English as their first language. I have tried to describe the essence of what is learned during each phase of development, from the earliest stages of babbling through to the early development of grammar and up to the creative use of certain discourse structures (as in the telling of jokes). Throughout the chapter I have drawn attention to the contexts in which children are using and learning English, and to the role of other people (parents and other caregivers) in children's language development.

Although I have focused on the acquisition of English, I have also tried to indicate something of the variety that exists in human language learning by pointing to some significant ways that children's early language experience can differ according to the language and culture of their homes and communities. The following chapter continues and extends this discussion, examining children's learning of different varieties of English, and English alongside other languages in bi- and multilingual communities.

Reading A

LANGUAGE ADDRESSED TO CHILDREN: LINGUISTIC AND CULTURAL ASPECTS

Elena V.M. Lieven

This reading is a brief extract from a much longer chapter on crosslinguistic and crosscultural aspects of language addressed to children. In the chapter as a whole, Elena Lieven reviews evidence on the importance of child directed speech for language learning; the role of conversational partners such as brothers and sisters, and other children; and the extent to which adults explicitly teach appropriate language to their children. As the reading makes clear, comparisons between children from different linguistic and cultural backgrounds serve as a test of theories of language learning. Useful further reading on this topic can be found in Lieven's chapter itself, and in one of the collections she cites, Slobin (1985).

Just as systematic individual differences between children learning the same language have to be accounted for by theories of language development, so differences between languages and between language-learning environments will condition the claims of any theory of language development to universality. Our theories of how children learn language are largely based on the acquisition of English by children from middle-class or upper-middle-class environments in the United States or the United Kingdom. These need to be tested against studies of language development in cultural settings other than those of the middle classes in advanced industrial societies and for languages other than English.

There are two 'straw positions' which can be used to characterize the extremes in approach to crosscultural studies of language development. First is the idea that child-centred 'motherese' is universal and therefore, *ipso facto*, of central importance in children's learning of language. The second is that there are cultures in which speech is never addressed to language-learning children and that therefore it must be possible to learn to talk simply by listening to adults talking to each other. Even if the empirical parts of these two positions were true, the conclusions drawn from them need not be ... Probably nobody subscribes fully to either position, but stated in this way they demonstrate why looking at language development in a very wide range of cultures is an essential constraint on theory building.

The following questions [are of interest]:

1   What is the range of environments within which children learn to talk?

2   Do adults from other cultures and subcultures see themselves as adjusting their language to children and, if so, to what purpose?

3   How, if at all, might these adjustments relate to the child's task of learning language structure?

By 'environment', I mean the characteristics of the interpersonal surroundings within which young, language-learning children spend their time. Is it dyadic or polyadic, mainly alone with the mother, with other adults, with siblings, with a group of children? By 'culture' and 'subculture', I mean a community defining themselves or defined by others as having a coherence of both living style and ideology. In referring to 'our culture' or 'children from the type of background usually studied', I mean families from middle-class backgrounds in which one or both parents have post-school education, living in urban and technologically advanced settings. All these terms are approximations and all would give any self-respecting sociologist and anthropologist nightmares. Also, as already mentioned, children from the same backgrounds can be significantly different in their approaches to learning language (Lieven, Pine and Dresner Barnes, 1992; Pine, 1994) ...

Major methodological problems are involved in the comparison of language-learning studies crossculturally. Studies of children learning English (and, to some extent, other languages originating in Europe) tend to have larger numbers of subjects and to be conducted by developmental psychologists or psycholinguists. It is usually possible to get some idea of the relative quantities of various types of talk by both adults and children; but they are often almost completely unreflective about the culture within which the child is growing up, and this is particularly true of the studies of children learning English. Studies of children from non-industrialized cultures and/or learning non-Indo-European languages tend to pay much closer attention to the entire context in which children are learning to talk, but they rarely take a quantitative approach. This is often because the researcher is a native English-speaker observing the culture 'from outside' and also because s/he is more likely to be an anthropologist or cultural linguist. In addition, there are all the dangers more generally associated with comparisons across cultures: for example, how can we be sure that what look like similar behaviors are actually fulfilling the same functional role in the two different cultures? These factors make it difficult to draw definitive conclusions, but they do generate material which can make an important contribution to current debates in the field ...

Theories of environmental influences on language learning have tended to be built upon the study of the mother–infant dyad. In fact, of course, most children in the world grow up in polyadic situations. So while these children spend little time in dyadic conversation with one adult, they spend a lot of time in one of the following situations: with the mother and other siblings/children; with older children or others acting as caregivers; sitting around with a group of adults and children. This is not only true of children in non-industrialized cultures; in many economically advanced societies childcare arrangements may be less dependent on the mother staying at home with the children. Thus Berman (1985) reports that Israeli children spend a good deal of time with other children and with caregivers other than the mother. There are also subcultures within highly industrialized countries in which children spend the day surrounded by other adults and children, sometimes with their mothers and sometimes not (see Heath's 1983 study of the African-American 'Trackton' community, one of two rural working-class groups she studied in the southern United States). More polyadic patterns of childcare are very typical of children raised in rural, economically traditional societies. The children in Schieffelin's (1985) study of the Kaluli of Papua New Guinea spend their time with their mothers and siblings, while Ochs (1985) reports that, among the Samoans, elder children are set to look after the young child but usually in sight of the mother. Nwokah (1987), in her study of a rural Nigerian village, reports that young children are looked after during the day by male or female 'maids' (eight- to twelve-year-old children) while the mothers go to market or work in the house, and that these maids usually take the children to a communal space in the village, largely frequented by children. Bavin (1992) also says that the Warlpiri-speaking aboriginal children in her study spent their time in communal groups surrounded by other adults and children.

We know that all these children learn to talk and Slobin's edited volumes (1985) describe the course of their development. But we know considerably less about how to characterize the speech that they hear and how they might make use of it. Studies of some of the cultures mentioned above state that there is little or no speech to infants until they themselves start to talk. In other cultures adults do talk to children, but in ways normally regarded as unhelpful by child language researchers (e.g. elicited imitations). Finally there are cultures in which, despite being very different from those of the standard studies, adults appear to use something very like child-sensitive speech.

References

BAVIN, E. (1992; reprint forthcoming) 'The acquisition of Warlpiri as a first language', reprinted in SLOBIN, D.I. (ed.) *The Crosslinguistic Study of Language Acquisition*, vol. 3, Hillsdale, N.J., Erlbaum.

BERMAN, R. (1985) 'The acquisition of Hebrew' in SLOBIN, D.I. (ed.) *The Crosslinguistic Study of Language Acquisition*, vol. 1, Hillsdale, N.J., Erlbaum.

HEATH, S.B. (1983) *Ways with Words*, Cambridge, Cambridge University Press.

LIEVEN, E.V.M., PINE, J.M. and DRESNER BARNES, H. (1992) 'Productivity in multi-word utterances: analytic and synthetic solutions', paper presented at the 1992 Child Language Seminar, University of Glasgow.

NWOKAH, E.E. (1987) 'Maidese vs. motherese: is the language input of child and adult caregivers similar?', *Language and Speech*, 30, 213–37.

OCHS, E. (1985) 'Variation and error: a sociolinguistic approach to language acquisition in Samoa' in SLOBIN, D.I. (ed.) *The Crosslinguistic Study of Language Acquisition*, vol. 1, Hillsdale, N.J., Erlbaum.

PINE, J.M. (1994) 'The language of primary caregivers' in GALLOWAY, C. and RICHARDS, B.J. (eds) *Input and Interaction in Language Acquisition*, Cambridge, Cambridge University Press.

SCHIEFFELIN, B.B. (1985) 'The acquisition of Kaluli' in SLOBIN, D.I. (ed.) *The Crosslinguistic Study of Language Acquisition*, vol. 1, Hillsdale, N.J., Erlbaum.

SLOBIN, D.I. (ed.) (1985; third volume forthcoming) *The Crosslinguistic Study of Language Acquisition*, 3 vols, Hillsdale, N.J., Erlbaum.

Source: Lieven, 1994, pp. 56–9.

Reading B
THE CHILD'S EXPANDING SOCIAL WORLD

Michelle E. Barton and Michael Tomasello

Most Western middle-class children have mothers as primary caregivers. Most of these mothers converse with their children in a particular way: they adapt their conversation to the child's competencies and needs, and they make frequent attempts to solicit the child's active participation in conversation from a very early age. They are able to do this well because they know so much about their individual child's knowledge, experiences, and language practices, and because they are highly motivated to engage their child in interaction and to show off her/his particular skills. This style has been shown to be conducive to the child's acquisition of a number of important linguistic skills. But by virtue of their high levels of knowledge and motivation, mothers are also likely on many occasions to anticipate their child's needs before they are linguistically expressed, to fill in gaps in incomplete or poorly expressed child utterances, and to preempt the child's participation in talking about a difficult topic. The maternal style may thus not be as conducive to the child's acquisition of some other types of communicative skills.

If mothers were the only people infants needed to communicate with, interaction with them alone would be sufficient for the child to become a communicatively competent member of her/his culture. There would develop a variety of idiosyncratic communicative devices that would subserve their communication needs quite well, and the need for devices more widely adapted socially would be minimal. But children do need to communicate with other people, even those with whom they share few or no common experiences – and this is the point of language.

Language is a set of social conventions designed to facilitate communication with other persons who have acquired the same linguistic conventions, whenever and wherever they may have done so. Natural languages are constructed so that they do not depend on an extensive amount of shared knowledge or experience of particular events. For example, what is expressed by a simple pointing may be expressed in other ways when the intended item, place, or activity is not physically present, and there are grammatical devices for indicating who-did-what-to-whom in the absence of a shared experience of the event as well. In a very interesting survey of several language groups and the social structures they evolved in, Parisi (1983) in fact argues that obligatory grammatical devices are associated precisely with those societies in which members must communicate with unknown interactants with unknown backgrounds and habits, and there are even some languages in which grammatical marking is obligatory in those contexts in which it is clear that the listener could not reconstruct the intended who-did-what-to-whom relations on her/his own without marking. The problem for young children is that they are learning to communicate and acquiring language as a means of communication all at the same time. New communicative partners are constantly presenting them with new challenges that require them either to deploy their existing communicative skills in new ways, or else to acquire new skills that will help them to meet these challenges effectively.

To be a competent communicator, then, the child must learn to communicate in user-unfriendly as well as user-friendly environments, and this is where, on our hypothesis, fathers and siblings enter the picture. Fathers and siblings are not necessary features of the language acquisition process – or else single-parent children and only children would not acquire language normally, which they do. But if children are to communicate effectively with adults and children they have never before encountered, it would be very helpful if they had first had some practice with other adults and children with whom they have an affective bond and with whom they have a fair amount of previous social experience. The data we have reviewed … support the view that both secondary caregiver fathers and preschool-age siblings are less fluent conversational partners for young children than are primary caregiver mothers, and hence provide the children with opportunities to modify their speech for a less familiar partner. In particular, both fathers and siblings interact with nascent language learners such that, compared to mothers, they are:

1   less conversationally responsive, ignoring more often the child's linguistic overtures;

2   less conversationally supportive, providing the child with fewer conversation-maintaining devices such as questions and turnabouts;

3   less conversationally competent with the child in the sense that they experience more breakdowns, fewer successful repairs, and overall shorter conversations;

4   more directive of the topic of conversation and the child's behavior.

Thus, as their social worlds expand during their toddler and preschool years, children receive important feedback about their language skills from fathers and siblings who are familiar to them as interactants, but who on many occasions genuinely do not understand them. Clearly, the communicative styles of both fathers and siblings require the language-learning child to make adjustments and develop a variety of pragmatic skills. Although the outcomes of these experiences remain speculations at this time, it is plausible to expect that fathers and siblings play different roles in the infant's communicative development. Fathers may encourage the development of more linguistic means of communication (using language to serve a conventional referential function) *via* their lexically demanding style. Siblings, on the other hand, might conceivably lead to the development of more social and pragmatic skills for communication (using language to serve a social-regulatory or expressive function) *via* their directive style and the competition for the caregiver's attention they engender in the multi-child context. It is experiences such as these, then, that are proposed to serve as bridges, each in its own way, to the child's communication with other adults and peers with whom the child has not already established familiar routines of communication.

We have really just begun to document the different kinds of linguistic experiences that children have outside the mother–child context. There are as yet many unanswered questions, for example, possible differences between primary and secondary caregiver fathers as conversational partners, the role of birth spacing in sibling–child conversations, and the precise way that interactions with fathers and siblings might facilitate communication with other types of linguistic partners. These would be difficult questions to answer even with the full battery of experimental methods. But in the context of the real world, we must rely on the converging methods provided by naturalistic studies of children's linguistic interactions with different conversational partners, correlational studies that relate what happens in these interactions to the child's subsequent language skills or style, and experimental training studies that investigate the effects of particular kinds of interactions. Synthesizing information from all of these types of investigation will be necessary if we are to understand more thoroughly the various roles of the social-linguistic environment in the child's acquisition of communicative competence.

Reference

PARISI, D. (1983) 'A three-stage model of language evolution' in DE GROLIER, E. (ed.) *Glossogenetics: the origin and evolution of language*, Chur, Switzerland, Harwood.

Source: BARTON and TOMASELLO, 1994, pp. 131–4.

2 ENGLISH IN THE REPERTOIRE

Barbara Mayor

2.1 INTRODUCTION

In the previous chapter the focus was largely, but not exclusively, on children growing up in families and communities where only English is spoken. In this chapter the canvas widens to include children learning to speak English alongside other languages, as well as children learning to distinguish between several different varieties of English – in other words any child with two or more distinct means of expression.

I begin the chapter looking at children growing up bilingual, who, at the same time as learning to distinguish English from their other language or languages, also have to learn when it is appropriate to use the one or the other. I go on to consider the extent to which some of the same factors may be at play for a monolingual speaker in learning what it means to talk like, for example, a middle-class girl from Scotland or a working-class boy from Australia (i.e. learning to use linguistic means to signal membership of social groups). This is far from being a matter of simple determinism: I examine how we exercise personal linguistic choices in order to express our individual identities and to achieve personal goals. And throughout the chapter I consider the available evidence for when and how these various skills develop.

In our everyday lives we play a variety of social roles, and it is often through spoken language (or silence) that we signal shifts in our social identity or relationship with others. Sometimes we *unconsciously* converge towards or diverge from the speech patterns of others, either within or beyond our community; at other times we may make a *conscious* choice to emulate or mimic another person or social group. This chapter explores how, as children and young people, we develop such a **repertoire** of linguistic behaviour.

The theatrical metaphor here ties in with the concepts of roles and scripts, actors and audiences, which figure prominently in studies of social interaction and are discussed more fully in the second book in this series, *Using English: from conversation to canon* (Maybin and Mercer (eds), 1996).

2.2 LANGUAGES FOR LIFE

❖ ❖ ❖ ❖ ❖

Activity 2.1 *(Allow 5–10 minutes)*

Consider the following exchanges and try to identify what is actually happening between the participants. What role do you think the English language – or a particular variety of English – is playing? What effect do you think the speakers are trying to achieve?

Scene 1: The home of an ethnically Chinese family in Newcastle upon Tyne in the north-east of England.

Mother:	*Oy-m-oy faan a? Ah Ying a?*
	(Want some rice?)
Daughter:	(no response)

Mother:	*Chaaufaan a. Oy-m-oy?*
	(Fried rice. Want or not?)
Daughter:	(after a 2 second pause) I'll have some
	shrimps.

(Li Wei, 1994, p. 86)

Scene 2: A youth club in an English south Midlands town.

I was standing behind the snack bar. Ishfaq [a 15-year-old British boy of Pakistani descent] came into the club soon after it opened and in our first exchange of the evening, he came up to me at the counter and said in a strong Panjabi accent: 'Ben Rampton can I help you?' Though it was me doing the serving, I sustained the joke and asked for 20 Mojos (chews). Then in his ordinary voice he placed an order for 10 Refreshers [sweets].

(Rampton, 1996)

Scene 3: Outside a family home in New Zealand.

Father:	Tea's ready Robbie.
	(*Robbie ignores him and carries on skateboarding.*)
Father:	Mr Robert Harris if you do not come in immediately
	there will be consequences which you will regret.

(Holmes, 1992, p. 47)

Comment

Here are my own conjectures about what *may* have been happening.

In the first extract it appears that the daughter is resisting the mother's choice of language (Chinese) by responding initially with silence. Her eventual response in English seems to be doing more than simply indicating a preference for one *food* over another, but rather making a statement about how she relates to her mother and/or her mother's culture.

In the second extract Ishfaq seems to be consciously mimicking a stereotype of British Asian English to role play a kind of mock 'colonial' relationship with Ben Rampton (who is a white Englishman). He then reverts to his 'ordinary' voice to re-establish a more equal relationship.

In the final extract the father, having failed to achieve the desired outcome in informal language, opts to address Robbie in a pseudo-legal register, in this case explicitly signalled by a formal term of address 'Mr Robert Harris'. Whether or not this was effective would depend not only on Robbie's understanding of the words uttered, but also on his reading of the double-edged message (i.e. this is only *half* a joke ...).

In all three extracts, of course, it is possible that the participants may have intended something different from or additional to what I have construed – it is conceivable for example that Robbie's father may have been simply sharing a joke about the speech style of an elderly friend of the family. The complex meanings of any social situation may be lost on an observer, especially one relying only on a written transcript.

❖ ❖ ❖ ❖ ❖

Whether we consider ourselves monolingual in English or bilingual, in our interactions with others most of us have access at any given time to a range of different language varieties to signal our shifting attitudes and identities. Kamwangamalu has formulated this as three dilemmas which we face each time we open our mouths:

Who am I?

How am I perceived by others?

How would I want to be perceived?

(Adapted from Kamwangamalu, 1992, p. 33)

A key question addressed in this chapter is how and at what age children and young people learn, alongside the more formal aspects of language structure, to negotiate these aspects of their own identity and attitudes towards others through the medium of English and other languages.

Growing up with English

Mine had been an English-speaking upbringing, my father had insisted on it, as that was the language that would 'give us the world'. But here [at the elite Malay College] was the Malay world, and in all its diversity of regional tones; Kelantanese in particular was a delight to the ear, but virtually incomprehensible. This being North Peak, however, most of us from the rest of the country would soon shade into the particular patois of Northern Malay in our speech, adopting with ease its rotund simplicities.

English remained, thankfully for me, the medium of our instruction, as it had been throughout our education so far. But soon after I went home for the first term holidays, I overheard my father tell my mother, his voice thick with disgust, 'You hear the boy? He sounds like a Sayong Malay!'' (Sayong being a decrepit little village buried amidst banana groves across the river from Kuala Kangsar.)

I think he meant for me to overhear the exchange, rather than address the point directly to me. I think he understood that the damage done to my speech was the result of a young boy's effort to fit in with his peers in an alien environment …

My niche was, what had seemed such a liability and embarrassment when I first got there, the English language. I became a school debater and a fixture in the College magazine. English, for our generation, was an effortless alternative language, yet there was still considerable respect for those of us most fluent in it. It set a certain seal on the Malay College's quality, that our English debating team could hold its own against those of the nation's other great schools, notwithstanding their more expansive resource of Chinese and Indian youth. For a mere Malay to stand up and strut the oratorical boards, his argument prevailing, his eloquence and arrogance more than match for those of his Worthy Opponents.… there was some pride in that.

… I held my own, helped my school satisfy its addiction for winning, and was as a result largely forgiven for my cultural deficiencies as a Malay. Rehman (what kind of name is that? 'Raymond'? You sure it's not a spelling mistake?) might not have been able to extricate himself from the slightest literary tangle in Malay, but in *English*, ho, you should have heard him! That guy could *talk*!

(Rashid, 1993, pp. 81, 84–5)

'Cooperative conversationalists'

As you have seen in Chapter 1, all babies, whatever the language or languages by which they are surrounded, begin by learning what it is to communicate, and only gradually learn how to use human language to accomplish this. In the words of Evelyn Hatch, 'One learns how to do conversation, one learns how to interact verbally, and out of this interaction syntactic structures are developed' (Hatch, 1978, p. 404). So language acquisition is initially a matter of learning the rules of social behaviour and only later a matter of learning the grammatical rules by which these are realized. Even at the preverbal stage there are many ways in which the discourse patterns differ according to the culture or cultures in which children are being brought up.

Some of these patterns will be specific to adult–child interaction itself. Suzanne Romaine (1984, p. 164) summarizes a range of anthropological findings on different cultural attitudes to children's talk, ranging from the Koreans, who (like the Victorian Britons) reputedly stress silence as a part of good behaviour, to the Samoans who treat baby talk as if it were a foreign language, to the Luo and Koya people of Kenya who are not responsive to the language mistakes made by children but do give explicit instructions on the social appropriateness of speech. I would add to this the British (and, to a lesser extent perhaps, the North Americans) who, to outsiders, appear obsessed with inculcating the social rituals of *Hello, Good-bye, Please* and *Thank-you*. Susan Ervin-Tripp (1971, p. 34) reports a child playing with a toy telephone and engaging in a rudimentary 'conversation' which consisted only of *Hello, fine, goodbye!* Kenji Hakuta (1986, p. 112–3) quotes an entertaining example of an American infant who learned to say *Phew!* as a greeting because it was the first thing her mother would say as she entered the room and caught the smell of a dirty nappy [diaper].

Social routines of family life

It is often the social routines of language that we learn first. Anthea Fraser Gupta quotes the following example of a typically Singaporean 'checking sequence' between a father and his daughter (aged 2 years 11 months). (Note the use of the 'pragmatic particles' *meh* and *a* in the questions – an influence of Chinese languages on Singaporean English.)

'Aunty' here is a general term used to refer to any adult female friend of the family.

Girl:	*Aunty wear red red one, the Aunty wear red shoes.*
Father:	*Who wear red shoes?*
Girl:	*Aunty.*
Father:	*Aunty wore red shoes meh?*
Girl:	*Red red.*
Father:	*Red shoes a?*
Girl	*Yes.*

(Gupta, 1994, p. 81)

Contrast the following exchange between an American mother and her 5-year-old son:

Mother:	*How was school today? Did you go to assembly?*
Son:	*Yes.*
Mother:	*Did the preschoolers go to assembly?*
Son:	*Yes.*
Mother:	*Did you stay for the whole assembly or just part of it?*

(Berko Gleason, 1973, p. 162)

Heath's study was concerned particularly with differing 'literacy practices' and is referred to again in the next chapter. Literacy practices in English are also discussed in the second book in this series, *Using English: from conversation to canon* (Maybin and Mercer (eds), 1996).

Both children, in their different ways, are being exposed to what it means to carry on a conversation. Children are, to quote Hatch (1978, p. 384) 'cooperative conversationalists'. And, as we have established, language learning evolves out of learning how to carry on conversations, rather than the other way round.

In certain contexts it is a matter of learning when *not* to speak as much as when to speak. The children of Trackton, a poor black American community documented extensively by Shirley Brice Heath, were explicitly taught by adults to be as 'uncooperative' as possible in conversation with strangers whose purposes in the community were not known (Heath, 1982b, p. 115).

Communicative competence

In the 1960s the American theoretical linguist, Noam Chomsky (1965), drew a distinction between: linguistic **competence** – the knowledge of the language system which the speakers of any language have (arguably in differing degree), enabling them to distinguish utterances which are grammatical in the language from those which are not; and linguistic **performance** – the frequently un-grammatical and/or imperfectly delivered actual utterances of language in use. This distinction was soon challenged by the applied linguist, Del Hymes, on the grounds that performance is itself rule governed, and that speakers need to acquire distinct skills in performance, such as knowing when to speak, which variety of language to choose, what is the socially appropriate turn of phrase to achieve the desired effect, etc. He termed this **communicative competence.** In other words, as well as learning the sounds and structures of particular languages, children are learning the discourse strategies of their communities.

> A child who might produce any sentence whatever – such a child would be likely to be institutionalized: even more so if not only sentences, but also speech or silence was random, unpredictable. For that matter, a person who chooses occasions and sentences suitably, but is master only of fully grammatical sentences, is at best a bit odd. Some occasions call for being appropriately ungrammatical.
>
> We have then to account for the fact that a normal child acquires knowledge of sentences, not only as grammatical, but also as appropriate. He or she acquires competence as to when to speak, when not, and as to what to talk about with whom, when, where, in what manner. In short, a child becomes able to accomplish a repertoire of speech acts, to take part in speech events, and to evaluate their accomplishment by others.
>
> (Hymes, 1979, pp. 14–15)

In the sections that follow, I look at how even very young children who are learning English alongside another language acquire the communicative competence to use their two languages appropriately. I go on to consider evidence for similar social and stylistic variation among children with only varieties of English at their disposal.

2.3   BILINGUALISM: A SPECIAL CASE?

Some children are brought up in homes where both English and another language are in daily use.

Bilingualism in daily use – Singapore and Wales

❖ ❖ ❖ ❖ ❖

Activity 2.3   *(Reading A)*

Reading A is by Sylvia Rojas-Drummond and Hugh Drummond, a Mexican British couple who chose to educate their twin sons bilingually in Spanish and English.
Read this now and as you do so, make notes on the following.

- The ways in which the twins' language use fluctuates over time, especially:

    possible motivating factors for using English or Spanish at particular points;

    any indications of *passive* knowledge as well as active skills;

    the extent of (and reasons for) language mixing.

- The apparent (or purported) relationship between the twins' languages and other kinds of allegiance, especially:

    points in the text where a link is assumed between language, culture, nation, etc;

    any factors which would seem to challenge the existence of such fixed links.

- Any particular kinds of knowledge or skill the twins may have been learning in addition to those usually acquired by monolinguals.

Comment

As the evidence for the first of these points is to be found in a close reading of the article, I don't propose to expand on the detail again here. However, do keep a note of your observations and compare them with some of the evidence I present later in this chapter, to see how far the twins' behaviour is typical or how far it is idiosyncratic.

The evidence for the second point is a little more embedded, but note that it is assumed that the twins will be exposed to 'both languages and cultures' (p. 71) in the home and in the school, and the reference to 'mixed-nationality social groups' (p. 74). In everyday conversation we may (like the authors of the article) use the terms language/culture/nationality in an interchangeable or interconnected way, implying for example a direct link between bilingualism and biculturalism. In practice the relationship between these terms is a complex one but we need to recognize that there is a *conceptual* distinction, and there are times when it is useful to distinguish between them. For example, it may well have struck you that – even putting language aside for a moment – our legal nationality may not correspond to either our place of birth or our place of residence, let alone anything so nebulous as our 'culture'. Hugh Drummond is British born, but he was entitled to acquire Mexican nationality by virtue of his marriage. He has also spent a considerable time in the USA, as well as in Mexico with its own mixed cultural heritage. In addition to this, 'British culture' (itself a nebulous concept) has moved on during the years of Hugh's absence. (It is commonly observed that cultures in 'exile' are frequently more conservative than those left behind.) So how much culture does he actually still share with his father or nephews from the south of England? Note also that American teachers have, for at least some of the time, been entrusted with the task of conveying 'British culture' in a notionally 'British' school (p. 72). How all these issues relate to the English *language* itself is yet another question, and one which I continue to explore throughout this chapter.

With regard to the third point, I would want to argue that there is very little linguistic knowledge or skill that is *unique* to the bilingual learner. During the course of the chapter I hope to be able to demonstrate that *all* children need to develop in two important aspects:

- they need to recognize their various languages or varieties of language as separate *systems* (of sounds, grammar, meaning, etc) in order to keep them apart as and when necessary;

- they need to learn how to use their various languages or varieties of language appropriately, according to who they are talking to and what they're talking about – what Gupta (1994) calls the 'appropriate environments' – in order to achieve particular effects.

Children learning English 'monolingually' (who may in fact command several varieties of their single language) are also learning to make such distinctions and choices among the language varieties available to them. However, bilinguals represent a particularly stark case of the general phenomenon. As Romaine puts it, 'A choice between different forms of one language ... can convey the same kinds of social meanings as a choice between languages... What distinguishes bilinguals from monolinguals is that bilinguals usually have greater resources ... The skilled monolingual is one who is able to summon the maximum of pragmatic resources within one language' (Romaine, 1989, pp. 155, 157). We also need to remember that bilinguals normally have access to more than one variety within *each* of their languages, so that their overall repertoire encompasses both of these aspects.

❖ ❖ ❖ ❖ ❖

'Bilingualism as a first language': acquiring competence in two formal systems

So what are the key differences between the experience of learning English monolingually and that of learning it bi- or multilingually from birth? What of those who, to quote the Canadian linguist and educationalist Merril Swain (1972), have 'bilingualism as a first language'? The answer hinges on the relative extent to which the child experiences *language* as an undifferentiated phenomenon, or recognizes *languages* as separate systems. To a large extent this will depend on maturation. The monolingual baby learns how to talk (in the sense of physically articulating sounds) at the same time as learning to distinguish the sounds of one particular language and learns to make sense of language *per se* at the same time as learning the rules of one particular system, in this case something called 'English'. The bilingual baby who acquires two languages simultaneously will be in a similar situation, except that the corpus of incoming data will be broader. Much of the research in this area has concentrated on whether the baby is apparently separating the languages into two distinct systems at all (see, for example, the classic studies reproduced in Hatch, 1978, and the later overview in Romaine, 1995). In practice, separation of vocabularies and of the sound systems seems to begin earlier than separation of the grammatical systems, but the details vary from language to language and from child to child, and opinion is still divided on the issue.

Behavioural studies have been undertaken to try to ascertain whether languages are separately organized in the brain; if you are interested in this issue, you will find a good overview in Romaine, 1995.

Several researchers (e.g. Volterra and Taeschner, 1978, and Deuchar and Quay, 1994) have argued that, in the first stages of development the bilingual or multilingual child has a single semantic (i.e. meaning) system across the two or more languages. For example, Marianne Celce-Murcia (1978, p. 50) quotes her daughter Caroline at 2 years 4 months as having a regular preference for the French word *couteau* and the English *spoon*. (She speculates that this was because the English 'knife' and French 'cuiller' were more demanding to pronounce.) Significantly, in those cases where the child has a word in *both* languages for a single referent, it tends to have a slightly different meaning in each language – in a similar way to so-called synonyms in a single language (Imedadze, 1978, p. 129).

Indications that parallel vocabularies are becoming established in the child's two languages seem to be closely followed by a recognition of the distinct semantic coverage of terms, that is, the different range of meaning in the two languages. David Deterding (1984, p. 30) quotes a telling example from his son, Alexander, who was growing up bilingual in Taiwanese Mandarin Chinese and English. When at 2 years 3 months the boy learned to tell his English *sheep* from his English *goat*, he also learned that this particular distinction was not relevant in his Chinese (where *yang* may denote 'sheep' or 'goat'). Compare Robbins Burling's son, Stephen, who was growing up bilingual in English and Garo, a language of northern India: 'When ... at 2;9 he suddenly grasped the meaning of color terms and was able to consistently call a red thing red, he was able to do so in both English and Garo simultaneously' (Burling, 1978, p. 69).

A major task for both the monolingual and the bilingual child consists in learning which contrasts (phonemic, tonal, grammatical, semantic) within a language are significant. The bilingual child must additionally learn in what ways these rules can be generalized across the two (or more) languages and, if not, whether the languages differ in any systematic way. Chapter 1 discusses how there are certain patterns in the acquisition of English grammar and phonology that are followed by most children. Because of the different grammatical and phonological structure of different groups of languages, this pattern is not automatically replicated across languages. However, there is evidence (see Burling, 1978) that once a bilingual child has become aware of a particular structure or concept which can be applied to either language (anything from the voiced/voiceless contrast in consonants to the concept of spatial relationship) this will be reflected simultaneously in both languages, regardless of the one through which it was acquired. On the other hand, aspects of language which are specific to only one of the child's languages (such as grammatical gender and verb tense rules, polite terms of address or the significance of tones) will need to be specifically 'tagged' to the language concerned.

Having observed where some of the differences between the two languages lie, the bilingual child will naturally try to predict a regular pattern of differences in much the same way as the monolingual child will predict regularities within a single language. For example, in the case of two closely related languages such as English and German, there will be a systematic pattern of phonological and morphological contrasts which may help bilingual children to predict the form of a word in one language if they know it in the other, for example: *learn/ lernen, fall/ fallen, deep/ tief*. (This is not unlike the way in which a monolingual may mimic a dialect other than their own.) Thus we find W.F. Leopold's bilingual daughter, Hildegaard (see Leopold, 1978, p. 31) creating a hypothetical word *steep* with the meaning 'stiff', by analogy with the German *steif*, just as a monolingual child might produce *mouses* by analogy with *houses* – both wrong as it happens, but an understandable attempt to minimize the learning load and a valuable stage

Note that, in the research literature on language acquisition, ages are often given in the form 2.7 or 2;7 to indicate 2 years 7 months. This book uses the latter convention, although the texts quoted may use others.

in working out the rules. Hildegaard also tried to create a 'German' word [kandl] simply by adapting the phonology of the English word 'candle' – just as an adult language learner with a reasonable instinct for languages might improvise in another language. As German was the weaker of Hildegaard's two languages, 'there remained an influence of English on her vocabulary, idioms and, to a limited extent, syntax, but practically none on sounds, morphology and word formation' (Leopold, 1978, p. 32).

Acquiring English as a second language

Children growing up in bilingual homes are, however, vastly outnumbered by another group of English learners. Because of its international status, English is acquired as a second language by many children around the world as part of their encounters with the wider community outside the home. How does this affect their experience of learning the language?

Issues relating to the *teaching* of English as a second or foreign language are discussed in Chapter 7.

As we have seen above and in Chapter 1, the various aspects of language develop at a different rate throughout life: in very broad terms, there is a rapid development of the sound system at an early age, overlapping with and followed by a rather slower development of grammatical sensitivity, and a development of meaning and the strategies of discourse which continues throughout life. Depending on the age at which English is encountered, therefore, these different aspects will be more or less established in the child's first language.

Because even quite young children learning English as a second language have already progressed beyond the 'two-word' stage in their first language and are capable of retaining brief stretches of speech in their short-term memory, they are often able to articulate accurately whole clusters of words in English. Because they have some social experience, they are usually able to deduce the social meaning of these clusters from the communicative context, without necessarily analysing them into their component parts. Examples include: *Come on* and *Please push me* (Yoshida, 1978, p. 96); *Get out of here!* and *Good-bye, see you tomorrow* (Huang and Hatch, 1978, p. 122); *Don't do that!* and *That's not yours* (Hakuta, 1986, p. 126); *Shaddup your mouth* and *Knock it off* (Fillmore, 1979, p. 211).

It has been argued that such prefabricated chunks of language (also known as 'formulaic speech'), because they are socially embedded and so highly memorable, play an important role in motivating the learner. It is only gradually that the internal structure of the units (i.e. the meaning of the individual words) is recognized, and the child begins to manipulate the components to express a personal intention.

It is not surprising that learners of second languages sometimes misjudge and transfer into the second language specific, inappropriate, features of the first language. This is usually called **interference**. It can vary from the most extreme 'foreign' accent to the occasional import of an idiom, and can include pragmatic aspects like when to speak, how loud to talk and so on.

However, the notion of interference is not always helpful, since many errors made by second language learners of English, particularly the very young, resemble the developmental stages of first language learning, such as simplification of syntax, over-generalization of rules, and so on. For example, Roar Ravem (1974) studied the acquisition of English *wh-*questions (i.e. questions beginning with who, what, which, where or why) by his Norwegian-speaking son and daughter over a period of four months in Britain. He found that, like monolingual

For a fuller discussion of learners' grammars of English, see Chapter 1.

children, they used structures like *Where Daddy go?* and *Where Daddy is going?* before they produced the mature form *Where is Daddy going?* According to Ravem, this did not reflect interference from their native Norwegian, which would probably have led to a form like *Where go Daddy?* Instead they produced *Where Daddy go?* just like first language learners (Dulay and Burt, 1976, p. 69).

Some provisional 'errors' made by second language learners of English, particularly children of school age, do not appear to be strictly attributable either to interference or to developmental processes. Rather they result from the interaction between the two languages, and the developing bilingual's attempt to integrate the new system with the old. Dulay and Burt (1976) have described this as 'process transfer' rather than 'product transfer', that is, such children transfer general language-learning *principles* from their experience of their first language:

> Children learning English as a second language create somewhat different and more sophisticated rules than those created by first language learners. For example, second language learners probably know a language requires certain frills, such as grammatical morphemes. It is natural, then, that when learning a second language, they should tend to *overuse* or misuse some of these frills, since their past experience tells them that a language requires frills. This results in error types not typically made by first language learners. For example:
> He not eats.
> She's dancings.
>
> (Dulay and Burt, 1976, pp. 72–3)

'Error' in second, as in first, language learning, is best regarded as a sign of active learning – evidence that learners are applying their own provisional rule systems as opposed to merely imitating. As learners have access to more and more linguistic input, their provisional hypotheses will gradually be refined until their language approximates more closely to idiomatic usage. Hakuta quotes a good example of this process from a 5-year-old Japanese girl called Uguisu ('nightingale' in Japanese) whose development in the English language he documented:

> Uguisu's development in English contained some intriguing examples of transfer from Japanese. Her use of the English word *mistake* is an example. In English, the word is most frequently used as a noun, as in *You made a mistake.* In Japanese, the word is most frequently used as a verb, *machigau.* Uguisu's initial use of *mistake* was as a verb, the way she used the concept in Japanese. She used utterances such as *Oh no, I mistake, Don't give me more because you're mistaking, Because I just mistake it,* gradually changing to the more native-like use, such as *I made a mistake.*
>
> (Hakuta, 1986, p. 114)

Naturally, languages will differ in the extent to which they share common features with English. A large part of the bilingual learner's task consists in developing a sensitivity to what the two language systems have in common and where they differ. On the basis of experience in another language, the child may begin by expecting certain linguistic cues (what Dulay and Burt above call the 'frills') which are absent in English, or vice versa. But this is all part of an active strategy. As Corder (1978) says, 'It is one of the strategies of learning to find out just how far down the scale it is going to be necessary to go before starting to build up again' (p. 90). Thus, a speaker of, say, Cantonese is going to have to go a great deal further 'down the scale' to find common linguistic rules with English – whether of pronunciation, grammar or vocabulary – than is a speaker of a more closely related language such as, say, Spanish.

This phenomenon of gradual approximation of idiomatic usage has been dubbed **interlanguage** and will in most speakers be a transitional stage. However, age is a significant factor, and much will depend on the learner's linguistic identity in the first language, and their attitude towards English and English speakers. Although there is much individual variation, the evidence points to a greater resistance to forming such new identifications beyond puberty. This point has been well captured by Christopherson:

> The small child is unformed as a person and is keen to model his behaviour on that of his elders in order to become a member of their social group; but gradually a consolidation of the personality sets in which may inhibit the kind of submission to a new model that second language learning requires. Moreover, it may be difficult for the older person to see the necessity for the effort required, since he is already a member of a social group.
>
> (Christopherson, 1973, pp. 50–1)

The problematical nature of the concept of the 'native speaker' is discussed in the first book in this series, *English: history, diversity and change* (Graddol et al. (eds), 1996). Chapter 7 in this book discusses the educational provision for different 'non-native' learners of English.

Thus some older learners, while acquiring communicative competence in English, effectively declare themselves as 'non-native' speakers. As Haugen has put it, '*communication* may be satisfied by a relatively modest mastery of the second language; *social identity* … may require something approaching native command' (1956, pp. 96–7).

Codeswitching and language choice

In societies where English functions alongside other languages, there may be an elaborate pattern of appropriateness which either dictates or strongly influences the choice of one or other language in particular contexts outside the home.

Thus English and other languages, or particular registers of these, may become polarized to cover different ranges of experience: English, for example, might become the language of literacy and formal education, whereas another language might be used for commercial transactions, and yet another perhaps for popular entertainment, and so on. Not all situations, however, will be so clear-cut – and the bilingual always has the option of choosing against the norm for special effect. In the company of other bilinguals, moreover, the bilingual speaker has the further option of incorporating features of one language within the other or even of changing language completely within a single utterance, that is, **codeswitching**. Indeed codeswitching 'may itself form part of the repertoire of a speech community' (Poplack, 1980, p. 614). In this way even a single speech act can serve to express 'the multiplicity of identities of the speaker' (Kamwangamalu, 1992, p. 45) or what Heller (1992, pp. 134–5) has called 'double affiliation'.

For a fuller discussion of the use of English alongside other languages and of bilingual codeswitching, see the earlier books in this series, *English: history, diversity and change* (Graddol et al. (eds), 1996) and *Learning English: development and diversity* (Maybin and Mercer (eds), 1996).

Thus, in addition to the complexity of learning to manipulate the systems of two or more languages, the bilingual child is also learning how to use the languages appropriately, how to manipulate all the available linguistic resources in order to achieve the desired effect (choosing the right language for the right occasion, knowing when to mix languages and when to keep them apart, and so on).

In some bilingual families, as in some communities, there are more regular patterns of interaction, in which particular languages are used with particular people – for example, one langue with the mother and one with the father – and children will often challenge their parents in particular for using the 'wrong' language. One of many well-attested examples of this comes from Redlinger and Park (1980), who quote the startled reaction of Danny (aged 2 years 4 months) to his mother's utterance of a German sentence in the company of a German-speaking researcher: '"Nicht Vogel! … Du sag birdie." ("Not bird!…You say birdie.")' (p. 342). This clearly affronted the normal rules of family interaction.

In other families, the choice of language is open to negotiation according to the topic and/or the effect a speaker wants to create. Li Wei (1994), quoted earlier in Activity 2.1, has made extensive recordings among the Chinese community in Newcastle upon Tyne, England. He observed the way in which family members' choice of language (and in particular the decision to follow or diverge from the preferred language of other participants in the interaction) could be carefully calculated to achieve pragmatic results. He quotes the following exchange between a mother and her 12-year-old son, who is playing on a computer:

Mother:	Finished homework?
Son:	(two second pause)
Mother:	Steven, *yiu mo wan sue?* (want to review (your) lessons?)
Son:	(1.5 second pause) I've finished.

(Li Wei, 1994, p. 163)

Li Wei comments that 'in some senses the mother knows that by choosing the preferred language of the child [English] instead of her own preferred language [Chinese], she is turning a simple question into an indirect request for the child to do his homework before playing with the computer, an implicature evidently understood by the child. Had the child not interpreted the meaning of this particular choice correctly, one assumes that he could have been ordered by the mother to pack up his computer games and do his homework' (Li Wei and Milroy, 1994, p. 25).

In either of the above types of family situation, the child will become sensitive to the normal patterns of interaction, and may manipulate these to achieve personal goals or particular pragmatic effects. Harrison and Piette quote a range of vivid examples of even very young children demonstrating these skills to good effect:

Ioan [is] a bilingual Welsh/English boy of 3;3…. In his extended family Ioan could, in his third year, tell which relatives were bilingual, like himself, and which inserted odd bits of Welsh but lacked fluency. In a transcript of Ioan … he switches into English on seeing his monolingual English grandmother come into the room where five people had been talking Welsh. Before she says anything he announces, 'I don't want to', evoking the response, 'Well I say that Ioan – ought to go to bed'. Five turns follow in English and are all about his reluctance to go to bed. Then another adult asks in Welsh if he wants to stay, and Ioan replies in Welsh. Subsequently the talk moves to another topic. Ioan remains. At a point when his grandmother is talking, in English of course, with his father, Ioan selects Welsh to tell his mother he does not want to go to bed … Arguably we have here switchings that are so framed as to help bring about what Ioan wants … Apparently his bilingualism is a tool for discourse.

(Harrison and Piette, 1980, p. 222)

Romaine (1989, p. 111) has argued that in codeswitched discourse of this kind all linguistic choices can be interpreted as an index of the 'social relations, rights and obligations which exist and are created between participants in a conversation'. Erving Goffman (1981) has defined such shifts in personal alignment as changes in 'footing' and the boundaries of the events themselves as 'frames'. These are evident in children's role play, where the children effectively take on the perspectives of imaginary others in imagined situations.

Fancy footwork at play?

In storytelling as well as in joking [Hawaiian Polynesian girls, aged 5–7 years] nearly always dramatize by voice intonation and imitation of speech. This means that they will imitate … accents, alter their voices to indicate age, sex, and personality of a character, or distort their speech to insult a target child or group.

(Watson-Gegeo and Boggs, 1977, p. 83)

At age 8.11 Mario and Carla [Spanish American children] were playing cowboys and conversed entirely in English, as cowboys would be expected to do … Whenever they stepped outside these roles and gave instructions on how the play-acting was to proceed, or to offer protests, they switched to Spanish [see Fantini, 1985]. When children assumed a position of authority, they issued a command in Spanish. … If a child got hurt, he would be comforted by an older child in Spanish, even though an immediately preceding interaction between the children might have been in English [see McClure, 1977].

(Romaine, 1989, p. 205).

In their play [the ethnically Chinese children] reflect the language patterns of their school: when they pretend to be Malay girls in the class they speak Malay … When they address the teacher, or play at teacher–child interaction, they speak English. They even make an effort at using Standard English in their imitations of the teacher. They sing a 'goodbye song' in Mandarin.

(Gupta, 1994, p. 169)

We can see from the bilingual examples in the box that the young bilingual children are already able to associate the English language with particular kinds of practices. English, we may deduce, is something spoken in school, especially by teachers, and is the language of cowboys or possibly people in films more generally. The children's other languages seem to be associated with the management of play and with personal relationships. But even among these children, there are differences in the roles played by English. Some of them do choose to use English spontaneously during play. Some of them, moreover, are already familiar with more than one variety of English and are aware of different social meanings between varieties.

However, this still begs the question of whether particular languages – even in a given setting – are automatically the bearers of fixed sets of cultural values. Do we have any evidence that, in acquiring the English language, children are automatically being inculcated into a particular culture – or is the language amenable to new uses by new speakers? Gupta argues that, in Singapore at least, it is possible to decouple the several official languages from any direct association with particular cultures:

> When children learn or develop their English they are becoming like
> high status members of their own community … A child growing up
> speaking English, Mandarin, Hokkien and Cantonese in Singapore is not
> going to sound, or want to sound, like someone from England, Beijing,
> Fujian and Guangdong, but like a Singaporean speaking four languages
> … these languages are all seen as part of a single identity.
>
> (Gupta, 1994, p. 181, 65)

Gupta compares her own study of children's language use with an earlier study
carried out by Muriel Saville-Troike (1986), both of which seem to demonstrate
that ethnically Chinese children use English in a distinctively 'Chinese' way:

> [In Saville-Troike's study] two Chinese brothers aged 3 and 4 years …
> used strategies of argument [in English] involving temporization,
> compromise and moral argument which were also used extensively by
> Japanese and Korean children, but rarely or never by 'English speakers'.
> In my naturalistic data, arguments were frequent: the English-speaking
> Chinese children in my study seem to have a sophisticated argumentative
> style, and like Saville-Troike's subjects they invoked moral argument.
> This may be caused not only by cultural differences, as Saville-Troike
> suggests, but also … by the explicit marking, mainly by [Chinese]
> pragmatic particles, of interpersonal discourse features … It may be that
> the explicit marking of interpersonal discourse features which relate to
> such areas as whether or not you expect the interlocutor to agree with
> you, facilitate the use of reasoned argument.
>
> (Gupta, 1994, p. 58)

2.4   LEARNING SOCIAL AND STYLISTIC VARIATION WITHIN ENGLISH

As I state at the outset of this chapter, it is not only bilinguals who are able to apply
their linguistic repertoire to social acts: monolingual English speakers have access
to a range of different language varieties to signal their shifting attitudes and
identities and to achieve particular goals. Again the key question we consider is
how and at what stage these skills are acquired by children.

Pioneering research on social and stylistic variation in English was conducted
in the 1960s by the American sociolinguist, William Labov. Not all of Labov's work
was with young people, but one influential study among the black male adolescent
street gangs in Harlem, New York, focused on the subtle and systematic way in
which an individual's orientation towards the gangs was reflected in the forms of
language he used (Labov, 1977). Labov described the use of language in these
circumstances as a 'fine-grained index of membership in the street culture' (1977,
p. 255). Labov's approach has since been widely replicated elsewhere (e.g. Reid,
1978; Cheshire, 1982; Youssef, 1991), and continues to be constructively critiqued
and extended.

Labov's original hypothesis had been that young children were not sensitive
to social variation in language and did not learn to make stylistic choices themselves until early adolescence. Specifically he claimed that children pass through
predictable stages of linguistic development in the acquisition of Standard
English and that it is not until the age of 11 to 12 years that full 'stylistic variation' is

achieved, where 'the child begins to learn how to modify his speech in the direction of the prestige standard' in more formal situations, such as reading out loud or an interview with a stranger (Labov, 1964, p. 91). How far do you think this claim can be sustained in the light of the evidence above from young bilingual children and from your own experience? Leaving aside the question of what variety serves as the 'prestige standard' for a given child in a given situation, we do not have to look far to find counter examples to Labov's claim, where even very young children show themselves sensitive to contextual variation in language.

'Talkin nice'

In the tradition of Labov, Valerie Youssef (1991) conducted a longitudinal case study of three small children between the ages of 2 and 4 years on the Caribbean island of Trinidad, where the characteristic differences between speakers are 'not outright distinctions in the use of particular forms, but rather differences in proportional usage of those forms' (p. 89). During the course of the study the speech of the three children diverged along predictable social-class lines, with the most middle-class boy, Kareem, using increasingly more Standard English features and the most working-class boy, Keeshan, using increasingly more Trinidadian English features as time went by. This already throws into question one of Labov's original assumptions, namely that increasing awareness of social

variation would automatically cause children to orient towards a more standard form of English. The other significant finding was that all the children were clearly sensitive from the outset to contextual features according to the social context. Thus Janet (the 'middle' child of the three in terms of social class) at the age of 3 years 9 months produced 100 per cent Standard English past tense verb forms in conversation with her mother (who was very particular about the use of Standard English, as the language of 'advancement'), but only 54 per cent with the family helper (a Trinidadian English speaker), 47 per cent with her brother, and 40 per cent when playing with her peers out of her mother's earshot. The middle-class boy, Kareem, from the age of 2 years 10 months 'started to attend a preschool in which he learned about what he referred to as 'talkin nice' and increasingly acquired Standard English features which he varied stylistically according primarily to addressee' (Youssef, 1991, pp. 94, 90). He was exposed to Standard English stories from an early age, and gradually incorporated the past tense forms into his own narratives, though still with due regard to his addressee. The following (oral) account was produced at the age of 4 (Standard English verb forms are italicized; we may presume that 'comed' is an instance of child language rather than the adult Trinidadian form):

> When we *finished* we comed out. We dress up an we bathe an we *went* by the Tobago airport and wait for the aeroplane ... We *went* by a shop to buy some flying fish to eat ... We *had* to wait long and long.
>
> (Youssef, 1991, p. 94; original italics)

Youssef concluded that 'Overall [the children's] development reflected the extent and nature of expected usage of the respective markers for the social circumstances in which each lived' (p. 93).

Similar findings emerge from two studies (Romaine, 1975, and Reid, 1978) conducted in a very different social context indeed: urban Edinburgh in Scotland. Both Romaine and Reid found considerable evidence of both social class and stylistic variation among their young subjects. In the case of Reid's 11-year-old boys, there was also a significant 'school effect'. Moreover, Reid found that most of the boys in the study were already fully aware of the need to switch varieties of language, particularly the boys from the 'posh' school, who used a broader vernacular when interacting with their peers elsewhere:

[Kevin]	... that's what we're really here [at this school] for ... to talk nice and that.
[Michael]	... up at X school once, playing basketball ... they started to take the micky out of all of us ... because of the way we speak ... [so] you just keep your mouth shut and you don't say much.
[Ian]	I talk with a bit of a Scottish accent when I'm out in [one of the outlying towns] ... I don't really go from ... clean ... straight to dirty ... it's just a slight change in the way I talk ... if I talk to them with a sort of clean accent ... they'll think ... a bit of a bore really ... if you talk with the same accent as they do they'll just think ... you're one of us in a way.

(Reid, 1978, p. 169–70)

They were also aware of the pressures exerted on them (by mothers in particular!) to be more careful about their speech in other people's houses:

> [Kevin]   ... especially when their mother's wi them ... ken [you know] ... they just gie them a wee [small] flick ... to tell them to talk nice.
>
> (Reid, 1978, p. 169)

All of this led Reid to conclude that:

> It is as true of these eleven-year-old Edinburgh boys as of older inform-ants investigated previously that there are features of their speech which relate in a systematic way to their social status and to the social context in which their speech is produced.
>
> (Reid, 1978, p. 169–70)

Romaine was less willing, on the available evidence, to venture a statement as to the factors at play in influencing her rather younger subjects to vary the density of certain features in their speech. However, at different points in an interview, she elicited some very different stretches of talk from a 6-year-old girl.

Throughout this section Scots words which may not be obvious to speakers of other varieties of English are glossed in brackets.

❖ ❖ ❖ ❖ ❖

Activity 2.4 *(Allow about 5 minutes)*

Consider for a moment what factors might be at play in causing the 6-year-old quoted in the passages below to use such different styles of delivery at the two points (1 and 2) in the interview. We obviously only have a transcript on which to base any deductions, so they can only be tentative. To make the passages more intelligible the spelling conventions have been slightly adapted from the original with the author's permission.

1   I fall oot [out] the bed. She falls oot the bed and we pull off the covers. I fell oot the bed so D says 'Where are you J?' I says, 'I'm doon [down] here'. She says 'Come up. Babies dinnae [don't] do that. They should be in their co' [cot]' So she gets oot the bed. She falls oot cause she bumps her head on the wall and she says, 'Oh, this is a hard bed too' so she says, 'Oh, I'm on the fler [floor]'.

2   It's a house, my house that I live in now, cause I fle'ed [flitted, Scots for 'moved house']. The house is still in a mess anyway. It's still got plaster and I've no fireplace now, all blocked up. Workin men plastered where they used to be, there and there, and they did the same to the fireplace. They just knocked it all ou' [out].

(Adapted from Romaine, 1984, p. 100)

Comment

My own interpretation is that the first passage represents a humorous narrative in a relatively informal context in which the girl is clearly very engaged, and in which she includes stretches of direct speech quoted from another vernacular speaker. Both these factors, as well as the obvious hilarity of the original situation (I can almost hear the giggles!), are such as to produce the girl's most relaxed style. The second passage, by contrast, represents a more sober account, possibly in a more formal context, where a more standard style might be expected. It is conceivable also that the girl may be unconsciously echoing whole phrases she has heard uttered by adults about the building work.

❖   ❖   ❖   ❖   ❖

Like Reid's schoolboys, Romaine's young subjects were often quite lucid about their language practices. The following extract is taken from an interview with a 10-year-old girl:

Interviewer:	Does your Mum ever tell you to speak polite?
Child:	[If] there's somebody poli' [polite] in. Like see, some people moved en. There's new people in the stair [local vernacular for 'tenement flats'] we've moved up tae [to] and they come in and I'm always sayin 'Doon Shep', cause it's my wee dog, so I say 'doon'. My Mum say 'That's not wha' you say' she says, 'It's "Sit down, Ken"', cause she doesn't like me speakin rough.
Interviewer:	Why do you think she doesn't like it?
Child:	Well, if I speak rough she doesn't like it when other people are in because they think that we're rough ta'ies [tatties, i.e. potatoes] in the stair.

(Adapted from Romaine, 1984, p. 126)

Learning to be a child: relative status in the family and beyond

Halliday (1978, p. 1) has argued that 'A child creates, first his child tongue, then his mother tongue, in interaction with that little coterie of people who constitute his meaning group'. In other words, the child begins by learning what it is to speak like a child and only gradually experiments with other roles.

The baby's first experience of language is likely to be in dialogue with a parent figure. As described in the previous chapter, adults in many English-speaking cultures tend to use a particular style of language when communicating with babies, usually referred to as 'baby talk'. This has been well summarized by Jean Berko Gleason, who carried out her studies in the USA:

> Briefly we can say they raised the fundamental frequency of their voices, used simple short sentences with concrete nouns, diminutives, and terms of endearment, expanded the children's utterances and in general performed the linguistic operations that constitute baby-talk style. There was a lot of individual variation in the extent to which all of these features might be employed. One mother, for instance, spoke in a normal voice to her husband, a high voice to her 4-year-old, a slightly raised voice to her 8-year-old and when she talked to her baby she fairly squeaked.
>
> (Berko Gleason, 1973, p. 160–1)

Berko Gleason had set out to research baby talk, and in particular the extent to which older siblings were able to vary their speech to accommodate the communicative needs of younger siblings. During the course of the research she found evidence for some of the things she was looking for, but also made some unexpected findings:

> The children in our sample ranged in age from infancy to 8 years. By and large we were not primarily looking for evidence of code switching or stylistic variation in the children under 4. These children were included in the sample because we wanted to get examples of the adults and older children talking to them for evidence of baby-talk style. Some things did seem readily evident from observing the very young children and talking to their parents, however. The first is that even the tiniest children make some distinctions. The basic, earliest variation is simply between talking and not talking. Very small children will frequently talk or jabber nonsense to their own parents or siblings, but fall silent in the presence of strangers. When the parent tries to get the baby to say, 'Hi,' or 'Bye-bye,' to the interviewer, the baby stares blankly; and the mother says, 'I don't know what's wrong. He really can talk. He says bye-bye all the time.' The baby remains silent. After the interviewer leaves, surrounded once more by familiar faces, the baby suddenly springs to life and says a resounding 'Bye-bye!' So the first variation is between speech and silence.
>
> Another, more obviously stylistic variation we have seen in the language of the children under 4 as well as those over 4, has been the selective use of whining, by which I mean a repetitive, insistent, singsong demand or complaint, and not crying, which is very difficult for little children to inhibit. The whining basically occurs to parents and parent figures, and a child may abruptly switch to a whine at the sight of his parent, when he has previously been talking to someone else in a quite normal tone. In the nursery school I visited, for instance, one child was talking with his friends when his father arrived. At the sight of his father, he abruptly altered his tone and began to whine, 'Pick me up' at him …
>
> The children's language to the babies in the families was also examined for evidence of baby-talk style. While most of the features of peer group code appeared in the language of the entire 4- to 8-year old sample, there were age differences in the ability to use baby-talk style.

The older children were in control of the basic features of baby-talk style – their sentences to the babies were short and repetitive, and uttered in a kind of singing style. In one family I asked an 8-year-old to ask his 2-year-old brother to take a glass to the kitchen. He said:

'Here, Joey, take this to the kitchen. Take it to the kitchen.' (Baby-talk intonation, high voice).

A little while later, I asked him to ask his 4-year-old brother to take a glass to the kitchen. This time he said:

'Hey, Rick, take this to the kitchen, please.' (Normal intonation). This is clear evidence of code switching in the language of this 8-year-old child.

On the other end of the spectrum, the 4-year-old, Ricky, whom I followed about, did not use baby-talk style to his 2-year-old brother. He typically did not use either a special intonation or repetition. He said to the baby: 'Do you know what color your shoes are?' in just the same way he said: 'What's the name of the book, Anthony?' to his brother; and 'I don't think he know how to climb up' to his father.

Somewhere in between no baby-talk style and full baby-talk style lies slightly inappropriate baby-talk style, which we saw particularly in some 5- and 6-year-old girls …

The original aim of this study was to see if, indeed, children talk in different ways to different people. The answer is yes; infants are selective about whom they talk to at all. Four-year-olds may whine at their mothers, engage in intricate verbal play with their peers, and reserve their narrative, discursive tales for their grown-up friends. By the time they are 8, children have added to the foregoing some of the politeness routines of formal adult speech, baby-talk style, and the ability to talk to younger children in the language of socialization.

(Berko Gleason, 1973, pp. 163–7)

Some older siblings demonstrate great social sensitivity to the communicative needs of younger brothers and sisters. Here, two Singaporean brothers, aged 7 years 8 months and 4 years 5 months respectively, are attempting to assemble a plastic skeleton. The older boy is aware of the need to use Standard English with the interviewer, but switches to a more friendly Singaporean English to address his little brother (note the use of the pragmatic particles *ah* and *lah*):

Elder brother	[*to adult interviewer*] I don't know whether he knows how to do it.
	[3 sec pause] [*then to younger brother*] A- all this are bones ah?
Younger brother	Yah.
Elder brother	All this are human bones lah.

(Gupta, 1994, p. 77)

Sensitivity to relative status in relationships is particularly apparent if we look at children's developing recognition and use of the different ways of asking questions, making requests and issuing commands in English.

Shirley Brice Heath looked particularly at the use of questions among members of the poor black American community she was researching. The ability of the children to mimic the adult style of firing questions at them was impressive. For example:

Mandy, a child 4;1 years of age, was observed playing with a mirror and talking into the mirror. She seemed to run through a sequence of actors, exemplifying ways in which each used questions:

> How ya doin, Miss Sally?
> Ain't so good, how you?
> Got no 'plaints. Ben home?
>
> What's *your* name, little girl?
> You a pretty little girl.
> You talk to me.
> Where's yo' momma?
> You give her this for me, okay?

When Mandy realized she had been overheard, she said 'I like to play talk. Sometimes I be me, sometimes somebody else.' I asked who she was this time; she giggled and said, 'You know Miss Sally, but dat other one Mr Griffin talk.' Mr Griffin was the insurance salesman who came to the community each week to collect on insurance premiums. Mandy had learned that he used questions in ways different from members of her community, and she could imitate his questions. However, in imitation as in reality, she would not answer his questions or give any indication of reception of the messages Mr Griffin hoped to leave with her.

(Heath, 1982b, p. 119)

It would appear that English-speaking children, at least in North America, take some time to develop sensitivity to the full adult repertoire for 'getting people to do things'. Choosing the socially appropriate expression entails not only an awareness of the range of linguistic formulations available but also an accurate prediction of the likelihood of compliance on the part of the addressee. Even very young children – perhaps because of explicit teaching – seem to be sensitive to the effect of 'please'; but, with or without 'please', they tend to favour *questions* or explicit *statements* of their own need. Although they understand only too well the force of adult commands, because of their relative lack of social power children are rarely in a position to issue *instructions* or make direct *requests* themselves, unless it is to even younger children. When this rule is flouted, it occasions comment:

7-year-old [boy to 11-year-old girl]: *Bring your li'l self here.*

[Bystander]: *Who you think you are?*

7-year-old: *I think I'm somebody big.*

(Adapted from Mitchell-Kernan and Kernan, 1997, p. 204)

When addressing adults, however, children usually resort to the more indirect means of getting what they want, such as asking questions or making hints. According to Craig Lawson (in a 1967 unpublished paper from Berkeley, California, entitled ' Request patterns in a two year old'), even 2-year-olds have acquired rules for the social distribution of requests according to age and rank.

'I think I'm somebody big'

Thus, a 2-year-old girl gave almost entirely simple imperatives to her peers, but with adults and older children she used a mixture of desire statements, questions and permission requests. Shuy (1978, p. 272) relates how 5-year-old Joanna got herself invited to dinner by making three 'statements': about the absence of the family car, the fact that her mother worried if she missed meals, and finally 'You know, I eat almost anything'! In the words of Ervin-Tripp (1977, p. 188), 'wide use of tactful deviousness is a late accomplishment'. Interestingly, when one researcher tried to turn the tables on a child, it was almost as if they were speaking different languages:

> One type of statement [by the children] intended to function as a directive took the form *You gave Jimmy a nickle* or *You let Beverley take the tape recorder home.* This type of hint occurred so often in the course of the research that it became a source of humor. On one occasion one of the authors said to a boy of 11, in an accusatory tone similar to the one the children often used when hinting in this way: *Oh you washed Karen's car.* The child responded with a puzzled look and it was a few seconds before he realized that the researcher was jokingly requesting that he wash her car. It would appear that the success of this stratagem is tied to role relations.

(Mitchell-Kernan and Kernan, 1977, p. 200)

Tellingly, the 2-year-old girl studied by Lawson, who was rather unkindly 'set up' at the tea table to ask for some milk, exhibited strikingly different behaviour to her mother than to her father. To her mother she came straight out with *Mummy I want milk*, whereas to her father she beat about the bush with such expressions as *What's that? My milk, Daddy. Yours, Daddy? It's milk, Daddy. You want milk, Daddy? I have some, thank-you.* This brings us to the subject of the next section, which is how children learn gendered roles and relationships in English.

Learning to be an English-speaking girl or boy

At the same time as we are learning what it is to be a child, we are also in most societies learning our increasingly demarcated gender roles, and these too are reflected in girls' and boys' increasingly differentiated use of language. There is some evidence that, after a brief burst of directness, girls (like adult women) in many English-speaking societies revert to more indirect language. In an article full of vivid case studies, Carol Gilligan describes how previously bright and mischievous American girls like 8-year-old Diane (who literally blew a whistle at the dinner table whenever she got interrupted) and 8-year-old Karen (who walked out of the classroom when her teacher refused to call on her to answer) progressively lose their voices until, around adolescence, they are repeatedly heard to say 'I don't know', when in fact they *do* know, or even, like Iris 'If I were to say what I was feeling or thinking, no one would want to be with me. My voice would be too loud' (Gilligan, 1995, p. 207).

Other studies have found that certain interactional features (e.g. interruptions, direct requests) are associated more with boys and men, whereas others (conversational support features such as *mmh*, *yeah* and *right*, and indirect requests) are associated more with girls and women. The evidence is often striking, but needs to be interpreted with caution: people's use of interactional features varies between contexts and depending on what they are trying to achieve as they talk. Marjorie Harness-Goodwin (1990), in a study of black working-class children aged 8–13 years in Philadelphia, found that when playing in single-sex groups, girls' interaction was collaboratively organized. They made use of indirect request forms that drew in other participants (*Let's ask her, Maybe we can slice them like that*). This was in contrast to boys' use of more direct forms: *Gimme the pliers.* But the girls were perfectly capable of using direct commands when they needed to, as when one girl told a younger child *Don't put that down! Put that back up! It's supposed to be that way.*

There is a great deal of evidence that girls – particularly as they become adolescent – will adopt more standard varieties of speech than their male counterparts, when they judge that the occasion demands this. As one of Reid's 11-year-old Scottish boys observes, 'some girls … when they talk to their teacher, they talk sort of posh … and when they talk to their pals … they just talk normal' (Reid, 1978, p. 169). Interestingly, in an experiment conducted by Edwards (1979), this tendency for girls to talk 'posher' sometimes led to middle-class boys' voices being mistaken for girls' voices and working-class girls' voices being mistaken for boys' voices. Macaulay (1978), in a study of 10-year-olds, 15-year-olds and adults in Glasgow in Scotland, looked at the interaction between age, sex and social class, and found that the speech of the children diverged according to social class as they got older, with the 10-year-olds of all social classes speaking more like each other than the 15-year-olds. Among the 15-year-old middle-class children, the girls already sounded much more like middle-class women than middle-class boys, and the boys sounded rather more like working-class men than middle-class men. In other words, the girls' class and gender identities appeared to reinforce each other, whereas for the boys there was more of a tension between the two.

The perception of vernacular English as more 'masculine' starts at an early age. You may remember from the beginning of this section the case of Keeshan, one of the Trinidadian preschool children studied by Youssef (1991), whose language became 'broader' as the study progressed. One of the factors to which this was attributed was his growing identification with men in his community (*dem fellas* as he called them). Youssef quotes the following typical exchange between Keeshan, aged 4, and his mother on the male preserve of smoking (note the use of the vernacular future form *go*):

Keeshan	I want to go in Sports an buy a cigarette an a match to smoke. I go smoke just now. Let me buy a baby cigarette.
Mother	That will not burn.
Keeshan	It won't burn me. I go hide it tomorrow. I go take a baby fire an put it in the smoke thing, right. I go hold the match.
Mother	Youz Daddy doz smoke?
Keeshan	My Daddy doz smoke just now. Uncle Tolly smoke.

(Youssef, 1991, pp. 99–100)

Further evidence of the link between masculinity and the vernacular is available from Australia, where Edina Eisikovits (1989) conducted a study of sex differences in the speech of two groups of working-class inner-city adolescents, from school years 8 and 10 (average age 13 years 11 months and 16 years 1 month respectively). In common with other studies of a similar kind, she found more evidence of social conformity, including stylistic variation, among the girls; among the boys she found a strong preference for the vernacular third-person negative *don't* (as in *He don't wanna work so he told 'em down the Dole office he wanted to be an elephant trainer!*) and for swearing:

> Among the older girls there is a serious and conservative acceptance of the responsibilities of adulthood. All are concerned with fitting in with society and its expectations rather than, as two years earlier, with the conflicts with it. No longer are they rebellious in their attitudes towards family, school, and society in general. All see themselves as having 'grown up' – a process which for the girls means 'settling down' ...
>
> Among the boys, however, a rather different perception emerges. They, too, see themselves as having grown up, but for them this does not necessarily mean settling down or conforming to family or societal expectations of 'good' behaviour. Instead, it is more usually seen as a movement towards self-assertion, 'toughness' and an unwillingness to be dictated to ...
>
> Clearly, different behavioural norms as well as different social perceptions exist for the two sexes. Given these differences, it is hardly surprising that the two groups differ in their attitudes to and use of language.

That [the older girls'] new conservatism is extended to attitudes to language may be seen in A's changed view of swearing. Asked what her fights with her boyfriend are about she replies:

A: Oh, petty things. Like, oh, sometimes he swears at me and I don't like swearing anymore. An he'll swear at me so we have a fight about that ...

Interviewer: You don't think about that when you're 13 or 14 doing it yourself.

A: No, you don't. When you get older, you think, 'Oh Jesus, what did I ever say that for?' ...

The boys on the other hand tend to move in a contrary direction:

Interviewer: Did you used to get beltings when you were a kid?

B: Oh, swore once when I was about five an I was belted off me mother. Tried to wash me mouth out with soap ...

Interviewer: What about now?

C: If I swear in front of me mother now she don't say nothing ...

That such prestige value is attached to non-standard forms by the males in this study may be seen from the direction of their self-corrections. Unlike the older females who self-correct towards standard forms, for example:

D: Our Deputy-Principal was really nice and he sort of let my group, the kids I hang – hung around with, get away with almost anything.

E: An me and Kerry – or should I say, Kerry and I – are the only ones who've done the project.

the older males self-correct in the opposite direction, favouring the non-standard over the standard form. For example:

F: I didn't know what I did – what I done.

G: He's my family doctor. I've known im ever since I was a kid. An 'e gave – give it to me an 'e said, 'As long as it's helping you, I'll give it to you' you know.

That such consciousness of external prestige norms is only just developing among the older girls is evidenced in the contrary direction among the younger girls who self-correct in line with the males, for example:

H: It don't work out anyway – it don't work out noways.
(Eisikovits, 1989, pp. 42–5)

What we need to remember in the case of Eisikovits' research – indeed any research which looks at the effect of social variables – is the possibility that the gender/class/ethnicity of the researcher may itself skew the results in a particular direction. For example, in this case, the girls, identifying with Eisikovits' gender, may have consciously or unconsciously accommodated to her more middle-class speech, whereas the boys may have diverged in an effort to assert their masculinity.

There are several different ways in which the English language, and the use of English, may be described as 'gendered'. The relationship between gender and the use of vernacular and 'prestige' accents of English is briefly discussed in the first book in this series, *English: history, diversity and change* (Graddol et al. (eds), 1996); the second book, *Using English: from conversation to canon* (Maybin and Mercer (eds), 1996), discusses gender and interactional style, and women's writing in English.

But where do children get their notions of femininity and masculinity from? Carole Edelsky (1977) asked three groups of children, aged 6–7, 8–9 and 11–12 years respectively, and a group of adults to judge whether a series of statements (originally developed by Lakoff, 1973) were more likely to have been made by a man or a woman. The youngest group could only really agree about two things: that women were more likely to say *adorable* and that men were much more likely to say *damn it*. This perception that 'women don't swear' remained strong until at least the age of 11, when it was accompanied by a second strong assumption, that women are more likely to say *please*. Interestingly, though, there was far less consensus among the adults (who no doubt had a far wider base of personal experience on which to make such judgements!). This led Edelsky to speculate that, where children's judgements overshoot those of adults, it is because they have been explicitly *taught* the stereotypes.

Acts of identity: learning to express *oneself*?

The picture emerging from this section so far may appear overly deterministic. Are English-speaking children indeed locked into set paths according to their social class, ethnicity, gender, etc? Sociolinguistic work has generally concerned itself with the way in which language variation can be correlated with social factors of one kind or another, in other words with the *systematic* social variation of language in use. But, as Robert Le Page and Andrée Tabouret-Keller have pointed out, this assumes that *distinct* languages and *fixed* membership of social groups can be taken as given. Their influential book *Acts of Identity* (1985) sets out to:

> throw some light upon the ways in which such concepts as 'a language' and 'a group or community' come into being through the acts of identity which people make within themselves and with each other ... in other words, how the individual's idiosyncratic behaviour reflects attitudes towards groups, causes, traditions ...; and how the identity of a group lies within the projections individuals make of the concepts each has about the group.
>
> (Le Page and Tabouret Keller, 1985, p. 2).

The point about 'projections' is a key one: unless we have a keen shared sense of the *stereotypical* linguistic behaviour of other social groups we will have no fixed models to aspire to or flee from.

However, Le Page and Tabouret-Keller have drawn attention to the fact that our acts of identity may be constrained by the extent to which:

(i)   we can identify the groups

(ii) we have both adequate access to the groups and ability to analyse their behavioural patterns

(iii) the motivation to join the groups is sufficiently powerful and is either reinforced or reversed by feedback from the groups

(iv) we have the ability to modify our behaviour

(Le Page and Tabouret-Keller, 1985, p. 182)

Whereas children may take some time to achieve the first of these as their circles of interaction gradually increase, they will have a distinct advantage over adults in terms of the last.

Research studies have revealed evidence of both peer group pressure and individual idiosyncrasy. Lesley Milroy (1980, pp. 60–1) mentions the case of a boy who, having on one occasion shifted his speech style to suit a formal interview situation, was so laughed at by his peers that on the next occasion he moved sharply in the direction of the vernacular. Reid (1978, p. 165) quotes a humorous instance where he had made the assumption that a playground context would elicit the most relaxed – and, therefore, he assumed the most nonstandard – forms of language from his young male subjects. However, he had not bargained on the fact that the boys would rise to the situation by producing their best imitation of TV sports commentators, Scottish, English and American!

Further evidence of the role of individual choice is apparent in the findings of Arvilla Payne (1980), who was interested in the extent to which young children will acquire the accent of their peers rather than that of their parents. Payne conducted a survey of families who had moved from a variety of locations into a middle-class suburb of the US city of Philadelphia; she was looking particularly at the characteristic local pattern of pronunciation of a particular vowel sound. Her general conclusion was that children arriving after the age of 8 stood a far lower chance of sounding like a 'local' than those who arrived before. In other words their linguistic identity by this age had become relatively fixed. However, she found that, whereas a handful of children (particularly one teenage girl who had arrived at the crucial age of 8) had been strikingly successful in acquiring the local vowel pattern, and the majority had been somewhat confused about it, one family of five boys originally from New York City (who had moved to Philadelphia at ages ranging from 0–9, and were aged 10–20 at the time of the study) had been strikingly resistant to the pattern. It is fascinating to speculate why this might have been the case – and you may like to reflect on it now. However, what is important for the argument here is that there was nothing *predetermined* about the outcome, and one may assume that the family was exercising not only sensitivity to the social variables themselves but also a degree of personal/collective choice.

Trudgill (1986), reviewing a range of evidence from different parts of the English-speaking world, comes to the following conclusion:

> Labov … has argued that, while children younger than eight appear to be certain to accommodate totally, there can be no assurance that, after the age of eight, children will become totally integrated into a new speech community. I would also add that, after the age of 14 one can be fairly sure that they will not. The problem years are eight to 14, with the degree of integration depending on many different social and individual factors.
> (Trudgill, 1986, pp. 33–4)

So where does this leave us with regard to Labov's earlier claims, quoted at the beginning of this section? His ideas were obviously useful in identifying key stages in a child's sociolinguistic development, and – along with others – he was correct in identifying puberty as the stage when children's social identity through language becomes more self-conscious. However, his research had been based in relatively stable communities with a single local vernacular against which an individual could progressively measure any encounters with the Standard English of the wider world. Where the original hypothesis fell down was in generalizing from the monolingual and (relatively) monodialectal childhood experience. In cases where children are exposed from a young age to more than one variety of language, or where they move between language communities, perception of the different social values attached to each language variety is likely to develop in infancy, in tandem with their developing sensitivity to linguistic forms. Indeed the evidence is that, far from becoming more flexible around puberty, they are likely to become *less* so, as they become more committed to a particular set of identifications.

2.5   CONCLUSION

You may find it useful at this point to reconsider the three questions posed by Kamwangamalu (1992, p. 33):

Who am I?

How am I perceived by others?

How would I want to be perceived?

In this chapter we have already seen how young speakers may:

- unconsciously adopt (i.e. converge towards) the speech of others because they identify with it (e.g. Keeshan from Trinidad with 'dem fellas', or the Rojas-Drummond twins with their cousins from England); or
- consciously emulate the speech of those groups they wish to be close to or to impress or to get something out of (e.g. the Scottish girls who talked 'posh', or the Spanish American children who wanted to comfort each other); or even
- consciously mimic the speech of others – or more precisely, their *stereotypes* of others – while at the same time distancing themselves from the stereotype (e.g. Ishfaq in his humorous exchange with Ben Rampton quoted at the start of this chapter).

In his book *Crossing*, Rampton (1995) explores some of these complex phenomena with particular reference to adolescent ethnic identity.

The last of these may look like an intricate feat to accomplish, but it is something that we do every time we adopt a 'funny voice' in order to get away with saying something ironic or comical or provocative. There are various linguistic and paralinguistic devices, such as intonation, rate of speech or facial expression, which we may use to proclaim that it is not our own 'true' voice and that we are merely acting a part – but there is usually a convenient degree of ambiguity involved!

All of these acts of social 'positioning' then may be accomplished in English at a variety of linguistic levels, from sounds (accents or pitch) through vocabulary or grammar to choice of language itself.

❖   ❖   ❖   ❖   ❖

Activity 2.7   *(Allow at least 20 minutes)*

You may find it useful, by way of consolidating your work on this chapter, to prepare a matrix similar to the one below, drawing on examples from the chapter as well as on your own experience and observations. To start the process off, I have placed the examples just mentioned in the relevant cells.

	Accent	Vocabulary	Grammar	Language choice
Unconscious convergence	Rojas-Drummond twins (Reading A)	Keeshan? (Youssef, 1991)	Keeshan (Youssef, 1991)	
Conscious emulation	Scottish girls? (Reid, 1978)		Scottish girls (Reid, 1978)	Spanish American children (McClure, 1977)
Conscious mimicry	Ifshaq (Rampton, 1996)			

❖   ❖   ❖   ❖   ❖

We have seen that children start to learn the communicative norms of their community even before they learn their first word. From a very early age, whether bilingual or monolingual, they become aware of the social significance of different varieties of language, including different varieties of English, and learn how to vary their own language according to the perceived context and the desired outcomes. However, before bilingual children can manipulate their two languages to express social meanings, they first need to recognize them as two distinct systems: different aspects of the languages appear to 'separate' at different stages in the child's development.

Different identities and social meanings are expressed in some communities via different dialects, in others via different languages, whereas in others codeswitching allows hybrid identities to be expressed and mixed messages to be conveyed. Up to adolescence children are learning to use these different varieties and mixtures of language to express their identities and achieve their goals, both as members of social groups and as individuals; sometimes these different identities may reinforce each other, sometimes they may be in conflict. Adolescents are also becoming aware of increasingly subtle aspects of language variation, as they become increasingly sophisticated actors in and on the world.

Reading A

RAISING OUR TWINS BILINGUALLY

Sylvia Rojas-Drummond and Hugh Drummond

We are an Anglo-Mexican married couple resident in Mexico City and working at the National Autonomous University for over twelve years. Sylvia is a native Mexican who studied English in school and university, then did her doctorate in the USA and returned to Mexico. Hugh is a native Englishman who moved to Mexico after completing university in England, then picked up Spanish as an adult, in social contexts. He also did his doctorate in the USA. Each speaks the other's language quite fluently, but with some errors of syntax, vocabulary, pronunciation and so on.

When our twin boys Alan and Ian were born in Mexico City in July 1985, we established as a central goal that they should learn both languages and be exposed to both cultures as much as possible. They need spoken and written Spanish to participate fully as Mexican citizens and members of the international Spanish-speaking community; likewise, they need spoken and written English to interact successfully in Britain and the USA and to gain access to much scientific and technical literature. We expected it to be difficult to achieve full fluency in both languages, since the boys would presumably tend to speak only the language that prevails in most contexts (usually Spanish), and they might even confuse the two languages. We know many adults from homes with two native languages who failed to learn one of their parents' languages (and resent the failure). Hence, we adopted an explicit policy of exposing the boys to both languages and cultures, and of encouraging them to speak English in particular (the 'endangered language' in the Mexican context), while at the same time keeping the two languages separate by context.

At the time of writing Alan and Ian are 9 years old and they are in the third grade of a bilingual primary school that aims to expose children to both languages and both cultures, in all areas of the curriculum. It is populated mostly by Mexican children but a majority of children have one or two native English-speaking

Ian and Alan aged 6 years

parents. About 60 per cent of class time is with a British or American teacher who speaks English and aims to refer principally to British culture; 40 per cent of class time is with a Mexican teacher who speaks Spanish and refers principally to Mexican culture. In the playground the children speak almost exclusively in Spanish, and most third graders continue to struggle with English, even after several years of exposure (including preschool).

Alan and Ian currently speak Spanish with native-speaker proficiency and accent; they speak English very fluently but with a slight Mexican accent and some errors that are typical of native Spanish speakers. Also, their vocabulary in English is mostly British, but they use some American terms (more possibly than Hugh). Their fluency in English has enabled them to act frequently as classroom interpreters. However, they have not always been bilingual: both have together been monolingual Spanish speakers and monolingual English speakers, in dramatic response to their changing social and linguistic circumstances. Furthermore, the boys' willingness and ability to speak each language have fluctuated (in a very coordinated fashion for both) as the family has moved back and forth between Mexico and England.

Although we have lived mostly in Mexico since the twins were born (a total of eight years), during the year that the boys were 3;1–4;1 the family lived in Oxford, England, since Hugh and Sylvia were academic visitors on sabbatical. On the basis of these geographic moves, the boys' linguistic development divides naturally into three phrases: infancy in Mexico (0–3;1), the one-year interval in England (3;1–4;1), and five years back in Mexico (4;2–9;2).

Ages are given here in the form:
3;1 = 3 years 1 month
4;1 = 4 years 1 month.

During their infancy in Mexico, Alan and Ian spoke only Spanish, even though they had considerable exposure to English: Hugh always spoke and read to the boys exclusively in English, whereas Sylvia used Spanish, and they spent nearly as much time with Hugh as with Sylvia. The boys understood English as well as Spanish and they relished English rhymes and fairy tales, but their emerging language production was all Spanish. Hence conversations with their father were habitually bilingual: he spoke English and they spoke Spanish, with excellent mutual understanding. Now and then Hugh would ask the boys to say something in English and they would comply with a few hesitant self-conscious words, then revert promptly to Spanish.

Why did the boys choose Spanish? Probably this was not a result of a greater attachment to Sylvia, since Ian (but not Alan) actually appeared more attached to Hugh during the first two or three years. We suspect the boys' choice was a natural response to differential exposure to the two languages, and an adaptation to their social environment: not only the boys' mother, but their nanny, their Mexican relatives and all strangers spoke Spanish, so English may have represented only about one third of total input. Thus, during this period all their productive speech was in Spanish, although they could understand English. This monolingual situation changed radically after they turned 3 years of age.

When our family moved to England we spent the first month staying in Hugh's parents' home in London. On the very first day both boys started uttering phrases and sentences in English! It was as if their capacity for producing English had developed to some degree but in a latent state, and it became manifest when the context called for it. As they had been expecting, English language was all around them, and they responded by speaking more and more English, both to parents and grandparents. Initially they seemed shy, and Ian would mutter softly into his chest, but confidence came very quickly and within a few weeks both boys were speaking English nearly as fluently as they spoke Spanish, and rapidly building their active vocabulary.

Near Oxford, the boys attended a village playgroup and frequently interacted extensively with their English-speaking friends. Now they were living in an environment where their mother and a Spanish *au pair* were the only people using Spanish; none of the children in their playgroup knew any Spanish.

As the weeks passed, their English increasingly lost its touch of Spanish accent (although never completely), and they even began using English for talking together. The language they speak between them has been over the years the best indicator of which language is dominant for them. This rapid orientation towards using English for communication was accompanied by an increasing unwillingness to speak Spanish. Now even if Sylvia spoke to them in Spanish they would reply in English. Also, when Sylvia took them to the nursery and as they were approaching their friends, they explicitly asked Sylvia not to speak to them in Spanish, since they did not want to appear different from the others. We think that it was the social pressure, as well as their own need to communicate and integrate to this new culture as fast as possible, that brought on the dramatic change from being monolingual in Spanish to being effectively monolingual in English.

This year was to be Alan and Ian's big opportunity for becoming fluent in English. For this reason, combined with their evident reluctance to speak Spanish, Sylvia spoke to them in English too. Now only the *au pair* ever spoke to them in Spanish, and they almost always replied in English. So we decided to stop actively monitoring the development of this language, and assumed, incorrectly, that their skills in producing Spanish were simply dormant. We were therefore astounded when their Uncle Robin unwittingly tested their Spanish production one day by asking them to translate an English sentence – and found that they apparently had none. Just five months into our stay in England, the boys were apparently unable to translate simple sentences from English into Spanish. At first we thought it was translation itself that they couldn't manage. However, over time we became aware that Alan and Ian no longer expressed themselves in their first language, although they clearly could understand when spoken to in Spanish. This was not a cause of alarm; after all, within half a year we would be back in Mexico and immersion in Spanish would soon restore their performance.

In September 1989 the family returned to Mexico. Alan and Ian had just turned 4 years of age and were by then speaking English like ordinary English children of their age and with a British accent. We remember vividly when our Mexican family (including the boys' cousins, uncle and aunts) picked us up at the airport; they all looked astonished when they spoke to Alan and Ian in Spanish (as they had always done), and the children simply declined to reply! During the car journey to our home the children eventually produced a few short phrases in Spanish after being instigated to repeat them, but only with a lot of difficulty and shyness, as well as with a strong 'foreign' accent. Their capacity to produce Spanish had definitely become rusty.

Once back in Mexico, Hugh continued to speak to Alan and Ian in English and they consistently replied in the same language. Sylvia, on the other hand, went back to using Spanish. For a short while after our arrival, although the children showed signs of understanding what Sylvia said, they responded in English. A few weeks later, however, both children used Spanish when spoken to in that language, as they related more to their Mexican family and friends. Impressively, the strong 'foreign' accent they had displayed when speaking Spanish on their arrival only persisted for the first month or so. Then it gradually decayed and within roughly four to five months the children were speaking Spanish fairly fluently, and without a foreign accent.

The Rojas-Drummond family at the time of writing

A few months after returning to Mexico, then, the children showed their first truly bilingual production: consistently, they spoke quite competently in Spanish with their mother, relatives and friends, and English with their father. Interestingly, they continued speaking English together for up to seven months! But then a switch to speaking Spanish together came, very rapidly and dramatically.

Hugh was absent doing fieldwork for a month between March and April 1990 when they first spoke Spanish together. As Sylvia recalls, it was as if the switch happened from one day to the next, sometime in the middle of that month. And since that day they have rarely spoken English together.

When Hugh returned, he was surprised to see that, not only were the children now speaking Spanish together, but they were reluctant to speak in English to him. Within a few weeks, however, and through Hugh's insistence, they became again willing to speak to him in English. From this time onwards, the boys have shown an increasing bilingual capacity, accompanied by a growing consistency for choosing the contexts for speaking either language and automatic switching of codes in mixed-nationality social groups.

Although at present the children are quite fluent in both languages, apparently the two underlying language systems are not kept completely apart. Influences have been evident in both directions throughout the boys' development, and occur at different levels. Some examples are phonetic, as when they have pronounced certain words as they would be pronounced in the other language, or when reading or writing 'phonetically' in English (as is done correctly in Spanish). Others are morphological, like Ian incorrectly saying *atachadas* in Spanish – drawing on the English root *attach* and adding the Spanish morpheme *adas* to refer to the past participle, feminine gender (i.e. *attached*), or his invention of the Spanish word *superba* – from the English *superb* with the feminine gender morpheme *a* added. Still others have been syntactic, like Alan referring to some blue shoes in Spanish as *los azules zapatos* – using the English word order for noun and adjective, or his saying in English *Till when are you coming back?* from the Spanish 'Hasta cuando vas a regresar?'.

At school, as well as at home, Alan and Ian are gradually becoming literate in both languages too. At the beginning both children read and wrote English and Spanish 'phonetically', (which, as mentioned above, is appropriate for Spanish but not for English). This tendency in English has persisted for quite a while, but they are gradually reading and writing better in both languages, and particularly in English, which is the more difficult language to grasp in the written mode given the lack of close correspondence between writing and speech. Gradually, also, the children have come to discriminate when reading in each language and to adapt their strategies accordingly. When this differentiation started to take place, Alan would explicitly ask which language a certain text was in before starting to read, apparently so as to adapt his reading strategy to that language. Nowadays their reading in both languages comes increasingly naturally and easily. Here again, in general Hugh reads to them and they read to him in English, while with Sylvia these activities are carried out in Spanish.

A nice example of the children's handling of both languages in the written mode happened recently when they were asked to put books in English on the right hand side and Spanish on the left hand side of a bookcase. The children carried out this activity by themselves very accurately, and even subclassified the books into types within languages spontaneously, labelling them in the corresponding languages (e.g. they wrote the labels 'stories' and 'science' and attached them to the corresponding English subcategories, while adding the labels 'cuentos' and 'ciencia' for the corresponding subcategories in Spanish).

Another interesting example of the boys' capacity for automatic codeswitching happened recently when Alan was reading the book *Charlie and the Chocolate Factory* to Hugh in English in Sylvia's presence. After reading for a while in English, he would turn to Sylvia and narrate or explain to her previous events from the story in Spanish so that she could follow the parts he was reading. Then he would continue to read in English to Hugh, stop to explain again to Sylvia some events in Spanish and return to reading in English to Hugh, oscillating back and forth spontaneously and accurately. Both children show this capacity in various situations, as when speaking in turn to Hugh and Sylvia, naturally, rapidly and accurately switching back and forth between languages.

The children's accents in English seem to us to be essentially British (resembling Hugh's north-east London accent), with some influence from Spanish and American English. However, we recently experienced a striking example of the children's tremendous linguistic adaptability. At Christmas Hugh's father and two nephews came from England to spend a month with us. Just one week after their arrival, we could see signs of the boys, especially Alan, picking up a stronger southern British accent, as well as a rapid incorporation of new phrases and vocabulary in their productive speech. By the end of the month this influence was more evident still.

Experiences like this give us confidence that the children would be quite capable of adapting linguistically and culturally again if we were to live in England. Indeed, on a recent visit to the USA, they conversed freely and fluently with many Americans. At the same time, however, it reminds us that we must frequently seek out opportunities for them to practise their English and relate to British culture if we want them to continue growing up bilingual and bicultural – a challenge we face for many years to come.

This reading was specially commissioned for this book.

3 LEARNING TO READ AND WRITE IN ENGLISH

Pam Czerniewska

3.1   INTRODUCTION

This chapter is about children's early experiences of English as a written language and the first stages of their development as literate language users. Becoming literate, in English or any other language, is not simply a matter of learning how language is represented in writing, but also involves learning how written language is used in the home and community. In the first part of the chapter I use examples to show how children can be involved in the literate world around them from their earliest years, and long before formal schooling begins. I discuss children's early involvement in literacy as a social activity, and then go on to look at studies of how they first learn to read and write. I end the chapter with a brief discussion of how early literacy experiences relate to children's entry into the education system.

3.2   FIRST ENCOUNTERS

In their interactions with others and in an environment of printed language, children try to work out the many forms, functions and meanings of **literacy**. Before they go to school, most of them will have encountered different ideas about what learning to read and write involves and will be aware of different expectations about when they will be accepted as readers and writers by those around them. Children will use many strategies to work out what adults are doing with newspapers, books, pens, word-processors and all the other things associated with literacy, and will join the adult literate world in different ways. The anecdotes below (the first from my own experience) capture some of the conclusions that young children have reached along the way to becoming literate in English:

> A 4-year-old was drawing at his kitchen table when he began saying his mother's name over and over again. 'You're reading' his mother exclaimed, realizing that he was reading aloud from a label. Delighted, the child rushed out of the room. A few minutes later he returned holding a favourite book and said: 'No, I can't read properly yet'.

> In an Australian nursery, four-year-old Heidi drew a large detailed picture of a dog. Down the side she wrote some letters (many from her own name). Asked by her teacher what her writing said, she replied, 'I don't know'. 'Well, you wrote it', her teacher replied; 'I *know*', said Heidi, 'but I can't read yet'.

> (Adapted from Cambourne and Turbill, 1987, p. 12)

> Alison, aged 4 years, attending a nursery school in Newcastle upon Tyne (in the north of England), discovered that it was not her turn to join her favourite 'Soft Play' activity. Several minutes later she went to her

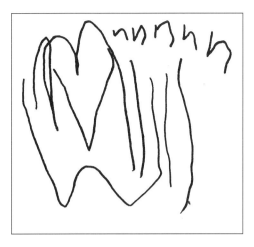

Figure 3.1   Alison's list

teacher and presented her with a piece of paper saying: 'I can go to Soft Play because I'm on the list. Look!' (see Figure 3.1).

(National Writing Project, 1989b, p. 13)

In a London school, a child who recently arrived from Hong Kong was very surprised to be given a book that she could not yet read to take home for her parents to read with her. Her experiences of reading had taught her that books are the reward for learning to read the words and that you do not start with the book.

(Gregory, 1992)

The children in these examples have already had many lessons about literacy. Some may be familiar to you from your own memories of learning to read and write or from helping young children to learn. Others may sound less familiar. Through their daily interactions at home and in the community these children have developed some reader-like and writer-like behaviours. They are beginning to understand how reading and writing are defined by their community, how it affects people's lives and what literacy will do for them. The young child's first discoveries of reading and writing have been termed **emergent literacy** by some (e.g. Teale and Sulzby, 1988), an expression that captures how children who live in a literate community are *in the process of becoming literate* almost from birth. They are learners who are participating in the language around them, finding out what it means to be a speaker, reader and writer in the community in which they live.

A collaborative venture

The child is not alone in this discovery of literacy. As Bruner (1986) puts it, children are not on solo flights mastering a set of skills but are involved in a collaborative venture:

> I have come increasingly to recognize that most learning in most settings is a communal activity, a sharing of the culture. It is not just that the child must make his knowledge his own, but that he must make it his own in a community of those who share his sense of belonging to a culture. It is this that leads me to emphasize not only discovery and invention, but the importance of negotiating and sharing.

(Bruner, 1986, p. 127)

The range of sociocultural contexts in which English-speaking children develop as writers and readers is very great and researchers are only just beginning to examine the effect of different cultural settings on how children learn to produce and to understand texts. Each child will acquire a personal history of interactions with different language varieties, different speakers, readers and writers. When a finding is reported based on one child's reading and writing, we need to question the extent to which those findings can be generalized to children's learning in other communities. There is much diversity among communities in which children learn to write and read English and any conclusions that I draw in this chapter can only be partial.

Contexts for literacy

Studies of different communities demonstrate the broad range of **literacy practices** available. Schieffelin and Cochran-Smith (1984), for example, have looked at literacy before schooling in three very different cultures: a Philadelphia nursery school in the USA where children's parents were literate in English and who placed high value on reading and writing activities; a Kaluli community in Papua New Guinea where some adults learned to read English at the local mission but where literacy played no part in the home activities and was not seen as important for the children to engage in; and, thirdly, a Sino-Vietnamese refugee family in Philadelphia who were literate in Chinese but whose literacy priorities focused on the functional need to learn English.

Schieffelin and Cochran-Smith found that the concept of literacy has many different meanings and many implications. The children and adults that they observed were learning 'a number of different kinds of literacy in different ways and for different purposes' (Schieffelin and Cochran-Smith, 1984, p. 21). For the Philadelphia nursery children, literacy was a range of activities in which reading and writing were seen (among other things) as important for self-expression, for learning about and telling others about their world, and for social transactions between friends and adults. This view of literacy was in sharp contrast with the Kaluli literacy practices in which literacy was not indigenous but brought in by members of a radically different culture (Christian missionaries teaching from the Bible) who had their own agenda for its use. In Kaluli homes, literacy did not play a significant part nor was it encouraged among children – in fact parents were found to discourage children's interest in books. In the third community studied, Schieffelin and Cochran-Smith observed that for the Sino-Vietnamese families in Philadelphia, an English literate tradition is being added to an even older Chinese one. For recently arrived refugees, the acquisition of **functional literacy** in English is a priority. Their involvement in English literature for personal expression and enjoyment was not evident, and its eventual development was not certain. The authors conclude that 'being literate' can mean quite different things in different communities. As they put it: 'Clearly, it is crucial that we do not equate the form, function, and meaning of literacy events across cultures, communities, or social groups' (Schieffelin and Cochran-Smith, 1984, p. 22).

One consequence of this diversity is that it is difficult to describe the process of becoming literate in English in general terms.

Introducing literacy

How parents and community members introduce literacy to children or new arrivals is rarely discussed outside academic circles. This is perhaps surprising given the amount of attention paid to literacy once school age is reached. Hall (1987), in his discussion of emergent writing, suggests that parents often fail to notice children's very early writing and that researchers (mainly from the UK, USA and Australia), who have collected hours of oral language from pre-schoolers, have not amassed anything like as many examples of mark-making activities. Similarly, while much has been said about the language styles adopted by adults while talking to young children – often known as 'motherese' or 'baby talk' – there is little equivalent data on the forms for introducing children to writing practices.

What writing and reading practices do children see during their early years and how do their early experiences of literacy affect their development as writers and readers? Denny Taylor made an intensive study of literacy practices among educated, literate households in the USA. She observed a range of **literacy events** – social events in which reading and/or writing play a significant role – and described the ways in which adults introduce literacy to young children as 'an idiosyncratic process which can result in very different experiences for individual children who are nevertheless successful in learning to read' (Taylor, 1983, p. 13).

Adults' styles of talking to infants are discussed in Chapter 1.

❖ ❖ ❖ ❖ ❖

Activity 3.1   *(Allow about 10 minutes)*

A useful way to consider the range of literacy practices in a literate community is to begin by thinking about all the literacy events that happen during the course of a day in your own life. Jot down some of the literacy events that you encountered today before settling down to this chapter.

Comment

The list of literacy activities for my first hour of a day in my life at home in England looked like this:

- checking the calendar for the day's appointments;

- helping my child with his reading book;

- reading over my older child's homework;

- glancing at yesterday's paper;

- looking up the TV schedule and setting the video;

- completing a coupon on a cereal packet and addressing an envelope for it;

- writing a shopping list;

- opening and reading letters;

- flicking through a mail-order leaflet for books;

- signing a birthday card.

❖ ❖ ❖ ❖ ❖

The flow of literacy

The list I provided for Activity 3.1 could easily be added to – the morning's breakfast activities at my neighbour's house would include reading tea-leaves! Characteristically, in a literate community, a set of literacy-related activities would be familiar and well rehearsed within a particular home, some even ritualistic. In this way, it is argued, they become well learned by children from an early age. Many of the interactions with print will happen in combination with different types of talk – oral reading of a family letter, discussion of the day's events, or argument over a cereal packet offer perhaps – and many will combine both reading and writing. Importantly, most of the activities are not about reading or writing *per se*, but rather they concern the social organization of people's lives. Some activities will be compulsory (e.g. completing tax forms), others will be associated with particular family members (e.g. grandpa always does the crossword), and a few may have restricted access (e.g. letters may be written in a language understood by only some family members). Together, the events provide a 'filter through which the social organization of the everyday lives of the families is accomplished' (Taylor, 1983, p. 26). Taylor makes the point that children are not only learning about reading and writing, they are learning a lot about family life and the purposes that reading and writing serve.

Chapter 2 in the second book in this series, *Using English: from conversation to canon* (Maybin and Mercer (eds) 1996), is about literacy as social practice.

An enjoyable example of this came from my son when he was 4 years old. At breakfast one day, a letter came addressed unusually to *Pamela* Czerniewska – I'm always known as *Pam*. My daughter who was sorting out the post remarked on this and I explained that my full name was only used in very formal documents so this was either bad news or it could be the long-awaited (small) tax rebate. It was, luckily, the cheque. Some weeks later, my son called to me, 'Pamela, Pamela come here'. He never uses my first name and *Pamela* was unheard before. I obeyed and he presented me with 2p, saying, 'Here's your money. I called you Pamela because that's what you're called when you're given money.' The incident underlined for me how written language does not simply represent a visual message, but, like spoken language, it is part and parcel of our interaction with experience. Literacy makes a difference to the kinds of experiences we have and to the patterns we find in them.

From the very beginning, children growing up in communities where literacy plays an important part, act and react to the experiences around them, making sense of its functions and forms. Examples show how taking part in literate activities does not depend on being able to read and write in the adult sense. Favourite product labels, restaurant signs and notices about missing cats and so on may be recognized long before individual letters are known. Where children are encouraged to experiment with writing even before their marks are intelligible to others, they will often produce 'pretend' shop signs, shopping lists, telephone messages and newspapers (see Figure 3.2 for example). The function of these texts can usually be understood by the context. One 4-year-old, unable to read or write, insisted on making and taking a newspaper when he was going out to a café. Interestingly, he called his paper the *Daily Planet*, the name of Clark Kent's (*aka* Superman) paper, illustrating the influence of television on a child's thinking about literacy.

Accounts of children learning to talk (as provided in Chapter 1) show that children are very highly motivated to work out how the language system works. For example, Donaldson (1984) argues that speech offers so many opportunities for achieving personal and functional ends that, not surprisingly, children want to learn how to use oral language: 'In short, children have some good reasons

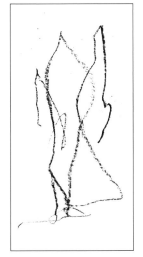

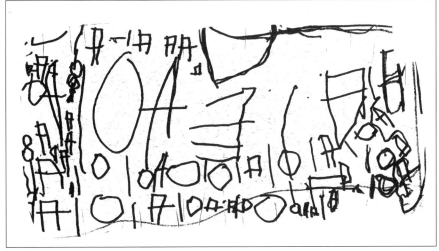

(a)   A shop sign
(Christopher aged
2 years 10 months)

(b)   An invitation to a party (Alexandra aged 3 years 10 months)

Figure 3.2   Examples of early writing

to want to learn and some good opportunities for doing so' (Donaldson, 1984, p. 178). However, she goes on to question whether writing will be seen as valuable to young children, as it 'usually presents itself impersonally and is inscrutable as to function' (Donaldson, 1984, p. 178). The studies by researchers such as Taylor, quoted above, would argue against her, showing the very observable nature of literacy events in many homes and how children actively participate in reading and writing practices they see around them. Children's early understanding of the nature of literacy activities may be shaky – one child, aged 3 years, thought that all the letters put in the post box (including those she 'wrote' herself) were for the postman. But these constructions of how things work serve to show how children follow individual paths of literacy development. They are working out, through their interactions with the practices of their community, how reading and writing function, albeit making quite a few mistakes as they go.

Taking different paths to literacy

The paths taken to literacy, as the earlier examples from Schieffelin and Cochran-Smith showed, vary from context to context. Different communities will mesh written and spoken language together in different ways for any literacy event, and the types of practices that are encouraged for different members of a community will vary as will the value placed upon literacy. A number of ethnographic studies have been published over the last decade or so showing differences in literacy practices. For example, Anderson and Stokes's study (1984) of preschool children's experiences of literacy in San Diego, USA, categorized their data into **domains of literacy** that included: daily living; entertainment; school-related activity; religion; general information; work; literacy techniques and skills; interpersonal communication; and storybook time. There were three different ethnic groups represented in the study – black American, Mexican American and Anglo-American – and Anderson and Stokes found considerable variation in the experiences that families had with literacy across the domains. All had some contact with print and the differences in the types of literacy experience were not determined by the ethnic background of the families. Where differences in patterns of literacy activity did emerge between families was in the length of time spent on an activity. The Anglo-American child tended to participate in a larger number of print-related activities but would not spend more time overall involved with print. Put the other way, children from Mexican or black American homes tended to engage in fewer literacy activities but these could be expected to last longer.

Shirley Brice Heath's work (carried out a little before Anderson and Stokes's) is perhaps the best known for its unearthing of differences in English literacy practices among three US subcultures. Whereas differences between Kaluli and Philadelphia families that Schieffelin and Cochran-Smith observed might come as no surprise, the contrasts in behaviour between three literate and geographically close communities that Heath (1982a, 1983) found caused conceptions of preschool literacy to be radically revised. Her focus was on 'any occasion in which a piece of writing is integral to the nature of the participants' interactions and their interpretive processes' (1982a, p. 93). Thus it included events from filling in a form to singing with a hymn book. She observed closely three communities in the American Piedmont Carolinas that she called Trackton, Roadville and Maintown. All of the communities were English speaking and all the observed literacy was in English. Her findings showed how children learn from their culture different means of using and making sense of print and different ways of relating their knowledge of the world through talk and writing. In her words, communities introduce children to different 'ways of taking' meaning from literacy events.

Children in the middle-class community in her study, Maintown, learned about literacy in an environment filled with print and with information derived from print. From six months on, these children heard and responded to books and referred to book-related incidents in their interactions. As they got older, Maintown children learned certain rules about book reading, such as when

interruptions are allowed and the types of questions that can be asked. They also learned ways of talking about texts and began to use the types of language structures more often heard in books than in speech. All this acted as a useful introduction to the practices they later encountered in school.

At first, Maintown seemed to have much in common with Heath's second community, Roadville, a white working-class community whose members had worked for four generations in the textile mills. Here, as in Maintown, books played a central role in children's lives and their rooms were full of alphabet friezes, mobiles and the like. The difference that Heath notes is in the use of books as teaching opportunities, times when children 'got it right', rather than as opportunities for stories to be explored. The world of books entered far less into 'real life', and book reading was less interactive between adult and child, especially when a child reached school age.

The third community, Trackton, provided a further set of contrasting uses of language. Trackton has a black working-class community, historically connected with agriculture but more recently with the textile mills. A Trackton child did not experience the baby paraphernalia of mobiles, friezes and pop-up books. The rich language opportunities came not from books, but from adult talk and oral narratives. A child who experimented with adult reading and writing behaviours was not seen as doing anything of special interest. But the environment was far from lacking literacy and children often arrived at school able to recognize much environmental print. Reading in Trackton was not a private affair, it was highly social, a time for discussion and negotiation of meaning. A letter, a set of instructions or a story might be interpreted, reshaped and reworked through a lot of talk.

The types of contrasts drawn among the different communities reflect the range of interactions possible under a label such as 'reading a book' or 'writing a letter'. Each of the three communities intertwined talk and writing in very different ways. Such evidence questions any simple oral–literate division, suggesting rather a set of features that cross-classifies the groups. For example, Maintown and Trackton valued imagination and fictionalization, while Roadville did not. Direct teaching about language was valued in Maintown and Roadville but not in Trackton. Negotiation over the meaning of a book or letter happened in Trackton and to some extent Maintown, but was not valued in Roadville. Children were seen as needing their own specially designed reading materials in Maintown and Roadville but not in Trackton. When children, with their different experiences of interacting with print, enter school they will find that only some of their literacy practices are valued. For some children, then, school literacy may seem very different from the literacy found in their own homes.

The children in Heath's research were becoming literate in only one language, English, the dominant spoken language, but her findings show how varied monolingual language learning can be. Often the children, especially once they begin school, will be learning to switch between different 'ways of taking', which, as Romaine (1989) in her overview of bilingualism has concluded, may be more complex than switching language.

In the chapter so far, I have tried to convey a picture of children, from their earliest years, encountering print with its many functions, forms and purposes. Communities vary in the types of literacy events that are thought important and in the ways that people interact with print-related activities. Children appear highly motivated to work out the part that literacy plays in their immediate world, and

This last point is taken up again below when story-reading practices are examined more fully.

many lessons about literacy will have been learned before formal schooling begins.

I will now go on to look closely at the writing system that children learning English need to work out, and give examples of very young writers' behaviour. After this, I offer a broad overview of young children's reading development with a particular focus on story-time. Finally, my discussion moves briefly into school settings and raises a few questions about current educational practices.

3.3   BECOMING A WRITER

A 5-year-old, whose first language is English, came home from school and told his mother that in Egypt in the old days they wrote in pictures. That was how he was going to read and write, he said, because it would be easy. He proceeded to draw a picture with the 'hieroglyphics' for 'mag' and 'pie' in the top right-hand corner (Figure 3.3) and then he read it aloud to everyone.

This anecdote – and many similar ones could be provided – illustrates the long and often complicated routes that children take before discovering how the writing around them is organized. They will try out different ideas about writing – testing, through their interactions with adults, what works and what does not. Some hypotheses will be appropriate for their own writing system, some more appropriate for writing in another language. Often there will be more than one writing system used in their home, and differences in their form and functions will be explored and sorted out. The writing that goes on in these formative years does not consist of unstructured doodles; rather it provides evidence of children's search for the principles underlying the adult system(s).

Figure 3.3   Writing in hieroglyphics – 'magpie' (Christopher aged 5 years 11 months)

A child's-eye view of print

To find out about the child's search for the system, it helps if the world of print is seen through a child's eyes. Adults learn to filter out much of the print that surrounds them, often ignoring symbols from other languages that they don't understand and unconsciously categorizing symbols into different sorts of writing. A walk along a local shopping street will demonstrate the diversity of written symbols from which children can begin to construct the adult writing system.

The book *Describing Language* (Graddol et al., 1994) provides an introduction to symbolic writing systems.

For example, in my local shopping area (north London, England), there are street signs, posters, shop names and flyers which use **alphabetic** script predominantly, though they also include **syllabic** symbols, numbers and abbreviations where letters and symbols represent syllables (e.g. The Broadway N8; George Bros. Ltd; 3lbs for £1). Just as noticeable are **logographic** symbols such as 'H' for hospital and 'M' for Macdonalds. In addition, there are the **pictograms** such as road traffic signs and assorted symbols for ladies' and gentlemen's lavatories. A child's orthographic experiences will also include many non-English scripts such as, say, Chinese and Arabic which might be used in their own homes or seen displayed on shop fronts and menus. It is clear that what children observe about their community's writing system involves much more than the written script used in one particular community. Temple, Nathan and Burris (1982) summarize the learning process for US children learning to write English like this:

> discovering how to write in English involves making choices from a very large range of alternatives. Children may very well be more aware of the alternatives than adults are, because our long experience with alphabetic writing tends to blind us to the possibility that there may be ways of representing words with symbols that are different from the ways we do it.
>
> (Temple et al., 1982, p. 15)

Examples of English children's early writing illustrate some of the possibilities that children explore. Numbers, letters, musical notation, non-English symbols and their own invented signs all occur in collections of emergent writing.

The example in Figure 3.4(a) overleaf was produced shortly after Hallowe'en. The arrangement of ghosts strongly resembles a pumpkin, traditionally a symbol of Hallowe'en. This combination of pictures and symbols occurs frequently in children's early writing and seems to indicate that children are not simply learning to produce a written script but are grappling with the many different iconographic elements of a cultural event. The example in Figure 3.4(b) was produced by a monolingual English-speaking child with one bilingual parent, who had seen Chinese characters at school while learning about the Chinese New Year. He was adamant about the relationship between his made-up Chinese characters and the English words. For him, learning to write was not confined to learning the literacy of his home and school, it involved an exploration of different writing systems.

Bissex (1984) found in her studies of children's writing that development in pictorial representation and use of symbols was highly noticeable in many children's early writing. She makes quite ambitious claims for children's literacy learning when she concludes:

(a)   *'Ghost Song' using letters and musical notes*

Figure 3.4   Further examples of early writing
(Christopher aged 5 years 1 month)

(b)   *Exploring Chinese symbols*

Often we [adults] do not appreciate the forms, used in other times and places, that children independently explore but must unlearn as part of their schooling. We tend to see our writing system as a given and children as developing toward it. Yet if we step away to gain a broader perspective in time, we see the writing system itself developing; we see that the child's literacy learning is cut from the same cloth as mankind's written language development.

(Bissex, 1984, p. 101)

Working out the English writing system

The English writing system to the young child may well have a much broader definition than it would to adults. It might well include pictures, like the heart in car stickers such as 'I ♥ New York'. The division between pictorial symbols and written symbols is a blurred one, so it is not surprising if children's definitions of writing do not immediately match those of adults. To understand better how children learn to write in English, the English writing system needs to be looked at in relation to other systems. Of the many possible ways of representing language, what does the child need to select as English?

Most researchers restrict the term *writing* to visual symbols that represent language and that do not represent objects and events directly. But like many definitions this one is prone to leak! Two principles are usually identified as the basis of the different writing systems: that symbols should represent *meaning* or that symbols should represent *sound*. More frequently, scripts are a combination of the two. The different writing systems can be categorized into three, fairly distinct, groups:

- logographic writing systems such as Chinese, where symbols are based on meaning more than sound;

- syllabic systems which use symbols to represent syllabic units of sound (e.g. Japanese uses a syllabic system, though it also includes meaning-based and alphabetic units);

- alphabetic systems such as modern European languages where sound units predominate, though by no means exclusively.

English has an alphabetic system which is mainly sound based, using an alphabetic script, but it also employs logographic and syllabic symbols. As I mentioned earlier, children may be more aware of the different systems used in English than adults are.

Is English easier or harder to learn than other languages?

Downing (1973) and Downing and Leong (1982) asked the question: how does the child's experience of the task of learning to read vary from one language to another? They looked at fourteen different languages, including English, and identified some major tasks facing the young learner. One critical task is to work out which unit of speech is coded by their language.

Describing Language (Graddol et al., 1994) explains the concept of 'morpheme'.

In Chinese, the predominant unit on which writing is based is the **morpheme**. This is a linguistic unit that refers to the minimal unit of meaning. It relates closely to a word, but is not always equivalent. For example the word *write* is one word and one morpheme, while *writer* is one word but two morphemes: *write + er*, while *writers* is three morphemes: *write + er + s*. The Chinese child, therefore, has to work out the relationship between the marks on paper and the morphemes in the spoken language. A logographic language like Chinese will need many more characters than, say, an alphabetic system – that is, there are many more morphemes in a language than there are speech sounds. It has been thought that this makes the learning task far harder involving considerable memorization. However, most Chinese characters also contain information about their pronunciation, a fact that, as Barton (1994) points out, dispels the myth that Chinese children have to learn by memory 40,000 unrelated squiggles.

In contrast with Chinese, Japanese writing uses a predominantly syllabic system. Again, however, it is more complicated than that statement might suggest, as four different scripts are used: hiragana, katakana, Chinese characters and Roman letters. Downing (1973) points out that first reading materials use syllabic characters exclusively, and only later will children need to learn the other characters. However, following the argument in the last section, it is likely that Japanese children will have experienced many different writing systems in their home and local environment and will have explored the possible relationships between speech and writing some time before they reach the specially designed readers.

Alphabetic systems mark a further contrast in the learning task. By alphabetic is meant that written symbols largely represent the **phonemes** of the language. The term 'phoneme' is used rather than 'sound' because alphabetic letters represent only those sounds which make a difference in meaning. For example, the [p] sounds at the beginning of *pot* and the end of *top* are different phonetically, but this difference is not used to make a contrast in meaning – so they are classified as one phoneme /p/ represented by one letter *p*.

In some languages, for example Finnish, there is a very close relationship between the phonemes and the letters. This means that a fluent reader familiar with alphabetic systems would soon be able to read aloud in Finnish, though unless they knew some Finnish they would not understand what they read. Although English is a predominantly alphabetic writing system, it may take a reader much longer to work out the relationship between letters and sounds.

As the many jokes about English **spelling** demonstrate, the symbols in English often do not bear a direct relationship with the sounds. Within English, there are many letter combinations which have to be memorized as though they were logographs (e.g. *knight, through*) and others as though they were syllabic-based (e.g. the ending *-tion*). The English spelling system also often contains information about the grammatical relationships between words at the cost of losing phonetic information. For example, the past tense is commonly represented as *ed* in the spelling, even though its pronunciation varies: compare, for example, the pronunciation of *-ed* in *wanted, laughed* and *called*. The young child learning to read and write English seems to face a more challenging task than, say, the Finnish child.

Apart from the task of working out how speech is coded in writing, Downing pointed out other aspects of the task that differ between languages. One difference is in the way the temporal order of speech relates to its spatial order. For example, in Hebrew, sounds are represented from right to left on the page, while in Chinese, the arrangement of characters is from top to bottom. In Japanese, printing can be either vertical or horizontal, while in English it is left to right. Another difference is in the design of the symbols. Arguably, simple shapes are harder to remember than more complex ones; a view supported by the many confusions learners of English have with the stick-with-loop symbols p, b, d, and with g and q. Lastly, Downing looked at possible task differences resulting from the relationship between characters and their names. Some letter names in English have strong clues about the sounds they represent (for example, K *kay*, M *em*, S *ess*), while others contain few such clues (for example, W *double-you*, and Y *wy*). However, the significance of this difference is unclear as many children will learn to read and write without knowing the letter names.

In a similar way to Downing, Barton (1994) asks whether different writing systems have advantages for the young learner: are some easier for the young reader or writer to learn? It seems that logographic systems like Chinese are easier at first for the reader to learn. Interestingly, a child who begins to read English by recognizing whole words by sight (i.e. without analysing their individual letters) is effectively interpreting English as logographic. Syllabic systems such as Japanese appear easier to read than alphabetic systems, and Japanese children are reported to experience fewer reading problems. The advantage of alphabetic and syllabic systems is that once the initial breakthrough happens, any new word can (more or less) be worked out, while the learning of new logographs has to continue for many years.

It is not clear whether there are advantages in the different systems for beginner writers. Learning to write English is problematic because of the vagaries of the spelling system, but children can be very inventive and produce complex messages that are intelligible to the reader. Other alphabetic systems are far more systematic in their correspondence with the spoken language (e.g. Finnish mentioned above, or Polish). However, where the script is predominantly sound based there is often also a complex grammar for the young reader/writer to learn. The conclusion seems to be that the English writing system is different from other scripts in the advantages and disadvantages that face the learner, but the effects are too complex to assess.

Children's answers to English spelling puzzles

Downing's and Barton's comparisons are written at a very general level, starting with the differences between writing systems and hypothesizing the implications for learners. Investigations that start by looking at the writing of young learners reveal some ways in which children tackle the learning task, and can show up features of different languages that account for children's behaviour. Read (1975), for example, showed how some English-speaking children used their knowledge of speech, of letter sounds and of letter names in order to produce their own invented spellings. Some invented spellings can be worked out fairly easily by the adult reader – MI = 'my', KAM = 'came' – as they draw on knowledge of letter sounds and letter names. Similar knowledge is apparently used to produce the less obvious spellings, like WHT for 'watched'. A reasonable guess is that the child has linked the 'ch' sound with that in the letter name for H 'aitch', and has used T to represent fairly accurately the sound of the final 'ed'.

Later research by Read (1985) indicates some of the complexity of children's understanding of language. He observed that in their early spellings, English-speaking children often leave out preconsonantal nasals, that is, nasals that come immediately before consonants as in *nt, mp* or *nd*. Thus children write *bopy* (bumpy), *plat* (plant) and *agre* (angry). They do not omit the nasal sounds in initial and final positions (as in *nit* and *tin*) which suggests that children are trying to represent a phonetic fact in the language which, as adults, we do not notice. Most adult English speakers are probably unaware that the nasal sounds that occur before consonants are considerably shorter than the ones at the beginning and ends of words. A similar phonetic difference in nasals occurs in Dutch, and children again omit the nasal letters in their early spellings. However, when Read looked at the early spellings of French-speaking children, he found that there were far fewer omissions of nasal consonants. At first, this seemed surprising. The only real difference between Dutch, English and French to account for the spelling patterns used was that only French has syllable-final nasalized vowels, as in *bon* [bõ]. It might be, Read suggests, that this salient feature in French would lead teachers and parents to point out to children this feature of their spoken language and its special relationship to written language. Whereas adult English speakers are unlikely to notice the difference between the nasals in *net* and *bent*, French speakers are likely to notice the difference between the spelling of *bon* and its pronunciation and explain it to learners. As Read puts it:

> Each language poses certain puzzles for the beginning speller while making other choices easy. Only by studying a range of languages can we have much confidence in our hypotheses about why children make the choices they do.
>
> (Read, 1985, p. 401)

English writing is more than letters

As adults, we may think of the written word as quite distinct from other kinds of symbol systems. But, for children, the world of print is not limited by the adult divisions into writing and not-writing. Mathematical and musical notation, map signs, computer graphics, bar codes, punctuation marks, road signs and so on are there to be worked out by children for their meaning and their place in the adult system. Numbers, for example, are syllabic-based symbols which children learn to read and write alongside the alphabetic system of relating sounds to letters. Young English-speaking children often use the words 'number' and 'letter' fairly interchangeably and they need to learn that, in English, whereas the numeral *6*, say, stands for the whole word 'six', the visually very similar *b* is a letter that has no individual meaning. These other notation systems are rarely recognized as part of the literacy learning process. A very simple example illustrates one child's perception of the writing system:

> A 5-year-old announced that he could write *No*. He went straight to the table and wrote: "*NO MuM*. This was what was written in a book he'd just read, including the opening quotation mark. He added that he wrote *MuM* better than in the book because he put big letters at both ends.

It rarely occurs to adults to point out which are the bits of writing that refer to the language and which are peculiar to writing itself. Often it is the errors that provide clues about the task that young learners engage in.

To summarize the argument so far, children learning to read and write in English face, like all children, the task of sorting through the available information about writing in order to work out the principles underlying their home/community writing system. For many children, there will be languages other than English used in the home and local community and these may not be the same as the scripts used in school. Many children will become biliterate at an early age while others will narrow down the system to just one written script.

Working out the principles of writing: some examples

Various researchers have looked at samples of children's writing and tried to describe what children are doing. Marie Clay (1975), for example, who has studied writing development extensively in New Zealand, talks about various principles that she observed children exploring in their writing. These included:

- the *message* concept – when children start writing down messages;

- the *copying* principle – when children start copying symbols;

- the *directional* principle – when children start writing in a particular way across and down the page; this principle is often explored further with experiments in mirror writing;

- the *inventory* principle – where children list all the symbols they know;

- the *space* principle – where children explore ways of separating words, for example with spaces or dots.

Principles like these do not appear to happen in any particular order, nor do all children exhibit them (though I imagine that much evidence gets lost or goes unnoticed in most people's houses). The examples in Figure 3.5 overleaf were produced over a five-week period by my English-speaking daughter, Alexandra – they are samples from a particularly productive period in her writing development before she went to school, and show how much goes on at the same time. She experienced no direct teaching, though writing materials were always available.

Yetta Goodman (1984), whose studies were mainly based in the USA, also identifies principles that guide children's emerging writing. (As with Marie Clay's work, the term 'principle' seems to be used rather loosely – 'strategy' might be more appropriate.) Her framework suggests three overlapping principles controlling writing development: functional, relational and linguistic. The *functional* strand refers to a child's learning about how language is used – for example, labelling pictures or sending invitations. The *relational* strand captures a child's attempts to find out how written language corresponds with the world – for instance, whether there is a relationship between the size of an object and the length of a word. Thirdly, the *linguistic* principle includes children's explorations of how different types of language require different types of language structures – for example, *Dear Granny* marks the beginning of a letter while *Once upon a time* marks a story. Goodman views the children's writing development as a process of hypothesis making, experimentation and then refinement of hypotheses. As Clay put it: 'The young child, who in the past was assumed to be incompetent, has emerged as an active participant in the process of becoming a writer' (Clay, 1983, p. 259).

While different researchers have come up with a variety of classifications of early writing, all the descriptions recognize a child's commitment to working out

ALE+ANDRA

(a)   Directional/message principle, written from top to bottom and from left to right

(b)   Inventory principle

Figure 3.5   Examples of Clay's principles. Alexandra produced (b) when she was 4 years 8 months, and the other two examples at 4 years 9 months

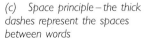

(c)   Space principle – the thick dashes represent the spaces between words

the writing system. Harste, Burke and Woodward (1981) describe this commitment after observing the writing of 3- to 6-year-olds in the USA:

> It is as if, among the 48 children studied, every convention that has been adopted by written language users worldwide was being reinvented and tested by this group of very young language users. Some tried writing right to left, others bottom to top, and a not surprising majority, given the culture they were in, wrote left-to-right, top-to-bottom. The use of space in relationship to placeholding individual concepts posed difficult problems for these children. Some used space and distance freely about the page, others drew dots between conceptual units, some drew circles around sets of markings, others wrote in columns to preserve order, while still others spaced their concepts using what we would see as the conventional form for this society ... The symbol system itself proved no less interesting. Children's markings, while having many English language features, ranged from pictorial graphs to symbol-like strings.
>
> (Harste et al., 1981, p. 137; cited in Bissex, 1984, p. 101)

Cut from the same cloth?

The discussion of children's early writing development has, so far, drawn mainly on samples of English-speaking children, often from monolingual/monoliterate homes. Bissex (1984, quoted on p. 87) writes about universals of literacy learning, and about literacy learning being 'cut from the same cloth as mankind's written language development'. Such broad statements may lead researchers to ignore the complex range of literacy practices and distinct literacy histories that exist in many communities. A child can experience many diverse forms and functions of writing. Mukul Saxena (1993), for example, in his study of literacy practices of Panjabis in Southall, London, reported the many choices available to the community for spoken and written communication. The dominant language in Britain is English with its alphabetic Roman script. But the three main cultural groups – Muslims, Hindus and Sikhs – use predominantly Urdu, usually written in Arabic script, Hindi, normally written in Devanagari script, and Panjabi, normally written in Gumurkhi script – though each language can be and is written in the script of another. Factors such as religion, age, schooling and social roles all affect the language(s) used in both speech and writing, with many speaking and writing more than one. Literacy events in the home and community will involve a complex interaction of different spoken languages and literacies. In planning a letter, for example, people might discuss the contents in one language and write the letter in another, even switching between languages and scripts within a letter.

When we look at the early writing explorations of children learning English, it is clear that young children who have the opportunity to do so are able to develop two or more literacy systems alongside each other. An example of this comes from an east London primary school whose pupils are nearly all bilingual, most speaking Bengali as their first language plus some speakers of Urdu, Panjabi and Gujerati. As part of their involvement in the National Writing Project (1990), Jacqui Clover and her team, which included bilingual teachers, worked with 5- and 6-year-olds, developing their confidence as writers and their awareness of the functions of writing. The children made books, and worked alongside adults who wrote with them and for them in a number of different scripts.

Figure 3.6   Raki's text
(National Writing Project, 1990, p. 40)

The writing produced by the children showed their considerable knowledge of various writing systems. Raki's piece of work includes English, Urdu and Bengali (Figure 3.6). Interestingly, all were written left-to-right; she had not yet adopted Urdu right-to-left orientation.

In another east London school, Lorna Drummond and Sati Sen observed the children's writing in a number of classroom play contexts, such as a post office, newsagent, hospital and café. Rujina Nessa (aged 6) wrote a letter to her cousin in Bangladesh inspired by the pretend 'post office' (Figure 3.7). The text demonstrates the parallel development of writing in her two languages: her Bengali text is very similar to her English text; in both she combines consonants and vowels to make words.

Overarching questions

In this part of the chapter I have tried to describe some aspects of the process that the young child engages in when learning to write in English. In order to do this it was necessary to show how English relates to other writing systems and the choices children have to make about what belongs to English writing and what to other languages. The complex cognitive processes involved need to be looked at, too, as the child works out the forms and functions of English. As Bissex says: 'To understand child mind in its engagement with written language, we need to be not only psycholinguists, but comparative and historical linguists and cultural anthropologists' (Bissex, 1984, p. 101).

A longer quote from the same article by Bissex acts as a summary to this section. It emphasizes how, while the focus here is on becoming literate in English, the child engages not just in learning the bits and pieces of English but works on the overarching questions about the nature of language.

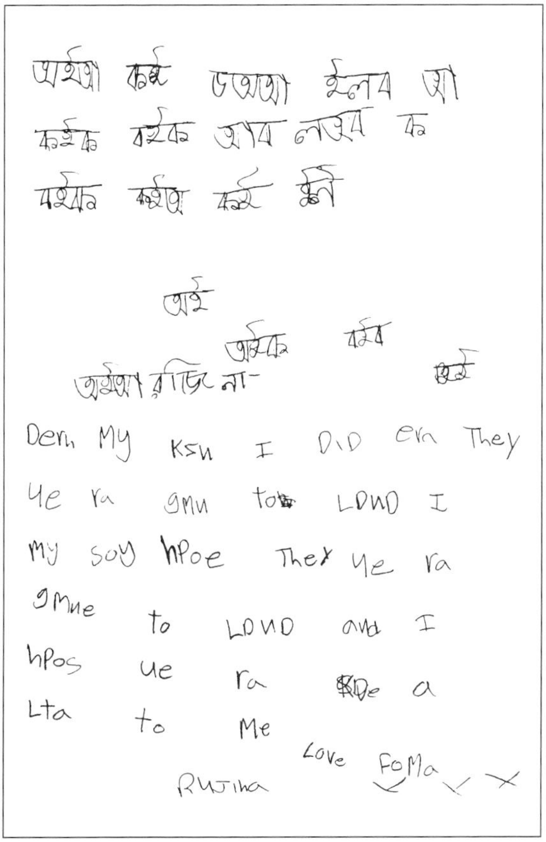

Figure 3.7   Rujina's text
(National Writing Project, 1990, p. 42)

To look closely at child mind is to take it seriously. Children are small; their minds are not. Child mind is human mind. Its contents are different from adult mind because it has had less time to gather information, to gain knowledge from experience, to develop certain kinds of thinking and means of expression. And, probably because it is not yet completely acculturated, it is more of a world mind in the sense that it is open to trying options that other cultures have developed, for example, in their writing systems … Although these options, whether conventions used in writing (such as dots rather than spaces between words) or principles (such as letters representing syllables rather than sounds), are discarded as part of the child's literacy learning in his or her own culture's system, exploring them may function to define for the child the characteristics of the system he or she eventually adopts. They not only reflect the scope of the child's intellectual explorations but enable those explorations and the asking of those unarticulated but overarching questions about the nature of written language.

Children reconstruct their language systems, both spoken and written. You cannot reconstruct a system by accumulating bits and pieces of information; you reconstruct it by discovering, through all the specific information you know about it, what its principles are – the rules by which it works. Children, in searching for order, assume order exists in the world. *Independently* they all invent virtually the *same* systems – for syntax, for example, or invented spelling – which bespeaks something more at work than immature minds in isolation. The immediate context in which learning takes place has been attended to in recent ethnographic research, but there exists also a broader context of historical and universal dimensions, which somehow is internalized. Or let us say that child mind possesses structures isomorphic with historical and universal ones. This is not surprising, since human intellectual history has been shaped by the same human mind in which child mind participates, and because language universals *are* universal by virtue of their greater cognitive simplicity.

(Bissex, 1984, p. 100)

3.4   BECOMING A READER

Many of the arguments about children's early writing development in English can also be offered to explain the processes involved in learning to read. Children develop a network of understanding about literacy, one that helps them discover principles of reading and of writing. It builds on the understanding usually already developed about spoken language and is part of the 'continual process of experimentation, risk-taking and negotiation, in purposeful, intentional ways' (Wray, Bloom and Hall, 1989). With a developmental perspective, the child is seen as actively involved in working out the literacy practices before schooling begins and without qualified instructors. This is not to deny the importance of schooling but refocuses attention on the ability of children to use their interactions with family and community members as the starting point for their literacy development. There is plenty of evidence that children do not wait until school before they start reading. Parents will often testify to a child's ability to recognize their favourite ice-cream from an advertisement and many will 'read' the labels as they go round the local shops or recognize street names and signs. They might not know the relationships between English symbols and their sounds but they have no problem in reaching the meaning. Children's understanding of environmental print is seen as an important route to literacy (Goodman, 1984) though not the only one. 'Multifaceted' is a term often used for the reading process and perhaps its many different sides account for the heated arguments that often occur about the most effective ways to teach reading.

Reading development and phonological awareness

There is an interesting line of research on early literacy development which has linked children's ability to read English to the extent of their awareness of the constituent sounds of the spoken language. One of the leading researchers in this field, Peter Bryant, explains the principal hypothesis behind this research as follows:

Most literate people (or at any rate people who read and write an alphabetic script) are well aware that words and syllables consist of smaller units of sound. This form of awareness is usually called 'phonological awareness', and there is a strong possibility that it plays an essential role in learning to read.

(Bryant, 1994, p. 2246)

The kind of evidence that Bryant and others have offered to support this view includes the following:

- measures of young children's sensitivity to sounds in words before they learn to read – for example, their ability to recognize rhyming words – are good predictors of how well they will succeed when they begin to read (Goswami and Bryant, 1990);

- many people designated as dyslexic (i.e. people without relevant physical handicaps whose reading falls far behind their other intellectual attainments) have been found to have very poor phonological awareness (Ellis, 1984; Snowling, 1985).

Some researchers, including Bryant, have studied the effects of teaching young children to recognize the constituent sounds of words, and concluded that it does in fact help their reading progress (Bryant and Bradley, 1985). They argue for the importance of talk activities which focus children's attention on the phonemic structure of English words, such as reciting nursery rhymes and playing other rhyming games (Bryant, Bradley, Maclean and Crossland, 1989).

What do children think readers and writers do?

One strand of the network of literacy understandings that has intrigued (and amused) researchers is the perceptions children have about reading/writing and readers/writers.

❖   ❖   ❖   ❖   ❖

Activity 3.2   *(Ongoing)*

If you have access to a young child, you might like to try to find out what they think you're doing while you are reading. You'll need to be quite subtle in your questions but most children enjoy saying how adults behave. You might try sitting reading to yourself and when this attracts interest ask the children what they thought you were doing.

❖   ❖   ❖   ❖   ❖

Gillian Lathey (1992) tried doing the type of investigation described in Activity 3.2 in her attempt to uncover some of the ways in which 3- and 4-year-olds thought about the process of reading. Armed with a pile of picture books and her own books, she stationed herself in a London nursery's book corner reading silently. Children's natural curiosity helped her get into conversations like this:

Lathey:	You know when I'm reading something like this – what do you think – what do you think happens? How do I do it?
Ben:	By talking like this: (*he holds the book and runs his finger backwards and forwards along the fly-leaf*) Chatter chatter chatter chatter chatter chatter

(Lathey, 1992, p. 74)

Ben, like a number of children, associated reading with talking. After all, for many children hearing books read aloud will be the most familiar experience. Some, though, made a distinction between oral and silent reading. Two children's sophisticated understandings are expressed in this extract:

Lathey:	I'm just going to read this bit to myself. You watch me. (*There is an interested silence as she reads.*) Now then. Do you think I was reading that, Ben? (*Ben shakes his head.*) Ben doesn't think I was. Do you think ...? (*Sade and Oleuwaseun nod.*)
Sade:	Yes I think you ...
Lathey:	(*to Ben*) Why do you think I wasn't reading it?
Ben:	Because you weren't talking.
Sade:	No, because you didn't *hear* her talking.
Lathey:	But, sometimes, you know when grown up people read books like this, they don't talk do they? Or do they always talk do you think?
Sade:	No.
Oleuwaseun:	They don't have to. They can if they want.
Lathey:	And what do you think is going on in their head when they're reading it silently like that, Seun?
Oleuwaseun:	Some people read quietly.
Sade:	They – they're reading it in their head they are.
Lathey:	They're reading it in their head are they?
Sade:	In the brain. They go dm dm dm dm dm dm dm dm dm ...
Lathey:	Do they?
Sade:	... talking ...
Lathey:	So, they're reading it in their brains and it's going dm dm like that inside is it?
Sade:	Yes.

(Lathey, 1992, p. 75)

Sade's and Oleuwaseun's construction of silent reading must, Lathey argues, have been influenced by the adult models at home – each one had a parent who was a college student. Other children had picked up less accurate ideas about reading from their observations: one child insisted that proper reading involved following the line of print with your finger. Some ideas will need to be modified later, like Yassin's surprise that an adult from outside could know the story in a book that was found inside the nursery. Children's perceptions can change quickly and can be affected by the conversations adults have with them. Lathey concludes that nurseries have a role in providing models of adult reading and in talking with children about the processes involved.

What do authors do?

With a similar interest in children's understanding of literacy practices, Sue McCaldon and Linda Jones (1989) asked 4- and 5-year-olds in Manchester, England, about writers: who they are and what they do. Their classrooms, one in a middle-class suburban area, the other in an inner-city area, with children from many different ethnic groups, were linked by their common curriculum emphases on authors and being an author. Attention was always drawn to the authors of books read in class and the children were encouraged to see themselves as authors of their own books: of recipe books, storybooks and so on. The teachers observed that children were often able to link books by author. One child, for example, said, 'He wrote *I'm Coming to Get You* didn't he?' while the teacher read Tony Ross's story *The Enchanted Pig.* Some of the responses were less clear:

Tariq: It's by Tony Ross 'cos he's an author.

Teacher: If Tony Ross is an author what does he do?

Tariq: Brings books, he sleeps in a bed.

(McCaldon and Jones, 1989, p. 75)

It is unclear, the teachers remark, whether Tariq's understanding of authors is somewhat abstract or whether he is unable to express his understanding. As with all studies of children's perceptions you need also to ask what sense the child made of the adult question – no doubt, Tony Ross does sleep in a bed! The children's responses to other questions revealed how well children use all the available evidence to reach their conclusions – even though they may not match the adult definition. For example, authors were closely associated with illustrators (the two often are the same for picture books). An author is:

'someone who colours books'

'a person who can make books. A man that paints flowers
and pictures.'

(McCaldon and Jones, 1989, p. 75)

Authors also faced difficulties similar to those confronted by the children. They needed to be clever 'because they have to be careful with the things that they do, they are not allowed to rub out' (McCaldon and Jones, 1989, p. 75). They also made books by 'folding pieces of cards and making pictures' (1989, p. 75). The children were very positive about themselves as authors with remarks such as: 'I'm an author, because I make lots of books. Mummy writes the words and I do the pictures. I tell her what to write.' (1989, p. 77).

When asked whether a monkey could be an author, children were quite sophisticated in their reasoning against this idea. Two 5-year-olds explained: 'No, monkeys can't write … they haven't got the right sort of head … No, they're pets, animals can't write.' A 6-year-old elaborated: 'No … because monkeys are animals … people can talk and animals can't.' (McCaldon and Jones, 1989, p. 76)

These examples of children's perceptions of reading and writing demonstrate, once again, the interest children have in the literacy process and their continual engagement in the task of making sense of it all.

Makers of meaning

The picture of the child that emerges from studies like these is of a 'maker of meaning'. This is in contrast with models of learning which see the child as a 'receiver of knowledge'. The theories about reading development over the last 20 years, particularly those emerging from US, UK, New Zealand and Australian studies, have shown a marked shift away from reading as a skill to be acquired towards reading as a system of meaning to be discovered by the child. US researchers such as Frank Smith (1978) and Kenneth and Yetta Goodman (Goodman et al., 1978) were influential in the 1970s in many English-speaking countries for their then radical views about the role of the child as the central agent in the reading process. Reading happens, they argued, not because children have been fed information about shapes, sounds and words, but because they approach any text with the assumption that it is going to make sense and that they can work out that sense by using everything they know about spoken language when attacking written language. From this perspective, a child who looks at a page that says *The elephant walked out of the gate* and reads 'The elephant went out of the zoo' knows an awful lot about language and reading, whereas a child who reads 'goat' instead of 'gate' in that context may know about initial consonant sounds but is not using her or his knowledge of language to produce a sensible text.

Kenneth Goodman wrote about reading as a 'psycholinguistic guessing game' with children's errors being seen as windows for the researcher into the reading process. Smith and others argued that children were 'readers' as soon as they looked at all that print around them and began making sense of it. They should be welcomed as new members to the reading club, joining the community of readers and writers (the language Smith uses is very seductive!). Following their lead, various new approaches to the teaching of reading have developed. One argument that follows from the emphasis on the child's role in finding meaning from print is that any reading activities that remove the sense of texts, such as meaningless exercises in letter sounds, or the use of reading primers with highly controlled vocabularies, will mystify rather than help the apprentice reader. UK and US teachers, in particular, have moved over the past few years towards the use of **real books** and **reading schemes** as opposed to specifically designed basic texts that often use artificial language. There has been and will no doubt continue to be considerable controversy about the 'real books' approach.

Time for telling

In the discussions about the child as the meaning maker, the importance of literacy practices that involve interaction with family and community members is often singled out. Bedtime stories, shared reading sessions at school, and television programmes like *Sesame Street* that expect children to join in, are viewed as valuable learning experiences. Storybook reading in particular, it is argued, is able to provide all the conditions you need for learning: enjoyable, motivating content; intimate adult–child interaction; potential for the child to see what adults do and to exchange roles when appropriate; a variety of stories available to suit different needs and prevent boredom; and a potential close link between home and school practices helping the child's transition to school. Some of these claims are examined more closely below. However, it should be remembered that researchers such as Brice Heath, and Anderson and Stokes (see section 3.2) showed that bedtime stories are only a small part of the literacy domains that children experience. Furthermore, children's interactions with print may be rich and varied even when story-reading happens infrequently.

❖   ❖   ❖   ❖   ❖

Activity 3.3   *(Reading A)*

Now read the article by Henrietta Dombey, 'Some lessons learnt at bedtime' (Reading A).

Before reading, you might like to think about any bedtime story sessions that you have shared with a child, or experienced yourself as a child.

❖   ❖   ❖   ❖   ❖

Henrietta Dombey writes: 'It is hard to see significance in the comfortable and familiar'. But Dombey's close attention to the language interaction, her observations that include and go beyond the intimate moments between mother and child, reveal many significant events. A primary lesson, she concludes, is the one about relationships between parent and child. Often the emotional experiences of story-reading begin for children as young as 6 months, 'as mothers and some fathers read to their children, enveloping the child and the book together into an emotionally satisfying literacy event' (Y. Goodman, 1984, p. 138). Many children, too, will have learned that bringing a book to a busy parent will often ensure getting her/his full attention for a few minutes at least.

Book reading in these contexts does not begin with the deliberate intention of teaching the child how to read. Parents may assume that it will help in some way but it is probably separated in their minds from what will go on later in school reading lessons. Dombey shows how Anna and her mother's verbal interaction is very unlike that found in many school settings. Exchanges between pupils and teachers in British classrooms have been shown to be characterized by the teacher introducing a topic often with a question (**initiation**), the pupils giving an answer (**response**), and then the teacher acknowledging the pupil's response (**feedback**) (Sinclair and Coulthard, 1975). Such an IRF exchange might go like this:

> In Chapter 4 of this book, Neil Mercer discusses IRF exchanges and other features of English as a classroom language.

Initiation	Now then, do you think the fox can get out of the way?
Response	Yes
Feedback	Good, he could get out, couldn't he?

Importantly, pupils rarely initiate these exchanges and even more rarely would they give further feedback to the teacher's response. In the exchange between Anna and her mother, there are no such conversational rights nor specific 'teaching' demands:

> Her mother does not see her job as ensuring either that Anna has 'understood' each new word or structure, or that she can give a literally faithful account of the events of the story. Indeed, there is an implicit assumption that to do any of these things would be to distract attention from the central activity.
>
> (Dombey, 1992, p. 34)

A transcript such as Dombey's cannot capture, as she points out, all the nonverbal interaction which is so essential to story-time; it is an intimate time, where children can learn the rhythms of texts that will, according to Dombey, support their later reading and writing development.

Margaret Meek, another British researcher who values story reading highly, discusses the importance of children hearing stories that are written by 'those who

take children seriously as readers' (Meek, 1988, p. 14). Texts that help children to read, she argues, do more than tell a story. They 'recruit' children's imaginations as Bruner (1986) puts it, letting them play around with possible worlds. In Dombey's article, Anna and her mother speculate about other endings for the fox and hen, 'mother and child are creating a story world and moving about inside it, making judgements on its elements and exploring its possibilities and laws' (Dombey, 1992, p. 33).

Creating new meanings

The story-times that Dombey and others are calling attention to are times when new meanings are created. For the parent and child in the example there is not one meaning, not one way of reading the book. Rather, there is the opportunity of many different meanings developing through the connections made between text and life experiences. 'In this way literacy becomes implicated in the creation of ways of thinking' (Barton, 1994, p. 147).

Carol Fox (1989) has looked at the way stories can create new meanings from a slightly different starting point. She has analysed the oral stories of young UK children that were collected by their parents. The influence of stories the children had heard was obvious, but what was fascinating was the way their stories demonstrated how story structure can support and generate new knowledge. The story extracts below demonstrate how well young children could express concepts of size and shape, and use mathematical operations that, in a school context, they would probably find more difficult:

> 'there's witches all around our country'
>
> 'There's ten witches in our country'
>
> 'Oh God, there's three in our country so we'll have to kill thirteen now'
>
> *Josh, 5:9*

...

and they have houses shaped a diamond with triangle windows and square doors, not oblong ones like you do have, square ones

Sundari, 5:7

...

and the choodya [*a monster*] came but it was very small for us [*children*] but big for them [*teddies*]

Jimmy, 4:9

(Fox, 1989, pp. 30–1)

Fox says of these examples: 'Telling a story makes cognitive demands which push children towards new relationships and decentred viewpoints so that they reach beyond their age in development' (Fox, 1989, p. 31). Because they can immerse themselves in their imaginative storytelling, new exciting kinds of thinking can emerge.

Creating conflict

There is an assumption in what Dombey, Fox and others write that books and their possible worlds are unproblematic. But children can face considerable conflict in the stories that they read, especially if what they read in a dominant language does not represent their own community's culture. There is also the assumption that the attitudes to reading found in one community will be the same in another. Reading in the research described above is, without question, seen to be fun and emotionally satisfying. But what happens when reading is defined differently by adults? Solsken (1993) for example found in her study of children in the USA that not all parents treated reading as fun. For many parents, reading was viewed as 'work' and, furthermore, it was often seen as a female activity. As a result, boys, in particular, were sometimes found to resist reading activities. A closer look at the assumption that bedtime reading is a 'good thing' for children's later success at school reveals that a more complicated relationship exists between literacy practices at home and at school.

3.5 LITERACY PRACTICES AT HOME AND AT SCHOOL

The focus on bedtime stories in the previous section may seem to put an unfair emphasis on a set of social practices peculiar to a specific group. Such a bias may seem to devalue all the other equally important domains of literacy or to ignore the many other uses of literacy, such as those mentioned in the first part of the chapter, and those described by Heath in the communities she studied. The significance of bedtime stories, for the purposes of this chapter at least, is the links that are made between them and later success at reading in school in many English-speaking countries. It is a connection that was made around 90 years ago by Huey (1908) when he said: 'The secret of it all lies in the parents' reading aloud and with the child' (Huey, 1908, p. 332).

'Bedtime-reading families' are often made synonymous in the UK and USA with school-oriented families, with a direct correlation being assumed between stories read in family settings and confident readers in primary classrooms. In the city of Bristol, England, during the 1970s and 1980s, a research team led by

Gordon Wells made a careful and detailed study of 128 young children's preschool language and literacy development. They also followed 32 of the children right through the years of primary schooling. Wells reported that listening to stories was significantly associated with two literacy measures: a 'knowledge of literacy' test at age 5 and a test of reading comprehension two years later. On the basis of this study, which included children only from English-speaking families but from a range of social backgrounds, Wells (1986) drew some conclusions about what kinds of experience at home were important for encouraging children's literacy development. Some of these conclusions are set out in the reading by Wells.

❖ ❖ ❖ ❖ ❖

Activity 3.4   *(Reading B)*

Now turn to 'What's in a story?' by Gordon Wells (Reading B). As you read, pay special attention to the reasons why Wells believes that stories – that is, written stories read aloud by an adult to a child – are particularly important for helping children enter the world of literacy. Notice, in the transcript of the talk between David and his mother, what kind of questions David asks, and what they are about.

❖ ❖ ❖ ❖ ❖

Wells draws very strong conclusions on the basis of his research about what kind of home experiences prepare children well for the literacy practices of school. You will have seen that, in the parent–child talk Wells transcribed, the reading activity encouraged David to ask several questions about the meaning of things in the text. In a US study that began by identifying early readers and looking for possible factors affecting that learning, Clark (1976) drew similar conclusions, having found that early readers had a strong desire to read and that their parents were keen readers who involved their children in storytelling and a range of other literacy-based activities.

Heath's comparison of three communities, discussed in the first section of this chapter, identified the middle-class Maintown families as the ones whose story-reading activities prepared them best for school activities; though her findings were more complex than that. In Roadville, the white working-class community, children experienced story-times in similar ways to those already discussed. However, when the child was about 3 years, there was a shift in emphasis away from the adult–child dialogue with a book, to one where the child was expected to listen and learn from books and to answer adult questions afterwards. Maintown children experienced a similar shift in interactional styles towards one associated with local US classrooms (including many initiation–response–feedback (IRF) exchanges as described above). In comparison with Roadville, however, Maintown parents used many more questions to make links between the text and the child's real-life experiences. Furthermore, at the end of a book, there would be discussion not only of what was learned but also of the child's reactions to what had been read. For the Trackton children, the black working-class community, there was far less continuity between home and school literacy practices. Book reading was less common and rarely just between one adult and child. Storytelling was more usually associated with an individual interacting with an audience. The correlation studies and ethnographic comparisons that link being read to and later literacy success have been used by those planning the school curriculum (in the USA and UK particularly) to promote story-time as the key to helping every child succeed in learning to read.

Is it that simple?

Many reception classes today in Britain take this message seriously. Most UK primary classrooms indicate the high value that is placed on storytelling. There will often be a book corner with soft chairs, carpet and inviting display of picture books; story sessions during class with all children gathered around the teacher; small group shared reading times with a teacher or volunteer 'listener', and, often, books that can be taken home. The approach has much support among the UK teaching profession. But questions need to be raised about some of the underlying assumptions. Eve Gregory (1992) puts the question this way:

> Decisively, it is often implied that learning to read in school retains the same characteristics and can be learned in the same way as at home. By immersing non-school-oriented children in the cultural practice of story-reading in school and through the provision of 'good books', they become acculturated into literacy in the same way as young school-oriented children are at home. But is this necessarily so? By overlooking or rendering unproblematic the situational context and believing she is modelling a cultural practice as it exists at home, the teacher may be doing something very different from what she intends.
>
> (Gregory, 1992, p. 40)

Gregory, who spent two years observing urban multilingual reception classrooms in the UK, concluded that you cannot take one cultural practice and assume that it will remain the same in a new context. Bedtime stories at home are what they are because of where they are and whom they involve. Once these constituents are changed – different places, different people, different relationships and histories – then the practice changes too. Whereas at home the central purpose of story reading is usually to enjoy the story together, at school the focus is on teaching about reading. The teacher will choose books that are enjoyable, but story-time is primarily a means towards a specific curriculum end. As such, a teacher will be aiming to develop the pupils' knowledge and understanding about literacy. (This way of interpreting the event of story-time draws on the work of Vygotsky, 1978, who observed how language acts as a cultural tool to help us make sense of experience.) Gregory argues, from analysis of her observations, that children come to school with different experiences of shared reading and some may find it hard to work out the teacher's 'ground rules' for story-times – when the teacher is talking about the story and when about their own life experiences; what comments about the story are acceptable and what are not; what kind of reactions to the story they should make. For some children from cultural backgrounds very different from that of the teacher, the 'ground rules' may be particularly problematic. An example of this can be found in one of the opening anecdotes to this chapter about a child recently arrived in England from Hong Kong who had learned that books are the reward for learning to read the words and that you cannot start with the book.

The new literacy in education

Many current reading and writing activities found in English-speaking schools, particularly in the UK, USA and Australia, assume that school literacy practices should build on children's early experiences with reading and writing. They form part of a view of teaching that, to quote from Margaret Meek, begins by finding out 'what parents, teachers and children say about reading; how they do it together, what they like, what they find difficult and at the same time what they know about language as a system, and what they do with it' (Meek, 1990, p. 152). Meek and others would agree with statements like: literacy teaching must begin with a child's own language experiences; reading should be based on 'real' books; children should be helped to think of themselves as readers and writers; language learning should be interactive; children should be engaged in uncovering meaning in texts; they should explore the purposes and functions of reading and writing and thus discover its organization; teachers should see themselves as facilitators and enablers of a child's literacy development rather than as an instiller of knowledge ... The list could be added to. These propositions represent the shifts in thinking about children and about learning that recognize the child as an active participant able to draw on complex networks of understanding about literacy from a very young age. They also make assumptions about the nature of classrooms and of the relationships between child, teacher and texts.

Where recent educational approaches have differed from earlier ones is in the boundaries that are drawn between home and school, teacher and child, and between oral language, reading and writing. 'New literacy' approaches, as Willinsky (1990) calls them, still have much to learn about those boundaries. For example, they have sometimes failed to recognize the effects of school contexts on the construction of literacy (e.g. Gregory's work discussed earlier). They have also been accused of becoming an orthodoxy, with children having no more control over literacy activities than they did in more traditional approaches. The debates will no doubt continue, but future ones are likely to give an increased role to the many and various literacy experiences that children bring with them to school and will reflect the complex relationships that exist between home and school communities, children, adults and literacy practices.

3.6   CONCLUSION

What are the main conclusions which can be drawn? First, many young children have a continuous involvement with literacy from their earliest years. Literacy is part of their social world, and many children will experiment with its forms and functions long before they are formally introduced to it in school.

Second, the learner of a written language has to sort out how literacy is used in a particular culture. Learners can take different paths to this understanding, but they will do so by trying to make sense of the written texts they encounter and the literacy events they observe and become involved in. Literacy events are important not only for helping children attend to significant features of written English (such as the relationship between phonological features of the spoken language and its alphabetic writing system, the distinctive styles and rhythms of written language, and the relationship between pictures and texts), but also because they encourage children to perceive the written language as a valuable means of representing and communicating ideas.

Third, certain early literacy experiences have been identified as especially significant for later educational success. The reading of bedtime stories is a good example.

Reading A
SOME LESSONS LEARNT AT BEDTIME

Henrietta Dombey

Few professionals who have given the matter much thought maintain that children begin to learn to read only when they start school. Instead, we all see that learning to read has a long pre-history. In the industrialised world pre-school children spend their lives in print-saturated surroundings and learn much of the form and function of written language before they start school. Some children learn even more. The experience of hearing stories read aloud is widely recognised as one which gives uniquely powerful lessons about literacy (Holdaway 1975, Scollon and Scollon 1979, Meek 1982).

In psycholinguistic terms, the listening child is developing a familiarity with the meanings and linguistic forms of printed texts which will materially assist her in later attempts to read, that is to make sense of written texts on her own. Through her experience of stories read aloud, she is developing a store of useful 'information in the head', to use Smith's term, that will enable her to be less dependent on the 'information on the page' (Smith 1971). In sociolinguistic terms she is learning something of the functions that written language can perform, something of what Halliday calls the 'functional extension' that written language can provide (Halliday 1978). And, of course, she is learning the powerful literary satisfactions that books can give. But exactly what happens in such 'listening' sessions has not been thoroughly explored ...

I would like to examine what is happening in one [literacy] event: a story reading between a parent and child in a home similar to those of [Shirley Brice Heath's] 'Maintown' in terms of its social class, educational background and expectations of literacy.

It is hard to see significance in the comfortable and familiar. Certainly, most readers ... will have experienced similar bed-time story sessions, as children, baby-sitters or parents. But the commonplace merits examination: through such commonplace practices as these, children develop significant cultural competences and understandings. To look closely and systematically at the complex patterning of the verbal to and fro between mother and child reveals how this enables the child to come into possession of the language and meanings of this particular written genre. I want to suggest that such a story reading is a complex social interaction through which the child is learning how to make 'readings' of a narrative text.

Anna is three and a half, and her mother is reading her Pat Hutchins' *Rosie's Walk*, which Anna has heard four times before. There are only two sentences in the printed text, but the reading of these is surrounded and interspersed by thirty-nine conversational utterances. These merit examination. They are not an irrelevant distraction, but the means through which Anna takes on the narrative they surround. This conversation has clear boundaries. The announcement of the title at the beginning and the references to bed-time at the end function as a frame, setting limits on what is said. And although this may not be apparent initially, within these limits the conversation has a coherence quite untypical of conversations with young children in other situations.

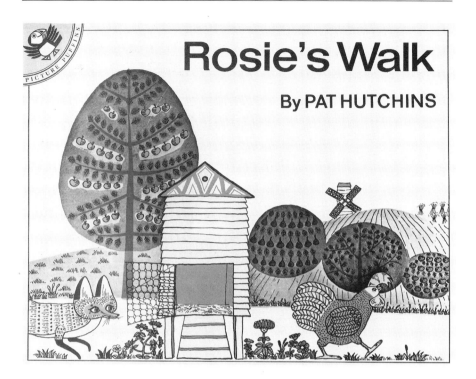

The transcript extract [in Figure 3.8] shows the first half of this story reading. The printed text is shown on the right side of the page, and asterisks indicate indecipherable speech. Omitting the narrative utterances, I have grouped the conversational utterances into exchanges, numbered on the extreme left of the page.

At first sight, it looks far from orderly. Even if we exclude the indecipherable speech, many of the exchanges between mother and child lack the formal completeness of exchange structure models such as those proposed by Coulthard and Brazil (1981) or Berry (1981). Not one has the complete Initiation, Response and Feedback format identified by Sinclair and Coulthard (1975). Indeed, of the nine exchanges in this extract, only six include a verbal response as well as an

IRF exchanges are discussed in Chapter 4 of this book.

Rosie's Walk   Pat Hutchins   (Puffin, 1970)
(Third of three stories that session)

E1	1	M	C'mon 'cos I want to go and have my supper.
	2		Hurry up.
	3		Rosie's Walk
	4		Rosie the hen went for a walk
E2	5	A	A fox is following her.
	6	M	Oh!

ROSIE'S WALK
   By PAT HUTCHINS
*Picture of carefree hen
walking through cluttered
rural scene, followed by
watchful fox
Cover*

*Picture of hen setting out
across picturesque farmyard
with fox eyeing her greedily
from under hen-house*
2
Rosie the hen went for a walk
1–2

7		Across the yard	*Picture of hen walking past fruit trees, unaware of fox jumping after her* across the yard *3–4*
8		Boum *****	*Picture of hen walking on unaware while fox bumps his nose on rake he has landed on* *5–6*
9 10	A	Around the pond, **** fish in the pond	*Picture of hen walking beside pond, unaware of fox jumping after her. No fish in picture.* around the pond *7–8*
11	A	Splash!	*Picture of hen walking on unaware of fox landing in the pond. No fish in picture* *9–10*
E3 ⌈ 12 		How they, how the fox just don't get out?	
⌊ 13	M	Oh I expect he'll climb out.	
⌈ 14	A	Why?	
⌊ 15	M	Why will he climb out?	
⌊ 16	A	Yeah.	
E4 ⌊ 17	M	Well, why d'you think he'll climb out?	
⌊ 18	A	Like when he wants, when he, the hen to eat.	
⌊ 19	M	Yes he wants to eat Rosie.	
20	M	Over the haycock,	*Picture of hen walking over haycock unaware of fox right behind her* over the haycock *11–12*
E5 ⌈ 21	A	Is, is he catching her?	
⌊ 22	M	*er turns page* no	*Picture of hen walking away from haycock unaware of fox buried in it* *13–14*
⌈ 23	A	Wh why?	
E6 ⌊ 24	M	(Laughter) 'cos he's a silly old fox, that's why	
⌊ 25	A	'cos he's gone in the hay.	
⌊ 26	M	Gone in the hay.	
E7 ⌈ 27	A	Could he get out?	
⌊ 28	M	um, Yes.	
29		Past the mill.	*Picture of hen walking past mill unaware of catching her foot in pulley rope, and of fox following her* past the mill *15–16*
30	A	He's doing that, doing that	
31	M	Is he?	
E8 ⌈ 32	M	*turns page* Aah!	*Picture of hen walking on unaware of fox submerged in flour behind her* *17–18*
⌊ 33		She doesn't even notice him, does she?	

Figure 3.8   Transcript of first half of 'Rosie's Walk' story reading

initiation. The remaining three are one-part 'exchanges', but of course Anna and her mother are face to face and share the same physical context: actions, gestures and facial expressions complete many of these apparently incomplete exchanges. Her mother needs no verbal response when she asks Anna to hurry up. There is no indication that either partner has failed to respond acceptably to what the other has said. But this coherence within the exchanges comes from the intermingling of words and paralinguistic communication, not from the words alone …

When we look at the interpersonal patterning of the exchanges we see that it is Anna who is taking the leading role. Anna initiates seven of the nine exchanges. She may be the novice in the matter of story-reading, but she is the one who decides what shall be talked about. This is a striking repetition of the interactive patterning found by Trevarthen to typify pre-speech communication between babies and their adult caretakers, and by Wells to be characteristic of conversational interaction between rapid language learners and their parents (Trevarthen 1979, Wells 1981).

To Anna's initiatives her mother acts as supporter rather than bystander, extending six of these into verbally complete exchanges, which follow the rules of reciprocity. Anna is less generous. Neither of her mother's two initiatives is granted a verbal response. Of course, embedded as these exchanges are in a shared physical context, as I have suggested, their lack of verbal completeness does not necessarily mean a failure to communicate. On the other hand, a high proportion of verbal completion surely shows a movement towards verbal self-sufficiency. Anna's mother treats her initiatives in a way that shifts the discourse towards the explicitness and formal completeness of written language.

This movement towards written language is also evident in the ideational structuring of the discourse. The only exchange whose commodity is not information occurs before the story title has been announced. In all the rest the commodity is information rather than goods or services: and with the exception of the final exchange, the information is all story-related.

Not only is there consistency of topic, there is also a more particular continuity in many of these story-related exchanges. Out of the nine exchanges, five are grouped together in sequences of two and three exchanges, where the initiation of the second and subsequent exchange is contingent on a proposition constructed in the preceding one. This development of story-related information results in a thematic consistency that seems rare in conversations involving young children. Mother and child are not flitting from topic to topic but constructing a series of closely related propositions.

These exchanges are, of course, centred on a narrative text. As they talk, Anna and her mother are not concerned to establish connections with Anna's first-hand experience (although this often plays a part in their readings) but to realise the narrative, to actualise its potential narrative structures and to build a complex, textured and coherent whole. In this story-telling this involves close interpretation of the pictures, for the printed text of *Rosie's Walk* is deceptively uneventful. The richer story, sharp with the constant threat to the innocuous hen of being pounced on and eaten by the unmentioned fox, is to be found in the pictures alone. To use Barthes' terms, the comments of both mother and child focus on the kernel events of the fox following Rosie and his desire to eat her; they ignore the satellite events of the frog on the lily pad and the goat by the hay (Barthes 1975) …

Their comments represent the actions and characters as operating in the present, not the past. What is in the picture is happening now, whereas what is in the verbal narrative has already happened. The ever-present sense of uncertainty about what might happen next is in marked contrast to the immutable certainty of the narrative. Mother and child seem to be concerned not simply to establish an invariant story, but also to construct a fictive world containing possibilities that extend beyond the invariant story of the spoken narrative. As they look at the pictures their intention seems to be to construe them not simply in order to identify elements in the story, nor just to supply elements missing from the verbal narrative. They seem instead to construe them in order to articulate a world where many things might happen. Just after this extract, Anna's mother says with apparent conviction,

I think he's going to get her this time

despite the fact that she has read the story to Anna many times before and both know that the fox will be perpetually frustrated in his attempts to catch Rosie. Anna reveals a similar concern with the possible story future rather than the certain story past when she asks whether the fox is able to get out of the hay. At the end she announces firmly that the fox can't get Rosie in her cage.

Through their conversational talk mother and child are creating a story world and moving about inside it, making judgements on its elements and exploring its possibilities and laws. Within this world there are many things to talk about, and as other readings of this story indicate, the topics chosen vary from one reading to the next. At each reading a different 'reading' is constructed. Yet where they talk of what might happen, their speculations are bounded by the limitations of the story world of this particular genre. There is no suggestion that the fox might get bored, that Rosie might get run over by the lorry from the egg marketing board or that the farmer might eat her for supper. For in this genre the characters behave autonomously and consistently, the significant events that take place are the outcome of this behaviour, and the social and mechanical complexities of the modern world are, by and large, kept at bay.

We cannot know in detail the extent to which the potential structures of the narrative are actualised for Anna. But an examination of the conversational utterances has shown us her concern to articulate the set of kernel events, to savour the hermeneutic tension, and not to overstep the bounds of the genre.

All this has taken place in conversational exchanges principally initiated by Anna, but in which her mother plays a vital, if self-effacing, role. Anna's mother does far more than deliver to her the words of the narrative, although her manner of doing this, in particular her use of intonation, is of key importance in giving it life. But if this were all that mattered Anna would be better served by tapes of stories read by justly celebrated actors than a hurried reading by a mother who wants her own supper. However, this personal reading is providing Anna with something no tape can give. For Anna's mother prompts, supports and extends her enquiries, enabling Anna to make the narrative her own.

Paradoxically, the loose and shifting structures of conversation permit mother and child to actualise the tighter and more complex structures of narrative. The discourse structures Anna is familiar with, and in which she plays the leading role, serve to elaborate and articulate the less familiar structures of the narrative, where her mother has control of the discourse. What is new is not merely juxtaposed with what is familiar: it is through the familiar that the new is given its coherence and significance and enters Anna's possession.

Anna is being initiated into the process of reading as a process of active meaning construction in which the reader makes a personal sense of whole texts. The text, of course, is markedly different from informal conversation and demands very different kinds of meaning making. Yet her mother makes no attempt to disentangle the various levels of linguistic and literary understanding of which such meaning making is composed. At one and the same time she is enlarging Anna's sense of the kinds of propositional meanings of which stories are composed, accustoming her to the narrow formality of the interpersonal meanings conveyed from writer to reader and extending her repertoire of the distinctive lexical and syntactic forms that realise these in narrative text. There is no pre-learning of the vocabulary, no preliminary session with adverbial phrases, nor any exclusive attention to the sequence of events *per se*. Their conversational interaction concerns none of these. Instead, all this learning of new forms and meanings seems to take place unobtrusively, even tacitly. The new forms are certainly not the object of their conscious attention. Their talk is organised and ordered by a central purpose, which is to produce, celebrate and give personal meaning to a whole narrative that brings its own semantic reward. Anna's mother acts on the expectation that this activity will be enjoyable to Anna, and that a determination to savour each story will impel Anna to make sense of the new forms as she constructs the new meanings. Her mother does not see her job as ensuring either that Anna has 'understood' each new word or structure, or that she can give a literally faithful account of the events of the story. Indeed, there is an implicit assumption that to do any of these things would be to distract attention from the central activity …

And there is no one correct internal narrative. What matters is that within the limits set by the text Anna should construct something pleasing to herself and that this pleasure should be shared between mother and child. That Anna sees a richer understanding as more rewarding is evinced by the questions she asks. And the explanations that her mother provides are in response to such questions: they are not items on a didactive agenda whose completion will indicate a correct reading of the text.

Re-reading will deepen Anna's understanding of narrative wholes and of their parts, of functions and of their forms, and make each narrative more firmly her own. As she comes to know a number of texts very well indeed and to apprehend (albeit intuitively) the relationship between the forms and meanings of which they are composed, she will be able to make satisfying sense of more complex texts and demand fewer re-readings. But all this learning is likely to be characterised by simultaneous and unconscious attention to a number of different linguistic and literary levels.

Her mother's mediation, through her use of intonation and her responses to Anna's initiatives, will assist Anna to conquer this new territory. As Anna's familiarity with new forms and new meanings develops, this mediation will become less necessary. It is likely already that Anna is using her familiarity with other stories to help her gloss new ones: familiar forms in new combinations help her construct new meanings, familiar meanings help her make sense of new forms. As she hears more stories she will have a richer stock to draw on and will be less in need of the mediation provided by a known and trusted adult. And with each new narrative her sense of the whole will be developed more from her own internal dialogue than from external dialogue with an experienced reader. But in all the stages of her progress towards a richer experience of narrative, she will proceed along a broad front organised by her intention to 'understand the story'. If the activity is to be intrinsically rewarding this is how she must go about it. For an adult to abstract one element from the narrative and 'teach' it to Anna would be to rob her of the pleasure of making the narrative her own. To borrow Rumelhart's description of reading, the process Anna is engaged in is simultaneous, multi-level, interactive processing (Rumelhart 1976).

The conversation with her mother provides Anna with an external model for the internal conversation with the author that is necessary to any but the most superficial reading of a narrative text. Thus, her mother helps Anna to do in partnership what she cannot yet do for herself. In her actions, she implicitly shares the view embodied in Vygotsky's much quoted observation:

> What the child can do in co-operation today, he can do alone tomorrow.
> (Vygotsky 1962)

Comfortable and familiar though they may be, bed-time story-readings such as this can teach us important lessons about the complex nature of literacy learning, and perhaps even give us a model for what we might do to advance it in school, not just in the primary years, but as long as students can be helped to read with greater power and satisfaction.

References

BARTHES, R. (trans. S. HEATH) (1975) 'Introduction to the structural analysis of narratives', *New Literary History*, vol. 6, pp. 237–72.

BERRY, M. (1981) 'Systemic linguistics and discourse analysis: a multi-layered approach to exchange structure' in M. COULTHARD and M. MONTGOMERY (eds) *Studies in Discourse Analysis*, Routledge and Kegan Paul.

COULTHARD, M. and BRAZIL, D. (1981) 'Exchange structure' in M. COULTHARD and M. MONTGOMERY (eds) *Studies in Discourse Analysis*, Routledge and Kegan Paul.

HALLIDAY, M.A.K. (1978) *Language as Social Semiotic*, Edward Arnold.

HOLDAWAY, D. (1975) *The Foundations of Literacy*, Ashton Scholastic.

MEEK, M. (1982) *Learning to Read*, The Bodley Head.

RUMELHART, D.E. (1976) 'Toward an interactive model of reading', *Technical Report no. 56*, La Jolla, California: Center for Human Information Processing, University of California, San Diego.

SCOLLON, R. and SCOLLON, S. (1979) 'The literate two-year-old: the fictionalisation of self', *Working Papers in Sociolinguistics*, Southwest Regional Laboratory.

SINCLAIR, J. and COULTHARD, M. (1975) *Towards an Analysis of Discourse*, Oxford University Press.

SMITH, F. (1971) *Understanding Reading*, Holt, Rinehart and Winston.

TREVARTHEN, C. (1979) 'Communication and co-operation in early infancy: a description of primary inter-subjectivity' in M. BULLOWA (ed.) *Before Speech: the beginning of interpersonal communication*, Cambridge University Press.

VYGOTSKY, L.S. (1962) *Thought and Language*, MIT Press.

WELLS, C.G. (1981) 'Describing children's linguistic development at home and at school' in C. ADELMAN (ed.) *Uttering Muttering*, Grant McIntyre.

Source: Dombey, 1992, pp. 29–35.

Reading B

WHAT'S IN A STORY?

Gordon Wells

Why should listening to stories be so much more beneficial as a preparation for literacy than looking at books and magazines and talking about the pictures, or attempting to represent ideas graphically through drawing and coloring – worthwhile though these activities are for their own sake? There are, I believe, a number of reasons.

First, in listening to stories read aloud at the age of 2, 3 and 4 – long before they can read themselves – children are already beginning to gain experience of the sustained meaning-building organization of written language and its characteristic rhythms and structures. So, when they come to read books for themselves, they will find the language familiar.

Second, through stories, children vicariously extend the range of their experience far beyond the limits of their immediate surroundings. In the process, they develop a much richer mental model of the world and a vocabulary with which to talk about it …

Stories can also provide an excellent starting point for … collaborative talk between children and parents …, as the parent helps the child to explore his or her own world in the light of what happens in the story and to use the child's own experience to understand the significance of the events that are recounted. Such talk and the stories that give rise to it also provide a validation for the child's own inner storying – that internal mode of meaning making which is probably as deeply rooted in human nature as is language itself.

The **GIANT** Jam Sandwich

Story & pictures by **John Vernon Lord**
Verses by **Janet Burroway**

All these positive features of sharing a story can be seen in the following extract from a recording of David (age 3 years), who has chosen to have *The Giant Jam Sandwich* read to him – obviously not for the first time. Notice how the mother leaves space for the child to offer comments and ask questions and how her contributions build on his, extending his understanding of both the matter of the story and the actual wording.

[*David is sitting next to his mother on the sofa so that he can see the book.*]

David:	The Giant Sandwich [*4-second pause*]
Mother:	Who's this here on the first page?
David:	The wasps.
Mother:	The wasps are coming [*Turns the page*] Here's some more, look. Wow! [*Reads*] *One hot summer in Itching Down* *Four million wasps flew into town.*
David:	I don't like wasps ... flying into town.
Mother:	Why's that?
David:	Because they sting me.
Mother:	Do they?
David:	Mm. I don't like them.
Mother:	They'll only sting you if they get angry. If you leave them alone they won't sting you. But four million would be rather a lot, wouldn't it? They'd get rather in the way. [*Reads*] *They drove the picnickers away ...*
David:	Mm.
Mother:	[*continuing to read*]: *They chased the farmers from their hay* *They stung Lord Swell* [chuckles] *on his fat bald –*
David:	Pate.
Mother:	D' you know what a pate is?
David:	What?
Mother:	What d' you think it is?
David:	Hair.
Mother:	Well – yes. It's where his hair **should** be. It's his head – look, his **bald** head. All his hair's gone.
David:	Where is it?
Mother:	Well, he's old, so it's dropped out. He's gone bald.
David?	Where's – Is that his hat?
Mother:	Mm. He's running, so his hat's fallen off. [*Reads*] *They dived, and hummed, and buzzed, and ate*
David:	D' they eat him?
Mother:	[*laughs*] I expect they might have tried to. I dunno. D' you think wasps eat people?

David:	No.
Mother:	What do they eat?
David	[*with relish*] They eat vegetables.
Mother:	[*laughing*] Vegetables.
David:	Yes.
Mother:	What sort? What do they like?
David:	They like [*5-second pause*] Um …
Mother:	What kind of vegetables were you thinking of?
	[*Long pause*]
David:	[*Looking at the illustration on the next page, which shows three male inhabitants of Itching Down, each attempting in his own way to get rid of the wasps*] Is that a spray to shoo them away? Is that a spray to shoo them away?
Mother:	Yes. It's probably some sort of insecticide, to get rid of them. And what's that net for, do you think? [*A butterfly net*]
David:	It's for catching them with.
Mother:	It doesn't seem to be much good though, does it?
David:	No. They come out the holes.
Mother:	[*laughs*] The holes are too big, aren't they? And what about this man? What's he got?
David:	He's – What's he got?
Mother:	What's that?
David:	A note. What does the note say?
Mother:	A note on a stick, is it? Is that what you think?
David:	Actually it's a sound.
Mother:	A what?
David:	A sound. What's it called on the – on the stick? What is it? What's that man got?
Mother:	Well you know, um–
David:	Yes … Sign.
Mother:	You think it's a sign? Yes it looks very **like** a sign with writing on, doesn't it?
David:	Yes.
Mother:	But it isn't. It's like Mummy's – um – fish slice [*slotted spatula*].
David:	What is it?
Mother:	It's a swatter. He's going to hit the wasp with it.
David:	How d' you hit wasps with otters?
Mother:	[*checking*] Swatters? Well, they're made of plastic usually –
David:	Yes.

Mother:	And they – you bang them down. See if you can squash the wasp. Looks very angry.
	[*5-second pause*]
	Anyway –
David:	Yes.
Mother:	[*reads*] *They called a meeting in the village hall* *And Mayor Muddlenut asked them all,* *'What can we do?' And they said, 'Good question,'* *But nobody had a good suggestion.* *Then Bap the baker leaped to his feet* *And cried, 'What do wasps like <u>best</u> to*
David:	<u>best</u>
Mother:	*eat? Strawberry*
David:	jam.
Mother:	*Now wait a minute.* *If we made a giant sandwich.*
David:	Yes.
Mother:	*We could trap them in it.*

What is particularly impressive about this last section is the timing. It is a truly shared recreation of the story, with David chiming in at exactly the right moment to fit the rhythm of the lines. It is also worth noticing David's interpretation of the picture of the man with the swatter: 'a note on a stick.' What power he attributes to written language. Even wasps can be vanquished by a sign with writing on it: 'WASPS, GO AWAY!'

To understand the full significance of having stories read aloud from an early age, however, we need to look more closely at the relationship between language and experience that is found in stories – and in most extended uses of written language.

In ordinary conversation, which is every child's first and most frequent experience of language in use, the meanings that are communicated arise for the most part out of the context of ongoing activity or out of past or future events about which the participants have shared knowledge or expectations. To understand what is meant, therefore, they can use the context to help them interpret what is said. Indeed, ... this is what makes it possible for the child to construct his or her representation of language in the first place. In conversation, too, the participants are usually face to face and so can provide immediate feedback on the success of the communication and engage in negotiation if problems occur. At the same time they also have to manage their interpersonal relationship satisfactorily. All of which means that, in conversation, attention is only partly on what is said. In seeking to understand each other's intentions, participants make use of a variety of other cues, and the meaning that is finally constructed is the outcome of a collaborative and negotiated interaction, which owes as much to other sources of information as it does to the actual words spoken.

In written language, by contrast, the situation is usually very different. Because writer and reader are not in face-to-face contact, and indeed probably do not even know each other, there is no need for, or even possibility of, a moment-by-moment monitoring of the interpersonal relationship. For the same reason, the writer can make no more than very general assumptions about the knowledge that the reader will bring to the text, and there is no context to support the writer's meaning other than that created by the text itself and the form in which it is presented. All of this leads to a much greater focus on the text alone as the carrier of meaning and to a need for greater explicitness if the intended meaning is to be unambiguously communicated.

This is not to ignore, of course, what the reader brings by way of general expectations and personal experience to the task of constructing an interpretation of the text, nor to underestimate the importance of the cues that are available to the mature reader in the genre form in which the text is presented – verse, dramatic script, newspaper editorial, etc. – or to the novice reader in the form of illustrations. However, even these cues are text-dependent, in the sense that it is only by attending to the text that their significance is recognized. Even when a story is illustrated, as for example in the case of *The Giant Jam Sandwich*, it is the text that gives a precise significance to the illustrations rather than vice versa.

In sum, the most important difference between typical instances of spoken and written language can be stated as follows. In conversation, and particularly in casual conversation around the home, what is said arises out of shared activity and only takes on its full meaning when considered in relation to that nonlinguistic context. The aim in conversational speech, therefore, is to make the *words fit the world*. In most writing, on the other hand, there is no context in the external world to determine the interpretation of the text. The aim must therefore be to use *words* to *create a world* of meaning, which then provides the context in terms of which the text itself can be fully understood. To understand a story therefore – or any other written text – the child has to learn to give full attention to the linguistic message in order to build up a structure of meaning. For, insofar as the writer is able to provide cues for the reader's act of construction, he or she does so by means of the words and structures of the text alone.

What is so important about listening to stories, then, is that, through this experience, the child is beginning to discover the symbolic potential of language: its power to create possible or imaginary worlds through words – by representing experience in symbols that are independent of the objects, events, and relationships symbolized and that can be interpreted in contexts other than those in which the experience originally occurred, if indeed it ever occurred at all.

Compared with the longer-term effects of this discovery, it is easy to see why drawing, or matching names or sounds to the letters of the alphabet, although useful, is of much less significance for later progress at school. The same is true of the learning that takes place when looking at picture books or catalogues and discussing the names and attributes of the objects depicted. No doubt this activity helps children to enlarge their vocabularies – at least for those things that can be pictured. It also gives them practice in answering display questions of a limited kind, and this may well give them an initial advantage if they find themselves – as many do – in classrooms where such skills are emphasized. But it is a short-lived advantage and one that is, in the longer term, restricting. For ultimately – and ideally sooner rather than later – they will need to be able to answer (and also to ask) questions that go beyond naming and rote recall. They will need to follow and construct narrative and expository sequences, recognizing causes, anticipating consequences, and considering the motives and emotions that are inextricably bound up with all human actions and endeavours. In a word, they will need to be able to bring the full power of storying to bear on all the subject matter of the curriculum.

Source: Wells, 1986, pp. 151–7.

4 ENGLISH AS A CLASSROOM LANGUAGE

Neil Mercer, with contributions from Douglas Barnes

4.1 INTRODUCTION

The three previous chapters deal with the learning experiences of young children as they become English speakers in the first few years of their lives. Those chapters also show how learning to speak English is in part a matter of learning to 'get things done' through the language, and also of using language to construct social identities.

This chapter is about the use of the English language as a medium for education in school, a setting which can have a powerful influence on the intellectual, social and linguistic development of older children. Most of the chapter is about talk in the classroom, but later I also discuss some aspects of written language. Two related themes are important throughout:

- the role of language in the process of teaching and learning;
- the relationship between English and other languages in the classroom.

4.2 LANGUAGE, TEACHING AND LEARNING

It is impossible to consider how English is used for the purpose of teaching and learning in schools without considering how language, in general, is used for that purpose. Nowadays, schools the world over have much in common in the ways that they function, commonality which is reflected in the language of the classroom.

One of the most obvious functions of spoken language in a classroom is for teachers to direct and control pupils' activities: they can tell pupils what they are to do, how they are to do it, when to start and when to stop. Teachers also use talk as a way of providing children with certain kinds of information which it would be hard to provide by any other means. They tell pupils stories, read poetry to them, describe objects, events and processes. They also assess pupils' learning through talk, as discussed below. But before we look at some examples of classroom language, let us look more carefully at what education is meant to be about, and at the role of language in it.

The essence of formal education is that one person, a teacher, helps another person, a learner, to learn to do things which the learner would not be easily able to learn without some help. The prime justification for setting up schools is to enable the process of teaching and learning to be carried out effectively. But formal education also has some specific aims. One is that children, or pupils, should acquire knowledge about particular subjects – science, arts, humanities and so on – represented by 'the curriculum'. And another aim, very relevant to our interests here, is that pupils should learn to use spoken and written language in 'educated' ways. What counts as 'educated' language use is something that is defined within particular societies, though there may be many common features across societies. Educated speakers of English are able to use the language in ways defined as appropriate within relevant **discourse communities** (networks of people with shared interests, purposes and ways of using language) when they explain ideas, describe events or processes, and construct arguments. They are able to use appropriate genres of English.

One way of defining a schoolteacher is as someone who guides his or her pupils into active participation in educated discourses (Mercer, 1995). The process of teaching and learning depends on the creation of shared experience and joint understanding. This is also very relevant to our interest in English as a classroom language. As a teacher and a class engage, day by day, in various activities and interactions, they are gathering a resource of shared experience which they can use as the basis for further activity. This is where the role of language is crucial. Without language, the opportunities for building and elaborating on shared experience would be extremely limited (as they are for other species). But teachers and learners can talk about what they have done, what they are doing and what they will do next; and as they do so the talk can thread together experiences shared over long periods of time. Each day's talk in a classroom forms part of a 'long conversation' (Maybin, 1994a) that may continue throughout the days, months or even years that teachers and pupils spend together in school. As we discuss below, the talk between teachers and pupils is usually recognizably 'educational' in its form and content.

Because the process of classroom education depends so heavily on language, one obvious requirement for the success of that process would seem to be that everyone involved has a good understanding of English or whatever language or languages are used in the classroom. In many parts of the world this requirement is not met. Later in the chapter I consider what happens in such situations. I also hope to show that there are other, less obvious aspects of language use in the classroom which are important and problematic for the process of education. Even children whose mother tongue is English have to learn certain things about how that language is used in school if they are to participate fully in the educational process.

The concept of 'discourse community' is also discussed in the second book in this series, *Using English: from conversation to canon* (Maybin and Mercer (eds), 1996 – see particularly Chapter 3). See also Chapter 6 of this book for coverage of a genre approach to teaching writing, and Chapter 8 for discussion of academic discourses and genres.

❖   ❖   ❖   ❖   ❖

Activity 4.1   *(Allow about 15–20 minutes)*

Sequence 1 below is a transcribed sequence of classroom talk. Read through it once, then go through it again and consider:

1   Who asks the questions?

2   What would you say was the main function of the questions?

3   Can you see any recurring patterns in the ways the teacher and the pupils interact?

Comment

You will have seen that all the questions in Sequence 1 were asked by the teacher. This is commonly the case in classrooms. The function of these questions seems to be for the teacher to learn what the pupils have been doing, and so be able to provide both some evaluation for what they have done and further guidance on what they should do next. You may have noticed a pattern in the talk between the teacher and the pupils which embodies these functions. The teacher uses a question to elicit information from one or more pupils. She then evaluates the reply given. There is a structural pattern to the talk: a *teacher's question* is followed by a *pupil response*, followed in turn by some *teacher feedback* or *evaluation*.

❖   ❖   ❖   ❖   ❖

Sequence 1

Sequence 1 was recorded in a secondary school in England where a class of 14-year-olds were engaged in computer-based communication with children in a nearby primary school. In a 'fantasy adventure' setting, the secondary students were (in groups of three) pretending to be a group of characters stranded in time and space. Using electronic mail, they told the younger children of their predicaments and asked for help. The younger children replied, and the older children used these replies when developing the adventure. The sequence is one small part of a much longer session in which the English teacher was questioning the various groups about the most recent communications with the younger children and about their future plans. (Note: Anne, Emma and Sharon are the girls in one group.)

Teacher:	What about the word 'dimension', because you were going to include that in your message, weren't you?
Anne:	Yeh. And there's going to be – if they go in the right room, then they'll find a letter in the floor and that'll spell 'dimension'.
Teacher:	What happens if they do go in the wrong room?
Emma:	Well, there's no letter in the bottom, in the floor.
Teacher:	Oh God! So they've got to get it right, or that's it! (*everyone laughs*) The adventurers are stuck there for ever. And Cath can't get back to her own time. What do you mean the letters are in the room, I don't quite follow that?
Emma:	On the floor, like a tile or something.
Teacher:	Oh I see. Why did you choose the word 'dimension'?
Anne:	Don't know. (*the three students speak together, looking to each other, seeming uncertain*)
Emma:	It just came up. Just said, you know, 'dimension' and everyone agreed.
Sharon:	Don't know.
Teacher:	Right, because it seemed to fit in with, what, the fantasy flow, flavour?
Sharon:	Yeh.
Teacher:	OK. Why do they go through the maze rather than go back? I mean what motivation do they have for going through it in the first place?
Sharon:	Um, I think that it was the king told them that Joe would be in the maze or at the end of the maze, and they didn't go back because of Joe, I think it was. I'm not sure about that.
Teacher:	You've really got to sort that out. It's got to be very, very clear.

(Mercer, 1995, pp. 30–1)

The structural element of classroom talk discussed in Activity 4.1 was first described by the linguists Sinclair and Coulthard (1975) and is usually known as an initiation-response-feedback (IRF) exchange. That is:

Teacher:	Why do they go through the maze rather than go back? I mean what motivation do they have for going through it in the first place?	**Initiation**
Sharon:	Um, I think that it was the king told them that Joe would be in the maze or at the end of the maze, and they didn't go back because of Joe, I think it was. I'm not sure about that.	**Response**
Teacher:	You've really got to sort that out. It's got to be very, very clear.	**Feedback or evaluation**

'IRF' exchanges (alternatively called IRE sequences, where the 'E' stands for 'evaluation', by Mehan, 1979) can be thought of as the archetypal form of interaction between a teacher and a pupil – a basic unit of classroom talk as a continuous stretch of language or 'text'.

See *Describing Language* (Graddol et al., 1994), for a fuller discussion of IRFs and of classroom talk as text.

However, they do not typify the pattern of talk in all classroom activities; other kinds of talk involving different patterns of exchanges (for example, in which students ask questions of teachers, or of other students) may happen too.

We can also see IRF exchanges occurring as slightly more complex, linked structures. So in the following example the teacher obtains three 'responses' to her 'initiation', and her second 'feedback' comment also functions as a further 'initiation':

Teacher:	Why did you choose the word 'dimension'?	**I**
Anne:	Don't know.	**R**
Emma:	It just came up. Just said, you know, 'dimension' and everyone agreed.	**R**
Sharon:	Don't know.	**R**
Teacher:	Right, because it seemed to fit in with, what, the fantasy flow, flavour?	**F/I**
Sharon:	Yeh.	**R**
Teacher:	OK.	**F**

IRFs of the kind illustrated in Sequence 1 have been observed as a common feature in classrooms the world over; and although the original research which established their existence was carried out in Britain by Sinclair and Coulthard (1975) and in the USA by Mehan (1979), there is no reason to believe that they are a feature of classroom life peculiar to those countries, or to classrooms in which English is spoken. Recent classroom research in several countries, including Brazil (e.g. Magalhaes, 1994), Botswana (Arthur, 1992) and India (Sahni, 1992; see also Reading A below), has revealed that similar patterns of classroom talk occur more widely.

Teachers' questions

Teachers have sometimes been criticized by educational researchers for relying so much on questions and IRF exchanges. Thus the educational researcher J.J. Dillon (1988) and the psychologist David Wood (1992) have both suggested that teachers' questions tend to suppress pupils' contributions to classroom talk, because they are usually designed just to elicit one brief 'right answer'. I recorded an example of a teacher doing this in a British school. It happened quite close to the beginning of the third of a series of lessons, for the class in question, on the geography of South America.

Sequence 2

Teacher: Argentina, what is the capital of Argentina?

Pupil 1:   Argentina City. [*Some pupils laugh, others say 'Sir, sir' and raise their hands*]

Teacher: [*To a pupil who has hand raised*] Brian?

Pupil 2:   Buenos Aires.

Teacher: Yes, good. Buenos [*writing on board*] Aires.

In this sequence the teacher asked a 'closed' question – one to which he knew the answer, which he had told the pupils in a previous lesson – and the pupils responded by trying to provide the 'right answer'. When one pupil failed to provide the only possible right answer, the teacher ignored the wrong answer that had been offered (thus providing 'feedback' of a kind) and went on to accept a second 'bid' for an answer from a second pupil. This particular kind of use of IRF exchanges – a teacher asking questions to which he or she knows the answer – is the most common in classrooms.

One obvious danger of a teacher relying heavily and continuously on such traditional, formal question-and-answer reviews is that students have little opportunity to make coherent, independent sense of what they are being taught. They are unlikely to be able to consolidate their understanding unless they have to recall and apply the relevant knowledge without the teacher's elicitations to prompt them. They also have little opportunity to develop and practise their own ways of using language as a tool for thinking with, by using it to reason, argue and explain. There are therefore some good reasons for agreeing with Dillon's and Wood's criticisms of teachers' dependence on the use of IRFs and of 'closed' questions.

However, if we look back to Sequence 1 we can see that the teacher there is *not* using IRFs in this way. Instead, she is asking questions to find out things that she does not already know: to find out about what the students have done and why they have done it. Notice the very different nature of the content and function of the teacher's and students' responses in Sequence 1, compared with Sequence 2. The first teacher's questions are 'open', in that she does not have only one possible correct answer in mind. She is asking pupils to *describe* clearly what they have done, to *account* for it, and is encouraging them to *review* their actions. She has joined a group of pupils in the middle of a sequence of work which they are carrying out by themselves. She is using her enquiries not only to assess her pupils' learning, but also to *guide* their future activity. Through questions such as

'Why did you choose the word "dimension"?' and 'Why do they go through the maze rather than go back?', the teacher is trying to direct the girls' attention to matters requiring more thought and clarification when they return to their work. In this way, she is not only focusing their attention on how effectively they use the English language to communicate with the young children in the primary school, she is also shaping their own awareness and understanding of what they are doing.

There are obvious similarities, then, in the *structure* of the talk in Sequences 1 and 2. However, if we also consider the *content* of the question-and-answer exchanges in the two sequences, and the *context* of the activities and shared experiences in which this took place, we can see quite different educational processes going on. So, while I have some agreement with the essence of Dillon's and Wood's critical analyses of how teachers use questions, I am suggesting that we must beware of equating *language structures* with *language functions*. Particular language structures – in this case IRF exchanges – can be used for more than one purpose and function according to the context in which they are used.

The use of IRF exchanges depends on teachers and pupils being familiar with the conventions of this kind of question-and-answer routine, and being willing to abide by those conventions. On the basis of research in classrooms in Britain and the USA, one would be likely to conclude that most children rapidly become familiar with the IRF structure of most classroom talk and participate in it fairly readily (Willes, 1983; Edwards, 1992). However, look now at another sequence. It was recorded by Ian Malcolm (1982) in an infant classroom in Western Australia, where the children (aged 5–6 years old) were all Aboriginal Australians. They have just heard their teacher tell a story in which a kitten is found by a girl and the teacher is trying to get them to talk about it.

Sequence 3

Teacher:	How do we know she liked the kitten?
	How do we know she liked the kitten?
	[*No responses from children*]
	No, you think about it, now. She got the kitten, I mean she found the kitten ... an' then she said to Mum and Dad she wanted to?
Child 1:	Keep it.
Child 2:	Keep it.
Teacher:	Keep it. So if she didn't want the kitten she wouldn't've kept it, would she? What d'*you* think, Brenda?
Brenda:	[*Silence*]
Teacher:	Well, you listen carefully.

(Adapted from Malcolm, 1982, p. 129)

Malcolm offers this extract as one which typifies many of the interactions he observed in Aboriginal classrooms. He found that Aboriginal children usually seemed extremely reluctant to engage in IRF sequences. He comments that:

As the children failed to perform their appointed roles in the discourse, the teacher engaged in an ongoing process of attempted repair or revision of her intended pattern. The result was, at first, an increased number of teacher speech acts, and later a premature abandonment of this speech event by the teacher for another in which the children were prepared to participate more readily.

(Malcolm, 1982, p. 129)

Malcolm suggests that the children's reluctance is not a matter of their lacking fluency in English. He offers instead a cultural explanation: in Aboriginal society such overt interrogations and demonstrations of understanding would not be considered polite. As Malcolm comments: 'the Aboriginal community favored and fostered reticence in speech, which is the very issue which underlies much of the communicative difficulty of the Aboriginal classroom' (p. 131).

Conversational styles in Aboriginal communities are discussed in Chapter 1 of the second book in this series, *Using English: from conversation to canon* (Maybin and Mercer (eds), 1996).

Research elsewhere – for example in Hawaii, and among native Americans in the USA and Mexico (Philips, 1972; Paradise, forthcoming) – has also shown that children from some cultural backgrounds find IRF patterns of question-and-answer alien and discomforting. But that research also shows that teachers usually tend, nevertheless, to try to uphold these conventions in the face of such reluctance or incomprehension. It is also often observed that schools normally make little effort to incorporate or exploit the language practices which children have had the opportunity to develop in their home communities, whether these be the storytelling of Irish travellers in Britain, the 'rapping' and 'toasting' of Afro-Caribbean teenagers (Edwards and Sienkewicz, 1990) or the imaginative story-poems heard among young children in working-class black American communities (Heath, 1983). Having spent more than ten years observing language use in Hawaiian communities and classrooms, Stephen Boggs describes some of the 'oral arts' which are an important part of children's informal social lives:

[The children] showed very close attention to the exact pronunciation of lyrics and rhythm when learning new songs ... I observed children in the third and fourth grades [aged 8–9 years] pronounce the lyrics of songs in Tahitian, Samoan, Maori – and even in Standard English! Particular Standard English phonemes not pronounced in everyday speech would be pronounced in songs, as in names ... This ... shows the close relationship between verbal learning and socially valued communication. Singing is a highly valued social activity.

(Boggs, 1985, p. 125)

He notes, however, that this interest and language ability on the part of children was only rarely exploited by teachers in school. Researchers have for some years pointed to the gulf which commonly exists for children between their experience of language in and out of school, in many parts of the English-speaking world (e.g. Edwards, 1976; Wells, 1986; Heath, 1983). But one should perhaps be cautious in drawing the obvious conclusion that if teachers made great efforts to incorporate children's out-of-school informal language practices into the life of the classroom, this would necessarily either be welcomed by the children or be successful as a strategy for teaching the curriculum. One of the vital qualities of children's informal language practices is that they belong to the children and are an integral part of life outside the classroom.

I have briefly considered how the cultural language practices of children's communities may affect their participation in classroom dialogue. Of course, language use in the classroom is shaped by cultural traditions; we have seen that the use of IRF exchanges can be related to an influential tradition of formal education. The influence of that and other traditions in classroom language is well illustrated in Reading A.

❖ ❖ ❖ ❖ ❖

Activity 4.2   *(Reading A)*

Read 'One cup of newspaper and one cup of tea' by G.D. Jayalakshmi (Reading A). The author describes her observational research in English-medium classrooms in an Indian secondary school. After reading the piece, consider the following questions:

1   What patterns of language use does Jayalakshmi observe in the Bhojpur classrooms?

2   To what cultural, traditional influences does Jayalakshmi attribute the style of teaching in Bhojpur?

3   Does classroom communication in Bhojpur have any features in common with those described earlier in this chapter?

Comment

You will see that Jayalakshmi suggests that in the secondary English-medium classrooms she observed, one can see the continuing influence of the traditional Indian styles of instruction and storytelling – styles which depended upon the performance of an effective storyteller (or guru) and a receptive audience (the students or disciples). These traditional methods have served Indian scholars well for generations and, as Jayalakshmi also points out, they have been combined with British influences to generate a distinct and well-established Indian style of classroom communication. Among other features, this style involves the frequent use of *rhetorical questions* by the teacher, marked by intonation, pauses or gestures, which the students are not expected to answer. Frequent use of such rhetorical questions may be a distinctive feature of Indian pedagogy: their use has not been reported in classrooms in other English-speaking countries. Likewise, students contribute to the generation of a distinctive style of classroom language use by *jointly reciting* what they learn in conjunction with their teacher. Up until the 1960s this kind of classroom language activity used to be common in most English-speaking countries, though it is not so universal today. However, note that Jayalakshmi also observes the frequent use of question-and-answer sessions at the end of lessons, usually organized in terms of IRF exchanges similar to those described earlier.

❖ ❖ ❖ ❖ ❖

The English of curriculum subjects

I want now to turn to a rather different aspect of the language demands made on children in school. As they go through their years of schooling, pupils encounter an increasing number of specialized technical terms. Learning these can be an important part of education: used effectively, the technical vocabularies of

science, mathematics, art or any other subject provide clear and economical ways of describing and discussing complex and abstract issues. A shared understanding of musical terminology, for instance – terms like 'octave', 'bar', 'key' and so on – makes it possible for two people to discuss, in the abstract, phenomena which otherwise would have to be concretely demonstrated. The discourse of educated people talking about their specialism is explicit only to the initiated. Becoming familiar with the language of a subject is therefore an important requirement for entering the intellectual communities of science, mathematics, literature or whatever.

In any classroom where English is the medium of instruction, an important part of a teacher's job is to help pupils learn and understand the specialized English of curriculum subjects. The use of technical language in the classroom frequently causes much confusion and misunderstanding. Teachers seem often to assume that the meaning of a word will become obvious to pupils as they hear or read it being used, while children are usually reluctant to ask questions about the meanings of words because to do so would reveal their ignorance. Some technical English words may be used only rarely in the wider world, but they may represent ideas which are not difficult for pupils to grasp because they can easily be explained or exemplified. (A good example is 'alliteration'.) Others may be impossible to explain through a concrete set of instances. This applies to many scientific concepts describing properties of matter (such as 'density') and processes ('evolution', 'photosynthesis', etc.). A consequence may be that many technical words become for children mere jargon, words which they know they are expected to use but which mean very little to them.

Educational research has provided many bizarre and salutary examples of how technical English terms may be misunderstood and most teachers will have their own collections. Two examples I have recorded are those of a 12-year-old who thought that 'quandary' meant a four-sided figure and a 16-year-old who, after saying that he had never understood 'subtractions', later commented that he could do 'take-aways'. Robert Hull, a British secondary teacher, has noted these kinds of problems among 14-year-old pupils:

> 'Animals harbour insects' meant they ate them. 'The lowest bridge-town' was a slum on a bridge … Expressions such as 'molten iron', 'physical feature', 'factor', 'western leader' were often insuperable obstacles to comprehension.
> (Hull, 1985, p. xi)

For children who are learning English as a second or additional language, the vocabulary and style of technical English may pose even greater problems. And if teachers themselves are not confident users of technical English, good explanations may not be available. For example, Cleghorn et al. (1989) found that Kenyan teachers who were teaching science through the medium of English were often unable to explain in English the meanings of terms they were using (such as 'parasite'). They comment:

> When teachers have to search for English equivalents of what is familiar but often not conceptually the same in the local language, the actual meaning of what is being taught can be altered.
> (Cleghorn et al., 1989, p. 21)

❖ ❖ ❖ ❖ ❖

Activity 4.3 *(Allow about 15 minutes)*

This activity is in two parts:

1   Think back to your own schooldays. Can you remember any terms which you never felt confident about using correctly, or any that you now know that you misunderstood? Do you recall teachers ever exploring the meanings of words in class, or discussing misunderstandings with pupils?

2   Look at the list of words below. All these words are expected to be learned and understood by children as part of the national curriculum for science in

British primary schools (i.e. for children aged 5–11 years). Could you explain their meaning to a child (or to another adult)?

evaporation	habitat
condensation	food-chain
insulator	cycle
conductor	precipitation
translucence	Newton (as a unit)
force	capillary

Comment

I asked three adults to do this activity. One had completed secondary and university education in England, and one had done so in Australia. Both were aged about 45. The third (aged 20) was currently studying science at a British university. All three said that they had no recollection of teachers explicitly discussing the meaning of technical terms, or of misunderstandings about them being publicly aired and resolved in class. The science student had little difficulty in telling me the meaning of the terms in part 2; the other two adults had some trouble with 'translucence' and 'force'. But all three commented on how little reason they ever had to use many (if any) of those words once they had left school.

❖ ❖ ❖ ❖ ❖

Pupils without a teacher

In several English-speaking countries, it has become increasingly common to set up activities in which pupils work and talk together without the continual presence of a teacher. There is no doubt that organizing students to work on their own in groups or pairs generates quite different patterns of talk from those which typify teacher–pupil interactions (Norman, 1992; Mercer, 1995; Barnes and Todd, 1995).

❖ ❖ ❖ ❖ ❖

Activity 4.4   *(Allow about 15–20 minutes)*

Look at Sequence 4, which is an extract from a discussion between a group of 9-year-old children recorded in an English primary school, on the topic of how they speak in and out of school. As you read the sequence, try to specify any ways in which the talk here is different from the examples of teacher-led talk earlier in the chapter.

Comment

Even though the children are responding here to questions set them by their teacher, you will no doubt have seen that the nature of their talk is quite different from that of the class discussions led by a teacher. Many of them make quite extended contributions. They expand on each other's comments. They are willing to express uncertainty to each other and to offer each other explanations (as in the later part of the discussion, about US English). In this sequence, talk is being used to share knowledge and construct joint understandings in ways that reflect the fact that the participants all have similar status in the discussion, as learners who can contribute from the wealth of their individual experiences.

❖ ❖ ❖ ❖ ❖

Sequence 4

The children in this group came from homes in which a variety of languages were spoken, including various Indian languages and US (rather than British) English. Their discussion was set up by their teacher, who provided the children with a set of questions about language use on cards. We pick up the sequence shortly after one of the children has read out a question from a card: 'Do you change the way you talk depending on where you are?'

G   At home I, uh, at home I talk, I talk Gujerati and in school and playground with my best friends Urdu.

A   I change the way in school and in the playground.

S   Me too.

M   In the class you know you talk quieter and everything.

A   Yes.

M   At play you can shout your head off so you can get … all the energy and that.

G   I can't, people look at me …
    [Laughter]

A   [Reading from the card] If so how do you change the way you talk?

S   I don't know.

A   Well I change the way I talk by being quieter.

M   If so how do you change the way you talk.

A   I change the way at school.

S   I speak politely at school.

A   At home I'm a right chatterbox.

S   Yes.

G   Yes, me too I keep talking …

S   When I'm angry with my parents I don't speak really politely.

M   When I'm at home talking with my mum …

A   Yeah.

M   I talk American because I'm used to it. When I'm around American people.

A   [Inaudible]

G   What?

A   I thought English was the same as American.

M   It's not.

S   It's not because in American our chips, they call chips French fries … and …

M   Biscuits …

S   And they call crisps chips …

M   … and they call biscuits cookies and we call trousers pants …

G   What do you call pants, trousers?
    [Giggles]

G = Ghazanfar
A = Abraham
S = Surjit
M = Melissa

S   And they call petrol ... gas.

G   Why do you call petrol gas?

A   Oh God ...

M   It's just our language Ghazanfar.

S   It's just changed a bit.

(Open University, 1991, p. C19)

Collaborative learning of this kind makes considerable demands upon the students' ability to use language as a way of thinking together. The thinking and the talking in these circumstances become inseparable: language is being used, in an educationally appropriate way, as a *social mode of thinking* (Mercer, 1995). The students have to talk about the task and to collaborate successfully, for they can no longer rely on the teacher to define a line of thought and guide them along it. But even when talking and working without a teacher, students are expected to use language in ways that are educationally appropriate. That is, when a teacher asks pupils to 'discuss' a topic, the teacher is usually expecting something quite specific of them – to provide explicit descriptions, formulate reasons and explanations, and agree on possible solutions to problems. One important part of becoming educated in and through the medium of English is learning how to generate such appropriate 'educated' styles of English discourse, and such discourse depends on more than just the appropriate use of technical terms (as discussed earlier). Similar points can be made about writing in school (a topic to which I return, briefly, later).

What pupils have to learn

I have described some of the ways that teachers use the English language in the classroom to direct and constrain the contributions that pupils are expected to make to the process of teaching and learning (though, as we all know from past experience, pupils make many contributions to talk in the classroom which teachers do not seek). We have also seen that entering the world of school education sets children certain kinds of language learning tasks. Imagine a child, any child, starting the first day at a school in which he or she will be taught in English. There are three kinds of learning task which that child may face and which are crucial to educational progress:

1   Pupils have to learn the special ways of using English that apply in school, because they are unfamiliar with educational conventions and the technical language of curriculum subjects.

2   Pupils may have to learn to speak and write in English if they have grown up speaking some other language.

3   Pupils may have to learn to use Standard English if they have grown up speaking a 'nonstandard' variety of English.

In reality, the task facing any particular pupil may not neatly fit any of these three descriptions (for instance, she may be fluent in spoken English, but not in the written language); yet this three-part distinction can nevertheless be helpful at this stage for making sense of reality in all its complexity.

4.3 ENGLISH-MEDIUM EDUCATION IN BILINGUAL AND MULTILINGUAL SETTINGS

In this section I consider the use of spoken English in classrooms where the main language of pupils is not English. There are two principal sorts of situation. The first occurs in countries where there is English-medium education, even though the mother tongue of most of the children is not English. The second is where pupils whose mother tongue is not English enter schools in a predominantly English-speaking country. I provide examples from both of these types of situation.

In any situation where English is used as a classroom language but is not the main language of children's home or community, teachers may have the multiple task of teaching:

- the English language;
- the educational ground rules for using it in the classrooms; and
- any specific subject content.

Jo Arthur (1992) has carried out observational research on teaching and learning in primary school classrooms in Botswana. As in the Indian secondary school studied by Jayalakshmi (see Reading A), English was used as the medium of education, but it was not the main language of the pupils' local community. Arthur observed that when teachers were teaching mathematics, they commonly used question-and-answer sessions as opportunities for schooling children in the use of appropriate 'classroom English' as well as maths. For example, one primary teacher commonly insisted that pupils reply to questions 'in full sentences', as shown below.

Sequence 5

[Teacher]:	how many parts are left here? [first pupil's name]
[First pupil]:	seven parts
[Teacher]:	answer fully. how many parts are there?
[Pupil]:	there are ... there are seven parts
[Teacher]:	how many parts are left? sit down my boy. you have tried. yes. [second pupil's name]
[Second pupil]:	we left with seven parts
[Teacher]:	we are left with seven parts. say that [second pupil's name]
[Second pupil]:	we are left with seven parts
[Teacher]:	good boy. we are left with seven parts

(Arthur, 1992, pp. 6–7)

You can see that this sequence is made up of a linked series of IRF exchanges. For example:

- how many parts are left here? [*initiation*]
- seven parts [*response*]
- answer fully [*feedback/evaluation*]

Her students therefore needed to understand that their teacher was using these exchanges not only to evaluate their mathematical understanding, but also to test their fluency in spoken English and their ability to conform to a 'ground rule' that she enforced in her classroom – 'answer in full sentences'. Arthur comments that for pupils in this kind of situation, the demands of classroom communication are complicated because their teacher is attempting to get them to focus on both the medium (English) and the message (maths). Arthur says that such dual focus is common in Botswana classrooms, as the following sequence from another lesson shows.

Sequence 6

[Teacher]:	in which continent is your country? in which continent is your country? give an answer
[First pupil]:	in Africa is my country
[Teacher]:	he says in Africa is my country. who could frame her sentence? in Africa is my country
[Second pupil]:	Africa is my continent
[Teacher]:	my question was. in which continent is your country?
[Third pupil]:	its continent is in Africa
[Teacher]:	it is in the continent of Africa. everybody
[All pupils]:	it is in the continent of Africa

(Arthur, 1992, p. 13)

Bilingual codeswitching in the classroom

Codeswitching among children is discussed in Chapter 2 of this book. See also the first and second books in this series, *English: history, diversity and change* (Graddol et al. (eds), 1996) and *Using English: from conversation to canon* (Maybin and Mercer (eds), 1996), for further discussion of codeswitching in other contexts.

In circumstances where English is being used as a classroom language but where the pupils' first language is not English, a teacher may **codeswitch** to the first language if problems of comprehension arise.

Sometimes the first language may be used only for asides, for control purposes or to make personal comments. However, when codeswitching amounts to the teacher translating the curriculum content being taught, its use as an explanatory teaching strategy is somewhat controversial. On the one hand, there are those who argue that it is a sensible, common-sense response by a teacher to the specific kind of teaching and learning situation. Thus in studying its use in English-medium classrooms in China, Lin (1988) explains a teacher's use of translation as follows:

> The teacher was anxious that her students might not understand the point clearly; she therefore sought to ensure thorough comprehension through presenting the message again in Cantonese which is the students' dominant language.
>
> (Lin, 1988, p. 78)

Researchers of bilingual codeswitching have sometimes concluded that it is of dubious value as a teaching strategy if one of the aims of the teaching is to improve students' competence in English. Thus Jacobson comments:

> the translation into the child's vernacular of everything that is being taught may prevent him/her from ever developing the kind of English language proficiency that must be one of the objectives of a sound bilingual programme.
>
> (Jacobson, 1990, p. 6)

It seems, however, that teachers often use codeswitching in more complex ways than simply translating content directly into another language. On observing classrooms in Hong Kong, Johnson and Lee (1987) noticed that the switching strategy most commonly employed by teachers had a three-part structure, as follows:

1   'Key statement' of topic in English.
2   Expansion, clarification or explanation in Cantonese.
3   Restatement in English.

Johnson and Lee found that teachers commonly did not provide simple translations of the initial English statement, but rather gave some information in Cantonese which would help pupils to make more sense of the statement when it was restated in stage 3. The implication here is that such teachers are pursuing the familiar task of guiding children's understanding of curriculum content through language, but using special bilingual techniques to do so.

An interesting study of codeswitching in bilingual classrooms in Malta was carried out by Antoinette Camilleri (1994). She showed that codeswitching was used as a teaching technique in a variety of ways. Look, for example, at these two extracts from the talk of a teacher in a secondary school lesson about the production and use of wool, based on a textbook written in English. The teacher begins by reading part of the text. (A translation of talk in Maltese is given in the right-hand column.)

Extract 1

England Australia New Zealand and Argentina are the best producers of wool *dawk l-aktar li għandhom* farms *li jrabbu n-nagħaġ għas-suf O.K.* England *tgħiduli minn licma post* England *għandhom* Scotland *magħrufin tant għall-*wool *u ġersijiet tagħhom O.K.*

they have the largest number of farms and the largest number of sheep for wool O.K. England where in England we really mean Scotland they are very well-known for their woollen products

Extract 2

wool *issa* it does not crease but it has to be washed with care *issa din importanti ma għidtilkomx illi jekk ikolli nara xagħra jew sufa waħda* under the microscope *ghandha qisha ħafna scales tal. ħuta issa jekk ma naħslux sewwa dawk l-i*scales *jitgħaqqdu ġo xulxin u indaħħal ġersi daqshekk ġol-* washing machine *u noħorġu daqshekk għax jixxrinkjali u jitgħaqqad kollu*

now this is important didn't I tell you that if I had a look at a single hair or fibre

it has many scales which if not washed properly get entangled and I put a jersey this size into the washing machine and it comes out this size because it shrinks and gets entangled

(Adapted from Camilleri, 1994)

Camilleri notes that the first extract shows the teacher using the switch from English to Maltese to *amplify* the point being made, rather than simply repeating it in translation. In the second extract, she explains the English statement in Maltese, again avoiding direct translation. Camilleri comments that the lesson is therefore a particular kind of literacy event, in which there are two parallel discourses – the written one in English, the spoken one in Maltese.

Studies of codeswitching in classrooms have revealed a variety of patterns of bilingual use (Martyn-Jones, 1995). For example, Zentella (1981) observed and recorded events in two bilingual classes in New York schools, one first-grade class (in which the children were about 6 years old) and the other a sixth-grade (in which the average age would be about 12). The pupils and teachers were all native Spanish speakers, of Puerto Rican origin, but the official medium for classroom education was English. One of the focuses of Zentella's analysis of teacher–pupil interactions was IRF sequences. Both Spanish and English were actually used by teachers and pupils in the classes, and Zentella was able to show that there were three recurring patterns of language switching in IRF sequences, which seemed to represent the use of certain 'ground rules' governing language choice. These are summarized in Table 4.1.

Table 4.1

	Rules governing language choice	Teacher initiation	Student reply	Teacher feedback
1	Teacher and student: 'follow the leader'	English Spanish	English Spanish	English Spanish
2	Teacher: 'follow the child'	English Spanish	Spanish English	Spanish English
3	Teacher: 'include the child's choice and yours'	English Spanish	Spanish English	both languages both languages

(Adapted from Zentella, 1981)

We can see that distinctive patterns of language use emerge in bilingual classrooms, overlaying the familiar patterns of teacher-led IRF exchanges. The extent to which features such as codeswitching between English and other languages occur in any particular classroom will depend on a whole range of factors including:

- the degree of fluency in English that members of a particular class have achieved;
- the bilingual competence of teachers;
- the specific teaching goals of teachers; and
- the attitudes of both children and teachers to the other languages involved.

Language policy and practice

Chapter 2 has more information about bilingual language learning.

The behaviour of teachers and pupils regarding the use of English and other languages in class is likely to reflect official educational policy on language use in school. Educational policy on the use of other languages in English-medium classrooms varies from country to country, and always has done. Policy and practice in schools are often influenced by ideas about the supposed cognitive and social effects on children of growing up bilingual.

Policies are also liable to change. The enforcement of a strict policy of prohibiting the use of a mother tongue in school was well documented in nineteenth-century Wales, where any children heard speaking Welsh on the school premises were reprimanded and made to wear round their necks a rope called the 'Welsh knot' to show they were in disgrace. By the late 1980s, however, both Welsh and English had become officially recognized as classroom languages in Wales. Some countries, such as Canada and various states in India, have longstanding policies of recognizing English alongside other languages in schools. On the other hand, at the point of writing (the middle 1990s), established policies of tolerance towards the use of Spanish and other languages in many state schools in the USA seem in danger of being overturned in response to a strong 'English first' campaign to establish English constitutionally as the only officially recognized language in the nation's schools, workplaces and public life. This brings us to a related issue: the choice of English as a classroom language.

4.4   THE 'CHOICE' OF ENGLISH AS A CLASSROOM LANGUAGE

So far, I have been dealing with the use of English in the classroom as if at the level of educational policy the choice of English, rather than another language, is obvious or inevitable. But of course English is only the obvious choice in situations where it is the sole official language of a country or state, or where it is spoken by the vast majority of people. Yet English has been chosen as the medium for classroom education in many countries where those conditions do not apply. One example is India where, as described in Reading A, many pupils receive their education in English even though it is not their first language. In officially bilingual countries such as Canada, choices have to be made at the level of state

Teaching science in an English-medium school in India

and city about whether French or English should be used as the main language in class. In such countries, educational policy may be framed to allow parents some degree of choice of classroom language for their children. Thus in Wales, the balance of Welsh- and English-medium schools is officially monitored and is supposed to be adjusted to suit demand.

Sometimes there is no real 'choice' about whether or not to use English or another language as a medium for education, because English is already the dominant language in a community. If a policy choice does have to be made about whether English or a community language should be used as the classroom medium in a country's schools, the decision may be a matter of political controversy. As Mazrui and Mazrui (1992) put it when discussing the use of English in African schools and other state institutions:

> Africa is ... a great battleground between Western languages and non-Western languages. English, French and Portuguese have had particularly wide-ranging influences ...
> Africa's ethnic heterogeneity finds its diverse differentiation in language. *Per capita* there is a wider range of languages in Africa than in any other region of the world. By a strange twist of destiny, there are also more French-speaking, English-speaking and Portuguese-speaking countries in Africa than anywhere else in the world.
> (Mazrui and Mazrui, 1992, p. 84)

Some of the reasons for controversy associated with policy decisions about the choice of which language to use as a medium of instruction are described by Josef Schmied (1991) in the book *English in Africa*, an extract from which is included as Reading B.

❖   ❖   ❖   ❖   ❖

Activity 4.5   *(Reading B)*

Read 'Arguments for and against English as a medium of instruction' by Josef Schmied (Reading B). As you read it, try to make your own evaluation of the strength of each of the arguments Schmied presents.

❖   ❖   ❖   ❖   ❖

Standard English as a classroom language

In all English-speaking countries, it is normally expected that in their writing students should try to conform to the conventions of English vocabulary, spelling and grammar for that country. It is also a fairly common expectation that students should use standard vocabulary and grammar in their spoken English in the formal business of the classroom – that is, when replying to teachers' questions, or making oral reports or formal presentations to an audience. In public examinations, marks may be lost if students express themselves in regional 'nonstandard' varieties. So here we come to the third of the tasks listed at the end of section 4.2: 'Pupils may have to learn to use Standard English if they have grown up speaking a "nonstandard" variety of English.' As the great majority even of native speakers of English use regional varieties of English – which are by definition nonstandard – in their out-of-school lives, this kind of learning is faced by the majority of pupils entering English-medium classrooms.

An insistence on the use of the official, standard variety of English in the schools of an English-speaking country may seem unsurprising, easy to justify and, at first consideration, uncontroversial. But this may become a heated and complex political issue, as has certainly been the case for many years in Britain. The more vociferous advocates of a policy which insists on the use of Standard English as a classroom language in Britain have sometimes argued that the issue is not simply one of a choice between which variety or dialect of English is most appropriately used in the classroom, but one of maintaining standards of *correctness* of English in school. People on the other side of this debate may adopt a variety of positions, but most share a concern about the effects that an official denigration and devaluation of the regional Englishes of local communities may have on the self-esteem of pupils who are members of those communities. Related to policy and practice about the use of Standard English as a classroom language is the issue of whether or not pupils should be expressly taught about Standard English and other varieties as part of the school curriculum.

See Chapter 6 for further discussion of the place of Standard English in the school curriculum.

4.5   TALKING AND WRITING IN ENGLISH: GENRES AND DISCOURSES

So far, I have concentrated on the use of spoken English as a medium for classroom education, and given little attention to writing. Just as one of the tasks facing all pupils being educated in English is that of learning certain educational 'ground rules' or conventions for using spoken English in the classroom, educational success also depends on pupils learning to use the conventions which are used by educated writers. However, research has shown that these 'ground rules' are rarely taught explicitly by teachers. Instead, students are expected to infer them from what the teacher says and does, and from whatever feedback the teacher provides on the students' work (Sheeran and Barnes, 1991). This kind of realization stimulated a group of Australian language researchers (Martin et al., 1987) to devise a new approach to the study and teaching of writing in the classroom, based on the work of the linguist Michael Halliday and now generally known as the **genre approach**. One of the aims of this approach has been to focus the attention of teachers and students on how written texts in English are expected to vary according to their nature and function. The founders of the genre approach argue that earlier influential approaches to teaching writing tended to leave the 'ground rules' of writing implicit, and so unclear to students.

❖   ❖   ❖   ❖   ❖

Activity 4.6   *(Reading C)*

Read 'Teaching writing: process or genre?' by Janet Maybin (Reading C). After you have done so consider the following questions:

1   What are the main distinctions between the 'genre' and 'process' approaches to teaching writing in terms of:
    •   their underlying models of language; and
    •   their implications for how 'educated' ways of writing should be taught?

2   What might be some of the possible dangers of applying the 'genre approach' too prescriptively?

❖   ❖   ❖   ❖   ❖

Genres across cultures

Academic English in higher education is discussed in more detail in Chapter 8.

Chapter 6 discusses some implications of genre analysis for the English curriculum.

The strength of the genre approach is that it offers teachers and students an analysis of how English or any other language is used in specific social contexts, and attempts to make explicit the 'ground rules' for producing socially appropriate ways of writing. The essence of most criticisms of the genre approach is that:

- it tends to encourage the teaching of narrowly defined models for specific kinds of texts, when 'educated' writing involves the development of a much more flexible and creative ability;

- it tends to support an uncritical view of how established, powerful groups in a society use English (or any other language); and

- learning 'powerful' ways of using a language does not necessarily gain the user access to power.

When we look at the use of English across countries and cultures, it also becomes apparent that genres may vary between countries or cultures. That is, the conventional expectations among teachers about what a 'story' or a 'scientific report' is differ in, say, India, Australia and the UK. I suggested earlier that when children enter an English-medium classroom, having grown up speaking another language and having had their education in a country with very different cultural traditions, it may be difficult for both teachers and children to distinguish between the first two 'learning tasks' listed in section 4.2 – acquiring a basic fluency in English and learning the conventions of particular genres of English which are used in school. This variation can become a problem for pupils who move from one country to another, and it can be difficult for a teacher to tell whether a new pupil (especially one who is not fluent in English) who appears to be having difficulties with the language demands of education is struggling with general aspects of using English, or is having difficulties with grasping the 'local' ground rules for using language in the classroom.

This kind of difficulty arises in relation to written as well as spoken English, and is well illustrated by the research of Alex Moore (1995), who has studied the progress of children of non-English-speaking immigrant families entering secondary schools in Britain. Moore observed teaching and learning over several months in several classes in two schools. One of his special 'case studies' concerns the progress of Mashud, a boy of fifteen who had been in Britain for a year since leaving his native Bangladesh (where he had been educated in Bengali). Moore focuses on Mashud's classroom education in writing English. Mashud had quite a few problems with 'surface features' of English such as handwriting, spelling and grammatical structures, but was an enthusiastic writer. However, both Moore and Mashud's teacher (Ms Montgomery) noticed that:

> his work had a particular idiosyncrasy in that whenever he was set creative writing – or even discursive writing – assignments, he produced heavily formulaic fairy-story-style moral tales which were apparently – according to information volunteered by other Sylheti pupils in the class – translations of stories he had learned in his native tongue.

(Moore, 1995, p. 362)

Despite being a willing pupil, Mashud seemed unable to transcend this traditional style of genre and write in the genres that his teachers knew would be required of him in the British education system and in wider society. Further consideration led Moore and Ms Montgomery to some hypotheses about why this was so:

> It has to be said that neither Ms Montgomery nor I knew enough about Bangladeshi or Sylheti story-telling traditions to be able to expound with any degree of confidence on the cause of Mashud's particular way of going about things. The key to our future pedagogy, however, ... lay in Ms Montgomery's very wise recognition that '*there could be* the most enormous gap between what Mashud has been brought up to value in narratives and what we're telling him he should be valuing'.
>
> (Moore, 1995, pp. 365–6)

This insight into Mashud's difficulties with genres of writing was supported by a more careful analysis of his texts, which had a linear, additive, chronological structure associated with oral, rather than literate, cultural traditions (Ong, 1982). This led to Moore and the teacher designing activities for Mashud:

> If we responded appropriately, Mashud would, we hoped, learn something of what was valued in expressive writing in his new school, and how that was different from – though no better than – what he may have learned to value at school in Bangladesh.
>
> (Moore, 1995, p. 368)

This approach apparently proved successful, as during the remaining period of Moore's research Mashud showed clear progress in coming to understand and cope with the demands of writing in the genres of English required in the British school system.

4.6   CONCLUSION

Classrooms generate some typical patterns of language use, patterns which reflect the nature of teaching and learning as a social, communicative process which takes place in the distinctive institutional settings of school. I have described some common features of classroom language, such as the IRF exchanges which take place between teachers and pupils. These common features reflect, at least to some extent, the common functions of schools the world over. I have argued, however, that we must be careful not to assume that particular language structures can be used for only one communicative, or educational, purpose.

According to their out-of-school experience, pupils may find the genres or discourses of a classroom more or less intelligible and/or acceptable. But I have argued that every pupil who is being educated in English is expected to learn to use English in special ways, which means following the 'ground rules' of spoken language use in the classroom, taking up the specialized vocabularies of curriculum subjects and becoming able to present ideas within the constraints of the accepted genres or discourses of spoken and written language.

Where teachers and pupils are using English as a second or other language, other distinctive patterns of language use in the classroom also emerge. Teachers and pupils may 'codeswitch' between languages in class, and the content of the talk may reveal teachers' concern with the learning of English as well as the learning of the curriculum subject being taught through English. When considering bilingual and multilingual settings, in general I have also suggested that it is often hard to separate the language demands that classroom education makes on pupils from its cultural demands.

All the indications are that the worldwide use of English as a classroom language is likely to increase during the twenty-first century. Given the key role that language plays in the process of classroom education, it is likely that policy decisions regarding the choice of English or another language as the medium of education will continue to be controversial.

Reading A

ONE CUP OF NEWSPAPER AND ONE CUP OF TEA

G.D. Jayalakshmi

In 1987, I spent two months observing the way English is taught to 16-year-old students in Central School, Bhojpur, in the state of Bihar in India. Although education in India is mainly a state responsibility (India is a union of 24 states), the central government in Delhi runs a number of schools throughout the country called Kendriya Vidyalaya or Central Schools. These schools are primarily meant for the children of employees who work in transferable central government jobs, and so the curriculum in all Central Schools is the same. Because central government employees come from different parts of the country, the children in these schools, and indeed in any one class, speak different languages at home, and almost none of them has English as a mother tongue. However, English was the medium of instruction for the pupils I was observing and most of them had studied it for ten years.

Of the two teachers I observed, I shall concentrate on one here: Dr Keval, the regular English teacher for the Standard XI class. My method of inquiry was ethnographic. I tape recorded all the English lessons of this class while I was at the school and transcribed them later. I also interviewed the teachers and the students periodically. The students wrote diaries where they recorded their impressions of the lessons. In my analysis (described in more detail in Jayalakshmi, 1993) I brought to bear not only my own classroom observation notes, but also my knowledge of Indian culture as one who was born and brought up, went to school and later taught in the country.

The most striking aspect of these lessons was the fundamental similarity, despite superficial differences, in the teaching styles of Dr Keval and his colleague, Mr Sridhar. It could be described as a hybrid of traditional Indian teaching styles and a nineteenth-century Victorian British style transported to India with the introduction of English as a medium of instruction (Jayalakshmi, 1993, Chapter 8).

The classroom arrangement

The teacher stood in front of the classroom with the students sitting in rows on either side. The girls, who were fewer in number, sat on the teacher's right and the boys were on the left as well as behind the girls. A central aisle separated the two sides. In arranging the classroom like this, Dr Keval and Mr Sridhar were doing no more than following the usual custom. In India today, as in Britain a generation or so ago, this is the normal arrangement of classrooms. It serves to give the teacher a dominant role and it sets up what Adams and Biddle (1970) call a 'central communication system', where there is basically a single speaker (the teacher most of the time) and everybody else listens.

To an Indian, the roots of such an arrangement lie at least as strongly in two Indian traditions – Harikatha and Gurukula – as they do in western systems of education. In a Harikatha (literally, 'the tale of the gods'), the storyteller either stands or sits in front of an audience which is seated on either side, with a central aisle separating the men from the women, much as in the school. This arrangement is eminently suitable for the transmission of legends and stories – the storyteller's central position ensures that the audience can see clearly and its attention is unwaveringly held by the performance of the storytelling.

Such an arrangement, and indeed an attitude of reverence towards the storyteller or teacher because they are seen as knowledgeable, can also be traced back to the Indian system of teaching known as Gurukula. Drawings and etchings which have survived from as early as 5000 BC show the 'guru' or teacher sitting on a raised platform under a tree with his students sitting in rows in front of him, acknowledging his authority and learning under his tutelage. The Gurukula system, too, depended on an oral transmission mode where the teacher explicated texts to his students and these were then learned by rote. Although the students in Bhojpur did not have to memorize their lessons, the education system seems to be similar – it implicitly recognizes the teacher's superior knowledge and points to his importance, centrality and authority. He is seen as a repository of knowledge and his task is to transmit this to his less knowledgeable students.

The structure of the lessons

The lessons I observed in Bhojpur all took the form of the reading and explication of chapters from a textbook, and followed the same pattern whether the subject matter was a poem, a short story or an informative piece of non-fiction. The data in the analysis that follows come from lessons conducted by Dr Keval on a chapter about Paul Julius Reuter, the founder of Reuters News Agency.

The lessons consisted of the teacher introducing an idea, reading a paragraph, explaining it and then moving on to the next paragraph until the whole text had been covered. Sometimes the teacher asked questions at the end of his explanations before he went on to read the next paragraph. This seems to have been in order to check students' understanding of his teaching. For the same reason, there was almost always a question–answer session when the entire chapter had been completed, before the teacher moved on to the next chapter.

The storyteller in the Harikatha tradition appears to follow an almost exactly similar pattern, lacking only those genuine questions that require an answer from the listeners. During Harikathas, the storyteller recites a passage from a holy text, explicates it, and then moves on to the next passage until the entire tale is told. The teacher's talk in the classroom was similar to this ritualized form of storytelling, not only in having a similar pattern but also because this pattern was rigid and highly predictable. As in any ritual, it exists irrespective of the individual presiding priest: all players in the ritual know what is expected of them and perform accordingly. So, on occasions when Mr Sridhar took over from Dr Keval, there was no ambiguity in the situation. The students and Mr Sridhar knew exactly how to behave and the class was undisturbed by a change of teacher. In western schools, by contrast, when one teacher takes over from another, for however short a time, the class has to make many more adjustments to the different ways of working introduced by the new teacher.

How do people know whether the Harikatha storyteller is good or not? Similarly, how do students rate the performance of the teacher? It seems to me that the criteria for both these 'performances' are similar. In Harikathas, after the basic text is recited, the storyteller draws upon his own experiences to embellish his tale, often departing completely from the text in order to recount other tales more immediately relevant to modern times. Finally, the storyteller returns to the text to recite the next few lines. A good storyteller is one who shows off his knowledge and wisdom as he explicates the text. It is the ability to move from the specific to the general and return to the specific that is much admired.

Similarly, in Bhojpur my interviews with students suggest that a teacher is judged according to his performance when he explains a paragraph. If he can use the paragraph as a springboard to elaborate his thoughts (even if there is only a tenuous link with what he has just read), then he is considered to be a good teacher. Within this framework, the task of the teacher is to bring his own personal understanding and wisdom to his explanations. This is what gives the class an individuality and flavour and makes one teacher's class better than another's. In this context the students found Dr Keval lively, entertaining and hence a better teacher than Mr Sridhar, whom they considered boring and pedestrian.

Teaching style

The following extract shows one complete flight of fancy by Dr Keval, from the point of take-off from the chapter to the point of landing again. Here he is elaborating on the statement that Reuter found book-selling a boring profession and sought excitement by turning to the idea of developing a news service.

Dr Keval: A book-seller is here and, a circus lady is there. A girl or a
                   boy working in circus. Who is having excitement in his
                   profession?

Dr Keval and
students: A circus girl.

Dr Keval   Or a circus boy. Once I was watching, just a, circus. And I   A question mark in
[*continues*]:   simultaneously started making a poem. Because I was   parenthesis indicates that
                  seeing (?) an exciting profession. In book-selling there is   the previous words are
                  no excitement, OK? Just reading and taking books.   spoken with a rising
                  There is no excitement. There is no excitement in taking   intonation and are
                  a food which is without salt. But there is excitement in   followed by a slight pause.
                  taking what (?) chicken. Well spiced, nicely spiced.
                  Understand? So, people should have excitement in their
                  profession. There are people who wish, who desire, who
                  crave for excitement in their profession. And this very
                  excitement is what (?) a life force, force of life, that, and
                  that is an energy, a wonderful energy that scientists may
                  well research about. So, Reuter didn't find excitement in
                  book-selling. [*Reads*] And he sold off his book-selling ...

(Lesson 1, 6 July 1987)

Like the Harikatha storyteller, Dr Keval takes examples of everyday life – watching a circus, eating chicken – to convey a sense of what excitement might mean. His use of near-synonyms (such as 'There are people who wish, who desire, who crave for excitement ...') also serves to build his image as a knowledgeable person. The ability to use several slightly different terms to convey the same sense has always been considered a mark of wisdom in India.

Another important respect in which Dr Keval impresses his erudition upon his students is in his use of Sanskrit proverbs, which few, if any, of the students will understand. Sanskrit is a classical language and is no longer spoken; nevertheless, it is used to express 'great truths'. This is because it is the language of religion

(Hinduism) and the language in which wisdom has been passed down through the ages. Dr Keval uses Sanskrit in his lessons for two reasons – first, to impress pupils with his wisdom; and secondly, because he believes that his function is to instruct students not just in language but also, more generally, in life. For example, when he explains the way in which John Griffiths helped Reuter secure his first client, he explains that Griffiths is clever because of the company he keeps.

Dr Keval: सत्सो गुणा दोषा:।

[Good company produces bad qualities]

(sic)

You might have come across this very saying in Sanskrit.

सत्सो गुणा दोषा :।

[Good company produces bad qualities]

(sic)

There I mean, we cultivate qualities by virtue of what (?) company. If we are in good company, we'll cultivate good things, good habits. If we are in bad company we'll be cultivating bad habits. So this will be our attempt to be in good company. Always have control over yourself. Try your best always for keeping good company.

(Lesson 1, 6 July 1987)

This is a particularly illuminating example, because Dr Keval's quote in Sanskrit is actually wrong. He undoubtedly meant to say

सत्सो गुणा निर्दोषा:।

(Good company never produces bad qualities).

Dr Keval may in reality not understand Sanskrit much more than the students do. He may well have learned the adage by rote, and now recalls it imperfectly. Nevertheless, he uses the misquotation to advantage, as the students appear impressed by his erudition.

In a subsequent interview, Dr Keval explained to me that he explicitly sees his job in the English classroom not just as teaching the language, but also as inculcating moral and ethical values in his students. In this, he seems to be heir to two of the traditions mentioned earlier. First, there is the Harikatha tradition, with declamation in an ethical vein, exhorting listeners to be morally and spiritually upright, much like Dr Keval's lectures. Secondly, and working concurrently with the first tradition, is the British tradition of teaching English. Dr Keval would have had no difficulty in transferring these Harikatha ideas and values to the English lessons because the inculcation of morality has been a central part of English teaching in India since it first began in the nineteenth century. Even as early as 1815, Lord Moira (the then governor-general of India) thought that the best method of educational improvement among the Indian masses was 'to furnish the village schoolmasters with little manuals of religious sentiments and ethic maxims conveyed in such a shape as may be attractive to the scholars' (quoted in Edwardes, 1967, p. 135). One of the major arguments that Lord Macaulay employed 20 years later to convince the British that an Indian administrative class needed to be educated in English followed a similar vein. He proclaimed the advantages of teaching English to the natives, asserting that English was pre-eminent even among western languages:

> It abounds with works of imagination not inferior to the noblest which Greece has bequeathed to us; with models of every species of eloquence; with historical compositions, which, considered merely as narratives, have seldom been surpassed, and which, considered as vehicles of ethical and political instruction, have never been equalled; with just and lively representations of human life and human nature; with the most profound speculations on metaphysics, morals, government, jurisprudence, and trade; with full and correct information respecting every experimental science which tends to preserve the health, to increase the comfort, or to expand the intellect of man. Whoever knows that language, has ready access to all the vast intellectual wealth, which all the wisest nations of the earth have created and hoarded in the course of ninety generations.
>
> (Quoted in Edwardes, 1967)

The teaching of English, thus, was meant not only to create a class of administrators to deal with the demands of empire but, as Tharu and I have argued elsewhere, to be part of a general, humanizing, civilizing influence, spoken of as having the force of secular Christianity (Jayalakshmi and Tharu, 1990). It is therefore not surprising that the teaching of English carries some of that burden even today.

Given the almost absolute authority of the teacher in the class, he cannot be seen to be either wrong or ignorant. How do the teachers in Bhojpur actually convey the sense of authority to their students, and maintain their control over the class? And how do they organize the pacing of their lessons and the dissemination of knowledge? One technique that I observed both teachers using was the use of rhetorical questions. Often they set up questions and in answering them, provided explanations:

> Dr Keval: As a cup of tea is essential, more than that is (?) a newspaper. Why? That is hot enough. Your father is very much curious, very serious, very serious for reading the newspaper. What for? Have you asked your father? Your father will tell you the importance of news service. This news service is very important for persons who are interested in political events. The news service is very important for business people who are interested in business news.
>
> (Lesson 1, 6 July 1987)

In the above example, in the first sentence, Dr Keval uses a rising intonation with a short pause as a rhetorical device to provide information. He also uses straightforward rhetorical questions, such as, 'Why?', 'What for?', 'Have you asked your father?', to explain that newspapers carry the latest news from several different fields and would be of interest to a very diverse audience.

A problem with such rhetorical questions is that the same format is used to check students' understanding, or at least attention, as in the following example a little later:

Dr Keval: Your father, and after a few years, you yourself, would like
                two cups hot. One cup of newspaper and one cup of (?)

Dr Keval
and students
together: Tea.

(Lesson 2, 6 July 1987)

The question then is: how do students know when to answer a question and when to keep quiet, allowing the teacher to provide an explanation? On looking at the transcript as a whole, one's first impression is that students do not answer or interrupt the teacher when he is in the middle of an explanation, but as his explanations draw to a close the students respond to the teacher's questions, indicating to him that they have understood what he has to say. How do students in the classroom know that the teacher is in the midst of an explanation rather than coming to the end of it? I would suggest that they do not so much *know* that the explanation is complete or incomplete as help to *make* it complete or incomplete. What seems to happen is that, by keeping quiet, they force the teacher to go on and continue explaining till they feel satisfied. They show their understanding and satisfaction finally by responding positively to the question that the teacher puts to them or by completing a sentence along with him. The status of an explanation as complete or incomplete, then, is not something that exists independently of the students' perceptions of it; it is created by negotiation and shared understanding between the teacher and the pupils about what sort of explanation is satisfactory and what is not. Of course, if the teacher feels that he is in the midst of an explanation, he has the option of simply ignoring students' responses to his rhetorical questions. Thus, although the use of questions and how they are answered is negotiated between the teacher and students, more power lies with the teacher. The students do have some power, however, in that if they do not reply to the questions the teacher puts to them, he is forced to continue explaining till they have understood what he has to say.

Student participation

By answering the teacher's questions simultaneously with him, students demonstrate that they have entered the same frame of reference as the teacher. In so doing, they provide him with verbal clues that indicate they have been paying attention and have understood his explanations. Their choral responses are again not unlike the responses of the Harikatha listeners. In Harikathas too, the audience participates either by repeating the last words of the storyteller before the storyteller moves on to the next section, or more formally, by chanting God's name (Hare Rama or Hare Krishna) at the end of an explanation. Along with the Harikatha tradition is the tradition of choral chants used in catechism, in Sunday schools and in primary schools all over India. This chanting itself has its roots in the introduction of western education, where typically children were made to chant 'Our Father which art in Heaven' and 'God Save the King' in school assembly every morning. In their own classrooms, young children are still taught to chant the English alphabet – A for apple, B for bat and so on. It seems to me that the choral response in Bhojpur is a vestige of this strong acculturation which takes place when students are very young.

Within such a formal context, the students do not seem to have freedom to initiate talk that may lead to interesting discussions. Almost all the student-initiated talk consisted of requests for the meaning of words and generally followed the pattern 'Sir, what is the meaning of …', asked either in English or in Hindi. Maybe the students know this is the only sort of question that will elicit a response from the teacher. Besides, such questions sit comfortably in a trans-mission mode of teaching where the purpose is to impart information.

Thus it appears that given the highly structured and controlled nature of classroom discourse, there is almost no opportunity for students to speak. The only way they can talk is by whispering asides to each other. This, however, is not part of the official discourse and is much frowned upon. It may be that both the students and teachers in Bhojpur realize that there is not much sense in the classroom practices as they stand, but compulsively abide by institutional norms for their own sake, thereby turning classroom procedures into a ritual.

References

ADAMS, R. and BIDDLE, B. (1970) *Realities of Teaching: explorations with videotape*, New York, Holt, Rinehart & Winston.

EDWARDES, M. (1967) *British India 1772–1947*, London, Sidgwick & Jackson.

JAYALAKSHMI, G.D. (1993) 'Video in the English curriculum of an Indian second-ary school', unpublished PhD thesis, Milton Keynes, The Open University.

JAYALAKSHMI, G.D. and THARU, S. (1990) *Empire and Nation* television programme, for the course *Literature in the Modern World*, Milton Keynes, the Open University Production Centre.

This reading was specially commissioned for this book.

Reading B

ARGUMENTS FOR AND AGAINST ENGLISH AS A MEDIUM OF INSTRUCTION

Josef Schmied

Although the position of English in education may vary considerably in different African states there have been attempts to strengthen or to weaken it in most of them. As the arguments used by supporters and critics are relatively similar in most nations, they can be summarized in the following general discussion. First, four arguments (E1–E4) in favour of English will be presented and then four arguments (A1–A4) in favour of African languages … Each argument will not only be presented but also scrutinized and challenged by counter-arguments.

E1: The 'high cost' argument

As the young nations of the Third World have been under heavy strain with respect to manpower and financial resources since independence, all major changes in the educational system (as the change to another medium of instruction would be), have tended to be avoided. Any such change implies not only changing the curriculum, but also teacher training programmes and the production (writing and printing) of textbooks and teaching aids – all at enormous additional cost to an expanding education system. This has led to the continued use of old (often still British) textbooks, teaching methods and curricula. Opponents of the status quo counter the high cost argument by saying that changes will have to come anyway or are – with the help of national school book foundations, etc. – already under way. Since books, methods and curricula must in any case be modified and adapted to the changing African environment, would it not be possible to change the language together with the content?

E2: The 'anti-tribal' argument

Since the process of nation-building is crucial for African nation-states, as many aspects of public life as possible should contribute towards this aim. The selection of an African language would threaten the unity of the nation-state, because only in rare cases (e.g. in Somalia) do all citizens share a common mother tongue. Thus supporters of this argument maintain that English is the only ethnically neutral language. Nevertheless, even if this argument is strong, its critics argue, this does not exclude the use of African lingue franche (such as Swahili), especially if they are spoken by more Africans as a second language than as a mother tongue.

E3: The technological argument

As modern terminology in African languages is still being developed, especially in the scientific and technical fields, it is held to be impossible to use these languages now and even doubtful whether conscious vocabulary expansion and propagation would improve their chances in the near future, since the efforts and costs involved would be enormous. The critics of this argument, who advocate the modernization of African languages, usually point out how much has already been achieved in certain cases. They claim that the case of Swahili, for instance, proves that African languages can speedily acquire a technical and scientific vocabulary.

E4: The 'international communication' argument

Supporters of this argument say that the world is shrinking because of world-wide communication, and that people need a common language more than ever before. As English has – through whatever historical and political processes – gained a unique status in the modern world, it would be foolish not to take advantage of this. As all attempts during the last hundred years to create an artificial world language have failed, a natural language might be more successful. On the other hand, supporters of African languages ask how many Africans are really involved in international communication and whether the small group that is would not better be catered for in special courses. Besides, they argue convincingly that this is rather an EIL [English as an international language] than an ESL [English as a second language] argument; in other words, it is not an argument for using English as a medium, but rather for teaching English and even for teaching it as thoroughly as possible. Furthermore, it is doubtful whether it really is an advantage for students when badly taught English is used as a medium of instruction.

A1: The psycholinguistic argument

Because psycholinguistic studies have shown that mother-tongue education is better for a child's cognitive development, numerous recommendations have been made for giving African children this chance of fuller development. However, as these studies mostly refer to early educational development, and since other studies seem to show that multilingual education triggers otherwise latent mental capacities, opponents of this argument maintain that there is no reason to believe that English in education is harmful, provided that early education (possibly including literacy) has been carried out in the mother tongue.

A2: The 'élitist' argument

Because English is only spoken by an educated élite in Africa, using English in education provides children from an English-speaking home with an initial advantage, which is unfair to the other pupils, who are disadvantaged anyway. It is, however, a fact that in at least some African countries it was the parents who demanded the early introduction of English-medium education on the grounds that this was the only way to compensate for initial disadvantages by the time the pupils competed for places in further education. Furthermore, as English is still the stepping stone to well-paid employment in many anglophone countries the expansion of English language teaching may be the only way to undermine its élitist character. Again, this is rather an argument for the efficient teaching of English as a subject than for its use as a medium.

A3: The 'linguistic imperialism' argument

Because the European languages were imposed on Africa by the colonial powers, adherents of this argument say that, the colonial powers having been driven out, it is high time for Africans to fight for complete independence and rid themselves of all remnants of colonialism, including the European languages. Opponents argue that the English language today cannot any longer be seen as the property of one or two imperialistic nations, but has, in its various forms, developed into a true world language, or at least a language which is the property of the world as a whole.

A4: The 'cultural alienation' argument

Because English is the language of a European nation and a Western culture it cannot carry the associations and connotations of an African identity. Education in English may therefore deracinate the African child and alienate it from its own cultural background. This argument can be countered by pointing out that modern African life has already incorporated so many features of modern 'Western', international life that English is only one of them. Furthermore, African writers have already proved that it *is* possible to convey African culture, life and even traditions in the English language if this language is appropriately 'adapted' ...

This brief review of some of the main arguments suggests that none of them is adequately backed up by research, and that either side can refute the arguments of the other, most of these being opinions and attitudes, though nonetheless important for that ... There have even been some practical experiments to find out which approach yields better results in terms of subject skills, verbal skills in English or in general or academic performance as a whole, but none of them is absolutely conclusive, either because they could not control certain variables (e.g. parents' use of English) or because they had much more favourable input conditions than usual (e.g. in terms of schoolbooks and dedicated teachers) ...

It goes without saying that there are many more arguments on either side, both sound and unsound, but the four main lines of argumentation presented by each group should now be clear. If there is any realistic solution to the problem of choosing a linguistic medium for African education today at all, it is likely to be a compromise. This would be in accordance with a long African tradition of multilingualism, which language specialists from predominantly monolingual European nation-states tend to forget.

Source: Schmied, 1991, pp. 102–5

Reading C
TEACHING WRITING: PROCESS OR GENRE?

Janet Maybin

Introduction

During the 1970s and 1980s an approach to teaching literacy, usually referred to as **process writing**, became influential in North America. Drawing on the work of Donald Graves and Donald Murray, this approach spread to Australia. Many ideas were taken up by the British National Writing Project and have now been incorporated into the National Curriculum. Process writing shifts the focus from the finished product to the processes which pupils need to go through as writers. It aims to give pupils a greater sense of ownership and enhance pupils' commitment to their work. This approach has been a major influence on policy and classroom practice in many schools. Since the mid-1980s, however, an alternative writing pedagogy has been gathering strength in Australia, and, at least in that country, looks set to replace process writing as the main teaching orthodoxy. The *genre approach* developed from the work of Michael Halliday and draws heavily on his theory of functional linguistics. Halliday argues that we have developed very specific ways of using language in relation to how certain things are accomplished within our culture, and that different contexts and language purposes are associated with different registers, or genres of language. Genres encode knowledge and relationships in particular ways through the use of different language structures. Learning about a particular subject discipline, therefore, involves also learning about specific ways of using language. We expect pupils to write in a number of different specific ways in school, and we assess them according to how well they manage to reproduce these different genres, but we never actually tell them how to do it. Proponents of the genre approach argue that making the genres explicit and showing how to write them will enable pupils to understand more fully how knowledge is constructed in different academic disciplines. It will also empower pupils to deal with the various written genres used in the adult world.

These two approaches suggest different responses to fundamental questions about teaching writing in school:

- What is involved in the process of becoming a writer?

- What are our criteria for good writing, and how are these communicated to pupils?

- When and how should teachers intervene in students' writing?

Process writing

Graves' initial premise, and the first sentence of his 1983 book *Writing: teachers and children at work*, is 'Children want to write'. He suggests that the writing process can be divided into a number of distinct stages, from the initial discussion of ideas through drafting, conferencing, revising and editing to publishing. The teacher plays a vital supportive role in each of these stages, but it is important that the writing topic is chosen by the pupils, and that they retain ownership of the writing throughout. Thereby, Graves suggests, students can find their own authentic writing voice and development of the craft of writing will come naturally, including attention to surface features like spelling and handwriting.

Graves suggests that teachers can support and check on pupils' progress through writing 'conferences'. Below is an example of a conference on 'working with the main idea' (conferences can be about any aspect of writing, from choosing a topic to punctuation, and can be held with groups of pupils as well as individuals). According to Graves, Mr Sitka suggests how Anton might move on in his writing while still leaving him in control of the piece through asking 'questions that teach'.

Mr Sitka:	Where are you now in the draft?
Anton:	Oh, I've just got the part down about when we won in overtime.
Mr Sitka:	So, you've just got started then. Well, it's probably too early to tell what it's about. What did you figure to do next with the draft, then?

Anton:	I don't know. I don't want to just write and wander around. I've written about when we've won but it sort of just has me stuck at that point.
Mr Sitka:	Tell me about that coach of yours.
Anton:	God, how I hated him! I almost quit three or four times maybe. I thought he couldn't stand me. He'd yell, catch every little thing I did wrong. We'd run and run until we couldn't stand up. Have some passing drills, then he'd run us some more. He'd just stand there yellin' and puffin' on his cigar. Course he was right. When we won the championship, I think it went way back to those early practices.
Mr Sitka:	The way you tell it sounds as though you have quite a live beginning to your story. Try just writing about early practices, then see what your piece is about.

In process writing pupils are seen as apprentice authors writing for real audiences. Their writing is published and put into the class library for other pupils to read. Classrooms become workshops and communities of writers, where teachers are also writing and encouraging pupils to develop particular kinds of behaviours for each stage in the writing process rather than focusing on specific skills in isolation. For many teachers associated with the British National Writing Project [NWP] (1985–8), Graves' work seemed to provide a structured way to support pupils' writing in accordance with the English curriculum model of personal creativity and growth through language (see Dixon 1967; Barnes *et al.* 1969).

In addition to assimilating ideas from process writing, the NWP tried to follow through some of the implications from recent research by anthropologists and cultural psychologists. This suggests that reading and writing should be seen as social practices rather than as collections of decontextualised skills, and that classroom methods should take account of the meaning and function of writing practices outside the school (e.g. Heath 1983; Street 1984; Scribner and Cole 1988). NWP teachers tried to build a range of real purposes and audiences into pupils' work, and to develop more explicit links with the outside world; for example pupils might be writing for senior citizens or to a newspaper, or exchanging stories and journals with pupils in other parts of the country.

Content and voice

There are many accounts by teachers of how an emphasis on process, ownership and real purposes can produce outstanding pupil writing and high levels of enthusiasm and commitment. A number of critics, however, have questioned how absolute students' control over the content of their writing should be, whether the notion of students developing a personal writing voice through process writing is sustainable, and whether students should not be receiving more direct help with the structure of their writing.

Pam Gilbert (1988, quoted in Czerniewska, 1992) suggests that sometimes the content of students' writing needs challenging, for example where they are uncritically reproducing sexist or racist stereotypes. She quotes a story written collaboratively in a process writing classroom by some 10-year-old boys in which most children in their class appear as characters who are attacked by marauding Efa Bunnies. In 'Bloodbath Efa Bunnies' the boys are represented as Rambo-like heroes while the girls are either killed or married off, with one exception. This girl, who was the largest in the class, jumps on the bunnies and the boys' text reads

'"AAAA! My God! Super Blubber!" they said as they got up. "Run!"' Gilbert suggests 'No need to kill off this female: her size and aggression have effectively excluded her anyway. (What worse fate for a girl than to be called Super Blubber?)' This story was duly typed, bound and added to the class library without any criticism or questioning. Particularly at a time when teachers are checking school resources for instances of sexism and racism, Gilbert suggests that we should be encouraging students to interrogate the social stereotypes they reproduce in their own writing, perhaps in the case of these boys through encouraging more consideration of the audience for whom the story is intended. (Interestingly, two days after 'Bloodbath Efa Bunnies' was placed in the class library, it mysteriously disappeared …) Janet White also criticises process writing for ignoring the cultural construction of writing practices within which pupils are differently positioned according to, for instance, their sex and ethnic background. 'Giving pupils power over the writing process does not necessarily mean that they are writing more powerful texts … (perhaps) all we have helped pupils to own are versions of cultural clichés' (in National Writing Project 1990).

Reproducing their own experience may also mean that students cover only a limited range of topics over a year, and produce an even narrower range of written genres. Martin *et al.* (1987) quote an aboriginal classroom where children's writing covered only four topics in the year: visiting friends and relatives, going hunting for bush tucker, sporting events and movies or TV shows they have seen. These events were all written about in the 'recount' genre – a simple sequential retelling of events. Rather than giving pupils freedom, Martin *et al.* suggest that this approach is actually restricting children's development, and denying them access to the writing skills which would provide them with power in the real world.

Graves' notion of how students develop a personal writing voice is also questioned by Gilbert. She suggests there are unacknowledged criteria that determine which 'voices' are acceptable to the teacher but that these criteria (which privilege a particular kind of class and literary experience) are never made explicit to pupils. Gilbert argues that, although the criteria become particularly important in relation to the assessment of students' work at secondary level, most students still have just to guess at what they think individual teachers will like.

Gilbert uses two examples of 16-year-olds' writing to explain why framing the purpose and audience for a writing task and providing resources and discussion still does not necessarily give students enough help with the style and structure required for the piece. Susan and Ken's class were asked to write a magazine article on the topic 'Are creative writers always abnormal?' They had a class discussion about what was abnormal and were given information sheets about various authors from which they could draw evidence. Their teacher also read them extracts from published magazine articles. The openings of Susan and Ken's pieces are given in Figures 1 and 2.

The teacher was disappointed that out of all the class only Susan had managed to produce 'that funny blend between personal writing and yet impersonal writing because it's in a newspaper', and she felt at a loss about how to help the other students organise pieces of information into an acceptable journalistic format, and take on the particular linguistic features which identify a journalistic style. Susan creates the effect her teacher was looking for through using first person plural pronouns, rhetorical questions and pairs of juxtaposed sentences, but Ken's assignment reads like a school essay and is based on the notes the teacher gave the class. In her comments on Ken's work, the teacher focuses on the surface features of his writing: 'Ken, you must proof-read *much* more carefully.

Are creative writers always abnormal ?

In many minds exists the notion of a creative writer. It may be the image of a budding poet, a ponderous youth, cramped in a dismal attic weaving webs of delight and love. Or perhaps it's the image of an erotic and demonic soul, volatile in temper, unrestrained, wild and bizarre in manner. Wherever your fantasy lies, the perception of a trouvère is that he is inspirational, sensitive or different, thus abnormal.

Yes, we the majority believe creative writers are abnormal. What is abnormality? Is it an exception to the rule, a contrary spirit, the non-conformist, or is it as the dictionary defines something not usual, a deviation from normal. Thus all masterful writers who have known the fruits of success earn themselves distinction and diverge from the essence of the human race. They become celebrities,

Figure 1   Extract from English assignment by 'good' student (reduced size)
(Gilbert, 1992)

ARE CREATIVE WRITERS ALWAYS ABNORMAL

Most Creative writers have been said to have been abnormal but some are normal. These abnormal writers have different ways of putting their works across to the reader of work. There have been many great writers of the past present who have been abnormal.

The great number of poets have shown their abnormality thru their writing + poetry. Some Example of these abnormal poets of the past were Wilde, Thomas, Coleridge, Byron just to name a few. Wilde was a poet and playwright at the end of the 19 Century. He used to dress irregular + odd which made

Figure 2   Extract from English assignment by less competent student (reduced size)
(Gilbert, 1992)

A magazine article cannot have such basic errors.' While these are undeniably a problem, Gilbert suggests that he also needs to be taught how to reproduce a specific written genre.

The genre approach

'Learning the genres of one's culture is both part of entering into it with understanding, and part of developing the necessary ability to change it ... Capacity to recognise, interpret and write genre is capacity to exercise choice' (Martin *et al.* 1987). Proponents of the genre approach argue that writing is very different from talk, and pupils cannot simply pick up the specialist linguistic structures involved: they need to be taught. Written genres tend to be more condensed and abstract, frequently involving the use of nominal forms, for example 'the *failure* of the crusades', 'the *precipitation* of the solid', 'the *betrayal* of Macbeth'. Our culture also requires that pupils learn to use genres which are differently structured depending on the purposes and audiences for their writing. For example, they need to be able to reproduce procedures, descriptions, reports, explanations, arguments and various kinds of narratives. These all have distinctive overall structures (for instance, a simple narrative structure involves an initial orientation, a complication, a resolution and a coda), and particular kinds of grammatical uses and vocabulary. To teach a specific genre the teacher is advised first to provide exemplars and discuss their particular features with the students. The teacher then jointly negotiates a piece of writing in this genre with the class, and after this the students research and draft a piece of writing in the chosen genre. There is further consultation with the teacher and finally the piece may be published for the class library.

The genre approach focuses strongly on how to construct particular kinds of texts. Unlike process writing, the teacher has a strong directional input at the beginning and explicitly scaffolds students' writing structures. Martin *et al.* (1987) perceive the example quoted above where Mr Sitka is helping Anton as an example of poor and unfocused conferencing which will not help Anton to shape the structure of his narrative, or to avoid 'just writing and wandering about'.

It may even be that a narrative is not the appropriate genre for Anton's piece. The Australian genre teachers argue that the emphasis on narrative rather than expository genres in many primary schools leaves children inadequately prepared for writing in secondary school, and unable to engage with knowledge in the different subject areas. Denying pupils access to the genre means denying them access to the subject. They are left, Martin *et al.* suggest, stranded in their own words, cut off from what history, science and so on are really about. (This is an almost directly opposite argument to the one mounted in Britain in the 1970s by Britton and Rosen, who advocated allowing students to use more personal and expressive language across the curriculum. For them, subject genres could set up artificial and unnecessary barriers which *prevented* students from engaging with subject knowledge.)

A number of criticisms have been made of the genre approach. First, although genre theorists claim to be treating texts as socially constructed out of particular contexts and relationships, proponents often make rather naive claims about empowering pupils through teaching them to reproduce particular genres of texts. As Barrs (1991–2) points out, it's not just knowing how to write that matters in this world, but

> being in a position to ensure that your writing reaches an audience, and then is noticed and read. We could all learn how to write certain powerful genres – such as high level memos – but this wouldn't increase our access to power by one jot.

Second, teaching about genre sometimes offers a rather impoverished model of learning, with little sense of process or development. Knowledge about genres is transmitted from teachers to students, with little opportunity for active student-led learning or collaborative work. Third, there is the question of who determines the genres which are to be taught in school and whether the values and power relationships which are encoded in dominant cultural forms and their associated genres should be accepted as 'given' by teachers and uncritically transmitted to their students.

Conclusion

The process writing and genre approaches derive from different theoretical models: the first treats language as a personal resource, and the second, language as a social construct. In the first, learning to write is seen as a natural process supported by the teacher who creates a motivating working context with real purposes and audiences. In the second, the teacher's responsibility is to equip students with linguistic skills so that they can read and reproduce the genres which will give access to subject knowledge and power in the outside world. Criteria for good writing in the process model emphasise personal creativity and effectiveness in terms of audience and purpose while genre teachers, although also wanting to ensure effectiveness, assess this through how successfully students have managed to reproduce particular genres of writing.

Both approaches claim to 'empower' students, the first through giving them ownership of their writing and the second through equipping them with important linguistic skills. Taking both these approaches together suggests that they could be seen as complementary rather than oppositional. There is a need to build motivation and learning opportunities into the process of writing, but also to ensure that students understand and can work with the linguistic structures needed for specific genres. In addition, we need to look at how writing practices in the classroom relate to those used outside the school, and at whether there is scope for extending the range of activities used with students. Finally, one of the distinctive qualities of writing in relation to oral language is that it enables one to stand back from and reflect on one's own ideas and understanding. This kind of metalinguistic activity is central to intellectual development and work with pupils on writing should include critical reflection, not only about process and structural aspects of their writing but also about its content – the values it expresses and how far it constitutes an engagement with real and important issues of learning and understanding.

References

BARNES, D., BRITTON, J. and ROSEN, H. (1969) *Language, the learner and the school*, London, Penguin.

BARRS, M. (1991–2) 'Genre theory: what's it all about?', *Language Matters*, no. 1.

CZERNIEWSKA, P. (1992) *Learning about writing: the early years*, Oxford, Blackwell.

DIXON, J. (1967) *Growth through English*, Oxford, Oxford University Press.

GILBERT, P. (1992) 'Authorizing disadvantage: authorship and creativity in the language classroom' in CHRISTIE, F. (ed.) *Literacy for a changing world*, Victoria, Australian Council for Educational Research.

GRAVES, D. (1983) *Writing: teachers and children at work*, Portsmouth, New Hampshire, Heinemann Educational Books.

HEATH, S.B. (1983) *Ways with words: language, life and work in communities and classrooms*, Cambridge, Cambridge University Press.

MARTIN, J.R., CHRISTIE, F. and ROTHERY, J. (1987) 'Social processes in education: a reply to Sawyer and Watson (and others)' in REID, I. ·(ed.) *The place of genre in learning: current debates*, Centre for Studies in Literary Education, Deakin University.

NATIONAL WRITING PROJECT (1990) *What are writers made of? Issues of gender and writing*, Walton-on-Thames, Thomas Nelson.

SCRIBNER, S. and COLE, M. (1988) 'Unpackaging literacy' in MERCER, N. (ed.) *Language and literacy from an educational perspective*, vol. 1, Milton Keynes, Open University Press.

STREET, B. (1984) *Literacy in theory and practice*, Cambridge, Cambridge University Press.

Source: Maybin, 1994b

A HISTORY OF ENGLISH TEACHING

A.K. Pugh

5.1   INTRODUCTION

The teaching of English has always been a controversial topic. There have been pedagogical debates about *how* English should be taught but underlying these has been the more fundamental question of *what* should be taught: what do children and young people, in schools and colleges, actually need to learn about the English language? The previous chapter began to examine this question by looking at English as a language of education – a language through which students in many parts of the world gain access to different types of academic knowledge. This chapter marks a change of focus: it looks at the history of English as a school and university subject and at changing definitions of 'English' in different historical periods.

❖   ❖   ❖   ❖   ❖

Activity 5.1   *(Allow about 20 minutes)*

Think about your own school experience of English as a subject. Jot down a list of the sorts of activities you did. Then try to assess the purpose of what you learned and how you have used the knowledge and skills you developed. If you are able to, compare your experiences with those of one or two friends or colleagues. (This activity assumes you studied English at school: if you did not, jot down your experiences of studying another language.)

Comment

You may well have found your own experiences differed from those of other people you consulted. The teaching of English has been characterized by considerable diversity, even in recent years. You can compare your experiences, and perhaps account for the origins of some of them, in reading about different approaches to English in this chapter.

When considering the purpose and relevance of what you learned, you may have noted that some activities seemed of little relevance in life after school. Did these have a place up to a certain stage of learning, or do they appear to be merely school exercises that were retained in the curriculum after their function had become less clear? Did you feel overall that your work in English emphasized creativity, individual development and a liberal education, or rather that it emphasized correctness, conforming, learning rules and adhering to standards? Your thinking about issues of this kind should help you orientate to this chapter.

❖   ❖   ❖   ❖   ❖

Our history begins earlier than most – with the learning of English as a vernacular language in Anglo-Saxon times. In order to allow this historical depth, we focus mainly on developments in the history of Britain, and especially in England. The chapter does, however, make reference to English teaching in some other countries in which English is (or has at some time been) an official language. Throughout this long history, the English curriculum has been affected by different aims and purposes that were perceived for the teaching of English; ensuring basic literacy, providing training for administrators and for merchants, and making generally available a liberal education have all competed as aims. These aims relate to broader purposes that include making a population more governable and a workforce more conformist, ensuring the existence of literate professional and business elites, or, alternatively, making the population less conformist, more critical and less at the behest of administrators, clerics, lawyers and so on.

A major theme that runs throughout the chapter is the influence of current social, political and economic factors on what constitutes 'English' and how it is taught.

5.2   ANGLO-SAXON AND MEDIEVAL APPROACHES

Until about 700 AD there was no English to be taught, in Britain at least. However, King Alfred (849–901 AD) (despite spending much of his time fighting off invasions) developed in his later years an educational system in which Old English had an important role. Redmond Burke (1993) notes that the need for such a 'state' system was related to the havoc wrought by plagues, Viking raids, and the decline in the church's educational provision that resulted from private purchases of abbeys. Britain's insular nature may also have contributed to the use of the vernacular for activities involving reading and writing, activities largely pursued in Latin on Christian mainland Europe.

You can read more about King Alfred, and about the history of English in general, in the first book in this series, *English: history, diversity and change* (Graddol et al. (eds), 1996)

Alfred himself translated, and had translated under his supervision, a number of Latin works into English. In addition he commissioned books in Anglo-Saxon. Schools that he set up were not exclusively for the children of nobles and a reading programme was established for all illiterate earls, bailiffs (king's representatives such as mayors and sheriffs) and thanes (broadly speaking, gentry) who were to lose their official duties and authority if they did not cooperate.

However, despite the considerable literary culture in Old English that Alfred encouraged, literacy in Latin was the goal, and learning to read in English merely a step towards it. An account of Alfred's own learning to read demonstrates this.

No consideration of Alfred's career could be regarded as complete which omitted the incident about his learning to read. A passage in Asser's *Life of King Alfred*, written in Latin, states that Alfred 'remained illiterate until he was twelve years old or more, although he listened attentively to recitations of Saxon poems which his retentive mind enabled him to remember'. That Alfred 'remained illiterate' means no more than that he did not know Latin, then the medium of communication in Western Europe. The Latin verb 'to read' (*legere*) is constantly used as 'to read Latin', not only in Asser's *Life of King Alfred*, but also

Asser was a Welsh priest who assisted Alfred in his work and who wrote his biography.

ALFRED ALLURED TO READ BY HIS MOTHER.

in other works of the Middle Ages. This interpretation seems logical
when one recalls that for several centuries a legal privilege known as
'Benefit of Clergy' used a Latin reading test to determine on the spot
whether an accused criminal was a clerk. There follows, in his biography,
the incident of Alfred's winning a book of Saxon poems by learning
to read them aloud to his mother. On one occasion she held out a
Saxon book to his tutor, who assisted him in understanding the poems.
Later Alfred returned to his mother with the book and read aloud the
poems to her.

(Burke, 1993, p. 15)

This account includes other interesting pieces of information. The method of
learning to read emphasized understanding meaning and the reading of large
units of text. It also shows that Alfred's mother had a role in his learning and it
highlights the use of 'illiterate' to mean not knowing the classical literature. It
does not tell us the age at which Alfred learned to read except that it seems to be
before he was 12 years old.

   We do not know if this method of learning to read was typical of Anglo-Saxon
approaches, but perhaps it was, since according to Asser's *Life of King Alfred* any
earl, bailiff or thane who had difficulty learning to read was to obtain help from a

son or relative 'to read aloud in Saxon books to him, day and night, whenever he had leave' (cited in Burke, 1993, p. 17).

The approach in the Middle Ages (about 1100–1400 AD) was rather different, founded as it was on Roman principles. Michael Clanchy (1984) describes these in a discussion of medieval literacy:

> The estimated extent of medieval reading ability is the more remarkable considering that the basic method of teaching made reading difficult to learn. The traditional starting point was Latin letters, in the sense both of learning to identify and pronounce the individual letters in the Roman alphabet and of learning Latin language and literature. The medieval 'literatus' was ideally a man of letters. The reason for starting with Latin was that before 1200 in Western Europe nearly everything that was written down, particularly the holy scripture, was expressed in Latin. (The British Isles were exceptional in writing in Old English and Celtic languages as well as in Latin.) The reasons for starting instruction with the individual letters of the ABC were embedded in medieval culture. This method was believed to be the old Roman way and it therefore had the sanction of antiquity. Furthermore, pronouncing individual letters gave each one a consistent sound which ensured that the Latin texts of the scripture were read or chanted in church correctly. Finally, the scholastic method of the medieval universities was based on the premise that everything should be broken down into its constituent parts in order to understand it: learning to read individual letters must therefore precede learning words.

'Man of letters': this emphasizes that it was mainly men who were literate in this sense, though Clanchy elsewhere in this article gives examples of mothers teaching their children to read.

> Special books for teaching children to read did not exist. As the Latin scripture was the essence of knowledge and the ABC was the starting point of learning, all that was required was an alphabet set out at the beginning of a prayer-book …
>
> The medieval 'primer' was not in origin a reading book for children. It was rather the primary or basic prayer-book. In its essential form it contained a selection of the 'Hours' or form of worship used throughout the day in the Latin liturgy, preceded by the 'Our Father', the 'Hail Mary', the Apostles' Creed and the Ten Commandments. From the latter half of the fourteenth century onwards these texts might be translated into English (or another vernacular) or expressed in a combination of Latin and English. Children started with a primer because it contained the elements of Christian belief and worship, which all parents were enjoined to instruct their children in, and not because reading was a desirable end in itself. The primary object of the exercise was not to acquire a wide competence in reading, as most medieval people would not have come across more than one or two books in a lifetime, but to express the elements of Christian teaching.

The term 'primer' is now used, especially in North America, to mean an initial reading book, often part of a reading scheme.

(Clanchy, 1984, pp. 33–4)

Latin as a language of initial learning was, however, already under threat. As the language of academic learning, of the Church and of administration it was firmly established, but for law Norman French and English were also necessary in the medieval period. Clanchy has elsewhere, in his important book *From Memory to Written Record* (Clanchy [1979] 1993), also shown how after the Norman conquest (1066) written records took over from the more oral culture of the Anglo-Saxons, so that literacy became more pervasive and necessary.

John de Trevisa translated
the *Polychronicon* from Latin
into English with an added
commentary. The
Polychronicon is often cited
as a source of
contemporary evidence of
the position of English in
education. See also
Chapter 3 of the first book
in this series, *English:
history, diversity and change,*
(Graddol et al. (eds), 1996)

There is a well known passage from John of Trevisa, writing in about 1380, about the replacement of Norman French by English as the language of learning in grammar schools. The Normans in England, as in Wales and Ireland, tended to integrate with those they had conquered and to lose their French (Curtis, 1950) . Other factors that favoured literacy in the vernacular languages of Europe as a whole include the invention of printing, the rise of Protestantism and the growth in trade.

In relation to this last factor, Michael Hyde (1993) has made a careful study of the correspondence of an Italian merchant family and indicates the considerable role for literacy in the business of a fourteenth- and fifteenth-century Florentine merchant. He refers to the specialist literacy employed, in particular to the unadorned plain style and the priority accorded to news (of financial matters), but says that different types of literacy should not be seen as exclusive – the merchants read widely in Latin and in the vernacular. In fact literacy encouraged by trade provided a market for secular writings in the vernacular language and the very rapid early growth of printing both required and nurtured this growth in literacy.

Nevertheless, trade gave rise to a functional tradition in education that has been described by Hébrard and Chartier (1990). They trace, for France and many European countries, two diverging traditions in education at the school level. One tradition has its origins in the Roman notion of a liberal education and was the education for lawyers, clerics, administrators and most professions. Originally, it was exclusively organized by the Church, for a long time used Latin as the language of learning, and was available to only a small proportion of the population. There is, however, another strong tradition that has its origins in the mercantile culture of Italy of the fourteeenth and fifteenth centuries. Here textbooks were in the vernacular language, emphasis was on more practical uses of mathematics and language (for example) and entry was less restricted. This tradition, though often seen as the academically poor relation, had (and still has) a large influence on education in many countries.

The Reformation was a
sixteenth century religious
movement in many parts of
northern Europe that tried
to reform the Catholic
church and eventually gave
rise to the Protestant
churches. It is important
for the history of English
because of its use and
promotion of vernacular
languages. See the first
book in this series, *English:
history diversity and change*
(Graddol et al. (eds),
1996).

During the Reformation, Britain cut itself off from many other European countries by its political break with the Roman Catholic church. There was not a clean break in religious doctrine and culture, however, and Latin remained of importance although there were many compromises. For example, although the Bible was translated, there was no encouragement for everyone to read it (as there was in other Protestant countries). Indeed, much of the population (including women, apprentices, most serving men, husbandmen and labourers) was forbidden by an Act of 1543 to read it. Private study of the Bible, unmediated by a priest, was associated with religious and political ideas that were regarded as dangerous to the government of the time.

In this section I have mentioned two rather different approaches to teaching reading in English: a holistic 'reading for meaning' approach that seems to have characterized King Alfred's early learning; and the medieval approach that broke written English into its constituent parts (letters, then words, then sentences). You can see later in this chapter and the next that there have been tensions between such approaches to teaching reading right up to the present day.

I have also mentioned the changing relationship between Latin and vernacular languages such as English, that would lead, eventually, to the establishment of English as a language of education, both as a medium of instruction and as a school subject.

5.3   SIXTEENTH TO EIGHTEENTH CENTURIES

The sixteenth century and the Reformation also saw a growth in 'grammar schools' established initially for the teaching of Latin grammar, and in colleges at Oxford and Cambridge universities. These were charitable foundations, often endowed by those who had profited from the privatization of church lands and the expanding overseas trade of the period. They were boys' schools; scholarships were provided for poorer students, but, in practice, they were attended mainly by the sons of wealthier townspeople and farmers. While English was used as a language of instruction in the grammar schools, Latin remained predominant in the universities.

The growth in grammar schools in itself created a demand for literacy in English, as pupils needed to be able to read and, usually, write in order to enter. This initial literacy was provided by schools of various kinds, many of them private or charity schools in England. In Scotland, a different strand in Protestantism led to more popular education, including, by the late seventeenth century the establishment of a school in every parish, organized by the Church of Scotland in a national system. Any of these parish schools could teach up to the level of entrance to a university, of which there were five in Scotland as opposed to only two in England until the nineteenth century.

Nevertheless, by 1600 the teaching of English as a subject appears to be fairly well established in England. Ian Michael (1987) finds the term 'English teacher' first used in 1587 and he lists a number of publications from 1591 in which 'English school master' appeared in the title. Cressy (1980) also comments on the flourishing of books on English (usually textbooks with a preface on teaching method). In these books, the medieval method of beginning with reading before, some years later, proceeding to learn to write was the most general approach. However, Michael mentions certain exceptions where the two were learned together. One advocate of such an approach is William Bullokar who introduced a method by which he claimed that a child of 5 years of age could learn to read and write within six weeks. His approach (Bullokar, [1580] 1966) involved the use of a modified alphabet of 37 letters (see Figure 5.1).

Michael's study of English teaching is based on a very detailed analysis of textbooks. This enables him to document the development of different aspects of English from the sixteenth to the nineteenth centuries. For instance, on literature:

> Some children had been reading, under instruction, doctrinal and scrip-tural matter, in English, long before the middle of the sixteenth century. From 1550, the date of the first interpretative rhetoric in English, they could meet a very little secular English literature in school. The amount of English literature in the rhetorics increased in time and could be supplemented during the early decades of the seventeenth century from the aphoristic anthologies [i.e. moral tales] and, to an unknown extent, by what it is convenient to call chapbook literature [popular literature]. By the middle of the seventeenth century pupils could be encouraged … to read English poetry from the school library, and the everyday spelling-books were beginning to include secular reading-matter such as proverbs and general knowledge. By 1717 the pupils could have an anthology of English verse designed for school use and aimed explicitly at helping them to appreciate poetry. By 1740 the spelling-books regularly con-tained secular verse and short anecdotes or fables.

(Michael, 1987, p. 379)

1500 is often given as the start of the 'early modern English' period. During the period discussed in this section, English began to be standardized; it became codified (represented in dictionaries and grammars); and it acquired the resources necessary to function as a literary language as well as a language of science and education. See the first book in this series, *English: history diversity and change* (Graddol et al. (eds), 1996).

This period saw the production of several descriptions of English, written mainly for educational purposes. For a discussion of these see the first book in this series, *English: history, diversity and change* (Graddol et al. (eds), 1996).

A 'rhetoric' was a book about analysing the structure of speeches or texts (compare a 'grammar' as a book about the analysis of sentence structure).

Figure 5.1   Extract from Bullokar, 1580, A Short Introduction or Guiding, *pp. 2–3. The extract explains Bullokar's selection of 37 main letters (with 3 additional letters) and illustrates these*
(Bullokar, [1580] 1966)

Michael provides the following tentative outline showing when the main components of English made their first appearance:

From early times	Reading, spelling and pronunciation; some oral expression; perhaps some drama, for which there is no textbook evidence
By 1525	Some written expression
By 1550	Snatches of literature
By 1586	Grammar
By 1650	More substantial literature; more sustained written expression
By 1720	Some explicit teaching of literature; linguistic exercises in, or derived from, grammar and rhetoric
By 1730	Elocution
By 1750	More substantial dramatic work
By 1770	More sustained teaching of literature; more attention to language and written expression
By 1820	History of the language
By 1850	History of literature

(Michael, 1987, p. 381)

Michael's study took no account of factors of the kind we mentioned earlier (political, social and economic) that are relevant to understanding debates about what constitutes English. His approach was not intended to achieve this purpose, although he acknowledges its importance in referring to the eventual need for a historical setting and in noting that teachers responded to movements in the culture of their times. In fact, up to 1800 a good deal occurred outside education, but that had bearing on it, to set the basis for the nineteenth-century debates that we examine in the next section.

❖   ❖   ❖   ❖   ❖

Activity 5.2   *(Allow about 5 minutes)*

As an illustration of this, consider Figure 5.2 below, which shows the gradual decline in illiteracy in England. What do you notice about this trend?

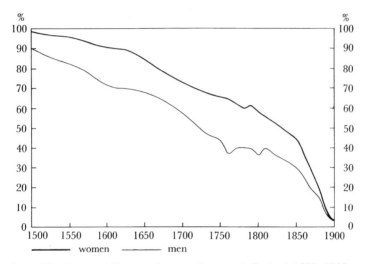

Figure 5.2   Estimated illiteracy of men and women in England, 1500–1900
(Cressy, 1980, p. 177)

Estimates are based on various sources of evidence and, after 1754, from data on ability to sign marriage registers.

My comments follow.

❖   ❖   ❖   ❖   ❖

The graph shows that, historically, women have had less access to literacy than men. Cressy (1980) relates this to differences in women's and men's lifestyles. For instance, he writes of the period from the late sixteenth century to the early eighteenth century:

> Most women did not need to be able to write. The domestic routine of cooking and sewing and child-rearing had little need for reading, and it scarcely afforded the time. There were, of course, exceptions, and several popular books were aimed specifically at a female audience. These were privileged women whose literacy was a social ornament, daughters who learned to read and write to please their fathers, and wives whose literacy matched that of their husbands. But we must not be misled

by examples of gentlemen's ladies and merchant's widows keeping accounts and conducting correspondence into thinking that such abilities were widespread. Even among those social and economic groups where the men had regular dealings with paper and ink, the women were usually illiterate.

(Cressy, 1980, p. 128)

While there has been a gradual decrease in illiteracy in England, as elsewhere in Europe, there are two rises against this trend; one in the middle of the seventeenth century and one around 1800 (just before for women, just after for men). The second rise has been attributed to the industrial revolution – I return to this in the next section. Cressy attributes the first rise to the effects on life and schooling of the English revolution, or Civil War, fought between Parliament and the supporters of King Charles I in the mid seventeenth century. This is despite the fact that high levels of literacy were associated with the revolutionaries; the vast majority of petitions and receipts of the parliamentary army, under the command of Oliver Cromwell, were signed, often by the men and sometimes by their wives (Cipolla, 1969).

Religion and literacy went together at this time with a strong emphasis among the religious sects that supported the Parliamentarian side on personal study of the scriptures. Trade was also associated with literacy as other evidence from Cressy shows. For example in Table 5.1 we see that, as might be expected, some economic activities were associated with very low levels of illiteracy.

Table 5.1   Clusters of illiteracy in rural England, 1580–1700

% illiterate	Economic activity
0–10	Retailers' distributors
14–33	Specialist crafts
37–52	Manufacturers' processors
56–58	Village crafts
73–100	Heavy manual trades

(Adapted from Cressy, 1980, p. 136)

However, trade and religion are not the only factors at work. There is also the influence of reading and writing seen as a 'consumer good' (or possession) that some groups of people desired more than others. In proposing this view Lacqueur (1983, pp. 46–7) provided some examples: 'No argument from necessity can account for the fact that 82 per cent of joiners and carpenters could write in the Lancashire of the 1830s, but only 55 per cent of foundrymen and iron or brass moulders. Why should 70 per cent of shoemakers be literate but only 50 per cent of hatters?' There may be answers to Lacqueur's questions, to do with the amount of reading and writing involved in these different trades in dealing with suppliers and customers, the extent to which some trades involved subcontracting, were more technical than others and so on; also there may have been traditions of literacy associated with certain trades, themselves often linked to religious persuasions and to the specific geographical areas and social milieu associated with certain trades. Nevertheless, Lacqueur's point is well taken, that there is no one simple explanation for the variations that are concealed by the apparent smoothness of the trend towards universal literacy.

In this section I have discussed the development of English as a school subject from the sixteenth to the eighteenth centuries. I have suggested that a wider range of topics came to be taught, and that these topics came increasingly to be recognized as aspects of 'English'. I have also indicated the importance of the social and political context for understanding developments in education. I drew on information about the gradual decline in illiteracy rates to illustrate the importance of context.

5.4   THE NINETEENTH CENTURY

I mentioned that the second increase in illiteracy shown in Cressy's graph (Figure 5.2), around the beginning of the nineteenth century, had often been attributed to the industrial revolution, the period roughly between 1760 and 1840 during which Britain was transformed from an agricultural to an industrial society, and which was accompanied by large population shifts as people moved from (relatively) stable rural backgrounds to find work in the cities. There is more to it than that. An increasingly literate population could be seen, and was seen, as a less manageable population and against the background of the French revolution vested interests everywhere were alarmed and threatened.

The French revolution (1789–99) was itself associated with the 'dangerous' writings that had been published, especially in Holland, in the eighteenth century. The growth of newspaper and pamphlet publishing permitted the spread of a range of opinions that had not been seen in England since the seventeenth-century revolution, so much so that the government rapidly curtailed press freedom. On the other hand, an increasingly industrialized society appeared to many to demand more widespread literacy and high levels of literacy as a consumer good (associated with access to the increase in publishing), as a means of social and economic advancement, and to many as a means of breaking down the old class barriers.

Language and class

Language and class have perhaps always been associated but this was particularly remarked and noticeable in nineteenth-century England. Phillips (1984) examines in detail, mainly from literary sources, the differences in the terms used for such everyday things as meals by different classes, but also points to the ways in which novelists were able to place characters by characteristics of their language. Of course, for novelists to do this readers had to share their hierarchical and class-based system of categorization. In this they were helped by the novelists themselves, as well as by books that helped them to learn what was 'proper'. One example of books on letter writing, *The Complete Letter-Writer for Ladies and Gentlemen*, published in about 1910 (Ward Lock, undated) devotes six pages to how to address people of different ranks before giving general advice (much of it referring to bad habits, to be avoided, and ignorance, to be concealed). There follow numerous examples of letters proper to all sorts of occasions (see Figure 5.3).

No. 66.—From a Lady requesting assistance in Parish Entertainments.

THE RECTORY, BROOMHILLS,
(Date in full————)

DEAR MRS. WILLIAMS,

It is our custom to provide a series of entertainments for the parishioners during the winter months, and I shall be very grateful if I may enrol your name among those willing to assist. Shall I impose too severe a strain upon your good nature if I ask you to be responsible for one such entertainment this season, arranging the programme and supervising its performance? It is, of course, understood that any out-of-pocket expenses you may incur in the matter will be a first charge upon the moneys taken at the doors.

With kind regards,

I am, dear Mrs. Williams,

Yours very truly,

MARY KIRK.

No. 67.—Answer to the above, Affirmatively.

ROSE COTTAGE, BROOMHILLS,
(Date in full————)

DEAR MRS. KIRK,

I shall be delighted to be of service to you, and if you will fix an evening in December I will invite one or two of my friends who are musically gifted to come down and take part in a concert. As soon as it is practicable I will draft a programme and submit it to your approval. In the meantime you may enrol among the names of those always willing to assist you when possible that of

Yours sincerely,

KATE WILLIAMS.

No. 68.—Answer Negatively.

ROSE COTTAGE, BROOMHILLS,
(Date in full————

DEAR MRS. KIRK,

I am sorry that I cannot undertake the arrangement of one of your village entertainments this year. We return to town early in September, and are unlikely to be here for more than a fleeting visit until the spring. I wish I could comply with your request, but I am sure you will prefer a definite answer in the negative to a provisional promise which at the eleventh hour I might, to your greater disappointment, find myself unable to fulfil. With kind regards,

I am, yours very truly,

KATE WILLIAMS.

Figure 5.3 Three examples from 'Letter writer for Ladies' (Ward Lock, undated, letter nos 66–8)

English reading and writing in elementary education

Throughout the century a classical education had the highest prestige in England and the universities only slowly introduced English studies. In the public schools too, even by the 1860s, English studies had very little role, and remained neglected for the rest of the century despite recommendations to the contrary from the governmental Taunton Commission of 1868 (Hollingworth, 1974).

Most of the population, however, could aspire only to a form of basic education, which for most children meant Sunday schools, evening classes or factory schools. In the earlier part of the century there were several views on English in such contexts and these need to be judged against the social, political and economic background mentioned above. One approach was to discourage the teaching of reading and writing to the mass of the population. Another was to teach reading but not writing. Quite different was the view, often seen as dangerously democratic, that literacy in English should be available to all, and that literacy meant more than a basic skill in deciphering and re-encoding. These arguments are not entirely dead either in Britain or elsewhere, though they were expressed with some considerable clarity at the time.

For example, Hannah More (cited in Lankshear and Lawler, 1987, p. 45), who founded Sunday Schools in the 1790s, countered the view prevalent in late eighteenth-century Britain that learning was dangerous by asserting that religion could help the social order, 'When each, according to his place, pays willing honour to his superiors ... when high, low, rich and poor ... sit down satisfied with his own place'. In her schools, she said 'I allow of no writing for the poor. My object is not to make them fanatics, but to train up the lower classes in habits of industry and piety'. Andrew Bell, founder of the Church of England system of monitorial schools (also quoted in Lankshear and Lawler, 1987, pp. 45–6) wrote in similar terms in the early nineteenth century: 'It is not proposed that the children of the poor be educated in an expensive way, or even taught to write and cypher'. The opinion of a 'representative of a Justice of the Peace' (quoted by Williams, 1961, p. 135) is similar: 'It is doubtless desirable that the poor should be generally instructed in *reading*, if it were only for the best of purposes – that they may read the scriptures. As to *writing* and *arithmetic*, it may be apprehended that such a degree of knowledge would produce in them a disrelish for the laborious occupations of life'.

This view continued well into the nineteenth century. Robert Lowe, a member of the Liberal party government, at the time of writing the equivalent of Minister of Education, and later to become Home Secretary and Chancellor of the Exchequer, wrote in 1861:

> The lower classes should be educated to discharge the duties cast upon them. They should also be educated that they may appreciate and defer to a higher cultivation when they meet it; and the higher classes ought to be educated in a very different manner, in order that they may exhibit to the lower classes that higher education to which, if it were shown to them, they would bow down and defer.
>
> (Cited in Gordon and Lawton, 1978, p. 183)

Not all did so defer, and given the associations between education, religion and class control, it is not entirely surprising that the majority of convicts transported to Australia resisted the considerable pressure on them, during the voyage and on arrival, to learn to read. It was thought it would help reform them and make them more useful to society. However, 'they had no use for the reading skills as they were presented to them, and no desire for the religious instruction with which they were identified. In the colonial penal system, no one had shown them any alternative reason for having to read' (Reeves, 1983, p. 72).

Perhaps the most cynical support for education for children of the poor was given by the Reverend H.W. Bellairs about 1850: 'It should be borne in mind that an ill-educated and undisciplined population, like that existing amongst the mines of South Wales, is one which may be found most dangerous to the neighbourhood in which it dwells; and that a band of efficient school masters may be kept at much less expense than a body of police or soldiery' (cited in Khleif, 1980, pp. 106–7).

Despite the views expressed above, a demand for writing led to its being taught in some schools, though usually only after a considerable time in school since the most common method in the nineteenth century for learning to read and write was still that described by Clanchy for the middle ages (see p. 162 above). Stephens (1987, pp. 158–9) writing of Sunday schools in the Midlands in the 1840s shows that some writing did take place, though there were objections to it from those who believed that the Sabbath (Sunday) should be kept as a day of worship and rest. The respect for the Sabbath may well have served as an unchallengeable reason covering other real motives concerning the supposed dangers of writing; but in Kidderminster, for example, from 1840 the Sabbath was kept and children were taught to write: the simple expedient was to move the writing class to Monday evening.

Elementary education refers to the basic education, usually up to age 13, available in nineteenth-century Britain. This was the education that became compulsory and, later, free by the end of the century.

It must be borne in mind that for much of the nineteenth century most children began work at an early age, typically 7 or 8 years. School attendance was limited to a small population; it was also brief and erratic. Even when elementary education became compulsory (1880) and free (1891) large numbers of children failed to attend school – nearly a million, according to Lance Dobson, (1984). Dobson provides a rather dismal picture of the teaching of reading and writing.

We know that 'alphabetism' – the mere recognition and copying of letters in sequence – was common. Children at school in mid-Victorian times were usually taught the letters of the alphabet first, then two-letter words, and went on successively to five- and six- letter words. Some never got past the first stage. The annual reports of the Committee of Council on Education – and the HMIs' [Her Majesty's Inspectors of Schools] reports on schools in particular – reveal the poor quality of the instruction given in schools and of the performance by pupils ...

From the records we cannot discover directly how many pupils had an indisputable facility in reading and writing, even when their Standard performance in the Inspector's examination was deemed passable. The H M Inspectors' reports ... provide a bleak picture. After 1862 children were prepared for the HMI's examination in reading by concentrating on a single book. Some teachers got their pupils to learn it by heart, and occasionally an HMI found a pupil reciting a passage for him with the book held upside down. Inspectors retaliated by requiring pupils to read from the text backwards. Writing was tested by dictation from the same reading book. Teachers and pupils conspired to deceive the Inspectors; HMIs were sceptical about the results and hypercritical of the school's efforts. One HMI brought with him into a classroom a book which he himself did not know at all and asked a succession of pupils to read from it; some could not attempt it, and the HMI had to listen to pupils totalling

NEW SCHOOL-ROOM, BOYS' HOME, REGENT'S PARK ROAD

GUTTER CHILDREN – THE FIELD LANE RAGGED SCHOOLS

one-third of the class who did read from it before he grasped what the content of the book was about. In 1852 Matthew Arnold, just before he was appointed as an Inspector, said that young pupil-teachers [older pupils used to teach younger ones] could not paraphrase a plain passage of prose or poetry without totally misunderstanding it or write half a page of composition without making gross blunders. Teachers used reading around the class as a standard method, and repetition was constant so that correction and memorisation could take place.

Most writing lessons were spent on exercises in copying from models provided by the teacher or taken from books, or else a script was dictated by the teacher.

(Dobson, 1984, pp. 43–4)

English and the Celtic languages of Britain

It needs to be emphasized that we have been mainly discussing education in England. English in education undoubtedly led to greater standardization in the English language, especially through the teaching of reading and writing, at the expense of regional dialects. In both Ireland (Goldstrom, 1972) and Wales (Khleif, 1980) the effects on children's own language were more severe because the use of English as a language of instruction in government-funded schools was accompanied by the suppression of Welsh and Irish, in part because of their associations with anti-English movements. In Scotland, too, that had for many years had consistently higher levels of literacy in English than obtained in England, English was used in schools and Gaelic was suppressed. If there was less resistance in Scotland than in Wales and Ireland, that may be attributed to the fact that many of the Gaelic areas had been deliberately depopulated in the seventeenth century and that English was less the language of an invader or colonial power. The suppression of the Celtic languages implied the suppression of their cultures also, of course.

> The history of English in Scotland is discussed in the first book in this series, *English: history, diversity and change* (Graddol et al. (eds), 1996).

English and Empire

In India and other parts of the British Empire, there was no attempt as in Britain to eradicate the local languages. British rule was less concentrated in India than it was in Ireland and Wales, and the approach used was a different one. In India, and elsewhere in Asia, English was introduced as the language of the elite and as the language of higher education. Its function was in some ways akin to that of Latin in medieval and Renaissance Europe in that it was the language of administration and of 'high' culture. English became, and remains, one of the national languages but it is the language of a small proportion of the population.

❖   ❖   ❖   ❖   ❖

Activity 5.3   *(Reading A)*

Please now read Reading A 'English and Empire: teaching English in nineteenth-century India' by Anthea Fraser Gupta.

While you are reading note down:

• how the purposes of teaching English in India at this time differ from those discussed for elementary education in England in this section (5.4);

• how the social class of the students differed and how this relates to differences in content;

• views on what was meant by learning a language;

• cultural effects of English studies and reactions to these.

After reading you might like to compare your notes with mine below.

Comment

In India the purpose for teaching English was to prepare an elite that would cooperate with the British and was not to ensure a literate population in English (or any other language). Hence the emphasis was not on the basic skills of decoding and handwriting, but very much on cultural as well as linguistic aspects. For this the Anglicists had to be successful so that English writings replaced those in other languages and literatures as a high status point of reference. In this sense there was a common policy of control, but applied to very different circumstances.

The Indian students were mainly boys from the middle and upper classes, whereas those in England included the poorest, boys and girls, but tended to exclude the wealthier who would have had a private education. The Indians were also older, but that is not the only reason for literature having a role in their studies, whereas such literature as there was in the English elementary school seems to have been used for (well-prepared) reading practice.

In India, the heavy emphasis on translation suggests a limited view of language learning, but one that was appropriate where the aim was cultural dominance. There were also 'moral' (really cultural superiority) justifications among the proponents of English in India and some justified concern about possible effects on established customs, morals and beliefs. In England too there was a moral tone, especially related to knowing one's place in society, together with a fear (echoed by the Indian upper classes) that too much learning might endanger social structures.

❖   ❖   ❖   ❖   ❖

Reading and writing in Canadian education

Harvey J. Graff (1979) writing of the English speaking areas of nineteenth-century Canada argues that even in monolingual situations literacy was used to devalue cultures other than that of the literate elite. In Canada, as in Britain, mass education was introduced in the nineteenth century. Graff (1979) gives the arguments used to support its introduction by Egerton Ryerson, the first Superintendent of Education for Upper Canada. These include, from his report of 1846, a strong moral tone, as in England, for education was defined as 'not the mere acquisition of certain arts, or of certain branches of knowledge, but that instruction and discipline which qualify and dispose the subjects of it for their appropriate duties and enjoyments of life, as Christians, as persons of business and also as members of the civil community in which they live' (p. 30). Ryerson did not exclude writing from the curriculum, but rather encouraged 'correct' and 'intelligible' writing in rather loftier tones as important to a mechanic, for example, as 'the vehicle of his thoughts, the instrument of all his intercourse with his fellow men and with the histories of other nations and of the past ages' (pp. 30–31). There was also a promise of personal advancement: in 1848 Ryerson asked 'How is the uneducated and unskilled man to succeed in these times of sharp and skilful competition and sleepless activity?' (pp. 70–1) and answered that 'every man, unless he wishes to starve outright, must read and write, and cast accounts, and speak his native tongue well enough to attend to his own particular business' (p. 31).

However Graff's detailed study showed that characteristics such as ethnic origin, social class, race, age and sex, had more effect on economic success than the possession of literacy. 'Among the unskilled and the semiskilled, very little economic advantage accrued to the literates. Literacy, though, had a greater role in the attainment of skilled or artisanal work and their commensurate rewards' (Graff, 1979, p. 198). Graff's overall conclusion (pp. 22–3) is that 'the provision of mass schooling; the working class acceptance of it, though a questioning one; and universal, public education all served this direction: promoting discipline, morality and the "training in being trained" that mattered most in the creation and preparation of a modern industrial and urban work force. These were the purposes of school – and one use of literacy'.

Elsewhere, too, in the nineteenth-century teaching of English there was the predominant emphasis on reading, a frequent suspicion of writing or an insistence on correctness in terms of adhering to 'correct' forms. For example, the large-scale and mainly well-intentioned programme in the USA to make the former slaves literate after their emancipation was deliberately phased out when it became apparent that they might become 'too literate' (see Morris, 1981).

An alternative approach to literacy

If formal education in English and literacy in the nineteenth century appear to have had as a major function maintenance of the class structure, or control of the Empire, there was nevertheless another approach. Lankshear and Lawler (1967) discuss at length the limited literacy available in formal education and contrast it with what they designate 'proper literacy'. This is akin to an older notion of literacy that involves not just knowing how to read and write, but especially refers to knowing the literature. It was not, however, a literary canon that concerned the Corresponding Societies that Lankshear and Lawler describe, but familiarity with political works about rights and freedom.

❖   ❖   ❖   ❖   ❖

Activity 5.4   *(Reading B)*

Please now work through Reading B, an extract by Lankshear and Lawler: 'The corresponding societies: working class literacy and political reform'.

While reading, note particularly the contrasts in both aim and method with elementary education in Britain and Canada. The emphasis here is on content and relevance of what is read, and on analysis and discussion, not simply on decoding. Indeed, those who could not read and write could participate. You might note similarities with other groups who have sought social change, such as more recent women's groups, in the approach to discussion. You could also consider how the aim and approach differed from that of English in India discussed in Reading A.

Note also towards the end of the article, how the initial successes of Corresponding Societies seem to have encouraged the action of churches and, later, the state in promoting mass literacy, while ensuring that it was taught in a limited way and emphasized the maintenance of a rigid social order.

❖   ❖   ❖   ❖   ❖

The Corresponding Societies, despite their suppression, also provided an important basis for the application outside the educational system of the basic skills sometimes learned there. The growing literacy of the working classes provided a readership for the emerging newspaper publishing (itself the subject of considerable government concern and suppression) and for the lively pamphleteering of nineteenth-century Britain. It remained an important challenge to the narrow reading, and sometimes writing, that the state provided; and the conflict continues, informing debates about the teaching of English, well into the twentieth century.

The development of English studies in the universities and in secondary education

The view, that we have earlier discounted, of English as a subject of only recent origin may well be based on its relative recency as a university subject. Lance Dobson provides a useful review of the development of English studies at this level.

The late recognition of English studies

The universities of Oxford and Cambridge did not teach English to their undergraduates until the end of the [nineteenth] century and saw no point in doing so. Those who were talented enough to read classical literature could easily broaden a cultivated mind by reading books in English at leisure, and neither university would admit a course in English studies which seemed to lack academic rigour and prestige. More initiatives appeared elsewhere during the nineteenth century, first at the University of London and later at the new provincial universities and university colleges, but the beginnings were slender ...

Professorships had been established in English at University College, London, in 1828, and in English literature and history at King's College, London, in 1835, and similar appointments were made at Owens College, Manchester, in 1866 and at Liverpool in 1882. But at the University of Durham, founded in 1832, no place was given to the teaching of English until the end of the century.

The tardy and reluctant acceptance of English at the universities has a simple explanation. English was not thought to be a proper academic study, an intellectual discipline, and its study, if countenanced at all, would have to rest on a basis of scholarship. Even at London and the provincial university colleges, the teaching of the subject followed the classical model. The teaching of English literature was frequently combined with history, and there were several joint Chairs in the two subjects. The number of students attracted by courses of study in English was comparatively small, and the subject was soon burdened with rigorous examinations, by which its sponsors sought to enhance its reputation, but which in practice only shrouded it in dullness. Moreover, the scope of English studies was gradually widened to include Anglo-Saxon and Medieval English, which led to an emphasis upon the historical and philological aspects of the subject, and this tended to warp its growth.

(Open University, 1981, p. 60)

In secondary education there was, as noted earlier, little study of English in the public (i.e. private) schools despite the general recognition that the subject was neglected and should not be so. For example, Matthew Arnold in *The French Eton* written in the 1860s comments on the studies in the French Lyceum:

It has the scientific instruction and the study of the mother-tongue which our school course is without, and is often blamed for being without ... In the study of the mother-tongue the French schoolboy has a more real

advantage over ours; he does certainly learn something of the French language and literature, and of English our schoolboy learns nothing.
(Cited in Hollingworth, 1974)

In the grammar schools and higher grades of elementary schools English studies were also neglected. As Dobson also showed (Open University, 1981), the Royal Commission on Secondary Education included in its report for 1868 the view of an Assistant Commissioner that the English Language was seldom taught systematically and in 1895 the Commission reported that the curriculum had been so distorted by the need to teach certain subjects in order to gain government funding that literary subjects had been very little studied.

Nevertheless, there was pressure to include English literature and the study of English language in the school curriculum. In Scotland from the 1870s there were many articles on the teaching of English at secondary level in the then very flourishing educational press. In England schools attempted to broaden the curriculum to include literature, although they were inhibited by the very restrictive national curriculum then in place that was tied to a system of grants, effectively based on payment according to examination results.

Developments towards the end of the nineteenth century

Literature was introduced with difficulty into schools at all levels. Even in the twentieth century the London School Board was taken to court successfully by the district auditor for effectively overeducating elementary school pupils by including literature in the curriculum of elementary schools (Gordon and Lawton, 1978, p. 20).

Despite the restrictions, and as a response to the frequent complaints from inspectors about low levels of reading that suggested a market existed for texts with some interest and meaning, many publishers introduced graded readers for elementary schools from the 1870s. In this, Scottish publishers such as Blackie, Collins, Oliver and Boyd and several others seem to have dominated, perhaps because English was better established as a subject in Scotland. However, the texts even in a 'literary reader' could be somewhat constraining and the reader was very much cast as subjective receiver of the text, rather than as someone who could actively interact with it. Nevertheless, these readers represented a move towards a broader English curriculum and they often included poetry and sometimes some quite lively stories among the odd mixture of jingoistic and moralistic tales, fables, accounts of explorations and so on. Figure 5.4 overleaf is an extract from Longmans' 'Ship' Literary Readers *The Fourth Reader*. It shows that morality and education do you good; the squire rewards the righteous who have fallen on evil times, wrong-doers are arrested, and it is placed in pre-industrial times – before the days of railways and telegraphs.

The conflicts and uncertainties in the nineteenth-century teaching of English were carried over into the twentieth century. There appears to have been widespread agreement that English was very important but a reluctance to introduce the subject beyond the elementary level. At that level the teaching was constrained both in content and scope, deliberately so for fear of the dangers of a truly literate population, and English (as opposed to reading and writing) did not become a full and compulsory subject in elementary schools until 1882, though it was permitted as an optional subject from 1875. At other levels in education there were so many competing strands that it was perhaps easier, as in

LESSON 9.

The White Pigeon.—PART II.

plague   nat'-ur-al   tel'-e-graph   rob'-ber-y
seized   es-pe'-cial-ly bor'-rowed   con'-sta-bles
threat'-en car'-ri-er   mes'-sa-ges   man'-aged

1. The boy's name was Frank Noble. When he had gone the squire asked the carpenter about him, and heard that his parents had not long settled in Somerton. They used to keep a farm; but, the cattle plague having carried off their cows, they were unable to pay their rent, and had now opened a small shop in the village. Everybody spoke well of them, and everybody liked Frank. "He will get on in the world," said the carpenter, "because he is never in idle company; and I've known him since he was two feet high, and never known him to tell a lie."

2. Mr. Somers was so pleased with this account that he made up his mind to help the Nobles. Meanwhile Frank had taken the white pigeon to the woman who owned it. But she would not take it. "You have saved its life, and I'll make you a present of it," she said.

3. Frank thanked her, carried the bird home, and soon grew very fond of it. He was so kind to it that it lost all fear, and would hop about the kitchen, and eat off the same plate as the dog. As he now wanted to know more about pigeons, he borrowed a book of Natural History, and by reading it he found that his was a carrier pigeon.

4. Frank lived before the day of railways and telegraphs. A bird which could take a message faster than any horse could gallop was therefore very useful then, and the boy thought he would try to train his pigeon. It took him a long time, but he managed it in the end.

5. Frank's pigeon became the talk of the country round, and the neighbours sometimes borrowed it to take notes for them. A gang of thieves to which Fox belonged heard of it, and they thought that it would be very useful to them. So young Fox, a fellow of nineteen, was sent to buy it.

6. But Frank would not part with his white pigeon, especially after young Fox began to threaten and bully him. When the thieves were

Figure 5.4 'The White Pigeon – Part II' (continued opposite)

the case of the public schools, to do little or nothing, given that it was not quite clear what precisely should be done.

Nevertheless, this was also a century in which the study of **philology**, of dialects and of Anglo-Saxon became well established. However, these more liberal studies were in a sense peripheral; according to Williams (1961) the shadow of class culture affected all nineteenth-century thinking on education, and had the effect of separating liberal education from the concerns of trade and industry. Oddly, in view of the century's emphasis on industrial efficiency, the elementary schools had an English curriculum that was, superficially at least, also largely irrelevant to the economic world of the time, though it was hardly liberal either. Graff (1979) and others have argued that it was in subtler ways that the limited English curriculum of the nineteenth century served the emerging industrial society. English literature had little role at any level during the century, which seems particularly strange given the importance it was shortly to assume.

I have suggested that the introduction of widespread education in English during the nineteenth century was a matter not just of teaching certain types of

Philology, coming from Greek *philos* (friend) + *logia* (learning) and meaning 'love of learning', was originally applied to the study of:
1 literature (often literature of an earlier period)
2 the language used in the literature.
Today, the term is most frequently applied to the scientific study of language and particularly to the study of the changes undergone by a language over a period of time.

(Todd and Hancock, 1986, p. 346)

told this one of them said: "Very well, if we can't have it by fair means, we'll have it by foul"; and, sure enough, a few days afterwards the bird was missing.

7. The gang at first took it to a part of the country some way off Somerton, and taught it to carry messages for them there. Then, when they thought that it had forgotten its old home and its old master, they ventured to use it nearer Somerton.

8. They sent it with a note to Fox's cousin, whom they wanted to join them in a robbery. But the pigeon flew straight to the Nobles' house, and tapped at the kitchen window as it used to do. Frank ran with the greatest joy to let it in. "O father," he cried, "here's the white pigeon come back; I must run and show it to mother."

9. At this instant the pigeon spread its wings, and Frank saw under one of them a dirty piece of paper. He opened it, and he opened his eyes also as he read: "Meet me at Crooked Billet, twelve to-night. Bring pistols. Squire away from home.—C. F."

10. "Why," cried Frank, "they are going to rob Mr. Somers!"

"Yes," said his father, "the note must mean that; let us go and warn him." Before they set out, however, they shut up the pigeon that it might be seen by no one but themselves.

11. Mr. Somers sent for the constables, and armed the servants. The thieves came about one o'clock, and easily broke into a house where every one seemed asleep. But as soon as they had entered they were seized and marched off to gaol.

12. Neither Frank nor his father would take any money from Mr. Somers, so he said: "Will you, my good lad, trust me with your white pigeon for a few days?"

"Yes, sir, and welcome," answered the boy.

13. A few days afterwards the squire called at the Nobles' house and bade father and son follow him. They followed him till they stood opposite the new shop. The carpenter had just put up a sign which was covered with a bit of carpet.

14. "Go up the ladder, will you?" said Mr. Somers to Frank, "and pull that sign straight, for it hangs quite crooked. There, now it is straight, so pull off the carpet and let us see what is under."

The boy obeyed, and saw a white pigeon painted on the sign, with the name of Noble in large letters underneath.

15. "Take care you do not fall and break your neck," called out the squire. "Come down, and wish your father joy of being master of the new shop, the White Pigeon. And I wish him joy of having such a son as you are."

COMPOSITION.—Make sentences showing why you think Frank Noble was fair, brave, truthful, unselfish, clever, and industrious.

(Longman's Ship Literary Readers, 1895, pp. 36–40)

knowledge and skills, but also of inculcating certain values and encouraging certain forms of social relations. This is evident in the use of literacy teaching to maintain the current social order in England and Canada; in the suppression of Celtic languages and culture in other parts of the UK; and in the promotion of European cultural values amongst an English educated elite in India.

5.5   ENGLISH IN THE TWENTIETH CENTURY

The twentieth century has seen English established as a major subject in schools and universities in Britain as well as, increasingly, elsewhere. For much of the time, literature has predominated, with philology in strong decline in universities and **linguistics**, often referred as the scientific study of language, enjoying only a relatively short period of rapid growth as a university subject in the 1970s and early 1980s. The concern with basic skills has continued and English teaching has in recent years become the topic of more political debate and disagreement than even in the nineteenth century. I begin this section by discussing two major government reports that both reviewed and attempted to influence development in English teaching. I then discuss some general approaches that have under-pinned English teaching for much of the century. Continuing developments in English teaching are considered in the next chapter.

Two major influences – the Newbolt Report and the Bullock Report

English teaching has had a variety of aims during the twentieth century. As might be expected given their separation in time, two of the major government reports of this century, the Newbolt Report (Board of Education, 1921) and the Bullock Report (DES, 1975) do not concur greatly on what should be taught. (The names of these committees reflect the common British practice of naming official committees after people who chair them – Sir Henry Newbolt and Sir Alan Bullock).

The Newbolt Committee was convened at the end of World War One and its membership included many well-known university critics of English literature, at that time not a well established subject. Its brief was to report on the position of English in the educational system, having regard to the requirements of a liberal education, the needs of business, the professions, and public services, and the relation of English to other studies. It reported at a time when Europe had been unsettled by war, against a background of the Russian revolution, other impending revolutions in Europe and, nearer home, the final secession of much of Ireland from Britain. It was also a time when the class structure of nineteenth-century Britain was under strong challenge.

A major emphasis in the report was on national unity. Taking a similar stance to that of the influential Victorian educationalist, Matthew Arnold, who claimed that 'culture unites classes' the Newbolt committee stated: 'We believe that such an education based upon the English language and literature would have import-ant social, as well as personal, results; it would have a unifying tendency' (Chapter 1, para. 15). This aim of unifying the nation was not simply a romantic aspiration. The report discussed how this aim could be achieved. In literature it involved English taking the place of the Greek and Latin classics as a literature to be studied, but this study was to involve personal appreciation and be separate from the analytical scholarship that had been taught alongside appreciation in studies of the Classics. In language it involved reducing the class-based distinctions in speech and writing and at the early stages involved:

> First, systematic training in the sounded speech of standard English, to secure correct pronunciation and clear articulation: second, systematic training in the use of standard English, to secure clearness and correct-ness both in oral expression and in writing: third, training in reading.
> (Board of Education, 1921, Chapter 1, para. 13)

Later there was to be a scientific study of language and of formal grammar but this was to be 'kept apart (so far as that is possible) from the lessons in which English is treated as an art, a means of creative expression, a record of human experience' (Chapter 1, para. 7). The main eventual aim was on literature as a 'channel of formative culture' and as 'a medium of creative art' all related to the enjoyment of a liberal education. To lead students from where they were, they should be encouraged 'to write in their local language and with the material offered by the scenes and life which are familiar to them' (p. 275). Other aims included gaining a certain command of the language essential to other subjects and for employment but these are given relatively little attention beside the theme of English as culturally unifying and the emphasis on English as a live subject in which the learner was personally involved.

One of the editors of the Black Papers was Brian Cox, later to be chair of the National Curriculum English Working Group (referred to in Reading C of this chapter).

The Bullock Committee which reported over half a century later, in 1975, was set up by Margaret Thatcher, then Secretary of State for Education, 'to consider in relation to schools, all aspects of teaching the use of English, including reading writing and speech'. The Report was commissioned as a direct response to a series of publications called the Black Papers, which claimed, as one of the themes, a decline in standards of literacy sufficient to damage the national economy. (Black Papers were unofficial reports contrasting in their aims with the governments's official White Papers.)

In membership the Committee was very different from that of Newbolt. It contained headteachers and university professors of education, but there were no representatives of University departments of English. There was also, as Crystal (1975) pointed out, no sociologist, psychologist or general linguist. Many members had primary school teaching experience, but those with experience of teaching literature appear to have been less well represented.

Despite expectations that it would be critical of current practice the Report found no evidence for falling standards in literacy, and supported much of the practice then current in English classrooms, although it is clear that the report takes issue with an unlimited diet of 'unchecked creativity' in the primary classroom, when other types of language work were 'neglected'. Similarly, in the secondary classroom, English was criticized when it became 'almost exclusively a source of material for personal response to social issues' (p. 7). Nevertheless, as Carter (1989) states: 'The report received an enthusiastic reception from the English teaching profession but received some public criticism for not advocating a concentration on basic skills of literacy by formal methods of language training' (p. 1). This refers to the Report's comment that 'Competence in language comes above all through its purposeful use, not through the working of exercises divorced from content' (p. 528). The Report did, however, restructure the thinking about English through its two major recommendations of a developing language programme from preschool to school leaving age, with reading as an integral part of the language curriculum, and the notion that all subjects had a responsibility for the development of 'language across the curriculum'. The immediate result was the creation in both primary and secondary schools of posts with responsibility for language across the curriculum (LAC). For a time, it seemed as if the definition of English might be extended to take on this additional dimension. In reality, the responsibility for LAC came to rest with the English departments, and despite the rhetoric, the reality continued to be that English departments were responsible for the development of pupils' language skills.

There are clear differences between the Bullock and Newbolt Reports in their aims for English. In the Bullock Report the emphasis is, following its terms of reference, on the use of English and on the monitoring of standards. Its aims for the teaching of English include enabling children to be sufficiently literate for employment (with a reference to the Newbolt Report where this was accorded less attention) and for higher education (paragraphs 1.2 and 1.3). Language competence is conceived of as growing incrementally through writing, talk, reading and experience and it is the teacher's concern to encourage this growth in a pupil as well as 'the technical control of his work'. Teachers of English should help, but only incidentally, in personal growth and social change (1.4) and in extending the range of experience (1.9). Finally, English has a role, shared with teachers of other subjects, in training the 'technical' aspects of communicating on a range of topics in a range of situations, including the study of other school subjects (1.10 and elsewhere).

Approaches to the teaching of English in England and Wales

John Dixon (1967, p.1) suggested that there were essentially 'three models or images' of English as a curriculum subject, embodied in British educational policy and practice. These were: the language skills model; the cultural heritage model; and the personal growth model. In the following sections I use Dixon's models to discuss some developments in the teaching of an English curriculum in Britain in the twentieth century.

Language and 'skills'

During the twentieth century primary schools became increasingly child-centred. In this they were guided from 1905 by a Ministry of Education series of *Handbooks of Suggestions for teachers and others engaged in the work of public elementary schools*. Interestingly, the influence came from the USA in the early part of the twentieth century, although by the 1970s the Bullock Report (DES, 1975) noted considerable interest from the USA in the British child-centred approach to primary education. As the then Minister of Education for England and Wales puts it in the 1959 Handbook, 'we have in this country a tradition of independence and vitality amongst the teachers which guarantees that new knowledge and experience is quickly translated into new courses' (HMSO, 1959, p. iii). The 'Prefatory Note' then indicates a major change in primary education: 'The 1937 *Suggestions* stressed the change in emphasis in educational thought and practice from the subjects of instruction to the child' (p. v). There is advice on language, including not only reading and writing, but also oral aspects (though rather little of any note is said) and on handwriting, that has a section of its own. The whole tone is gentle and tolerant and the suggestions very much permissive.

It seems from this publication that the Newbolt Report's proposals for the teaching of pronunciation were not implemented, at least by this time, except that, according to the Handbook, those with speech problems may need help as may Welsh children learning English. In other respects the approach to language is one of the child discovering with the teacher's gentle guidance.

By the early 1960s, the English language curriculum in secondary education was very much reading and writing (with, to exaggerate only a little) the writing known as language and the reading as literature. Even though most children did not take external examinations the demands of the English language ordinary level General Certificate of Education (GCE) dominated. There were several examining boards but all included the writing of essays, précis and comprehension; grammatical analysis had largely disappeared by the 1960s.

The GCE was the national education examination, normally taken at about 16 years (ordinary level) and 18 years (advanced level). The ordinary level has now been replaced by the General Certificate of Secondary Education (GCSE).

The Schools Council *Language in Use* project (Doughty et al. 1971; Doughty and Doughty, 1974) had attempted to integrate learning about language with learning how to use language. More recently, we can see in Britain a return to the study of language in use, what the Newbolt report called the scientific study of language, in the introduction of advanced level (i.e. pre-university) examinations on the study of English language including papers on such topics as 'Varieties of English'. This development is influenced by the growth of departments of linguistics in British universities in the 1960s and 1970s (though they have since declined considerably). Other developments which continued from the 1970s through the 1980s include the increased attention given to listening and speaking, influenced by the work of Andrew Wilkinson (1965) who coined the word 'oracy' as a parallel to 'literacy'. In the late 1980s the government set up a National Oracy Project. This encouraged teachers to give higher priority to the use and development of spoken English among their pupils.

Literature and 'cultural heritage'

The Newbolt Report had sanctioned and encouraged the teaching of literature in schools at all levels. However, the Committee appeared reluctant to have English substituted for the Greek and Roman classics and only proposed it on grounds of necessity. 'The Classics then remain, and will always remain, among the best of our inherited possessions, and for all truly civilized people they will always be not only a possession but a vital and enduring one. Nevertheless, it is now, and probably will be for a long time as far as we can foresee, impossible to make use of the Classics as a fundamental part of a national system of education'. This last sentence seems to suggest that, somehow, though in the perhaps far distant future, the classical languages might be learned by all rather than a select few: it is a measure of the Classics' predominance in British education well into this century that their subsequent rapid decline could not be predicted.

The second book in this series, *Using English: from conversation to canon* (Maybin and Mercer (eds), 1996), discusses the development of literary canons in English.

A member of the Newbolt Committee, Arthur Quiller-Couch, later Professor of English Literature at Cambridge, published *The Art of Reading* in 1920 and Ezra Pound, the poet and literary critic, published the *ABC of Reading* in 1934. Both of these books, and much other literary criticism of the time, are about the establishment of a **canon** of English Literature. The century has seen a considerable broadening in the lists of books deemed worthy for study, so much so that recent attempts in the national curriculum (mentioned later in this chapter and the next one) to prescribe only limited reading of highly selected great authors seem rather unfashionable and irrelevant.

However, one has to appreciate the conflict between English, with its almost infinite range of reading material, and the Classics which constituted a virtually finite selection. It was unlikely that many undiscovered Greek and Roman texts would emerge and those that had survived were sufficiently few in number for the literate to be conversant with them and to recognize each other's allusions to them. The study of the Classics in this sense provided a shared elite body of knowledge. How was the English curriculum to compete?

English studies initially competed by emphasizing discrimination. Whereas the Newbolt Committee had aimed at the formation of a national culture, influential literary critics at Cambridge, notably F.R. Leavis, showed increasing rejection of the unified culture that was becoming predominant. *Mass Civilisation and Minority Culture* (Leavis, 1930) and *Culture and Environment* (Leavis and Thompson, 1933) together with the journal *Scrutiny* had a considerable influence on the teaching of English, especially in grammar schools.

There was something in the radicalism of Leavis and his attacks on mass culture that fired his students. Fred Inglis, then a well-known writer on the teaching of English, now a professor of media studies, wrote:

> Leavis's students went out to teach, and to teach that industrial culture attacked and attenuated some of the deepest meaning of our lives; that these depredations were more visible in our everyday language and its many embodiments but particularly in its imaginative forms, and that the one true way to resist these advances was to counterpoise against them the redemptive forces of great literature. These gave you the test for the death of the living language in everyday life. To keep the English language up was sufficient purpose in a man's life, for language carries, defines, and makes universal the inaccessible meanings of a human community.
>
> (Inglis, 1977, p. 41)

In a similar vein, George Sampson, a member of the Newbolt Committee and often credited with having caused it to be set up, argued that 'it is the purpose of education, not to prepare children for their occupations, but to prepare children against their occupations' (Sampson, 1921, p. 11). This anticommercial strand, to be found also in the Newbolt Report, was to lead to an elitism derived from radicalism that worked *against* attempts at forming a common culture. Terry Eagleton (1976, p. 14) writing from a Marxist standpoint considered that 'the confusion of revolutionary "vanguard" and "elite" was the precise effect of *Scrutiny's* inherent contradiction, as an ideological force locked in complicity with the very society it spiritually castigated'.

Leavis's advocacy of **practical criticism** was, perhaps, more tangibly influential on the teaching of English than his other ideas. In *Education and the University* he argues:

> Analysis ... is the process by which we seek to attain a complete reading of the poem – a reading that approaches as nearly as possible to the perfect reading ... What we call analysis is, of course, a constructive or creative process ... Valid analytical practice is a strengthening of the sense of relevance: scrutiny of the parts must be at the same time an effort towards fuller realization of the whole, and all appropriate play of intelligence, being also an exercise of the sense of value, is controlled by an implicit concern for a total value-judgement.
>
> (Leavis, 1943, pp. 70–1)

In practical criticism a text was regarded as context free; knowledge of the author's background, purpose in writing and so on being considered irrelevant. The critic could exercise judgement without this 'irrelevant' knowledge. While such an approach was useful for examination purposes and served to distance English texts from life, much as the classical texts were distanced, it now seems to elevate opinionatedness and idiosyncrasy.

Literature was, of course, studied outside the Leavisite tradition, but the influence of Leavis has been considerable. Practical criticism is argued for in the Bullock Report, which devotes one of its chapters to 'literature, which to many teachers is the most rewarding form of the child's encounter with language' (DES, 1975, 9.1). The arguments for a shared literary culture have by then largely disappeared: the process of language has overtaken the content of literature, except of course for those specifically studying English literature.

'Personal growth'

This approach to teaching English is embodied in the words *Growth through English* (Dixon, 1967), the title of a report of an influential meeting between English curriculum specialists from the USA and Britain, known as the Dartmouth conference. It tends to emphasize children's personal writing (as opposed to functional writing) as a means of developing self-awareness and aesthetic sensitivity.

It has also included more social concerns, since if English is defined as a process of growth (rather than in terms of its content) then its subject matter can be very broad indeed. In one instance, a British teacher like Christopher Searle (1977) 'committed to a socialist transformation of society and the transformation of the nature of the school itself' could claim that the 'classroom is a vital powerhouse' for topics such as class conflict and racism. More commonly topic work, on a range of topics with children choosing their own, would form part of secondary English.

English has been seen as distinctive in the curriculum in that it is 'all pervasive and yet has relatively little subject matter of its own' (Central Advisory Council for Education (CACE), 1983, p. 159) – which makes it hard to be clear on what to include or exclude. Because of its large 'process' element English has been seen more recently as lending itself particularly well to an approach influenced by behavioural objectives, that set out specifically what children should be able to do. This is in strong contrast to approaches that emphasized personal development at the child's pace and often in a barely defined direction.

The three models I have used to discuss the content of the English curriculum are rarely found in a 'pure' state: various curriculum projects and reports, as well as the professional practices of English teachers, are often influenced by ideas relating to more than one model. A good illustration of such eclecticism from the latter part of this century is the National Writing Project, set up in the 1980s by the British Government. This was aimed at increasing teachers' understanding of their pupils' writing, so that they could develop pupils' own awareness of written English and their effectiveness as writers. In its philosophy, the project embodied much of the self-expressive, 'personal growth' philosophy of teaching English that has been promoted by writers like Dixon (1967); this can be seen in its emphasis on allowing children's literacy to emerge through experience (National Writing Project, 1989a). But with its equally strong emphasis on ideas like 'writing for specific audiences' (National Writing Project, 1989b) it also shared practical and functional concerns, though not the preoccupation with correctness often associated with the 'skills' model.

Later developments

Several social and political factors have influenced the development of the English curriculum in different English-speaking countries during the latter part of the twentieth century. In the USA and Canada there has, historically, been an emphasis on testing and that has had the effect of narrowing the curriculum. Also, in North America text book publishers have been very influential in shaping the curriculum and there has been little federal intervention or direction.

Developments in the Australian curriculum have come from a variety of sources, including federal initiatives, local initiatives within the States and

Territories, the concurrent development of the English teachers' associations in the States and the establishment of the (national) Association for the Teaching of English, which gave debates about English teaching both a local and a national voice. In 1989 a commonly agreed 'national framework' was established for eight key curriculum areas including English. The framework provides guidelines for the States and Territories to design their own syllabuses and assessment arrangements.

The New Zealand tradition of education has been characterized by Stuart Middleton, President of the New Zealand Association for the Teaching of English, as: 'one of liberal humanism embedded in a national obsession with assessment tempered by an almost intuitive capacity among New Zealand teachers of English to take an eclectic approach to language education' (in an unpublished speech).

New Zealand has always had a national curriculum, but this is now seen as a set of general guidelines; teachers have had considerable involvement in the development of the English curriculum and are also able to interpret this to meet the needs of their own students.

By contrast, the UK has seen increasing centralization in decision making about various aspects of the curriculum with the government's imposition since the late 1980s of a national curriculum for England and Wales (with distinct though related curricula for Scotland and Northern Ireland). English language teaching is now officially seen as consisting of four aspects: reading, writing, speaking, and listening. In England and Wales these aspects are assessed according to national criteria at regular intervals in a child's career, not only for diagnostic purposes but also so that information on the performance of schools can be published. The curriculum is set by the government through statutorily enforceable 'programmes of study' and by the national assessment. This is in great contrast to what was foreseen not very long ago even in official reports. *English in the 1980s* (Schools Council, 1979) begins (p. 11) by referring to the freedom of the teacher: 'there is probably no group of teachers in the world so free to work out what they regard as the most appropriate teaching for their pupils'.

❖ ❖ ❖ ❖ ❖

Activity 5.5   *(Reading C)*

Please now work through Reading C, 'The development of a national curriculum for English in England and Wales', by Sue Brindley. This provides a case study of recent educational policy development in Britain. Note, in particular, the change from a system characterized by diversity of practice to one in which the government has attempted to exercise far greater control over the curriculum; the process of policy development – for example, the tensions that developed between members of government committees/working parties and the politicians who had appointed them; and what aspects of the curriculum proved controversial.

Many of the controversies outlined here are revisited in the following chapter.

❖ ❖ ❖ ❖ ❖

5.6 CONCLUSION

This chapter has focused on several aspects of English teaching. I have discussed the varying status of English as a language of education: its development, in England, from a vernacular language where the eventual goal was an education in Latin, to a language taught in its own right; its association in certain contexts (Wales and Ireland were given as examples) with the suppression of other languages and cultures; its use in colonial contexts such as India, where it replaced the Indian classical languages and came also to be seen as a threat to modern Indian languages and to Indian culture.

Against this background, I have been concerned with the development of English as a subject: the continuing expansion of English in terms of its content; and debates, continuing through the nineteenth and twentieth centuries, about what should be taught, to whom, and for what purposes. I mentioned different approaches to the teaching of reading – a 'reading for meaning' approach as opposed to an approach that broke written language down into its component parts – that have been evident since the earliest times and that, as you can see in the next chapter, are still the subject of debate today. But the controversies surrounding English are not simply pedagogical: English teaching has been seen, to a large extent, as having to do with the transmission of cultural values. It has been concerned at different times (and sometimes among different groups at the same time) with the inculcation of 'discipline' and 'morality'; with keeping people in their allotted place; with providing access to political rights; with promoting national unity; and with providing a general, liberal education. The association between English teaching and cultural values is equally strong today, and is discussed further in the following chapter.

Acknowledgement

I am grateful to Greg Brooks for comments on a draft of this chapter.

Reading A

ENGLISH AND EMPIRE: TEACHING ENGLISH IN NINETEENTH-CENTURY INDIA

Anthea Fraser Gupta

When Britain, through the East India Company, edged its way into India over the eighteenth century, a new type of expansion had begun. At first the aim was to infiltrate the existing power structures rather than to overcome them. Indian structures, and the Indians, were manipulated to facilitate British rule. Later, Indians needed to be acculturated into their place in British India, and their education became a central issue. In nineteenth-century India, Britain first faced the possibility of having to teach English to a body of people who were important to Britain and to continuing British rule in India, and whose literary and educational backgrounds were in languages other than English.

At its greatest extent British India included modern Bangladesh, India and Pakistan, as well as Burma and other territories, including the Straits Settlements (Singapore, Penang and Malacca), all of which were administered from Calcutta.

Should English be taught?

The first major issue was whether it was desirable to offer Indians a European style of education using English, or to support the traditional Indian styles and languages of learning. This has come to be known as the debate between the **Anglicists** and the **Orientalists**. Some summaries give the impression that the Orientalists supported local languages and the Anglicists wanted to stamp them out. In reality it was more complicated than that. The Orientalists supported the continued use of the classical languages of Indian tradition (Sanskrit, Persian and Arabic), which were not spoken as native languages. The Anglicists gave support to English as the classical language. Neither the Orientalists nor the Anglicists were concerned with the suppression of the local *vernaculars* (languages that were spoken on an everyday basis and which also had a literary tradition): in both cases it was accepted that the first experience of education would be through the vernacular.

Britain had gained control of significant areas of India by the end of the eighteenth century. From the 1780s onwards, support was given to developing education in India in the Indian tradition. Orientalists established schools teaching Sanskrit, Persian and Arabic. Some of these schools were for Indians, while others, especially the Fort William College in Calcutta, were for East India Company officers. In the same Orientalist tradition, Stamford Raffles in 1823 planned for a college in Singapore, which would serve the needs both of the 'sons of the higher order of natives and others' and of the East India Company's staff who needed to learn local languages (especially Malay and Chinese). It would also serve to develop the local languages and preserve their literature (Buckley, 1902, p. 122).

Even in the eighteenth century, there were a number of English-medium schools in India (Nurullah and Naik, 1951), mostly under the control of missionaries, and many primarily targeted at European and Eurasian children, converts to Christianity, and orphans. The products of these schools were to provide the first generation of teachers. But only after 1835 was there sustained *official* support for English-medium education for other inhabitants of India and the Straits Settlements. In the Straits Settlements, the college Stamford Raffles had proposed opened in 1837 as an elite English-medium school, which it remains to this day.

The British found in India a situation that was quite familiar to them from Britain. Sanskrit, Persian and Arabic corresponded to Latin and Greek in Britain, while the vernacular languages corresponded to English in Britain. It seemed natural for education to begin in the vernacular, and for later stages of the education of the 'sons of the higher order' to develop the classical languages. It began to be suggested from 1814 (Sinha, 1957, p. 8) that the English language and European knowledge could be used to some extent, and that European texts could be translated into the Indian classical languages. From here it was a small step to the promotion of English as a replacement for the classical languages which in turn led to the virtual disappearance of the use of Persian in India, and to the retreat of Sanskrit and Arabic to limited, mainly religious, spheres. With the spread of English in the Empire, it also came to present a threat to the vernaculars. Gandhi (quoted in Nurullah and Naik, 1951, p. 564) referred to the pre-eminence of English as a 'canker' which had made Indians forget and devalue their mother tongues.

English for science and career opportunities

There were pragmatic reasons for boys (girls were not expected to have careers) to learn English: in 1774 English had become the language of the Supreme Court in Calcutta and opened up posts to those with English skills (Mittra, 1878, p. 4). As job possibilities grew in several governmental sectors for those with English skills, the advantages of learning English became apparent to many ambitious families. The government also saw the need for Indian public servants. The English-medium Hindu College (established in Calcutta in 1816) was a secular school, under the control of Indians. Only later did it receive official support.

In December 1823, when a new Sanskrit college was planned for Calcutta, Rammohun Roy, one of the prominent Indians involved with the Hindu College, wrote a letter to the Governor General, Lord Amherst, to request further official support for English education. In his letter he indicated that the main aim of English was to give access to European science:

> we understand that the Government in England had ordered a considerable sum of money to be annually devoted to the instructions of its Indian subjects. We were filled with sanguine hopes that this sum would be laid out in employing European gentlemen of talents and education to instruct the natives of India, in Mathematics, Natural Philosophy, Chemistry, Anatomy, and other useful sciences, which the natives of Europe have carried to a degree of perfection that has raised them above the inhabitants of other parts of the world.
>
> (Cited in Mittra, 1878, p. 9)

The earliest impetus for official support for English education did not come from government sources but from Indians responding to their perceived needs for their own social and educational development. By the early nineteenth century even the oriental colleges held classes in English, and English schools had been established by both missionaries and by Indian donors in many parts of India (see Sinha, 1957, and Mahmood, 1895).

English for the transmission of European cultural values

Many of the Europeans who promoted English saw it as likely to improve the moral quality of Indians. In 1824, the Committee of Public Instruction (these committees were established in 1823 to look into the Indian needs for education) gave the Hindu College a favourable report:

> A command of the English language and a familiarity with its literature and science have been acquired to an extent rarely equalled by any schools in Europe ... The moral effect has been remarkable and an impatience of the instructions of Hinduism and a disregard for its ceremonies are openly avowed by young men of respectable birth and talents, and entertained by many more who outwardly conform to the practices of their country men.

(Cited in Mittra, 1878, p. 34).

Indeed teachers and students of the Hindu College did give offence to Hindu orthodoxy by their exploration of beef eating, Christianity, and free-thinking.

The British saw Hinduism as idolatrous superstition, although they gave slightly greater respect to Islam. The weakening of Hinduism was seen as a sign of moral advancement, as, of course, was conversion to Christianity. While some schools were avowedly proselytizing, others were secular in intent. Both alternatives were likely to deter Muslims from sending their children to English-medium schools, where they were grossly under-represented (Mahmood, 1895). The extent to which the teaching of English was linked to the promotion of Christianity is a recurring issue (to this day), as is the wider issue of the exposure to 'European' or 'Western' values through texts in English. Phillipson (1992) discusses how aid to Third World countries in the form of English language teaching may still be seen as not only advancing scientific and technical education, but also as transmitting the cultural values of the donor countries (principally USA and UK), and creating new modes of thought. Whether this is evaluated positively or negatively will of course depend on the commentator's cultural values. For example, the language planning policy of modern day Singapore incorporates measures intended to neutralize what are seen as bad 'Western values' linked with English (including liberalism, welfarism, individualism, free speech, free love), while English is described as necessary for access to science, technology and world trade. In a reversal of the nineteenth-century European view it is the Asians who are presented as moral and the 'Westerners' as depraved.

The support of the government switched decisively from the Orientalist to the Anglicist position in 1835, when a resolution was passed which transferred government support to English education. Justification for this had been provided by the infamous Minute of Lord Macaulay, the new president of the General Committee of Public Instruction. Macaulay's Minute is generally quoted as the definitive statement of the Anglicist movement.

Macaulay argued that the wealth of literature and science in English, and its global spread, meant that 'of all foreign tongues, the English tongue is that which would be the most useful to our Native subjects' (cited in Mahmood, 1895, p. 50). He put forward a very strong version of the Anglicist position, that the native languages had 'no books on any subject which deserve to be compared to our own' and argued for English as a civilizing force. 'The languages of western Europe civilised Russia. I cannot doubt that they will do for the Hindoo what they have done for the Tartar' (cited in Mahmood, 1895, p.50). English education for the elite would have a trickle-down effect:

> We must at present do our best to form … a class of persons Indian in blood and colour, but English in tastes, in opinions, in morals and in intellect. To that class we may leave it to refine the vernacular dialects from the western nomenclature, and to render them by degrees fit vehicles for conveying knowledge to the great mass of the population.
>
> (Cited in Mahmood, 1895)

The promotion of English science and history would put accurate information within the reach of the natives, so creating an emergence from ignorance and barbarity, and the morals and religion of the natives would be much improved. In 1836 Macaulay wrote to his father:

> It is my firm belief that, if our plans of education are followed up, there will not be a single idolater among the respectable classes in Bengal thirty years hence. And this will be effected without any efforts to proselytise; without the smallest interference with religious liberty; merely by the natural operation of knowledge and reflection.
>
> (Cited in Trevelyan, 1909, p. 330)

Reading this extreme version of the Anglicist position, it is difficult to understand why so many Indians supported English education. However, some of the Anglicists held secular views which did not see the Indian tradition as entirely worthless. By the end of the century it was apparent that hopes of mass conversion to Christianity 'were entirely fallacious' (Mahmood, 1895, p. 70).

However, in some settings the Anglicist movement was linked with the promotion of vernaculars as in Bengal where it resulted in the flowering of literature and the arts which was to be known as the Bengali Renaissance (Sengupta, 1979, p. iv) and which was one of the roots of the nationalist movement in India. Indeed, even in the eighteenth-century opinion was divided as to whether exposure to European values would lead the natives to willing submission to British rule, or would lead to a desire to assert their independence (Charles Grant, cited in Mahmood, 1895).

English for the elite

What all the participants – Indian and European, Orientalist and Anglicist – shared was a principal concern with the education of the (male) elite. English medium education of a high quality was envisaged only for the 'respectable class of native'. Charitable schools existed for the benefit of orphans, and of poor Europeans, and their 'bastard children'. However, most children in English-medium schools were expected to pay fees, or win scholarships. The grant-in-aid system, established in 1854, required schools to charge a fee. The legacy of this elitist tradition is still with us, as in many of the postcolonial countries, including India, a high level of ability in English either indicates or defines an elite. Elites can secure the learning of English for their children, and skill in English gives admission to the elite. In many of the postcolonial nations English is still secured principally through private education.

Both elite Indians and Europeans were concerned that people should know their place in society. Mukherjee (1970) reports the fears of the Calcutta upper classes that the spread of English education would hurt their own interests, causing the lower classes to become dissatisfied. Others argued (Mahmood, 1895) that 'instruction of the lower classes' would promote 'sobriety and order'. In India, as at home, the Europeans made a sharp distinction between the classes, being happy to extend to the elite the best of European education. In many parts of the empire distinctions were drawn between different ethnic groups. In the Straits Settlements, the Malays were seen as suited for a life as fishers and farmers, and Malay-medium elementary education for them was supported by government, while their aristocracy were offered a European education (Bloom, 1986; Fraser Gupta, 1994). English-medium education was seen as likely to attract the business-minded Chinese. Africans were sometimes seen as likely to be limited to menial and clerical positions (Phillipson, 1992).

Few girls learned the classical languages in Britain, and similarly it was not expected that many Indian girls would learn English. The imperative was to give girls elementary education and at first any girls who went further had to attend boys' schools. The first post-elementary school for Indian girls finally opened (in Calcutta) in 1849. The President of the Council for Education, Drinkwater Bethune, emphasized that in boys' education the mother tongue had to be cultivated, while English was also resorted to 'on account of the superiority of its literature', but in the case of the education of girls 'we shall make Bengali the foundation and resort to English only for some of those subsidiary advantages and when we know that the communication of such knowledge is not in opposition to the wishes of the parents' (Sinha, 1957, p. 42). English-medium education was extended to very few Indian girls. Families whose sons had been given some English education early in the nineteenth century were not likely to extend the learning of English to their daughters until the twentieth. Mahmood (1985, p. ii) did not discuss female education because 'English education, especially of the higher type has made no perceptible progress among the Native female population of India.' In both India and the Straits Settlements, the girls' schools were predominantly attended by Eurasians, Europeans, Armenians, Jews and Parsis until the end of the century. The disproportionate presence of these minorities became more noticeable the higher the level of education (Nurullah and Naik, 1951, Gupta, 1994).

Teaching methods

There was a sometimes tacit, sometimes spelled-out, assumption that before beginning English education, boys would have mastered their own languages. In fact skill in Bengali was a requirement in some of the early English schools of Calcutta (Mittra, 1878, p. 51).

One would expect more concern with the methods of English education than we in fact find. In the early years translation seems to have been a main method, modelled on the teaching of Latin in Britain. Reading literature and science were the ultimate goals of learning English. After all, the aim was to teach English 'as a classical language, and as a means of acquiring a knowledge of the European discoveries' (Minute of 1823 by Mountstuart Elphinstone, Governor of Bombay, cited in Mahmood, 1895, p.39).

Macaulay made this clear:

> What is meant by teaching a boy a foreign language? Surely this, the teaching him what words in the foreign language correspond to certain words in his own vernacular language, then enabling him to translate from the foreign language into his own vernacular tongue and vice versa.

(Cited in Sinha, 1957, p. 24)

In the schools of the Straits Settlements, English was often taught through instruction in Malay, and students were examined in their ability to translate from Malay to English (Europeans were exempted); Figure 1 shows a page from *English*

347—Where do you live ?	347—Mana tinggal ?
348—Where does he live ?	348—Mana dia tinggal ?
349—What is his address ?	349—Mana dia tinggal ?
350—Which do you choose ?	350—Yang mana mau pilih ?
351—Which does he want ?	351—Yang mana dia mau ?
352—Who shot that deer ?	352—Siapa tembak itu rusa ?
353—Who stolè his watch ?	353—Siapa churi dia punia jam ?
354—Who tied them together ?	354—Siapa ikat ?
355—Who told you so ?	355—Siapa kata begitu ?
356—Whose fault is this ?	356—Siapa punia salah ini ?
357—What a lovely day !	357—Ini hari baniak bagus !
358—Why doesn't he speak ?	358—Mengapa dia tidak chakap ?
359—Why is he crying ?	359—Mengapa dia men-angis ?
360—Why, you ran away !	360—Tetapi lu sudah lari !
361—Wish him good-bye.	361—Kasih tabek sama dia.
362—Say good-bye to him.	362—Kasih tabek sama dia.
363—You don't say so !	363—Baniak heiran !
364—Your face is bleeding.	364—Lu punia muka berdara.
365—A tiger is very fierce.	365—Harimau baniak garang.
366—About twenty men were killed.	366—Dekat dua-puloh orang kena bunoh.
367—All his brothers are dead.	367—Samua dia punia abang adik sudah mati.
368—Am I to go now ?	368—Skarang sahya musti pergi ?
369—Are there no more left ?	369—Tada lagi ?

Figure 1   Extract from Hullett's book showing sentences glossed in Bazaar malay, the pidginized lingua franca of the Straits Settlements

Sentences with Equivalents in Colloquial Malay (Hullett, 1887) which was written as an introduction to English for the students at the premier boys' school in Singapore, Raffles Institution (mentioned earlier in this reading). The use of translation became hard where, as in the Straits Settlements, the pupils (and teachers) came from a variety of language backgrounds. By the end of the century, the 'direct method' of teaching, using only English, had become common and the advocation of this method was often linked with a desire to promote spoken English. The oscillation between 'foreign language' teaching methods and 'direct methods' has remained in the countries of the former Empire to this day, preference for one or the other depending on the language background of the students as well as on changes in fashion.

Acknowledgements

I would like to thank S.N. Mukherjee for his comments on an early draft of this article and Cassandra Yue Chee Tieny for finding Hullett's book.

References

BLOOM, D. (1986) 'The English language and Singapore: a critical survey' in K. KAPUR (ed.) *Singapore Studies*, Singapore, Singapore University Press.

BUCKLEY, C.B. (1902) *An Anecdotal History of Old Times in Singapore*, Singapore, Fraser and Neave. [Reference to the reprint of 1965, Kuala Lumpur, University of Malaya Press.]

GUPTA, A.F. (1994) *The Step Tongue: children's English in Singapore*, Clevedon, Multilingual Matters.

MAHMOOD, S. (1895) *A History of English Education in India: its rise, development, progress, present condition and prospects being a narrative of the various phases of educational policy and measures adopted under British rule from its beginning to the present period (1781 to 1893)*, Aligarh, Muhammadan Anglo-Oriental College.

MITTRA, P.C. ([1878] 1979) *A Biographical Sketch of David Hare* in SENGUPTA, G.G. (ed.), Calcutta, Jijnasa.

MUKHERJEE, S.N. (1970) 'Class, caste and politics in Calcutta, 1815–38' in LEACH, E. and MUKHERJEE, S.N. (eds) *Elites in South Asia*, Cambridge, Cambridge University Press.

NURULLAH, S. and NAIK, J. P. (1951) *A History of Education in India (during the British period)*, Bombay, Macmillan.

PHILLIPSON, R. (1992) *Linguistic Imperialism*, Oxford, Oxford University Press.

SENGUPTA, G. G. (ed.) (1979) *A Biographical Sketch of David Hare*, Calcutta, Jijnasa.

SINHA, N. (1957) 'Beginning of western education' in GUPTA, N.R. and P. (eds) *Hundred Years of the University of Calcutta*, Calcutta, University of Calcutta.

TREVELYAN, G. O. (1909) *The Life and Letters of Lord Macaulay*, London, Longmans, Green and Co.

This reading was specially commissioned for this book.

Reading B

THE CORRESPONDING SOCIETIES: WORKING-CLASS LITERACY AND POLITICAL REFORM

Colin Lankshear and Moira Lawler

Stimulated by middle-class initiatives for political reform and radical currents engendered by the American and French Revolutions – including the work of Thomas Paine and the reactionary backlash to his *Rights of Man* – the London Corresponding Society [LCS] was founded in January 1792 by eight men seeking a political association which would represent the working classes. The Society's general aim was to arouse nationwide commitment to pursuing political reform and to establish links between groups throughout Britain involved in reform struggle. Its specific goals were universal suffrage and annual parliaments. Membership was open to any man who, being proposed by two members, affirmed their belief that every adult had the right to vote and vowed they would promote the cause of parliamentary reform 'by all justifiable means'. Subscription was by payment of one penny per week, and the resulting income was used to foster correspondence with other societies and to publish literature which would promote political reform ...

To understand more fully the nature and role of literacy within the work of corresponding societies we must turn to their more overtly educational activity: in discussion meetings and publishing. The LCS provides the model here. Each division ran weekly discussion meetings. After new members had been admitted, the delegates had reported on the last delegates' meeting, and the division had voted on questions directed by the delegates' committee to the membership at large, members would listen to a reading of a reform pamphlet or newspaper article. (Many members were, of course, unable to read). Discussion would follow. In addition, political broadsides, pamphlets, and books were sold and circulated, and reform songs sung. This form of organized cooperative self-education was complemented by Sunday evening reading and discussion meetings and regular debates.

The nature and educational quality of the division meetings and Sunday evenings varied considerably. At their 'roughest' they seem unlikely vehicles for reflection and close analysis. 'Almost everyone speaks and there is always a great noise, till the delegate gets up. People grow very outrageous and won't wait, then the delegate gets up and tries to soften them' [Thompson, 1963]. At their most sophisticated, though, they reflect a unique and powerful pedagogy. Francis Place offers an inspiring account of the division meetings and Sunday evenings in which he personally participated. According to him the discussions and debates opened to members 'views which they had never before taken'. Members were compelled by these discussions 'to find reasons for their opinions and to tolerate others'. Sunday evening meetings were often held in members' homes and, in Place's view, 'were very important meetings and the best results to the parties followed'. These meetings followed a typical pattern.

> The chairman (a different man each Sunday) read aloud a chapter of a book. During the ensuing week, the book was passed around for the men to read at home. The next Sunday the chairman read the chapter again, pausing three times for comments. No one was to speak more than once

during the reading, and anyone who had not spoken during the first two pauses was expected to speak at the end. After that there was a general discussion during which no one could speak on a subject a second time until everyone who wished to had spoken once.

[Cited in Thale, 1983]

The material read and discussed had a definite radical and liberating flavour. Paine was a favourite author, although any work asserting the political and social rights of citizens, and analyzing how and why these were denied in daily life, was considered appropriate. In the words of a member of the Sheffield Society, reading and discussion were intended

> to enlighten the people, to show the people the reason, the ground of all their complaints and sufferings; when a man works hard for thirteen or fourteen hours of the day, the week through, and is not able to maintain his family; that is what I understand of it; to show the people the ground of this; why they were not able.

[Cited in Brown, 1918]

... The Corresponding Societies were also heavily involved in publishing. Webb speaks of the astonishing range of material which has survived, and produces evidence that publishing was on a very large scale. It is estimated that 200,000 copies of Paine's *The Rights of Man* had been sold before 1794. This massive circulation was assisted by the creative active literacy of corresponding societies. In Manchester, for instance, a radical leader was asked to abridge the book so that it could sell for less than a shilling. The Sheffield Society produced an edition for sixpence. Besides such larger works societies published their official addresses, pamphlets, radical newspapers and magazines, collections of political ballads, periodicals, satirical pieces, broadsides, printed handbills, and even catalogues of low priced reform publications. The outcome of this indigenous publishing activity was that working people had access to an enormous body of critical, innovative, (often humorously) penetrating, politically enlightening and inspiring literature. This freed working-class readers from the ideological grip of the upper class – whereby workers were immersed in a view of the world that reflected and enhanced the interests of their oppressors.

Unfortunately it is impossible to do justice here to the complexity, vitality, and richness of the Corresponding Societies. They merit study in their own right. Sufficient has been said, however, to situate empirically two central ideas. First, we have seen in the life and work of Corresponding Societies a literacy being forged in the context of a group (in this case a social class which was becoming increasingly conscious of itself as a distinct class) pursuing its interests and aspirations under conditions characterized by extreme inequality of access to structural power. Indeed, it was precisely the awareness of being completely excluded from formal political power by which to exercise some control over their social and economic conditions, and thereby promote their class interests, that drove these working men to actively pursue political reform: to get a hold on some formal power as a means to confronting and redressing their oppression. The conception and practice of literacy which emerged was tailored to pursuing the political enlightenment, organization, and mobilization of a social class.

'Proper literacy', a term coined by Lankshear and Lawler, refers to knowing about the literature (i.e. what is written) rather than simply being able to decode or re-encode a written text. It also involves not just reading but writing and enables people to operate more fully. It is close to the Latin 'literatus', which itself has influenced our modern term 'illiterate', which is often used as a perjorative term to mean ignorant (of books) rather than totally unable to read and write. The approach of Freire, a Brazilian educator, to functional literacy was to see it as enabling people to participate fully (e.g. politically) in society and particularly emphasizes writing, whereby people structure the world and influence others. This is in strong contrast to functional literacy programmes in, for example, the USA and third world emphasizing job related literacy.

Second, the literacy that involved was a proper literacy: indeed, it was a properly functional literacy in the manner of Freire. The form and content of reading and discussion – the *pedagogy* – was, at its best, a powerful force toward working people assuming greater control over their circumstances and destiny, and doing so in a rational and informed manner. 'Here were methods devised by a workers' society, of a kind to encourage self-confidence, clear thinking, and the capacity for self-expression' [Simon, 1960]. There may not have been much in the way of creating original abstract theory. (This, of course, is hardly surprising given that the working class was systematically denied all but the most minimal forms of formal instruction and intellectual development. Quite simply, working people lacked an organic intellectual tradition, a basis, from which to develop their own original theory). There was, however, a genius for transforming theories, ideas, beliefs, and arguments into active pursuit of class interests; a gift for political organization which gave material substance and real political force to newly won ideas.

These ideas, and the organized forms of political practice and activity – mediated by literacy – through which they were simultaneously acquired and expressed, became the basis of the working-class movement itself: the early foundations of political consciousness, organization and sustained struggle, which bore tangible fruits in the latter half of the nineteenth century and the early decades of the twentieth. 'The same practical genius which built up the trade unions in the nineteenth century is evident in the educational movement of the Corresponding Societies: in the system of division meetings, delegation and correspondence, as well as in the organization and control of mass meetings, and the adept use of the press, sympathetic booksellers and friendly publishers. Literacy – proper literacy – was both a vehicle and an outcome of this genius' Brown [1918].

In fact the literacy conceived and practised by Corresponding Societies helps us to specify more closely the ideal of proper literacy as extending people's control over their lives and enhancing their ability to deal rationally with their life decisions …

[There was, however, sustained oppostion to the Corresponding Societies; this took the form of legislation designed to prevent 'seditious' meetings; propaganda to counter reform literature; and the publication of alternative 'safe' reading matter for the poor.]

In the end coercion and hegemony prevailed. The Corresponding Societies were defeated. The distinctive literacy and pedagogical form devised and practised in this working-class association was driven out by a combination of legal repression, organized opposition, and stark political reality. The reference to 'stark political reality' is important. For all the ideological work undertaken by Corresponding Societies and their efforts to diffuse a proper literacy among the working classes, the established hegemony of church and king prevailed and continued to dominate *among the lower* as well as the higher social rankings. When it came down to it the majority of working-class people were aligned against reformers; even working-class reformers. The Corresponding Societies began the process of developing a consciousness among working people grounded in their own interests as a class rather than in the interests of classes which oppressed them. But it was just a beginning. Most of the working class remained immersed in a consciousness quite contrary to their own interests. That is, they remained hegemonized. And so, for example, Francis Place had no doubt that the Treason and Sedition Acts were extremely popular among oppressor and oppressed alike.

Infamous as they were, they were popular measures. The people, ay, the mass of the shopkeepers and working people, may be said to have approved them without understanding them. Such was their fear ... that 'the throne and altar' would be destroyed, and that we should be 'deprived of our holy religion'.

[Wallas, 1898]

If one literacy – namely, the proper literacy practised in Corresponding Societies – was a key element in giving rise to fears for the social and political order in the first place, a second literacy – practised in the original Sunday schools and enhanced by anti-reform tractarians – ensured that working-class sympathies were predominantly aligned *against* those who challenged the established order.

References

BROWN, P.A. (1918) *The French Revolution in English History*, London, Allen and Unwin.

SIMON, B. (1960) *Studies in the History of Education 1780–1870*, London, Lawrence and Wishart, p. 181.

THALE, M. (ed.) (1983) *Selections from the Papers of the London Corresponding Society 1792–99*, London, Cambridge University Press.

THOMPSON, E.P. (1963) *The Making of the English Working Class*, Harmondsworth, Penguin.

WALLAS, G. (1898) *The Life of Francis Place*, London, Allen and Unwin.

Source: Lankshear and Lawler, 1987, pp. 84–93

Reading C

THE DEVELOPMENT OF A 'NATIONAL CURRICULUM' FOR ENGLISH IN ENGLAND AND WALES

Sue Brindley

Until 1988, and the Education Reform Act, English teachers in England and Wales (and elsewhere in the UK) were, by and large, free to define English in the classroom in their own terms, within the constraints placed on them by exam syllabuses leading to the General Certificate of Secondary Education (GCSE) examination at 16 years of age. The balance of literature and language, the texts taught and the types of writing undertaken in the classroom were the teachers' choice. English was defined by English teachers, with the notion that the professional judgement of teachers would serve to ensure that pupils enjoyed a wide and varied experience of the subject.

This, inevitably, led to massive diversity in the teaching of English. English teachers' understanding of English as a subject, and their subsequent classroom practice, was shaped by a number of influences. Some teachers taught an English curriculum based on their own experiences of English as pupils. Others were deeply involved in professional debates on both content and pedagogy, many of which challenged fundamental understandings about the domain of English.

Despite occasional concern about English teaching, such as the concern about 'falling standards' in the 1970s that occasioned the setting up of the Bullock Committee of inquiry into the teaching of English, such diversity was not seriously challenged until the 1980s.

Education was high on the political agenda in the late 1980s, with the introduction of the Education Reform Act (1988) by the Conservative government of the day. Among other things, the act empowered the Secretary of State to introduce a common curriculum for pupils of compulsory school age in maintained schools. The selection of subjects for what was to be termed the national curriculum, the specific content of these subjects, their teaching and assessment all aroused some degree of controversy, with English provoking some of the most heated debate. The chart below sets out some of the main events in the development of English in the national curriculum: every stage of policy development detailed here was to prove controversial.

Chart compiled by
Joan Swann.

English in the national curriculum: a timetable of events

1987	Kenneth Baker, Secretary of State for Education, appoints committee of inquiry into the teaching of English chaired by Sir John Kingman. Committee remit is to recommend a model of the English language to serve as a basis for teacher training and professional discussion; and to consider in what ways this model should be made explicit to pupils.
1988	Education Reform Act establishes, among other things, a 'national curriculum' for England and Wales.
	'Kingman Report' submitted, 17 March; published 29 April.
	Working group established on 29 April to prepare proposals for English in the national curriculum; asked to build on the work of the Kingman Committee; chaired by Professor Brian Cox, a member of the Kingman Committee.
	Submission of first version of 'Cox Report', covering the primary years, at the end of September.
1989	Submission of final version of 'Cox Report', including the secondary years, in May.
1989–1990	Publication and introduction into the classroom of attainment targets and programmes of study for 'English in the national curriculum' (based on Cox Report recommendations).
1989–1992	Work carried out on Language in the National Curriculum (LINC) project, directed by Professor Ronald Carter; main aim is to acquaint teachers with the model of language represented in the Kingman Report. Teachers in every school in England and Wales involved in training. Project also produces training materials.
1991	LINC materials completed; these are released for teacher training purposes, but government permission is not granted for their publication.
1992	John Patten, the then Secretary of State for Education, commissions review of English in the national curriculum.
1993	Two versions of a revised English curriculum produced for limited consultation: one in April and one in September.
1994	Further consultation document issued.
1995	Publication of new version of English in the national curriculum.

As the chart shows the establishment of the national curriculum actually began with the setting up of the Kingman Committee of inquiry into the teaching of English in 1987. The Kingman Committee was set up by the then Secretary of State for Education, Kenneth Baker. Its remit was to recommend a model of the English language, whether spoken or written, which would:

i) serve as the basis of how teachers are trained to understand how the English language works;

ii) inform professional discussion of all aspects of English teaching;

iii) recommend the principles which should guide teachers in how far and in what ways the model should be made explicit to pupils, to make them conscious of how language is used in a range of contexts;

iv) recommend what, in general terms, pupils need to know about how the English language works and in consequence what they should have been taught, and be expected to understand, at ages 7, 11 and 16.

The committee's published report had significant implications for the definition of English. Where the Bullock Report, published in the 1970s, had supported language and literature in equal measures, Kingman drew the attention of English teachers to teaching about language in the classroom, and it gave rise to a project – LINC – with substantial government funding to develop materials for teachers. However, neither the report nor the materials had a smooth ride. Brian Cox, a member of the Kingman Committee, gives an indication of some of the to-ing and fro-ing that accompanies such policy development:

> The Kingman report was not well-liked by the Prime Minister [Margaret Thatcher]. When Professor Kingman discovered that his report's recommendations might be rejected, he used the Robert Robinson factor to cajole the civil servants. Robert Robinson, the popular and skilful host of the TV language game, *Call My Bluff*, was a member of the Kingman Committee and signed its recommendations. Would the Prime Minister really find it advisable to appear in public in opposition to the famous Mr Robinson?
>
> (Cox, 1991, p. 3)

The Kingman Report recommended explicit teaching of 'rules and conventions' of language use, in itself controversial because many people have claimed such teaching is unlikely to be effective. But it came out in favour of a modern descriptive approach that took account of language variation and change. It explicitly rejected the kind of traditional grammar teaching that 'gave an inadequate account of the English language by treating it virtually as a branch of Latin, and constructing a rigid prescriptive code rather than a dynamic description of language in use' (p. 3). According to Brian Cox, this did not sit well with the political climate of the day:

> The Kingman Report was not well received by right-wing Conservatives because they wanted a return to the traditional teaching of Latinate grammar, and the report came out firmly against this. Many politicians and journalists were ignorant about problems in the teaching of grammar and about the status of Standard English, and simply desired to reinstate the disciplines of study typical of schoolrooms in the 1930s.
>
> (Cox, 1991, p. 4)

The LINC materials built on and extended the Kingman model: they included discussion of variation and diversity in language use; they saw language as dynamic and changing, and as embodying social and cultural values; and they saw 'intimate connections ... between language and social power, language and culture and language and gender' (1991, p. 1). While the materials were released for teacher training in photocopied form, permission has never been granted for their publication. The box below contains an extract from the LINC reader, *Knowledge about Language and the Curriculum.* Ron Carter, national co-ordinator of the LINC project, discusses the differences between a traditional approach to grammar teaching and what he terms a 'new-style' (or more critical) approach to grammar.

'Old-style' and 'new-style' grammar

The following example from an O level GCE paper (1961) demonstrates clearly what kind of grammatical knowledge was required from school children and what view of the learning process was enshrined in the English curriculum at that time.

> Leaving childhood behind, I soon lost this desire to possess a goldfish. It is difficult to persuade oneself that a goldfish is happy and as soon as we have begun to doubt that some poor creature enjoys living with us we can take no pleasure in its company.

> Using a new line to each, select one example from the above passage of each of the following:

> (i)   an infinitive used as the direct object of a verb

> (ii)   an infinitive used in apposition to a pronoun

> (iii)   a gerund

> (iv)   a present participle

> (v)   a past participle

> (vi)   an adjective used predicatively (i.e. as a complement)

> (vii) a possessive adjective

> (vii) a demonstrative adjective

> (xi)   a reflexive pronoun

> (x)   an adverb of time

> (xi)   an adverb of degree

> (xii) a preposition

> (xiii) a subordinating conjunction

The main test here is of a pupil's ability to identify grammatical forms as a set of discrete items and to label them. Learning how to do this would have involved innumerable practice exercises and a commitment to memory of certain facts including an accompanying metalanguage. It is also not unlikely that this information would have been quickly forgotten after the examination, no matter how intensive the drilling exercises or transmissive the teaching strategies ...

An example of the differences between old-style and new-style grammar can be provided by an examination of the following headlines taken from British national newspapers in 1984 at a time when a national coal strike led to a not inconsiderable polarisation of political positions. The three headlines are taken from (1) the *Guardian* (2) the *Daily Express* and (3) the *Morning Star*.

1.   NCB chief fit after incident at pit
2.   Coal Supremo felled in pit fury
3.   MacGregor scraps pit visit in face of angry demo

There are several features of language which merit comment here. These include: the characteristic conventions of newspaper headlines such as omission of articles; the deletion of a main finite verb; abbreviations (*demo*) and alliterative patterning (*pit/fit*; *felled/fury*); the formality differences signalled by lexical choices e.g. *incident/demo* and by naming devices: *Coal Supremo*; *MacGregor*; *NCB chief*. And so on. Also relevant here would be features not immediately recognised when the headlines are laid out as above. These are such features as typography, the placement of the main caption in relation to pictures as well as to other headlines. Of some significance in this connection, for example, are the styles of sub-headlines which in some newspaper styles support the main caption.

But analysis of language in and for itself does little to reveal the contrasts between these headlines in terms of ideology. The relationship here between language and ideology is not a transparent one; it is signalled with some subtlety and works to subject the reader to a particular interpretation of events. In the case of headline (3), for example, MacGregor is placed in the role of main actor in the clause and is made responsible (*scraps visit*) himself for the act of cancellation (*scraps* is a transitive verb). There is no reference to his physical position or disposition. By contrast headline (2) represents MacGregor as acted upon (*coal supremo felled*) and underlines the lack of 'agency' by use of a passive verb, markedly emotive lexis (*felled/fury*) … Headline (1) seeks to be altogether more neutral by use of the word *incident* and the use of a complement structure (*NCB chief (is) fit*) avoids a passive/active distinction with its necessary assignment of agency. In other words, each headline inserts a different view of events. In (3) there is no suggestion that those taking part in the demonstration are directly responsible for action by MacGregor whereas in (2) MacGregor is the object of an action which we assume is initiated by the fury of the miners at the pit. In the opposition between coal supremo and miners the headline subjects the reader to a position which is limited by a preordained interpretation of events. In (1) there is no overt taking of sides, although in the case of such struggles neutrality signals greater allegiance to those social and political forces which seek to maintain a status quo. In all three headlines there is a relationship between stylistic choice, text structure and the ideological construction of a particular reading position. In each case different grammatical and other choices *encode markedly different ideologies*.

(Carter (ed.), 1990, pp. 104–8)

Controversy continued with the setting up of an English Working Party to advise on the requirements of the 1988 Education Act and the introduction of a national curriculum for English. The Working Party was to be chaired by Professor Brian Cox (a professor of English Literature at the University of Manchester). As mentioned above, he had been a member of the Kingman Committee, but was perhaps better known at the time as a co-editor of 'The Black Papers on Education' (1969–77). Cox himself concedes that these papers were 'supposedly traditional and right wing in their views of education' (Cox, 1991, p. 4), and he must therefore have been regarded as a strong supporter of traditional methods and values. Ironically, however, he was to become one of the government's most vociferous critics on educational policy. The Cox Committee identified five views on the purpose of teaching English:

- a personal growth view, which focuses on the child and emphasizes the relationship between language and learning in the individual child and the role of literature in developing children's imaginative and aesthetic lives;

- a cross-curricular view which focuses on the school, emphasizing that all teachers have a responsibility to teach language;

- an adult needs view, which focuses on communication outside of the school, emphasizing the responsibility of English teachers to prepare pupils for the demands of adult life, including the workplace;

- a cultural heritage view which requires schools to teach the 'classics';

- and a cultural analysis view, which helps pupils towards a critical understanding of the world and cultural environment in which they live.

This broad and rather eclectic approach to the English curriculum did not answer the requirements expressed by Kenneth Baker. Brian Cox states, 'When our first Report on the primary stages was submitted to Mr Baker at the end of September 1988, he felt that we had given insufficient emphasis to the teaching of grammar' (Cox, 1991, p. 7); and later: 'Mr Baker very much disliked the Report. He had wanted a short report, with strong emphasis on grammar, spelling and punctuation, which would have been easy for parents to read' (p. 11). Nevertheless, the 'Cox Report' was accepted, with some amendments, and formed the basis of the 1989 English national curriculum.

For the first time English was to be defined by content (programmes of study) with assessment at ages 7, 11 and 14 against specified 'statements of attainment'. The programmes of study were organized into speaking and listening, reading and writing, with knowledge about language as a strand running through each area. Several ongoing debates about English teaching were brought into sharp relief by the publication of the national curriculum. In the teaching of reading: What were the appropriate strategies? What was the position of phonics? In initial writing: How important was it to be able to use full stops and capitals correctly? What was the place of media, of information technology, of drama in the curriculum? What was the place of Standard English?

These debates persisted and in 1992 a review of the national curriculum was commissioned by the then Secretary of State for Education, John Patten. The review seemed destined from the outset to produce an English curriculum with an increased emphasis on 'basic skills' in reading and writing; the teaching of Standard English; and the identification of a common body of literary texts for study. The National Curriculum Council notes concerns that the current English Orders (i.e. the English curriculum):

(i) place insufficient emphasis on the requirement that all pupils should become confident users of Standard English;

(ii) do not define with sufficient precision the skills involved in learning to read, nor provide a clear and balanced framework to support the teaching of reading;

You can see some similarity between this list and John Dixon's three 'models' of English, written much earlier in 1967 and discussed in this chapter. The 'personal growth' and 'cultural heritage' views persist from Dixon's list; the 'cross-curricular' view, not mentioned by Dixon, emanates from the Bullock Committee's later recommendations on 'language across the curriculum'; 'cultural analysis' is related to the social concerns in Dixon's 'personal growth' (see p. 185); Dixon's 'language skills' model is not included as a separate heading by Cox, though it may be implicit in Cox's 'adult needs' view.

(iii) are not sufficiently explicit about how pupils can develop the habit of reading widely, and be introduced to the richness of great literature;

(iv) do not define clearly the basic reading skills and grammatical knowledge pupils need to master, and the variety of ways in which competence in spelling can be developed.

(National Curriculum Council, 1992)

The Cox curriculum had seemed to present a broad consensus about the teaching of English, so this review, only two years after its introduction, was met with dismay by many teachers. The revisions, however, went ahead, and after further (often heated) debate a revised (1995) version of the English curriculum was published. The English curriculum was organized into three programmes of study, speaking and listening, reading, and writing, with a paragraph emphasizing the interrelationship of these language modes. Each programme of study was organized using common headings: 'range' (i.e. the range of language activities children would be expected to cover); 'key skills' (the language skills children should acquire); and 'Standard English and language study' (ways of developing pupils' appreciation and use of 'Standard English', as well as what children should learn about the English language). The programmes of study were prefaced by general requirements, which included a requirement to develop information technology capability in all subjects, where appropriate, and a statement about access for pupils needing either support or extension work. The general requirements also outline certain features of Standard English as represented in the national curriculum.

It was emphasized that this was a minimalist curriculum, and that teachers were free to develop beyond this entitlement as they saw fit. In one sense, the definition of English was being opened up as an area again – but on this occasion with a clear core definition, in turn reinforced by a national assessment system, to be used by teachers at the end of one of the key stages (i.e. when children are aged 7, 11 and 14) to measure pupil achievement in the classroom. However, there is a fear that the assessments will be seen as so important as to effectively redefine the curriculum, leaving little room for flexibility in teacher initiatives.

References

CARTER, R. (ed.) (1990) *Knowledge about Language and the Curriculum*, Sevenoaks, Hodder & Stoughton.

COX, B. (1991) *Cox on Cox: an English curriculum for the 1990s*, London, Hodder & Stoughton.

LANGUAGE IN THE NATIONAL CURRICULUM (LINC) (1991) *Language in the National Curriculum: materials for professional development*, Nottingham, Department of English, University of Nottingham.

NATIONAL CURRICULUM COUNCIL (1992) *National Curriculum English: the case for revising the order*, York, National Curriculum Council.

This reading was specially commissioned for this book.

6 ISSUES IN ENGLISH TEACHING

Sue Brindley with contributions from Joan Swann

6.1 INTRODUCTION

Alex, a 7-year-old girl, has recently entered a new class in her primary school. She has been asked by her teacher to write a story on 'Friendship'. She begins her account:

> Mi best freind is Zoe and we play together we play in the playground and somtims she comes to mi hous and we play with mi computer. Mi other freind is Christine but she dus not come to mi hous.

If you were the teacher marking this, would your reaction be to ask Alex to tell us some more about her friends: for example, the ways in which Zoe and Christine are different even though they are friends? Or would you be more concerned that in an account of friendship, Alex should be able to spell *friend* correctly, and to write in sentences? Is it more important that Alex, at this relatively early stage of her school writing career, should write creatively and freely, with technical considerations coming low in her list of priorities for 'good' writing, or should she be trained straight away to consider grammatically accurate and correctly spelled work?

As Tony Pugh points out in Chapter 5, such dilemmas are about more than simply the effectiveness of different teaching methods. Different approaches to the teaching of English language are underpinned by desires for different outcomes: their advocates often suggest that a version of a future adult (and a future society) is being shaped by the decisions made by the English teacher.

English, as a subject, deals with values, culture and society: a potent combination. It has been a 'high stakes' subject, with powerful groups competing to control the definition of English and thereby the values being transmitted. Protherough and Atkinson have argued that 'Control of English is seen as one means of establishing ideological control over society and many pressure groups long to exert that influence' (Protherough and Atkinson, 1991, p. 2). Chapter 5 illustrates how such issues have been played out in nineteenth- and twentieth-century England, and also in India during the British occupation. Similar debates continue today in several parts of the English-speaking world.

The values that underlie debates about the English curriculum are an important theme in this chapter. We focus on three aspects of English teaching that have proved controversial: the role of Standard English in relation to other language varieties, and other languages in education; the teaching of reading; and the teaching of writing. In each case we examine some of the debates in these areas while also looking at illustrations of actual classroom

While this chapter, like the book as a whole, focuses on English language teaching and learning, the second book of this series discusses some aspects of English literature. See Using English: from conversation to canon *(Maybin and Mercer (eds), 1996).*

practice. The chapter, then, explores different approaches to teaching English; how these have been put into practice; and how discussion of such approaches and practices tends to broaden and encompass debates about different sets of values.

Teaching and learning English worldwide

Several contributors to a review of the English curriculum in different countries have stressed its ideological associations:

> What are these local problems and pressures with which English teaching in Australia has had to come to terms? First and foremost, there is the post-war migration, which has made Australia, after Israel, the most multicultural nation on earth. Allied with this has been an intensified search for a national identity as the common British heritage has weakened.
>
> (Davis and Watson, 1990, pp. 151–2)

> The 1970s in Canada saw a surging of interest in national identity. Many educators were asking a simple question: what does it mean to be Canadian? Some looked to literature for guidance and answers. In this search, the gaps in Canadian literature became obvious, particularly literature for young children and adolescents. It also became apparent that literature and culture were inextricably intertwined … [Certain writers] strongly advocated a cultural heritage model of literature. They presented this argument: Because Canadian literature is rooted in the social and political and historical setting, students will better understand their national identity through the reading of Canadian literature.
>
> (Robinson et al., 1990, p. 144)

> When key documents and retrospectives have been published on the teaching of English in the United States, their titles have consistently acknowledged a struggle: *Freedom and Discipline* (Report on the Commission on English, 1965), *Tradition and Reform* (Applebee, 1974), *Consensus and Dissent* (Farmer, 1986). The changing social and political fabric of the United States has pushed the operational definition of *English teaching* first toward one end of the continuum and then the other. The interim periods of momentary balance were usually disrupted by some socio/political event that reverberated beyond the political arena and into the educational one.
>
> (Simmons et al., 1990, p. 89)

Throughout the chapter we examine the teaching of English in what have sometimes been termed '**mother-tongue**' contexts: countries in which English is the first language of large sectors of the population and in which English is taught as a first language in schools. As this is a vast subject, we focus on only a few contexts – the UK (particularly England), Australia and New Zealand provide many of the examples – but there is also reference to other countries. Chapter 7 in some ways complements this one, focusing on issues that arise in the teaching of English to speakers of other languages.

6.2   WHICH ENGLISH?

Chapter 4 contains a brief discussion of the role of Standard English as a classroom language (that is, as a medium for teaching and learning in all subjects) but the issue has been particularly important for teachers of English as a subject.

One question that has preoccupied both policy makers and practitioners in several English-speaking countries is the place in the curriculum of Standard English and – a clearly related question – of other varieties of English. Debates centre not just on pragmatic concerns (such as, for instance, how widely used and understood different varieties are); as we saw in the introduction to this chapter, and as you might expect from your earlier reading in this book, social and cultural concerns have also loomed large.

Since 1989 Australia has had a 'national framework' for eight key areas of the curriculum, including English. The curriculum statement produced for English emphasizes the connections between language and national identity, as well as acknowledging diversity within 'Australian English':

> Australian English is the national variety of English in Australia, distinguished from other national varieties, such as British and American English, chiefly by pronunciation and vocabulary. It comprises standard Australian English, which is the variety used in schools, and a number of colloquial varieties. Students have any one of these varieties as their home language.
>
>   Whilst respecting students' home languages, English teachers have a responsibility to teach the forms and usages generally accepted in Australian English. The development of increasing proficiency in the uses of standard Australian English should be treated as an extension of, and an addition to, a student's home language. The goal should be to ensure that students develop an ever-widening language repertoire for personal and public use.
>
> (Australian Education Council, 1994a, p. 4).

(We are grateful to Paul Brock, from the Australian Language and Literacy Council/National Board of Employment, Education and Training, for helpful information on the Australian curriculum.)

In this extract Standard Australian English seems to be viewed as an entitlement, something which schools should make available to pupils. It is also something that can be added to children's language repertoire, without damaging their home language or language variety where this is different. The teaching of Standard Australian English is felt to be important because it is 'the language of formal spoken communication, the education system and professional life' (Australian Education Council, 1994a, pp. 10–11). However, the statement also emphasizes the equal status of both standard and home language practices. It points out:

> That the language used by a socio-cultural group is closely connected with its values, attitudes and beliefs, and that learning any variety of language involves understanding and interpreting the culture of which it is a part.

And

The Australian national framework provides guidelines on the teaching of English and other subjects. Documents such as the statement on English are not statutory and may be interpreted differently in different states.

> That although many languages and varieties of the English language are used in Australia, none is intrinsically superior to the other.
>
> (Australian Education Council, 1994a, p. 11)

A national framework for English in Australia

The Australian statement on English lists the following as the 'Goals of the English curriculum':

1   The ability to speak, listen, read, view and write with purpose, effect and confidence in a wide range of contexts.

2   A knowledge of the ways in which language varies according to context, purpose, audience and content, and the ability to apply this knowledge.

3   A sound grasp of the linguistic structures and features of standard Australian English … and the capacity to apply these, especially in writing.

4   A broad knowledge of a range of literature, including Australian literature, and a capacity to relate this literature to aspects of contemporary society and personal experience.

5   The capacity to discuss and analyse texts and language critically and with appreciation.

6   A knowledge of the ways in which textual interpretation and understanding may vary according to cultural, social and personal differences, and the capacity to develop reasoned arguments about interpretation and meaning.

Students come from diverse socio-cultural and language backgrounds. The school curriculum must recognise this diversity and the important part language plays in students' educational achievements.

(Australian Education Council, 1994a, p. 3)

In other parts of the English-speaking world it is also accepted that children should be given access, through formal education, to a standard variety of English: this in turn, it is argued, will give them greater geographical and social mobility (for example, access to higher education and professional employment) and will enable them to participate in more formal or public contexts of language use.

In Britain, where the long history of English has given rise to considerable regional and social diversity, Standard English is considered to be part of the curriculum for children aged 5–16 (it is a statutory component of the national curriculum in England and Wales, for instance). However, the teaching of Standard English has also been hotly contested in Britain, with the debate turning particularly on how Standard English is identified and how it relates to children's home language varieties.

One problem to which many linguists have drawn attention is the difficulty of drawing clear boundaries between Standard English and nonstandard varieties. Katharine Perera, a British linguist who has been involved in educational policy making (for instance, she was a member of the National Curriculum English Working Group, mentioned in Chapter 5, Reading C, and so had some influence in the early stages of developing the national curriculum), makes a classic linguistic distinction between grammar and vocabulary, and pronunciation: Standard English refers to the 'structure of the language, i.e. its

The development of the national curriculum is discussed in Chapter 5 (Reading C). Unlike the Australian 'national framework', the national curriculum has statutory force.

grammar and vocabulary', but it may be 'spoken in any accent' (Perera, 1994, p. 80). Perera offers the following characterization of Standard English. It is the variety that is:

(i)   *relatively* uniform throughout the English-speaking world;

(ii) used by educated native speakers;

(iii) used in public, formal contexts, e.g. Parliament, law courts, churches, radio, television, and particularly in education and published writing.

(Perera, 1994, pp. 81–2)

Unfortunately, as Perera points out, none of these characteristics is watertight. Standard English does show some variation and it is also constantly changing; educated speakers do not always agree about what are acceptable usages; and Standard English is also used informally: 'If this is not the case then it leads to the curious conclusion that when educated speakers of standard English are chatting casually with their friends they are no longer using standard language' (Perera, 1994, p. 84).

In practice, there is rather less scope for disagreement in the case of the written language, which has been codified in dictionaries and descriptive grammars and which has achieved considerable uniformity. But things are far less straightforward with spoken Standard English, which contains many informal features and has not been so fully described. Perera eventually resorts to a rather negative characterization on the basis of features that are 'widely stigmatised' by educated speakers:

> there is a rather small set of frequently occurring features which are recognisably non-standard and serve as social shibboleths. These include negative forms, e.g.
>
>> He ain't here
>> I didn't want no-one to hurt nobody
>
> verb forms e.g.
>
>> She seen him yesterday
>> They was laughing
>
> and pronouns and determiners, e.g.
>
>> He liked the play what I had wrote
>> I want them books.
>
> … Although this focus on stigmatised features probably captures a truth about spoken standard English, it is unappealing to have to define it in this negative way.
>
> (Perera, 1994, pp. 86–7)

For most purposes it matters little that spoken Standard English is hard to delimit – we could simply accept this as an interesting fact about the way language works. But when spoken Standard English is an explicit entitlement within the curriculum, the absence of an agreed definition becomes something of a problem. It is not clear how far Perera is speaking tongue-in-cheek when she remarks on policy making in the national curriculum for England and Wales: 'the National Curriculum requires that pupils are assessed on their ability to speak it, so it is essential to have some agreement about what it is' (Perera, 1994, p. 84).

❖   ❖   ❖   ❖   ❖

Activity 6.1   *(Allow 5–10 minutes)*

The extracts in the box come from *English in the National Curriculum* (Department for Education and Welsh Office, 1995). How do they compare with Perera's characterization of Standard English?

Standard English in the national curriculum for England and Wales

English in the National Curriculum outlines the following characteristics of Standard English:

- standard English is distinguished from other forms of English by its vocabulary, and by rules and conventions of grammar, spelling and punctuation;

- the grammatical features that distinguish standard English include how pronouns, adverbs and adjectives should be used and how negatives, questions and verb tenses should be formed; such features are present in both the spoken and written forms, except where non-standard forms are used for effect or technical reasons;

- differences between the spoken and written forms relate to the spontaneity of speech and its function in conversation, whereas writing is more permanent, often carefully crafted, and less dependent on immediate responses;

- spoken standard English is not the same as Received Pronunciation and can be expressed in a variety of accents.

(Department for Education and Welsh Office, 1995, p. 3)

The programme of study for 'Speaking and listening' at Key Stage 2 (ages 7–11) indicates how Standard English might be approached in the classroom:

> Pupils' appreciation and use of standard English should be developed by involvement with others in activities that, through their content and purpose, demand the range of grammatical constructions and vocabulary characteristic of spoken standard English. They should be taught to speak with clear diction and appropriate intonation. Pupils should be taught how formal contexts require particular choices of vocabulary and greater precision in language structures. They should also be given opportunities to develop their understanding of the similarities and differences between the written and spoken forms of standard English, and to investigate how language varies according to context and purpose and between standard and dialect forms.

(Department for Education and Welsh Office, 1995, p. 12)

Comment

The extracts make a conventional distinction between *dialect* features (for example, vocabulary and grammar) which do form part of Standard English, and *accent* features, which do not. The inclusion of spelling and punctuation in the list is more problematical – conventional orthography can also be used for non-standard varieties.

When it comes to providing guidance on practice, the national curriculum conflates other attributes ('clear diction', 'precision in language structures') with the teaching of Standard English. Such terms may be designed to connote desirable qualities: who, after all, would not wish children to speak clearly? They are, however, linguistically imprecise, and would not normally be regarded as having anything to do with different language varieties.

It is perhaps significant that the list in the first extract does not actually provide a definition of Standard English (nor is a straightforward definition attempted elsewhere in the documentation). Brian Cox, in *Cox on the Battle for the English Curriculum,* claims that '… when this [list] is read carefully it turns out to mean not much more than that Standard English is not the same as dialects' (Cox, 1995, p. 156).

❖   ❖   ❖   ❖   ❖

The first book in this series provides a fuller discussion of English accents and dialects, standardization in English and notions of 'correctness' in language. See *English: history, diversity and change* (Graddol et al. (eds), 1996)

In discussing Standard English in the same breath as clear diction and precision, the national curriculum is going beyond the view of Standard English that is accepted by linguists, and by many, if not most, educationalists (including those who drafted the Australian English statement): that, on a linguistic level at least, Standard English is not 'intrinsically superior' to other language varieties.

We saw earlier that, despite such different (and conflicting) views about what Standard English is, there has been a broad consensus that it should be made available to pupils. As mentioned in Chapter 5, the Newbolt Report on the teaching of English in England (Board of Education, 1921) stipulated that children should be taught spoken and written Standard English in the interests of national unity: a unified language would help to produce a unified nation. This link between language and national identity was also made in the (more recent) Australian curriculum statement cited above. The Australian document, however, also emphasizes respect for children's home language varieties, and this balancing act between respecting home language and providing access to a standard variety has also characterized policy and practice elsewhere. In 1975, the Bullock Report (see Chapter 5) took a similar line when it argued that teachers should accept the child's home language variety but that 'standard forms' should also be taught:

> The aim is not to alienate the child from a form of language with which he has grown up and which serves him efficiently in the speech community of his neighbourhood. It is to enlarge his repertoire so that he can use language effectively in other speech situations and use standard forms when they are needed.
>
> (Department of Education and Science, 1975, p. 143, para. 10.6)

Virtually all educationalists and policy makers recognize the importance of children's home language and few if any would argue that children should dispense with this entirely. There has, however, been debate about the extent to which children who speak nonstandard varieties of English can simply 'add on' another variety. Earlier chapters have pointed out that learning a language is not simply a question of acquiring ever more complex linguistic skills. In learning Standard English, children are necessarily aligning themselves with the language and culture of the school and it is debatable how far it is possible for certain speakers to do this without losing something of their cultural identity. Perera relates this dilemma particularly to the acquisition of spoken Standard English:

> Some children grow up amongst people who speak standard English and so that is the form of the language that they learn. When they are 3 or 4 they may well say things like *I digged a hole* but that is simply a transient form which will in time be replaced by the irregular past tense form *dug.* An important characteristic of standard English is that its functions and forms have been elaborated over time. This is especially true of its vocabulary. When children go to school, and particularly when they learn

to read, they become increasingly exposed to those words and grammatical structures of standard English that are characteristic of its more formal, public and written uses. For these children, learning standard English means extending the language that they have already begun to acquire.

Other children grow up in families where a non-standard variety of English is spoken. Naturally enough, they learn that variety. For them, the mismatch between the language of home and school is greater than for children who have standard English as their mother tongue. During the primary school years, as they are increasingly exposed to the forms of both spoken and written standard English, they begin to replace their non-standard features with standard features in writing (where there is time for planning and reflection). This replacement happens more slowly and erratically in speech. By about the age of 11, some pupils from non-standard language communities are likely to speak differently in the classroom with their teacher and in the playground with their peers. There is some evidence ... that girls take on these different speech forms more readily than boys. Certainly issues of attitude will be involved, since adopting a different language variety entails aligning oneself with the social group that speaks in that way; for some the loss of identity will be too big a price to pay for the not always apparent benefits of speaking a more prestigious variety.

(Perera, 1994, pp. 87–8)

Others have responded more critically to current policy on teaching Standard English. Like Perera, John Keen argues that children may face powerful social pressures to retain their use of nonstandard varieties of English. Keen maintains that, because people who learn Standard English must necessarily take on the values associated with this variety, the introduction of a widespread shift to the standard would require 'a parallel programme of social engineering' to shift social and cultural values. Furthermore, if access to Standard English were widened, what would happen to its function as a prestige variety? Keen predicts that middle-class speakers would need to adopt new forms of language to differentiate themselves from working-class speakers:

It wouldn't be long before you were reprimanding your offspring, 'Don't say "I've chosen my options for Year 10" like one of those children from the adventure playground; You should say: "I've chose my options" – after all, that's how Shakespeare would have said it' ('I have already chose my officer', *Othello*, I, 1)

(Keen, 1994, pp. 27–8)

More seriously, Keen points to the dilemmas that face English teachers:

Do we diminish the life-chances of working-class children if we accept the language norms of their speech communities? Should we try to increase the resistance of middle-class children to linguistic snobbery and provoke the wrath of government and media? Or should we press for Standard English and risk alienating a whole social class? How shall we advise children who want to get on in the world without feeling that they have betrayed their families and communities?

(Keen, 1994, p. 28)

Many teachers, faced with such dilemmas, have tried to educate children about their own language use, and that of others, by beginning to explore the characteristics of different varieties of English, how such varieties are used, and how they are evaluated by others. Children thus discover more about language and how it works but also, whether explicitly or by implication, they are confronted with the values associated with different varieties of English.

❖   ❖   ❖   ❖   ❖

Activity 6.2   *(Allow 10–15 minutes)*

Figure 6.1 contains a list of statements intended to promote discussion of language variation and diversity among secondary school pupils in Britain. You may care to try out the activity yourself, and perhaps discuss your responses with one or two friends or colleagues.

How useful are the statements for promoting discussion and encouraging you to examine your ideas about different varieties of English?

❖   ❖   ❖   ❖   ❖

Pupil Sheet 1a

Proper English?
Language Statements

Language Statements ✂

- In your group, read through these statements about language.

- Discuss them and decide which of them you agree with, disagree with or don't know about.

- Cut the statements up and stick them onto the large sheet of paper in three columns, 'Agree', 'Disagree' and 'Don't know'.

- Add to the 'Agree' column at least one statement each which you think is important and which has been missed out.

- • You need to speak properly to get on in the world.

- • Some accents sound 'nicer' than others.

- • It's wrong to make someone change their way of speaking.

- • Some people use their accents to put other people down.

- • Confidence in language matters more than correctness.

- • If teachers don't show pupils the mistakes they make in language, the pupils will never learn.

- • School can make children feel ashamed of their language.

- • Standard English is very important because that's the way we write.

Pupil Sheet 1b

Proper English?
Language Statements

- • Standard English allows powerful people to keep other people in their places.

- • Standard English has a lot to do with the power of books, newspapers, radio and television in Britain.

- • We change our way of speaking depending on who we're with.

- • People write differently from the way they speak.

- • Young people use more slang than older people.

- • There are differences between girls' and boys' language.

- • English is now the most important language in the world.

- • English is now an important world language.

- • It's important to be able to speak at least one language other than English.

- • Bilingual children don't get enough credit in school for what they can do.

Figure 6.1   Language statements

(English and Media Centre, 1995, pp. 218–9)

An English teacher, Jenny Leach, points out that such statements provide a starting point for discussion, raising issues that can be pursued in more detail: 'It's important that the statements cover issues that you intend dealing with in the lesson (or in subsequent lessons). I always used the same test at the end of a language studies unit to see how/in what ways pupils views had changed.'

We have focused so far on the teaching and use of different varieties of English, but similar issues arise in contexts in which English is used alongside other languages: should schools in 'English-dominant' countries concentrate on providing access to English as the language of the wider community? What should the attitude be towards children's home languages? Should these also be given formal recognition and support in schools? Such questions might seem particularly relevant to children learning English as an additional language, and in this respect they are followed up in the next chapter. But it has also been argued that all children, including native speakers of English, benefit when other languages are brought into the English curriculum. Gaik See Chew, discussing a project that explored the range of languages used by children in a multilingual classroom in London, noted that one of the aims of the project was:

> increasing knowledge about language, and about English as a mother-tongue. Knowledge about other languages and knowledge about English will give us valuable insight into language as a whole.
>
> (Gaik, 1992, p. 161)

Similar initiatives can be found in several parts of the UK. However, they receive limited support in *English in the National Curriculum*, which mentions the role of other languages only in relation to the acquisition of Standard English:

> The richness of dialects and other languages can make an important contribution to pupils' knowledge and understanding of standard English. Where appropriate, pupils should be encouraged to make use of their understanding and skills in other languages when learning English.
>
> (Department for Education and Welsh Office, 1995, p. 2)

This approach can be contrasted with the situation in those parts of Wales where education is available to children through the medium of Welsh; in this case there seems to be a rather more positive attitude to drawing on both languages within the English curriculum:

> The development of English and Welsh should be seen as mutually supportive. This may require modification of the teaching within the programme of study at Key Stage 2 [ages 7–11] but this will be slight and should ensure activities that:
>
> * build on the English language experiences of the home and of the community at large;
> * encourage pupils to transfer their skills in, and knowledge and understanding of, one language to the other;
> * draw pupils' attention, in a structured and systematic way, to the similarities and differences between the two languages;
> * assist pupils to acquire appropriate terminology that will enable them to discuss these similarities and differences purposefully;
> * develop pupils' understanding of the social contexts in which the languages are used;
> * provide a variety of reading material, eg *pupils' own work, the media, literature, reference books*, that will highlight these social contexts.
>
> (Department for Education and Welsh Office, 1995, p. 32)

The use of home or community languages in education has often proved controversial: this practice tends to flourish in contexts in which there is a general acceptance of diversity, or in which there is a supportive policy framework. In New Zealand, for example, an approach to language study has been devised which is based on comparative study of English and Maori. This comparison is intended to develop children's **metalinguistic knowledge**, that is, their knowledge about language and how it works. The proposal was first suggested prior to 1990, but following an outcry from some politicians and the press, who did not see it as part of the English curriculum, the proposal ran aground at that time. The proposal was subsequently revived and has been developed into a major teaching resource.

❖   ❖   ❖   ❖   ❖

Activity 6.3   *(Reading A)*

Now read 'Different voices in the English curriculum' (Reading A), in which Stuart Middleton, President of the New Zealand Association for the Teaching of English, and Principal of Aorere College in New Zealand, describes the approach to language study he helped to devise. Note in particular:

- the favourable policy context in New Zealand which makes such an initiative viable;

- the justifications for teaching students about Maori and English, as a means of promoting 'the values of biculturalism' as well as developing children's 'metalinguistic knowledge';

- the kinds of comparisons that can be made between Maori and English.

What is your own view of the use of such approaches in English lessons?

❖   ❖   ❖   ❖   ❖

6.3   PERSPECTIVES ON TEACHING READING

You may remember from Chapter 5 that another aspect of English teaching that has provoked debate over the years is the teaching of reading. Debates about the teaching of reading have, in fact, been high on the educational (and political) agenda in several parts of the world in recent years. The focus has often been on the early stages of education, and on how teachers should approach the teaching of children with very different interests, experiences and abilities in reading. The pupils in the photographs in Figure 6.2 will be at different stages in their reading competency; some may not yet be able to read without adult support. How should pupils be taught to read? What should the priorities be? Should the approach be that pupils come to see books as enjoyable and interesting, perhaps from looking at pictures, and want to find out what reading means? Or should it be that they are enabled from the very beginning to make sense of the marks on the pages, and that enjoyment stems from that? And how do teachers go about reconciling statutory demands, professional debates, their own expertise and actually teach children to read?

Figure 6.2   *Early primary children reading with each other and with older children, from published books, books they have made themselves and 'big books'*

Several aspects of the reading curriculum have proved controversial. At issue has been the content of children's reading: since books must be always about something, what topics are appropriate for young children, and how should they be represented? What values are (necessarily) being conveyed to children within their reading materials? Is the range of young children's reading sometimes over-narrow? How can a 'broad and balanced' selection of reading materials be achieved? Teaching methods have also been highly controversial, and it is on one particular aspect of this controversy that we now focus.

The debate about the most effective way to teach reading is often represented as polarized between two approaches: teaching reading through **phonics**, and using a **real books** approach. (See the box for an account of each approach.)

The debate about the values represented in teaching materials affects several areas of the curriculum. Chapter 7 discusses this in relation to materials produced to teach English to speakers of other languages.

Two approaches to reading

The **phonics** approach to literacy is concerned with the relationship of sound and symbol. Joyce Morris, a leading voice in the approach to reading through phonics, believes that pupils can be taught to read most effectively by learning the sounds that letters make, and joining these together to make words. In the following account, Morris explains the rationale for teaching reading through phonics:

> Briefly, English orthography is a system of systems and therefore 'polysystemic'. Basically it is 'alphabetic' in that the orthographic symbols (graphemes), whether single alphabet letters or letter combinations, represent the sounds of speech (phonemes) ... Therein lies the linguistic part of the rationale for a phonics approach to initial literacy with its highlighting of sound-symbol correspondence and word structure ... in many British primary schools, predominantly look-say, basal schemes form the 'core' of the reading programme for under-nines. This would suggest that ... the overwhelming research evidence in favour of phonics is being disregarded. If this is so, it could put many children at risk of not achieving their potential for literacy ... it could even be tragic for 'teacher-dependent' children who do not have favourable home circumstances and, generally, do not belong to that privileged minority to which most professional teachers originally belong; that is, children who are highly-motivated, verbally-gifted and therefore largely able to discover for themselves from their print environment how the traditional orthography of English works.

(Morris, 1988, p. 140)

Set against this is the **'real books'** approach, often exemplified through the work of Frank Smith, where children 'learn to read by reading':

> extensive research in many cultures has confirmed what many experienced teachers have known intuitively, that children become readers when they are engaged in situations where written language is being meaningfully used, much in the way they learn spoken language from their association with people around them who use speech in meaningful ways. This is the opposite of programmatic instruction ... (p. viii)
>
> The reason phonics does not work for children ... is that the links between the letters and the sounds cannot be uniquely specified ... our written language is provided with an alphabet of just 26 letters while there are about forty distinctive sounds in our spoken language. Obviously some letters must correspond to more than one sound. And, in fact, there is not one letter in our alphabet that is not associated with more than one sound (or with silence, like the *k* in *knot*). Nor is there any single sound of speech that is represented by only one letter. Spelling-to-sound correspondences are not one-to-one, but many-to-many... There may be half a dozen alternative ways of pronouncing individual letters, and no reliable phonic guide as to when each of the alternatives applies. (pp. 50–1)
>
> The system of 'phonics' is both cumbersome and unreliable, and only rarely produces an accurate pronunciation for a word not recognized on sight. Better ways of identifying unfamiliar words exist, such as asking someone, using clues from context, and comparison with known words of similar construction ... Reliance on phonics ... is dysfunctional in fluent reading and interferes with learning to read. (p. 75)
>
> Once a child discovers what a word is in a meaningful context, learning to recognize it on another occasion is as simple as learning to recognize a face on another occasion, and does not need phonics. (p. 140)

(Extracts from Smith, 1985)

❖   ❖   ❖   ❖   ❖

Activity 6.4   'Phonics' or 'real books'?   *(Allow about 20 minutes)*

Read through the extracts in the box. What are the main points made by Morris
and by Smith? How do these relate to discussions of learning and teaching
reading you encountered earlier in this book (mainly Chapters 3 and 5)? If you
have any experience of primary school classrooms, how do these approaches
relate to the ways teachers actually work in these classrooms?

Comment

Much of the debate, as expressed here at least, hinges on the extent to which
English sounds, or **phonemes**, correspond to **graphemes** (letters or groups of
letters). Morris argues that children need to be taught sound–spelling correspon-
dences; Smith maintains that, because of the lack of a one-to-one correspondence
between sound and spelling in English, a phonic approach will not work and may
actually be dysfunctional. You may remember from Chapter 3 that while there
is not a straightforward correspondence between phonemes and graphemes,
English spelling is not unsystematic: there are patterns that children can learn,
though not always at the phoneme/grapheme level.

   Though Morris is regarded as one of the most ardent advocates of phonics,
she seems nevertheless to recognize that some children can learn to read without
such direct instruction – even if they constitute only a 'privileged minority'. Smith
argues that *all* children learn best when they are 'engaged in situations where
written language is meaningfully used'. The approach advocated by Smith has
been termed 'real books' because of its emphasis on texts that provide a genuine
purpose for reading. It is broadly consistent with what Pam Czerniewska, in
Chapter 3, refers to as the 'new literacy' (see particularly her characterization of
this on p. 106). Tony Pugh, in Chapter 5, might well question the 'new', as he
claims that the Anglo-Saxon King Alfred acquired literacy in English by 'reading
for meaning'.

❖   ❖   ❖   ❖   ❖

Researchers have identified shifting positions on the teaching of reading over the
years. In charting developments in English teaching in Canada since 1965,
Robinson et al. note that an early preference for 'decoding methods' such as
phonics has given way to other approaches such as those advocated by Smith, and
to attempts to integrate reading with other aspects of language learning (Robinson et al., 1990, pp. 147–8). Davis and Watson include the teaching of reading in
their list of 'current problems' in English teaching in Australia:

> The battle still rages over the best method of teaching reading. There are
> some signs that the advocates of phonics (known to their opponents as
> 'phonicators'!) are losing ground to those who would advocate a more
> balanced approach. … In the last few years several infants and primary
> schools have had marked success with literacy-through-literature pro-
> grammes, that is, programmes which base the teaching of reading upon
> the wealth of magnificent picture and story books now available instead
> of on the synthetic texts of the typical reading scheme.
> (Davis and Watson, 1990, p. 168)

Ideologically, phonics has come to be associated with supporting a version of
English that is associated with skills-based learning and the need to be indoctri-
nated into particular ways of functioning in the classroom – the transmission of

information from teacher to pupil. A real books approach would claim to focus much more on the exploratory way of learning; the child 'reads for real', with the teacher supporting the child's learning through encouraging and extending the way in which the child constructs the reading activity. The knowledge is not transmitted from teacher to child, but developed by the teacher from the child's existing understanding. In the UK at least the debate has also acquired a political dimension: the phonics movement has come to be associated with a 'right-wing' approach to teaching, the real books far more with 'left-wing' beliefs about learning and pedagogy.

In practice, the associations of different methods are less clear-cut. For instance, an Open University pack on teaching reading attempts to broaden the notion of phonics, and to integrate this with other classroom activities. It suggests that, while reading in English does not work by 'sounding out' individual letters, 'there is also strong evidence to suggest that awareness of sounds, of letters, and of sound–letter relationships is associated with fluent reading' (Open University, 1994, p. 65).

The pack argues that children need to perceive words as separate units (rather than 'an unbroken string of sounds'), and to become aware of syllables, as well as individual sounds and letters. It suggests breaking up syllables into what have been termed 'onsets' and 'rimes' to help children see patterns in word structure. Such learning can be based on a number of games and routines, such as 'I Spy' to teach initial letters and sounds, and rhyming games to teach word endings.

Onsets and rimes

Marilyn Jager Adams explains ways of looking more closely at syllables, breaking them up into 'onsets' and 'rimes'. She suggests building up sets of words with matching rimes such as *bell, tell, sell, fell*; and of words with complex onsets such as *str-, bl-, spl-*

Word	Onset	Rime
I	-	I
it	-	it
itch	-	itch
sit	s-	-it
spit	sp-	-it
split	spl-	-it
splint	spl-	-int
spline	spl-	-ine
spilt	sp-	-ilt
spoil	sp-	-oil
pie	p-	-ie
spy	sp-	-y

(Jager Adams, 1990, p. 308)

These sets of words, and patterns of onsets and rimes, developed in class or group discussion, provide a good basis for later handwriting practice.

(Open University, 1994, p. 67)

English in the National Curriculum in England and Wales also advocates a mixed approach to teaching reading. At Key Stage 1 (ages 5–7), the programme of study for reading states that:

> Pupils should be taught to read with fluency, accuracy, understanding and enjoyment, building on what they already know. In order to help them develop understanding of the nature and purpose of reading, they should be given an extensive introduction to books, stories and words in print around them. Pupils should be taught the alphabet, and be made aware of the sounds of spoken language in order to develop phonological awareness. They should also be taught to use various approaches to word identification and recognition, and to use their understanding of grammatical structure and the meaning of the text as a whole to make sense of print.
>
> (Department for Education and Welsh Office, 1995, p. 6)

The following types of 'knowledge, understanding and skills' are mentioned:

> *Phonic knowledge*, focusing on the relationship between print symbols and sound patterns …
>
> *Graphic knowledge*, focusing on what can be learned about word meanings and parts of words from consistent letter patterns …
>
> *Word recognition*, focusing on the development of a vocabulary of words recognised and understood automatically and quickly …
>
> *Grammatical knowledge*, focusing on the way language is ordered and organised into sentences (syntax) …
>
> *Contextual understanding*, focusing on meaning derived from the text as a whole.
>
> (Department for Education and Welsh Office, 1995, p. 7)

Within the classroom, teachers will need to make decisions not only about the practical implications of the ideas we have been discussing, but additionally, how they can reconcile their own beliefs about the teaching of reading with statutory requirements (as set out in national curricula or profiles).

❖   ❖   ❖   ❖   ❖

Activity 6.5   *(Reading B)*

Now read 'Reading: an infant school's perspective' (Reading B), in which Lorraine Dawes, an advisory teacher for primary English in the London Borough of Redbridge in the UK, describes her own perspective on teaching reading. Note the different reading activities she sees children enjoying in the classroom. How do these correspond to the approaches outlined in this section?

Comment

In the school described in Reading B, the teachers have decided to use an approach which offers a variety of routes into learning to read. There is an emphasis on 'enjoyable experiences with books' and reference to 'real books'. Alongside this, 'Children are encouraged to see patterns in words and relate sounds to letters in their reading … ', and they also follow a structured reading scheme. The teachers are answering the requirements of the national curriculum by providing a 'broad and balanced' reading curriculum, but have clearly constructed their approach in line with their own beliefs about teaching reading. There seems to be an attempt here to reconcile the polarization of the debate over reading, represented earlier by the extracts from Morris and Smith.

❖   ❖   ❖   ❖   ❖

6.4   PROCESS OR GENRE IN WRITING?

Sean, a 14-year-old pupil, follows a timetable at school which is divided up into different subjects. On Tuesdays, he has science, where he has to write up a report, followed by history, where he has to present an argument supporting or opposing a case study on the causes of World War Two. In the afternoon, in English, Sean completes an assignment on creative writing and poetry, and his day ends in geography, with an account of the destruction of the rain forests in Brazil.

Sean's experiences illustrate the last issue we discuss in this chapter; a controversy over the teaching of writing that has become prominent in recent years. In his day at school, Sean undertakes four different writing activities: a scientific report, an historical exposition in the form of an argument, creative writing and a factual account. In teaching writing, should pupils such as Sean be taught to develop generic writing ability, or do they need writing skills specific to particular writing activities, such as scientific report writing?

You may remember this was one of the issues discussed in Chapter 4. In this case the focus was on children's language learning during the school years, but there are also implications for what, and how, English teachers teach, as Janet Maybin made clear in Chapter 4, Reading C.

❖   ❖   ❖   ❖   ❖

Activity 6.6   *(Reading)*

Look again at 'Teaching writing: process or genre?' by Janet Maybin (Chapter 4, Reading C), together with any notes you made on this reading. It provides extremely useful background information for the remainder of this section. Note in particular:

*   the distinction Janet Maybin makes between **process** and **genre** approaches to teaching writing;

*   the example of a process approach;

*   critiques of the process approach, and arguments put forward by proponents of the genre approach that children need to be taught the characteristics of different types of texts;

*   critiques of the genre approach – in particular the issue of how far teachers should simply 'transmit' genres, as opposed to encouraging children to question their use.

This last point is particularly important for the discussion that follows.

❖   ❖   ❖   ❖   ❖

As Maybin suggested, this particular debate in English emerged originally in Australia. Davis and Watson write:

> At the moment, a major controversy over the teaching of writing is looming. In the last decade, the Primary English Teaching Association (now the largest organisation of English/Language Arts teachers in Australia) has popularised the process-conference approach [note: conferencing is where pupil and teacher talk through the writing processes undertaken by the pupil]. Its energetic editor throughout the 1970s and early 1980s, Bob Walshe, produced a very helpful book, *Every Child Can Write* and many pamphlets; in 1980 the Association brought Donald Graves to Australia. While there have doubtless been some techers who have misapplied Graves's approach, there is no doubt that he and Walshe between them have transformed the teaching of writing: they have managed to persuade teachers to do their teaching during the process, where it is helpful to young writers, rather than rely solely on detailed marking of the product as the means of bringing about improvement. But now this approach is being challenged by a group of linguists who are arguing that learning to write is a matter of mastery of particular genres, and that teachers should provide direct instruction in the characteristics of each genre so that students can model their writing on the genre structure.
>
> (Davis and Watson, 1990, pp. 169–70)

❖ ❖ ❖ ❖ ❖

Activity 6.7   *(Reading C)*

Now read 'Learning written genres' (Reading C), an extract from the work of the Australian genre theorists, J.R. Martin, Frances Christie and Joan Rothery. Look particularly at the two examples they provide of a genre approach to teaching writing.

In each case, how do you think the teacher is attempting to support the child's writing? In particular, what aspects of the child's writing is the teacher paying attention to? And how directive is she being? It may help to answer these questions if you compare these examples with the 'process' example of teacher intervention cited by Maybin in Chapter 4, Reading C.

Comment

The activity you have just done is similar to one used with British teachers by the Language in the National Curriculum (LINC) project. LINC asked the teachers to evaluate the teaching in Martin, Christie and Rothery's second example (about the giant), alongside the extract from Graves discussed by Maybin. The following text comes from LINC's critical appraisal of the two examples. Compare it with your own interpretation:

The LINC project was set up at the end of the 1980s to identify a model of the English language that could be used in teaching and learning. It is mentioned in Chapter 5, Reading C.

> *[Martin, Christie and Rothery]*
>
> On the positive side, the teacher here is allowing time and space for a detailed response to the writing. She is engaging less with the meaning than with the structure of the piece. Her comments, however, are not cursory or restricted to surface features of spelling and punctuation, but

foreground the compositional problem of creating a satisfactory resolution to a story. This, then is a significant learning encounter between a pupil and teacher through a text.

Against this, the teacher does seem to wrest the ownership of the story away from the pupil in a rather unsubtle manner. Much of the initial discussion involves the pupil in 'guessing' what is in the teacher's mind rather than in giving further shape to a genuine fictive experience ...

The problem here may relate to the way in which the teacher is modelling her responsive role as a reader. She creates the impression that she is matching the story against abstract structural criteria rather than engaging with the meaning of the story itself. The pupil eventually latches on to this and meets the requirements of providing further 'complication' and 'resolution' .... The teacher's lack of concern about the substance of the actual story ending could be regarded positively as returning ownership to the writer. On the other hand, it could confirm suspicion that she is more concerned with teaching story structure than with entering the pupil's world of meaning and imagination ...

[Graves]

The focus of this exchange is different. Again this represents a significant experience for student and teacher, the latter giving Anton time to think through his priorities and to find the focus in the piece where his feelings and purposes as a writer are most deeply engaged. It appears that the open nature of the teacher's questions helps Anton to confirm his hunch that the most fruitful territory for the writing might lie in the powerfully ambivalent feelings and vivid memories he has about his coach.

Here the teacher is presenting writing as a journey of discovery or revelation where focus, shape and structure emerge gradually as the writer grapples with meaning through successive drafting. This is very different from [Martin, Christie and Rothery] where the suggestion is that essential structures can be laid down as a form of advanced organisation into which to fit meaning.

On the negative side, there does seem a strange falseness in the teacher ignoring his role as reader/collaborator. Here notions of ownership are kept so pure that the draft as text is not referred to, even though (presumably) it is on the table in view of both participants. Sustaining the writing process without any response to the effectiveness of the unfolding text as text seems somewhat bizarre, particularly as the student seems very conscious that he doesn't 'want to just write and wander around'.

(Language in the National Curriculum, 1991, p. 131)

❖ ❖ ❖ ❖ ❖

Fundamental to the genre and process approaches are different sets of beliefs about the way that children learn, that is, broadly speaking, a 'knowledge-by-transmission' model versus a 'child-centred' model of knowledge through exploration. (You can probably see a parallel here with the discussion of reading above. In each case, different approaches are underpinned by differing beliefs about how children learn.)

Genre theorists argue that children need an explicit **grammar** to help them construct appropriate texts. This is a 'genre-based' grammar, however – it is rather different from many other descriptive grammars that restrict themselves to the structure of individual sentences. Knapp and Watkins (1994) state:

> Grammar is a name for the resource available to users of a language system for producing texts. A knowledge of grammar by a speaker or a writer shifts language use from the implicit and unconscious to a conscious manipulation of language and choice of appropriate texts.
>
> A genre-based grammar focuses on the manner through which different language processes or genres in writing are coded in distinct and recognisable ways. It first considers how a text is structured and organised at the level of the whole text in relation to its purpose, audience, and message. It then considers how all parts of the text, such as paragraphs and sentences, are structured, organised and coded so as to make the text effective as written communication and in particular, how all parts are used to serve the purposes of the language users. ...
>
> Grammar is used here as a resource for understanding the different codings, or arrangements, that are used to construct text ... a knowledge of grammar of a text provides a way of gaining a detailed and critical understanding of the forms and meaning of a culture.

(Knapp and Watkins, 1994, pp. 8–31)

This type of grammar, operating at text level, has been found useful by many educationalists. The British LINC project, for instance, included material based on a similar grammar in its training materials. These developments in genre-based grammars derive from the work of the linguist Michael Halliday. For a brief outline of his work, and how it relates to other grammars, see *Describing Language* (Graddol et al., 1994)

Adherents to the process writing model, you will remember, believe that an understanding of the way language works is the result of writing (and speaking and reading) and that specific teaching about text structure is unhelpful, and can be counter-productive. Freedman (1995) argues that:

> the rules of our language have not yet been described accurately even by the most sophisticated linguists ... This is a fortiori true for the rules underlying written genres, where research and theory are still comparatively in their infancy ... the rules that are known are simply too complex and too numerous to be explicitly taught in the context of writing or language instruction (as opposed to courses devoted to linguistics or discourse theory) ... 'learning' (which involves the conscious learning of rules ...) and 'acquisition' (which entails the unconscious inference of rules on the basis of exposure to the target language) ... are separate processes ... with no interface between the two possible ... Conscious learning can be called on in language production – but only for use by ...the 'monitor' or editing function.

(Freedman, 1995, pp. 38–9)

Advocates of a 'genre' approach then, believe grammar teaching is essential to enable the writer to manipulate text successfully; whereas advocates of a 'process' approach believe grammar is an integral part of language usage, and that explicit teaching is both unnecessary and potentially harmful to pupils' writing.

In decisions over the place of grammar in teaching about writing, governments once again have a powerful voice. *A Statement on English for Australian Schools* carries the paragraph:

> By learning a language for talking about language, students are better able to discuss and analyse the linguistic structures and features of texts in relation to their use.

(Australian Education Council, 1994a, p. 12).

Figure 6.3   Do children need to be taught features of different genres?

Different levels of achievement are identified in the Australian English curriculum, but these are not directly related to children's age or year level at school.

In the Australian English profile under the heading 'Linguistic structure and features in writing', there are specific requirements relating to the teaching of grammar. So, for example, it is suggested that students at level four, should:

> Discuss with the teacher and peers how particular aspects of grammar are characteristic of particular text types and attempt to adopt these consistently in their own writing (use of simple present tense in reports and procedures, use of imperative in instructions, use of particular kinds of conjunctions).
>
> (Australian Education Council, 1994b, p. 83)

These proposals seem consistent with the approach of the genre theorists, and therefore carry implications about the ways teachers should approach the teaching of grammar.

The national curriculum for England and Wales also requires that in Key Stages 3 and 4 (ages 11–16) pupils need a knowledge both of 'sentence grammar' and the organization of whole texts. They should be given opportunities to analyse their own writing and to learn about:

> *discourse structure* – the structure of whole texts; paragraph structure; how different types of paragraphs are formed; openings and closings in different kinds of writing;
>
> *phrase, clause and sentence structure* – the use of complex grammatical structures and the linking of structures through appropriate connectives; the use of main and subordinate clauses and phrases;
>
> *words* – components including stem, prefix, suffix, inflection; grammatical functions of nouns, verbs, adjectives, adverbs, pronouns, prepositions, conjunctions and demonstratives;
>
> *punctuation* – the use of the full range of punctuation marks, including full stops, question and exclamation marks, commas, semi-colons, colons, inverted commas, apostrophes, brackets, dashes and hyphens.
>
> (Department for Education and Welsh Office, 1995, p. 24)

Again, it is specific teaching of grammar which is required, albeit to enable pupils to 'analyse their own writing'.

Within the UK, the teaching of grammar has frequently been invested with great significance. In developing the national curriculum, for instance, some politicians wanted a return to 'traditional' grammar teaching and, for some commentators, such demands go way beyond the quest for an effective means of describing language. In an article in the *Observer* newspaper, 'The decline and fall of English grammar', John Rae stated:

> The overthrow of grammar coincided with the acceptance of the equivalent of creative writing in social behaviour. As the nice points of grammar were mockingly dismissed as pedantic and irrelevant, so was punctiliousness in matters such as honesty, responsibility, property, gratitude, apology and so on.
>
> (Rae, *Observer*, 7 February 1982)

The first book in this series explores in greater depth the notions of 'good' and 'bad' English. See *English: history, diversity and change* (Graddol et al. (eds), 1996).

In exploring the teaching of writing in this section, the debate is once again overlaid with ideology: grammar as upholding an order not just in writing, but in society. The genre theory of writing has come to be seen by some as a part of a similar argument. Wayne Sawyer, for instance, has been highly critical of what he terms 'the stated and latent ideologies of the genre school':

> Theirs [genre theorists] is the rhetoric of social empowerment: if we don't teach working class kids and minority groups such as Aboriginals and ESL kids the genres that our society values then we are denying them access to power in our society …
>
> Here we have the rhetoric of the new hard, dry Left denigrating so-called 'progressive' teaching because of its denial of power to deprived groups. Note, too, that the power comes when we give kids a *conscious* knowledge of language structures.
>
> (Sawyer, 1995, pp. 16–7)

Sawyer argues that what he terms 'genre-ism' is a 'conservative ideology': teaching children how to reproduce powerful genres cannot lead to social change – it simply teaches them to 'do what they are told' (Sawyer, 1995, p. 17). He believes that teachers should challenge the status quo rather than teaching children how to reproduce it. Wayne Sawyer and Ken Watson (1995) develop this argument in relation to the teaching of 'scientific' genres. They make the following points:

- Are types of knowledge and specific forms of the English language indivisible? It is possible to write about the same subject (science in this case) in different ways, and within the scientific community itself there are alternative (for example, less impersonal) forms of writing. If one accepts that genres of written English are not fixed but variable, the basis of teaching specific forms becomes questionable.

- Even if specific 'scientific' forms are used between experts, expert-to-expert language is not necessarily the most appropriate for children, and can constitute a barrier to learning; children are not the same as experts and most will not go on to become practising scientists.

- Learning the specific characteristics of genres is not the same as understanding the principles embodied in that field of learning. In fact, an insistence on appropriate linguistic forms can exclude certain children: teachers may fail to recognise the validity of a child's contribution just because it is not expressed in an appropriate style.

The debate about whether, and how, students should be taught certain genres in English has affected teaching at all levels: Chapter 8 considers the teaching of English for academic purposes within higher education.

❖   ❖   ❖   ❖   ❖

Activity 6.8   *(Allow about 10 minutes)*

Look back over these debates about the teaching of writing and also those about 'phonics'/'real books' mentioned earlier. Note down any parallels which you may be able to identify.

❖   ❖   ❖   ❖   ❖

I suggested earlier that, in both cases, different approaches were underpinned by different beliefs about children's learning. But the parallel seems also to be ideological: it has to do with the extent to which teaching specific linguistic forms is a means of empowering children, or, alternatively, keeping them in their place.

While this section has focused on a debate about the teaching of writing, the more general question of whether children should be taught specific forms of English is one that runs throughout this chapter and, indeed, through several other chapters in the book.

6.5   CONCLUSION

It has been suggested in this chapter that the English curriculum is frequently the subject of controversy. We have focused on three aspects of the curriculum: the place of Standard English and other language varieties; the phonics/real books debate in the teaching of reading; and the genre/process debate in the teaching of writing, in order to illustrate different approaches to English teaching, and also to gain a sense of recent and current controversies.

Several issues seem to cut across these different areas of the curriculum. To what extent, for instance, should one teach formal structures of English (the forms of Standard English, aspects of word structure to aid initial reading, the characteristics of different written genres)? Is it better to take a more holistic and contextualized approach to the language, focusing on language processes and language use? The positions taken on such issues sometimes depend upon different views of the English language and how it is used: is phonics appropriate for a language that does not have a straightforward sound–spelling correspondence? Can one provide an adequate definition of Standard English? Do the characteristics of written genres identified by analysts adequately reflect practices within those genres?

It also seems, however, that different views of teaching and learning underlie some of these debates: is teaching about the transmission of sets of skills, or about encouraging children to explore their own and others' language use? A related point concerns the broader sets of values that underpin different approaches to English teaching. English teaching can be seen as providing access to powerful language forms and language practices: to Standard English, for instance, or to certain formal written genres. But what are the implications for children's sense of themselves and their personal identities? Does teaching such forms and practices actually empower children, or serve to keep them more firmly in their place? Should teaching be about reproducing powerful forms and practices or questioning them? Whether or not they address them explicitly, teachers need to negotiate a path through such issues in planning their own approach to the English curriculum.

In this chapter we have focussed on contexts in which English is taught primarily as a first language. But huge numbers of children and adults learn English as a second or additional language, and it is to this topic that we turn in the following chapter.

Reading A

DIFFERENT VOICES IN THE ENGLISH CLASSROOM

Stuart Middleton

> *Ko te reo te mauri o te tangata*
> Language is the essence of life

New Zealand/Aotearoa has a recent English-language history (perhaps 180 years) but a Maori-speaking history that is much longer. Both languages are, by act of parliament, the official languages of the country. This finds expression in policies that support and promote te Reo Maori (the Maori language) in different ways; initiatives have included the development of Maori language radio and television services, the provision of Maori language preschool units (nga kohanga reo/Maori language nests), support for bilingual programmes within primary and secondary schools, and the development of Maori language based primary and secondary schools (Kura Kaupapa Maori).

However, there is a clear responsibility on all subject areas in secondary schools to reflect and promote the values of biculturalism and to seek ways in which the rights and responsibilities established by the Treaty of Waitangi (a treaty between the British monarchy and the Maori people signed in 1840 and the basis for government policy and response) may be upheld. This is not without controversy and English as a secondary school subject has been at the edge of developments in this area.

The New Zealand Curriculum Framework and the syllabus statement *English in the New Zealand Curriculum* make clear the responsibility that schools and classroom programmes have in this. One of the key principles of the curriculum framework is that: 'The New Zealand Curriculum recognizes the significance of the Treaty of Waitangi.' It expands on this by affirming that:

> the school curriculum will recognise and value the unique position of Maori in New Zealand society. All students will have the opportunity to acquire some knowledge of Maori language and culture. Students will also have the opportunity to learn through te reo [the language] and nga tikanga [the culture] Maori. The school curriculum will acknowledge the importance to all New Zealanders of both Maori and Pakeha traditions, histories and values.

(Ministry of Education, 1993, p. 7)

The syllabus *English in the New Zealand Curriculum* is quite clear in its orientation:

> All students should be encouraged to appreciate New Zealand's bicultural heritage. In their approaches to learning and teaching, in the issues that are addressed and in their selection of spoken, written and visual texts, teachers should include Maori perspectives. New Zealand texts, including those by Maori authors and about Maori, should form a significant part of the wide range of texts that students will explore.

(Ministry of Education, 1994, p. 17)

In encouraging teachers to use languages other than English as a basis for language study it goes on to say that 'students can also explore language by comparing English with another language, such as Maori, or any other language spoken or taught in the school community'. It finds justification in encouraging this in what it calls 'New Zealand's unique linguistic situation [which] includes its own distinctive varieties of English and the indigenous language Maori' (Ministry of Education, 1994, p. 17).

Teachers of English have worked to incorporate this concern for te Reo Maori into English programmes; perhaps the most obvious way has been to use the work of Maori writers. Many Maori writers are used in programmes and both the content and the style of their writing enables teachers to reflect the concerns for language and culture. The writers work in different ways to effect this. For example, Witi Ihimaera tends to gloss Maori terms, as in the following extract.

> This held the whakapapa of the whanau, the genealogy of the people of the village
>
> (Ihimaera, 1972, p. 37)

On the other hand, writers such as Patricia Grace prefer to reflect the bilingual nature of Maori society more directly.

> 'Aue!' said Ben, and he flicked his arms above his head. 'Number ten.' And as the others nodded, sighed, he explained. 'Five fingers on this hand. And five fingers on this hand.' He showed them his hands. 'Era.' he turned to Raniera. 'You put your hands around the tuna like this. Na? Five and five are ten – Number ten. The fingers touched – Lucky Touch, the fingers touched.'
>   'Aee,' they agreed.
>   'Ko tera taku! I'll say!'
>   Raniera shook his head. 'Aue! Waste a good dream.'
>   'No dough for the Maori today.' said Monty. 'Ka hinga to tatau orate.'
>
> (Grace, 1975, p. 22)

Maori oral culture provides a clear comparison with English in terms of oratory. Custom and practice in oratory leads to a very stylized form of speechmaking: Maori speakers will greet the audience formally, they will refer to their genealogy and pay their respects to the dead and to the physical environment. They will then move on to the subject of their speech, concluding with formal proverbs and suchlike. This contrasts with the quick and inexorable logic of the English orators, who spend most of the time available talking about the 'topic'.

But perhaps the most controversial aspect of incorporating te Reo Maori into English programmes has been the proposal that a comparative study of the two languages would help to increase students' metalinguistic knowledge, that is, their knowledge *about* language, while at the same time meeting some of the social policy imperatives of the government.

There are sound reasons for such a study, in terms both of linguistic knowledge and of what we know about learning. The process of learning a language can lead to the development of a sound *metalanguage*: children learn how to talk about language by asking 'In what ways is this language I am learning different from or the same as the language I already know?'

The notion of metalinguistic awareness is also discussed in Chapter 1 of this book.

Example of a teaching activity that involves comparing Maori and Pakeha language and culture

A Form 3 (Age 13–14) class had been looking at a novel by a New Zealand Maori writer, Witi Ihimaera, *The Whale Rider* . It is a grand story about a young woman's encounter with the traditions of her tribe and with a whale, Paikea. At one point in the story the girl is taken to a marae (a Maori meeting place) and is introduced to her iwi (sub-tribe) by her hapu (extended family). It is an exciting meeting and the young girl sees the protocol of such a meeting graphically illustrated.

At about the same time there had been several formal assemblies in the school to welcome the Minister of Education among others. One of these had included the local kawa (protocol) for such meetings while the other had not and was conducted along conventional pakeha (European) lines.

The students were invited to develop a bilingual reader that had on facing pages a Maori meeting and on the other side a European meeting dealing with the same matter or event. They were encouraged to consider language differences (for example, Maori being used as opposed to English, the greetings, the ritual acknowledgement of ancestors, the dead, the physical surroundings etc.), differences in protocol (e.g. who gets to speak), the actual words being used, and so on. Clearly the more fluency students had in the two languages the easier it was. But by pairing students so that a student more competent in one language was placed with a student more competent in the other language the goals were achieved.

Where English is being learned as a mother tongue by students who are monolingual, this does not naturally occur. (It is often forgotten that well-educated users of English learned 'grammar' by going through such a comparative process as they learned one of the second languages that characterized 'academic' study.)

The Maori language is an ideal language to use for comparative purposes in English programmes in New Zealand:

- It is one of the official languages of New Zealand.

- It is used by a portion of the Maori population in their daily lives.

- It is the language which carries the culture of the indigenous people of the country.

Linguistically, the Maori language has significant differences with English and this adds to its value for comparative study.

The New Zealand Association for the Teaching of English, under contract to the New Zealand government, has recently completed a major resource *Exploring Language*. This will enable teachers to develop their metalinguistic skills and at the same time will provide a basis for the study of language by students in schools.

Students will be able to undertake a descriptive study of English through a comparative study of English and Maori. By asking that crucial question 'In what ways is this language different from or similar to the language I already know?', they will develop an understanding of language and how it works. In undertaking this study they will use an agreed terminology that has been standardized by and will be promoted through the resource.

The box below provides a brief illustration of just some of the elements in English that can be better understood through such a study.

Comparing Maori and English

Students may compare Maori and English in terms of their linguistic structure: they may look at differences in grammar, vocabulary, the sound system, the writing system. They may also look at historical changes to each language, at contemporary geographical and social variation, and at how the two languages are used. As an illustration, grammatical examples might include:

Word forms – inflections

English	*Maori*
Add -s for plural form:	The vowel is lengthened or the article is altered:
wheel → *wheels*	*te wiira* → *nga wiira*
house → *houses*	*wahine* → *nga wāhine*
Add -'s to show possession (or sometimes -' if a word already ends in 's'):	There is a possessive particle:
The girl's address	*te kurt a Hone*
James' notebook	*te whare a Hone*

Sentence structure

English	*Maori*
Word order is Subject–Verb–Object:	Usual order is Verb–Subject–Object:
Stephen has washed the dishes	*Kua horoi a Tipene inga pereti*
	(has washed Stephen the plates)
Word order in noun phrase is usually determiner–adjective–noun:	Normal order is determiner–noun–adjective:
The big basket	*Te kete rahi*
	(the kit big)

Idioms

English	*Maori*
good as gold	*Kei te tangi te tui*
	(He's in great form)
	Literally, 'The tui sings': usage restricted to orators

A comparison between the two languages not only increases understanding of how English works but also promotes an understanding that the systems and patterns of English are not the only ones that can be used and that there is a degree of arbitrariness about them. Trials with teachers working on this comparative approach suggest that it brings to the study of English a relevance that allows students to see the linguistic fabric of the world in which they live with greatly increased clarity, and without some of prejudices and confusions that sometimes arise in a linguistically diverse community. But most importantly, such an approach does seem to promote the understanding of the English language and the way that it works that is sought by the syllabus.

Ko taku nui
Taku wehi
Taku whakatiketike
Ko taku reo

My greatness
My inspiration
My elevation
Is my language

References

GRACE, P. (1975) *Waiariki*, Wellington, Longman Paul.

IHIMAERA, W. (1972) *Pounamu Pounamu*, Auckland, Heinemann.

MINISTRY OF EDUCATION (1993) *New Zealand Curriculum Framework*, Wellington, Learning Media.

MINISTRY OF EDUCATION (1994) *English in the New Zealand Curriculum*, Wellington, Learning Media.

This reading was specially commissioned for this book.

Reading B
READING: AN INFANT SCHOOL'S PERSPECTIVE

Lorraine Dawes

Oakdale Infant School places great emphasis on children becoming readers, and puts a priority on enjoyable experiences with books right from nursery. Shared reading with 'big' books encourages children to join in and retell. As teachers read with children, there is much talk, linking the pictures with the text. Some books become very familiar to the children, and they learn them by heart, which gives them confidence to enjoy the book by themselves and behave like readers. The first strategies they learn are related to the whole text – making meaning, relating to their own experience, predicting, reflecting. Focusing on the print is introduced through big books – first whole sentences and phrases, then focusing on the words they are learning through their writing – so phonics and word recognition are developed in the context of reading and writing. Storybooks are used as a starting point for activities across the curriculum.

Alongside the wide range of 'real' books, the school uses the *Oxford Reading Tree* [a structured reading scheme], and children first meet this through the large

Reading activities at Oakdale Infant School

flop-over books which introduce the characters. Children use the picture-only books to tell stories about the characters, and enjoy the various support materials – matching games, computer programs, and key word posters – as they read more of the books.

Broad and balanced collections of fiction and nonfiction books by popular authors and publishers are arranged in accessible class libraries. Children have time with these books each day, sharing reading; the sharing happens spontaneously as it is modelled by the teachers. They can take these books home, as well as their 'reading' book, and a library book which they change every week. Information books with high quality illustrations are used throughout the school, so the children become confident in using all kinds of books. They also make their own books, so they have reading resources in familiar language. Older readers make books to read to younger children. Children also often bring books from home. Reading is involved with many of the computer programs they use across the curriculum.

Parents are encouraged to read to their children, as well as hearing them read. There is a home–school book, in which parents make their own comments on their children's reading. Meetings are held for parents to discuss their role in their children's reading development. One afternoon, parents of Reception and Nursery children were invited into the school to learn about how teachers start children off with reading, and what parents can do to support them. They were given a short guide, *Helping Your Child with Reading*.

The classrooms are rich with print, and the children's attention is drawn to this, with the result that they consult the lists and posters, reading to each other and pointing out where to find words. Purposeful notices involving name cards provide meaningful reading, and in the writing area there are wordbanks and verbal stimuli and support for writing. Children are encouraged to see patterns in words and to relate sounds to letters in their reading and writing.

When hearing individuals read, teachers assess their confidence, fluency, reading strategies and response, so they know what key skills need developing. Children often re-read familiar books, gaining more from each reading. There are many smaller series of books (other than the *Oxford Reading Tree*) to which teachers may move readers, when they feel they need a period of consolidation. This avoids parental pressure for children to be constantly moving through the scheme. It is more important that they read with understanding. Meaningful intonation is developed through example from teachers and peers – mixed groups reading plays together provide good models for each other.

Children are encouraged to respond to the books they read, and support is provided: from choosing appropriate smiley/bored faces for early readers, to more complex review sheets for experienced readers.

Sue Borland has a Year Two class, with a wide range of reading development within it, including some able readers. She reads both fiction and nonfiction aloud to her class, with discussion to help them distinguish between story and factual writing. She has been reading Roald Dahl's *James and the Giant Peach* to the class; it fits in with their topic of minibeasts, and offers the more able readers an example of the kind of book they might soon be reading.

Julie has enjoyed *James and the Giant Peach*, and is reading *Charlie and the Great Glass Elevator*. She is a 'free' reader and chooses a variety of fiction and nonfiction. Sue guides her choice of reading by making suggestions and encouraging her to read other books by authors she has enjoyed. When Sue read *The Owl Who was Afraid of the Dark*, Julie bought it through the Book Club. Sue hears her read regularly once or twice a week, and Julie also reads to classroom assistants and parent helpers. With her teacher, she usually reads a couple of pages and they discuss it. Sue works on understanding: predicting, suggesting alternative endings, characters, thinking about the story, with prompts such as 'What sort of person do you think he is going to turn out to be?' She also focuses attention on effective language, especially description, that will support Julie in her own writing. Her reading record shows that over a two-month period Julie has read *The Sausage is a Cunning Bird* (poetry), *Teacher's Pet, Little Pig Goes to School, The Pig that Barked, Sir Undone, Monkey Business, Sir Undone* (again), *Tanya the Chicken, The Universe* (nonfiction) and is now reading *Charlie and the Great Glass Elevator*. She has also done lots of incidental reading, sharing books at the start of the day, library time, etc. Julie herself says of reading, 'I like it because it doesn't just make you enjoy the book, it tells you things as well. We have library every Wednesday and you can choose any book. I like this one – *The Universe* – it's about stars, and you can go back and look at books you've read before in earlier colours.' She likes to research topic work, using index, contents, etc. and is able to compose questions to offer to other children about what she has found out.

Helen is just beginning to make progress with reading after a slow start, and has just moved on to the Yellow Books in *Oxford Reading Tree*. Sue hears her read two or three times a week, and Hillary Hunwicks also works with her on reading twice a week. Sue has one afternoon a week when the children are involved with self-maintaining activities, so she is relatively free to concentrate on readers, but also she has to use part of her lunchtimes for hearing children read. Helen often asks to read to her teacher and is very keen at the moment. When Sue works with Helen, Helen reads first and Sue discusses the pictures and story with her. One advantage of the *Oxford Reading Tree* books is that Helen knows the characters so she can use her prediction skills; Sue does not like to have too much discussion before reading, in case it spoils the story. She tailors her practice to what the reader needs: earlier, and with unfamiliar books, she would go through talking about the pictures and helping Helen anticipate the story. Now the balance is the other way – text first, then pictures. Helen glances at the pictures for confirmation while she is reading. If she needs help with a word, Sue gauges whether she should tell her or help her work it out: for example, with the word *began,* Sue covered up the *gan* to help Helen get a start on the word. Helen still could not work it all out, so Sue told her. Sue prompts her to look at the pictures: 'Look at Biff's expressions.' Helen says, 'I like *The Magic Key.* Here's Biff and Chips. I can read it but sometimes I forget the names. Look, *Biff and Chip ran to the house. They looked in the window.* I liked *James and the Giant Peach.* It had lots of animals – caterpillar, greenfly, spider, ladybird and worm.'

Biff and Chip ran to the house.
They looked in the window.

Figure 1   *Biff and Chip. Extract from the* Oxford Reading Tree

On the carpet, when the class are sharing books in twos and threes, Helen tends not to choose a book but looks at those being read by other children. Sue often suggests that Helen and another child at a similar stage in reading look at a book together at odd moments during the week.

Helen made a slow start with reading, and her decoding of print started with books made for her about people in her family, using her own words. Although her whole-text strategies are mainly in place, her strategies at word level are slower to develop. She needs a lot of reinforcement with individual words, not being sure of some initial sounds and finding it difficult to retain words recognized on sight. She has an envelope of words that she can build into sentences about her family and home life, and for word games. (These words are drawn from her reading and writing, so are not decontextualized, but meaningful to her.) These activities help her focus on the words and draw on her developing phonic knowledge and sight vocabulary.

Sue's teaching of reading is grounded in a detailed knowledge of each child as a reader. Her whole-class activities (reading aloud, discussing books, focusing on sounds, drawing attention to effective language, difference between fact and fiction, etc.) are relevant to the range of readers in her class, but this is complemented by one-to-one teaching tailored to individual pupils' needs, as these two examples show.

The author thanks Hillary Hunwicks (language-coordinator) and Sue Borland of Oakdale Infant School, London Borough of Redbridge. Names of pupils have been changed.

This reading was specially commissioned for this book.

Reading C
LEARNING WRITTEN GENRES

J.R. Martin, Frances Christie and Joan Rothery

Genre-based approaches to writing development have been particularly concerned with curriculum genres, both from the point of view of assessing current methodologies and as well from the perspective of developing new genres which will teach writing more effectively to a wider range of children. In order to develop more effective genres it has been assumed that two critical factors must be addressed. First, ways must be found of introducing strategies familiar to children from their experience of learning to talk into their experience of learning to write. A place must in other words be found for interaction and guidance in the context of shared experience. Second, ways must be found to take into account the fact that written language is different from spoken language and that anything even vaguely approximating the kind of immersion experienced when learning to talk is out of the question. Writing is just too slow – exponentially so.

One of Rothery's early suggestions for a genre-based approach to teaching writing is outlined below. Stages 3 and 4 are oriented to developing shared experience as a basis for writing. Interaction is explicitly built into stages 3 and 6. And guidance is a feature of every stage.

1   *Introducing a genre* – modelling a genre *implicitly* through reading to or by the class; for example reading *Little Red Riding Hood.*

2   *Focusing on a genre* – modelling a genre *explicitly* by naming its stages; e.g. identifying the stages Orientation, Complication and Resolution in *Little Red Riding Hood.*

3   *Jointly negotiating a genre* – teacher and class jointly composing the genre under focus; the teacher *guides* the composition of the text through questions

and comments that provide *scaffolding* for the stages of the genre; e.g. in a narrative the following question might point towards a Resolution stage: 'How will x escape from the witch? Does she have to do it alone, or will someone help her?'

4   *Researching* – selecting material for reading; notemaking and summarizing; assembling information before writing (normally these skills cannot be assumed).

5   *Drafting* – a first attempt at individually constructing the genre under focus.

6   *Consultation* – teacher, pupil *consultation*, involving direct reference to the *meanings* of the writer's text; e.g. questions that help the writer to resolve the Complication stage of a narrative; young writers tend to find Complications easy, but resolving their characters' problems is hard; consultation involves getting into the text, not standing aside from it.

7   *Publishing* – writing a final draft that may be published for the class library, thus providing another input of genre models, and of course enjoyable reading.

… Stages 3 and 6 require special consideration. Stage 3 is based on work by Brian Gray (see Gray, 1980, 1985) on concentrated language encounters. The basic idea is for teachers and students to jointly construct a model of the genre in focus. An excerpt from one such negotiation is reproduced below.

Text [1]

(The Year 2 teacher and students have decided on the following opening – the general Classification in Report structure: There are lots of different kinds of ships. At the Maritime Museum we saw model ships. Joan Rothery is in the class and contributing to the negotiation)

T: *Tell me what you know about the ships. Or what we saw.*

C: *What do you mean?*

T: *Well, how can we go on now? Let's read what we've got.* (Teacher and class read first two sentences.)

C: *Do you mean Complication?*

T: *No, it hasn't got a Complication. That's the tricky part in this. This is not a Narrative. This is a Report. We have to say exactly what we saw and exactly what we know about what we saw.* (Teacher reads: At the Maritime Museum we saw model ships.) *Perhaps we could have what sorts of model ships.*

J: *I didn't see them. I'd like to know exactly what kinds of ships. Were they sailing ships?*

T: *That's what we need to do, isn't it. Remember who we're writing for.*

J: *I didn't go. You have to tell me about the ships you saw.*

T: *Remember writing a Report for Mr Campbell to put in his book about excursions. If someone picks it up they're like Mrs Rothery. They won't know what's there. But they'll want to say, 'Wow! That's great. Let's go there.' What can we say?*

C: *We saw the Endeavour.*

T:	*Right, We saw the Endeavour. What about the Endeavour? What can you tell me about the Endeavour? What kind of ship is it, Jack?*
C:	*It's an olden days ship.*
T:	(scribing) *It is an olden days ship. What else do we know about it?*
C:	*Captain Cook sailed around the world in it.*
T:	*This is a great Report.* (Teacher scribes) *What else do we know about the Endeavour, Gordon?*
C:	*He sailed to Australia. He discovered Australia in it.*
C:	*It was a pirate ship.*
C:	*No, it's not. He wasn't a pirate.*
T:	*No, he wasn't a pirate.*

(Negotiated text to this point: *There are lots of different kinds of ships. At the Maritime Museum we saw model ships. We saw the Endeavour. It is an olden days ship. Captain Cook sailed around the world in it. He discovered Australia in it.*)

Negotiations such as these are an extremely effective method of modelling genres for children. The text is based on shared experience, with the children assuming the responsibility of developing the field. The teacher's role is that of guiding them into the appropriate genre (in this case taking care to steer them away from recount and into report). This type of interaction makes it possible for teachers to provide scaffolding for writing in a way that is parallel to learning spoken genres. The responsibility for developing a successful text is assumed jointly, as when learning to talk.

Writing is of course, by nature, monologic discourse. And the purpose of providing jointly constructed models is to enable children to write texts of their own, when they seem ready to do this. However, as Graves' work (e.g. 1984) has demonstrated, it is possible to interact with children as they write. The text illustrates stage 6 in the genre-based model outlined above: consultation. This term is preferred to conferencing because it explicitly acknowledges the teacher's guiding role.

Text [2]

(A Year 2 writer consults with Joan Rothery, beginning by reading her text aloud.)

C:	*Once upon a time there was a big giant. He lived in a big hole in the woods and he was rich. He went out of the hole. He found a trap door. He went into the trapdoor and he got in trouble by a gigantic man.*
J:	*Is that finished?*
C:	*Yes.*
J:	*I think it would be good to know what happened to him. What sort of trouble did he get into?*
C:	*I don't know.*
J:	*Well, let's make it up.*
C:	*Well, I'll get a piece of paper.*
J:	*Don't write it down yet. Let's just say it into the tape. What sort of trouble might he have got into?*

C: *He might have got into trouble because he might have broken something?*

J: *Yes, like what?*

C: *Like what. Like a …*

J: *What might make someone very angry if you broke it?*

C: *Aaaah. There's a trapdoor. Perhaps it should be something … a vase?*

J: *A precious vase?*

C: *Yes.*

J: *So once he got inside he got into trouble.*

C: *Because he broke a precious vase.*

J: *And then what happened?*

C: *Then what happened …*

J: *Yes, what's going to happen to the giant. I mean he's just got into trouble.*

C: *Then the giant went back home.*

J: *Weell …*

C: *That can't be because it didn't get sorted out.*

J: *No, it didn't really, did it? He's got to get away from the gigantic man, hasn't he?*

C: *Yes.*

J: *We know that he got into trouble, he broke the precious vase …*

C: *Mmmm.*

J: *Is he going to escape?*

C: *He paid some money.*

J: (laughing) *That's not a bad idea.*

C: *Because he was rich, remember?* (Points to drawing that accompanies text.) *That's a big thing, full of money.*

J: *All right, so what will you say? That the giant was very rich and paid the man to let him go.*

C: *But what about when he broke the vase? I have to write about that too.*

J: *Yes, write about that first and then write about him paying the money so he could go.*

C: *Yes.*

J: *I think …*

C: *No, the man umm the man began to be his friend and they all lived happily ever after.*

J: *Oh, so they lived happily together. Oh, that's a good idea. OK. Let's play it back.*

Once again the child generates the field, with minimal guidance from Joan. But as far as genre is concerned Joan takes a very positive role, scaffolding the Complication/Resolution staging that is fundamental to this kind of narrative. It is this guidance that makes the teaching work.

References

GRAVES, D. (1984) *A Researcher Learns to Write: selected articles and monographs,* London, Heinemann.

GRAY, B. (1980) 'Concentrated language encounters as a component of functional language/literacy teaching' in MCCAUSLAND, T. and MCCAUSLAND, M. (eds) *Proceedings of the Conference on Child Language Development: theory into practice,* Launceston, Tas., Launceston Teacher's Centre.

GRAY, B. (1985) 'Helping children to become language learners in the classroom', in CHRISTIE, M. (ed.) *Aboriginal Perspectives on Experience and Learning: the role of language in Aboriginal education,* Geelong, Deakin University Press, pp. 87–104.

Source: Martin et al., 1987, pp. 67–72

ENGLISH FOR SPEAKERS OF OTHER LANGUAGES

Jill Bourne

7.1 INTRODUCTION

This chapter looks at the teaching of English to speakers of other languages. This is not a marginal issue. The vast majority of English users across the world have learned English as an additional language, and much of this learning has taken place at least partly within the formal confines of an English language classroom. Where is English taught to speakers of other languages? How is English presented to such learners? Who learns English, and why? What does it mean to be a second language learner of English? It may be that you learned English yourself as an additional language, or that you have taught English – in which case you will have a great deal of personal experience to bring to bear on these questions.

Teaching English to speakers of other languages may at first seem to be a much simpler activity than teaching English 'mother tongue', described in the last chapter. It might seem common sense that it is simply a question of teaching the system – the words, sounds, grammar and ways of using the English language, as codified in grammar books, dictionaries and textbooks – to those who have not before had access to this system. Put simply:

> we need to know the *words* that express our meanings and how to put those words together in *grammar* so that they make sense. We want to be sure that the *function* of what we are saying and our *pronunciation* are not only clear, but also appropriate in our *discourse* with other people.
>
> (Edge, 1993, p. 27)

However, as you will have expected, with language things are never that simple. First, few people come to English classes without some experience of English. The global spread of English has been powerful. It has left its mark not only in terms of the use of English for a variety of functions in many different societies, but also in its influence on other languages themselves, just as other languages have left their mark on English through this contact.

What this means is that it has become less and less easy to assume either a total lack of experience of English on the part of learners or that learning English will be for them a neutral, academic experience. Policies concerned with language in education seem to recognize this implicitly, often being ambivalent and contradictory. For example, Prodromou (1990) describes how, when there were strong moves to introduce English into primary schools in Greece, there were simultaneous moves to ban English shop names. Baldauf (1990) describes how in Samoa there was a desire to develop English language skills for 'progress' but at the same time a fear of losing traditional languages and cultures, resulting in positive policies on English being implemented in ways that were not effective.

Furthermore, a positive national policy towards teaching a language does not necessarily mean that an *individual* is equally positive about learning that language. Learners' attitudes towards English may be ambivalent. There may be material rewards and hence motivation for learning English, but learners may also have an emotional resistance where they feel, consciously or unconsciously, that the learning of the language is being imposed on them, or that they are excluded from a worthwhile role within an English-speaking society. As a teacher of a conversation class for immigrant women once asked, 'Why do they come if they will not speak?' (Mukherjee, 1985). English language learners have to balance costs against benefits.

I follow up these issues later in the chapter, but first I want to look more closely at some of the contexts in which English is being taught and learned around the world.

7.2   WHERE IS ENGLISH TAUGHT AND LEARNED?

English as a foreign language

The examples below illustrate the variety of contexts in which English is learned. They paint a complex picture of English language teaching and its connections to the whole-school curriculum and to policy at national level. Much of the data on which they are based is drawn from the British Council (1993).

Two important trends can be discerned globally. First, within the school system there is a general move towards more English classes for young learners at primary level (from 5 to 11 years). While in countries like Malaysia this is not encouraged within the school system, there is a growing demand both there and globally for private English classes for children, with many wealthy parents clearly willing to pay to ensure that their children get ahead on the ladder to social success in which they see English as a factor.

A second trend is the beginning of a shift away from a focus on the language alone towards what is called in the USA **language and content teaching**, or combining language teaching with curriculum content. In Germany, for example, a small but growing number of schools are setting up 'bilingual sections', which start by offering extra lessons in English and then introduce the teaching of an increasing number of subjects through the medium of English as the child progresses up the school. Similar developments are taking place in the former east European countries, most notably the Czech Republic and Hungary, where in recent years there has been a huge investment in the development of English teaching (to replace Russian as a first foreign language) supported by both the USA and the UK. In south-east Asia, Brunei, a neighbour of Malaysia, is also concerned over standards of attainment at university level where much of the reading is through the medium of English. Brunei is developing **bilingual education**: the medium in lower primary is Malay, then supported English-medium education is gradually introduced in upper primary – English language and subject classes are combined by, for example, the teaching of English through geography. Similar developments can be found in Hong Kong, another country where English retains an important presence. However, for the majority of children wherever they live English is still learned as a subject in classes that focus on the language itself.

In addition to the teaching of English in the school system there is a big demand for English for adult learners all over the world. In the examples below Brazil provides an example of this.

France

In France most pupils study at least three to four hours of English a week from the age of 11. While most classes focus on the teaching of the language, there is a pilot 'classes européenes' scheme in some lycées in which English is learned through subject content – taught through the medium of English. Since 1989 there have been pilot schemes for introducing English at primary level: by 1993, of the 30 per cent of children studying a foreign language in primary school 80 per cent were learning English.

Malaysia

Malaysia is a multilingual country. The main language groups include speakers of Malay, Chinese and Tamil. Bahasa Malaysia has been adopted as the country's official language, with English recognized as an important second language. Although English is a language used extensively for internal business, Chinese is an equally important trading language in the region. Because of the colonial history English was for many years the medium of education; however, Bahasa Malaysia was gradually introduced into the system until, by 1983, it had replaced English as the medium of instruction from the primary school through to the university. This policy led to concern that university students no longer achieved the competence in English they needed in order to work with the science and technical texts that were published mainly in English. Accordingly, in 1995 the national language policy was modified to allow universities to teach science and technical subjects through the medium of English.

Morocco

French remains the predominant foreign language taught in schools in Morocco, but a reading knowledge of English is becoming increasingly important at university level, even where courses are taught through the medium of Arabic or French. In addition, a new English-medium university has recently been opened – a development found in a growing number of countries. In 1993 the minister of education announced that 90 per cent of secondary students listed English as their preferred foreign language option. Until recently the emphasis was on spoken English, to enable school leavers to communicate with other speakers of English; however, new approved materials and methods are shifting the balance and giving greater importance to the development of reading and study skills in English.

Teaching adults in Brazil

In Brazil there are language schools run by both British and US cultural organiza-tions, with over 195,000 students attending classes. In addition, a huge number of registered private language schools teach English, and English language teacher training has a strong presence in the university system, which offers MAs for local teachers of English.

   Students have the choice of one of two varieties of English, British or US, depending on which language school they go to. For some, sociopolitical con-siderations appear to determine the choice of school, alongside practical factors such as expense and convenience. While the US variety would appear to be the most relevant, given geographical location, some Brazilians choose British English just because it seems to be more politically neutral in this context, or even to signal rejection of US power in the region.

The English language – a global industry

Private language schools, not tied to national syllabuses and often with unqualified teachers looking for guidance on teaching, have been prime customers for English language textbook publishers, whether for adults or children. In order to maximize profitability and hold down costs the publishing industry attempts to produce English language teaching textbooks, audiovisual material and teacher-training materials that will be acceptable across as many different countries as possible. Thus fashions and fads, and concerns about pedagogy in English-dominant countries, as well as carefully thought-through suggestions for effective English teaching, have swept around the globe through the medium of popular, best-selling language schemes, mainly from the UK and the USA.

While private language schools tend to work with small classes, English teaching in state schools often involves large classes with few resources. Pupils' and other teachers' expectations of the sorts of activity that should take place in the schoolroom are likely to place great constraints on English teachers. Nevertheless, techniques and materials developed in the private language-school context have often been recommended as models for state school teachers by visiting teacher trainers. I look at some of these trends later in the chapter, and consider arguments that this practice constitutes a form of 'cultural colonization' of other nations.

English as a 'second language'

❖   ❖   ❖   ❖   ❖

Activity 7.1   *(Allow about 20 minutes)*

Read the following case studies adapted from Jordan (1992). Jot down the ways in which the language-learning needs of these people are likely to differ.

1   Rafiq, aged 11, can speak, read and write Bengali competently, having completed five years at school in Bangladesh before moving to England. He is now taking his first tentative steps in the use of English. In his school, English language support teachers work alongside subject teachers; they provide training and support in organizing group work, and in planning lessons to give access to the curriculum for bilingual learners of English. Children like Rafiq, who need more support with reading and writing in English, also have extra small-group English literacy lessons.

2   Amina, aged 14, arrived in Australia as a refugee directly from the war zone in Somalia, where she had seen her brother shot. She was clearly traumatized, depressed and frightened of crowds. Amina's school arranged for her to join a small and sheltered 'induction' class for some weeks to support her and to help her to understand her new environment. Her school has also arranged for a Somali-speaking community volunteer to come into her lessons each

week and to accompany her for professional counselling. In her induction group she will learn to find her way around the school, learn 'survival' English, meet some of the teachers and gradually begin to join her regular class. Because of her age and the fact that her peers will soon be entering examination classes, Amina will probably attend English support classes for the rest of her time in school. These will not focus on English alone but will attempt to give access to the full curriculum and prepare Amina for making use of further education opportunities after she leaves school.

3   Lupita came to California from Mexico two years ago at the age of 7. She spoke no English but joined a school where over 90 per cent of the children and at least half of the staff were Spanish speakers. Lupita's parents were encouraged to place her in the 'bilingual' stream of the school. In the early years the curriculum here was mainly in Spanish, with classes in English as a second language. Just recently, the language balance of the class has begun to shift, with more and more work being done in English. By the time Lupita transfers to high school she will be working mainly in English, although she will also continue to improve her reading and writing in Spanish.

4   Leila is an adult political refugee to England from what she calls Turkish Kurdistan. She was a journalist there but, although she is a university graduate, she is now working as a clothes presser in a factory, where all her fellow workers are Turkish Kurds. Her original intention was to learn English quickly and become a journalist again, but she found she had to take a job for financial reasons, which limits time for study, and as she arrives tired for evening language classes her progress is disappointingly slow. She is trying to find an alternative job in a company which provides language support linked to skills training.

5   Thatch is from Cambodia. He was educated to primary level and worked as a driver there. On arrival in Australia he attended a short, intensive 'survival' English course in a reception centre. After several years in Australia he understands English well and can cope with everyday situations. He can read and write English a little. Many people he meets, however, still find his pronunciation of English unclear and sometimes do not understand him. As he was made redundant from his first job, he has time to go regularly to English classes to learn how to look for work and handle interviews, and to prepare for coping with specialist job training courses if he is fortunate enough to get a place on one. He particularly wants to improve his pronunciation.

6   Liu is a businessman working in a new Chinese 'joint enterprise'. He has been sent to Singapore for business studies as well as to seek new contracts and improve his English. He attends a twice weekly English course for businessmen in a private language school where he is taught one to one and in small-group classes.

Comment

In the first three case studies the emphasis was on finding ways of supporting the development of English while giving the children access to the full educational curriculum.

Rafiq, Amina and Lupita were lucky to go to school in areas that had built up their resources and developed expertise in working with bilingual children. This is certainly not the case everywhere, and many learners of English are left to sink or swim in a monolingual school curriculum (Bourne, 1989).

In Amina's case, English was not the immediate priority compared to dealing with her traumatized condition, but it remained an important element in coming to terms with life in her new surroundings. Cummins (1979) has argued that it can take around five years at least for a child to develop a new language to the level needed for cognitive/academic purposes; however, concepts established in the stronger language can easily be transferred into a second language as it develops. Children like those in the case studies cannot wait until they have learned enough English before they acquire literacy skills, learn mathematics, history, etc. and join in other classes, or they will lose their entitlement to an education.

This is a powerful argument for transitional bilingual education like Lupita's if full bilingual education is not possible or desired. However, the resources are not always available or the numbers of children speaking the same language may make such provision financially and organizationally impractical. Political policy decisions are involved here. Where the emphasis is on the integration of minority groups into the dominant society, provision for languages other than English may receive little attention. On the other hand, as in some states in the USA, political will and community activism may bring about provision for bilingual education like Lupita's where there are large groups of people sharing the same languages. In either context, special provision is likely to be made for some form of extra English language teaching, since most educationalists would accept that no child should be denied access to the language of the wider society and the power that goes with it.

It is important to remember the diversity of needs among English language learners themselves in English-dominant countries: they will have different prior experience of and access to English, different levels of education and literacy in their first languages, and different views of themselves as minority group members in the English-dominant society.

The three adults described in the case studies also have different needs from one another. Although the first two are both relative beginners in English, they look for different things in their classes. Leila would really like intensive English classes like the ones Liu receives, to take her to the high level she needs for journalism. However, she is willing to settle for English language development integrated into skills training in order to be paid while improving her English. Thatch also wants language linked to skills training but first needs help to handle the hurdle of job finding and interviews. Again, his needs are pressing, and slow progress in English will lead to disillusionment. Liu's private classes allow him to work at his own level and pace, while working in an English-speaking milieu at the same time forces him to make use of all the English he knows and to build up fluency.

❖   ❖   ❖   ❖   ❖

In making appropriate provision, teachers have to consider learners' needs and aspirations, the language skills they possess in both languages, other skills they may make use of, any barriers to learning and ways of overcoming them. Ideally, an analysis of this sort will lead to the planning and negotiating of an individual programme drawing on the courses and study-centre facilities on offer.

In the next reading Christopher Brumfit, professor of language and education at the University of Southampton, who began his own teaching career in

Tanzania, examines the distinctions usually made between teaching **English as a mother tongue (EMT)**, **English as a second language (ESL)**, **English as a foreign language (EFL)**, and **English for speakers of other languages (ESOL)**, and asks how far these distinctions are valid. In the second part of his reading he considers the question of varieties of English for different learners: which variety of English should be chosen for different contexts, and on what criteria?

❖ ❖ ❖ ❖ ❖

Activity 7.2   *(Reading A)*

Read 'English for speakers of other languages: which varieties of English for which groups of learners?' by C.J. Brumfit (Reading A). As you read, note down definitions for ESL, EFL, EMT and ESOL, and then answer the questions below.

- Why does Brumfit think the distinctions are problematic?
- Which variety of English does he suggest as the most appropriate learning target for each group of learners he discusses?

❖ ❖ ❖ ❖ ❖

Chapter 6 discusses some of the controversies surrounding the teaching of Standard English in mother-tongue contexts. An earlier book in this series, *English: history, diversity and change* (Graddol, Leith and Swann (eds), 1996), discusses varieties of English spoken in different parts of the world.

Brumfit suggests that serious thought needs to be given to the variety of English chosen for specific groups of learners. In most countries private language learners make a choice between US or British Standard English in their choice of schools. This is considered of some importance in parts of South America where people may feel ambivalent towards the type of English needed for work or study because of what they perceive as the political dominance of the USA. This can be resolved by seeking out a British course, or by focusing on British content. In south-east Asia some teachers promote Australian or New Zealand norms of English. Analysis of international textbooks indicates that these tend to adopt either British or US Standard English (Dendrinos, 1992) for all the reasons outlined by Brumfit in Reading A. However, these varieties are now generally labelled **international English**, a redefinition I find problematical because it makes a variety of English that is used by some appear to be the model of language for all. In practice teachers in regions such as south Asia or Africa tend to adopt the variety of English that is in use among the elite in the English-speaking countries in their region, such as, in these cases, Singapore or Nigeria. Brumfit argues that learners' goals should include an ability to understand the range of varieties with which they are likely to come into contact (British/US/Australian/local varieties): to speak and write at least one variety, perhaps a local one initially, and then to take on more 'standard' varieties higher up the education system.

7.3   HOW IS ENGLISH TAUGHT AND LEARNED?

Although different methods of English teaching have been fashionable at different periods, many of them survive to the present day, coexisting in a variety of guises and contexts even within the same classroom.

First, some experiences of learning English. The two passages below suggest that learners can respond quite successfully to different strategies for learning English, especially when the content meets their interests!

❖ ❖ ❖ ❖ ❖

Activity 7.3 *(Allow 10–15 minutes)*

Read through the quotations below about the strategies employed by two learners of English. The first, from *Quicksilver* by Marie Rambert, was first published in 1972 and the second, *Memories of Lenin* by Nadezhda Krupskaya, in 1930.

If you have ever learned English or another language as a second (or third) language, how did you go about it? Did you learn in class or informally?

Which strategies and activities seemed most useful to you inside and outside class? In what ways were your own interests engaged by the content?

> He taught me from a book by a man named Robertson, and I can remember exactly how it was laid out. There would be a short passage of some six or seven lines of English. I remember one that began: 'We are told that the Sultan Mahmoud by his perpetual wars abroad, and his tyranny at home, had filled the dominions of his forefathers with ruin and desolation and had unpeopled the Persian Empire.' Underneath each word there would be its literal translation into French, thus: 'Nous sommes dit que ...' And finally there was the translation into good French: 'On nous dit ...' Thus you had a clear idea of the relative construction of English phrases and French. It was a simple, but brilliant system. I was interested, and I learnt it all by heart in no time.
>
> (Quoted in Brumfit (ed.), 1991, p. 30)

> We thought we knew the English language, having even translated a whole book (the Webbs') from English into Russian, when we were in Siberia. I learnt English in prison from a self-instructor, but had never heard a single live English word spoken ... When we arrived in London we found we could not understand a single word and nobody understood us. At first this was very comical, but although Vladimir Ilyich joked about it, he soon got down to the business of learning the language. We started going to all kinds of meetings. We stood in the front row and carefully studied the orator's mouth. We went fairly often to Hyde Park, where speakers harangued the passing crowds on diverse themes ... We were particularly keen on listening to one speaker of this kind. He spoke with an Irish accent, which was easier for us to understand ... We learnt a great deal by listening to spoken English.
>
> (Quoted in Brumfit (ed.), 1991, p. 27)

Comment

Although I chose these passages to illustrate different methods of learning English, once I had brought them together I found it interesting to consider the *content* of the 'English lessons' they referred to. In one, English is used to learn about world history, although whether from an English or French perspective is unclear from the passage, while at the same time an explicit focus on the written language is provided. In the second, the emphasis is on learning the spoken language, and the vehicle is politics. I particularly enjoyed the reference to the Irish speaker as being 'easier to understand'. This contradicts the view that speakers of English as a first language need to learn *one* standard variety to be understood in the wider world!

These two experiences of learning English both belong to an earlier period than the present, before an industry of English language teaching grew up, before there was easy access to English-teaching textbooks and before there were teacher-training departments established to research and disseminate specialized methods. Yet is it inconceivable that people might adopt similar approaches today? You may have begun to learn a language mainly through listening to speakers in an informal setting, or perhaps through watching films and TV, or through listening to popular music.

❖   ❖   ❖   ❖   ❖

While it is usual to talk of changes in approaches to English teaching across the decades, when new trends appear they usually coexist with earlier approaches still in use in other classrooms, or in other parts of the world. The translation method of learning English used by Marie Rambert seems very similar, for example, to the extract shown in Figure 7.1 from a Japanese textbook on English (*Chuo English Studies Book 1* by M. Ueyama and D.C. Tamaki, reproduced in Grant, 1987). As with Marie Rambert's approach, a text is translated, but in the Japanese example this is either followed up or preceded by a number of exercises that focus on grammatical points from the passage. The content in the Japanese passage is simplified and

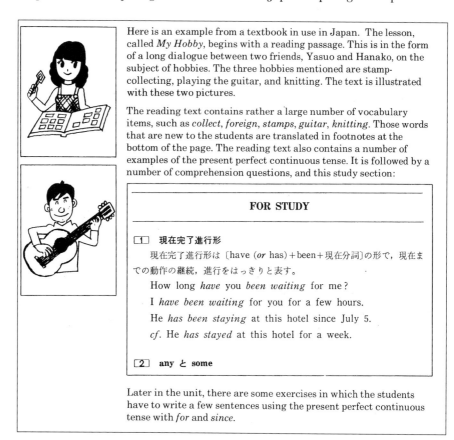

Here is an example from a textbook in use in Japan. The lesson, called *My Hobby*, begins with a reading passage. This is in the form of a long dialogue between two friends, Yasuo and Hanako, on the subject of hobbies. The three hobbies mentioned are stamp-collecting, playing the guitar, and knitting. The text is illustrated with these two pictures.

The reading text contains rather a large number of vocabulary items, such as *collect, foreign, stamps, guitar, knitting*. Those words that are new to the students are translated in footnotes at the bottom of the page. The reading text also contains a number of examples of the present perfect continuous tense. It is followed by a number of comprehension questions, and this study section:

FOR STUDY

〔1〕　現在完了進行形

　　現在完了進行形は〔have (*or* has)＋been＋現在分詞〕の形で，現在までの動作の継続，進行をはっきりと表す。

How long *have* you *been waiting* for me?

I *have been waiting* for you for a few hours.

He *has been staying* at this hotel since July 5.

cf. He *has stayed* at this hotel for a week.

〔2〕　any と some

Later in the unit, there are some exercises in which the students have to write a few sentences using the present perfect continuous tense with *for* and *since*.

Figure 7.1   Extract describing a Japanese textbook
(Grant, 1987, p. 47)

controlled, and so is less cognitively demanding than the one Rambert tackled. We will come back to the question of the content of English teaching later in this chapter.

In contrast to the emphasis on written English taken by this translation- and grammar-focused method, another approach – one that made an impact on English language teaching from around the turn of the century until the 1970s – focused on teaching spoken English first, through intensive **drilling** of language patterns. English alone was to be used in the classroom. Translation was thought to be appropriate only at advanced levels. Illustrations, mime and other visual aids were used as clues to enable students to grasp meanings. There was an emphasis on pronunciation and grammatical form, rather than on meanings. The box illustrates how oral drills could be put into practice.

It was in Standard IV that they began to learn English.

Lucia, Mwihaki's sister, taught them. They all sat expectantly at their desk with eyes on the board. A knowledge of English was the criterion of a man's learning.

Teacher	I am standing up. What am I doing?
Class	You are standing up.
Teacher	Again.
Class	You are standing up.
Teacher	(*pointing with a finger*) You – no – you – yes. What's your name?
Pupil	Njoroge.
Teacher	Njoroge, stand up.

He stood up. Learning English was all right but not when he stood up for all eyes to watch and maybe make faces at him.

Teacher	What are you doing?
Njoroge	(*thinly*) You are standing up.
Teacher	(*slightly cross*) What are *you* doing?
Njoroge	(*clears his throat, voice thinner still*) You are standing up.
Teacher	No, no! (*to the class*) Come on. What are *you, you* doing?

Njoroge was very confused. Hands were raised up all around him. He felt more and more foolish so that in the end he gave up the very attempt to answer.

Teacher	(*pointing to Mwihaki*) Stand up. What are you doing?
Mwihaki	(*head bent on to one shoulder*) I am standing up.
Teacher	Good. Now, Njoroge. What is she doing?
Njoroge	I am standing up.

The class giggled.

(Ngũgĩ wa Thiong'o, 1964, pp. 5–6)

❖ ❖ ❖ ❖ ❖

Activity 7.4   *(Allow about 5 minutes)*

In the boxed extract from Ngũgĩ what do you think Njoroge was learning about English, and about being a speaker of English?

Comment

This is a sharp observation of once fashionable 'English only' language teaching methods imposed on teachers through their training as 'scientific', 'correct' methods. Njoroge's teacher had been trained to ignore her bilingual skills, when they might so easily have helped to sort out learners' confusion. At the same time, the extract indicates the fundamentally authoritarian nature of this drill approach. Ownership of the language is firmly in the hands of the textbook writer. The teacher who is a non-native speaker simply has to manage the communicative event, and learners are discouraged even from using a dictionary to manage their own learning. Understanding the language becomes less important than producing it on demand: in the dialogues, pupils take on the role of the English characters in the text, rather than having any personal agenda.

❖ ❖ ❖ ❖ ❖

Although less popular today, oral drills still have their place among other activities in many modern textbooks. Echoes of the approach are seen, too, in a tendency to frown on the use of the first language and translation methods in English classes, and in an emphasis on developing spoken before written English even in contexts where students' priorities are for reading English (for example university entrants who need to handle science texts published only in English in order to graduate in their first languages in their own countries, as in Morocco, discussed earlier).

However, just like the 'translation' methods which have been so strongly criticized, and yet which seemed to work for Rambert and Lenin (even though supplemented by Speakers' Corner), drills may have worked well for some learners, providing them with a way into communication and an identity that suited them as English speakers.

Children's acquisition of communicative competence in English is also discussed in Chapter 2 of this book.

A major reaction to the use of oral drills arose from an interest in **communicative competence**, a term coined in the 1960s to cover everything a language user needed to know to communicate effectively. This embraced not only grammar, pronunciation and word meaning, but also knowledge of how to use language appropriately for different audiences, how to construct well-organized written texts or oral monologues, and how to integrate language with other appropriate communication systems – gesture, eye contact, and so on. In a famous phrase, communicative competence incorporated the 'rules of use without which the rules of grammar would be useless' (Hymes, 1979, p. 15).

Proponents of **communicative approaches** to language teaching suggested that 'errors' in early use of English were to be expected and welcomed as signs of the way the learner is hypothesizing about how the language system works. Rather than becoming bad habits, 'errors' would be corrected gradually as the learner gained more experience of the system (see for instance Corder, 1974). There was a demand for more interactive classrooms where learners could use English (develop 'fluency'), as well as learn its grammar (develop 'accuracy').

In the USA Krashen (1981) went further, suggesting that learning a second language was very like learning the first, and proposing a 'natural approach'. He argued that learners should simply be encouraged to participate in plenty of easily comprehensible activities in the 'target language', absorbing English just as a child learns its first language, and not be required to produce English (the 'silent period') until ready to do so. The teacher's job should be simply to provide 'comprehensible input' and activities which would encourage learners to use English, with feedback focusing on meaning rather than form. Teaching that focused on grammar or structures would be of little use. While Krashen's extreme position was controversial, debate for some time centred on how to balance 'accuracy' and 'fluency' activities most effectively in the classroom.

With the establishment of oral drill methods of language teaching in the 1960s the ESL teaching tradition had begun to diverge strongly from the concerns of teachers in 'mother-tongue' contexts. Methods were so different that during periods of large-scale migration to English-speaking countries, new teachers were thought to be required for learners of English as a second language. These learners were also thought to need separate classes since the teaching methods were so different.

With the 'natural approach', mother-tongue and second language teaching came closer together, influencing each others' practice in interesting ways, especially in a new emphasis on literacy and wider educational outcomes for bilingual learners of English.

EFL textbooks have also responded to demands for communicative 'fluency' activities alongside models of grammatical 'accuracy'. Hutchison and Torres (1994) compare textbooks of the late 1970s, which they say consisted almost entirely of texts, questions and substitution drills, with modern successors, often by the same authors, which contain integrated video materials, problem-solving exercises, role play, songs, the development of reading, writing and listening skills, games, grammar summaries and tape transcripts.

Where the learning context is one in which there is less English in the environment to be absorbed, and classmates share another, stronger language, learning English is obviously less 'natural' than learning a first language, and communicative methods have to be planned with care if they are not to degenerate into trivial games as meaningless as the oral drill routines described above.

7.4   WHO DOES WHAT IN ENGLISH?

Communicative approaches to language teaching suggest that learners need to be taught not only **language forms** but also **language functions**.

For instance, the sentence *Are those your books on the floor?* has an interrogative form. But functionally, it is ambiguous: it may be a question, seeking information; but it may also be an order (Pick them up!) or a complaint. Not all functions, however, are available to all speakers. As Foucault has written:

An earlier book in this series, *Using English: from conversation to canon* (Maybin and Mercer (eds), 1996), discusses certain functional approaches to language study.

> We know very well that we are not free to say anything, that we cannot speak of anything when and where we like, and that just anyone, in short, cannot speak of just anything.
>
> (Cited in Sheridan, 1980, p. 122)

❖ ❖ ❖ ❖ ❖

Activity 7.5   *(Allow 5–10 minutes)*

How many different ways can you think of to ask somebody to open the window? Jot these down, and consider which ones you would teach to a beginner with little experience of English. Why?

Comment

You may have listed forms such as:
- Open the window please.
- Could you open the window, do you think?
- Would you mind opening the window?
- Excuse me, I wonder if you could possibly open the window?
- Do you think it's getting a bit stuffy in here?

Look at your list again. What sorts of relationship between speaker and hearer do the different forms imply? In my list the first, 'Open the window please', is a simple structure to teach a beginner and, indeed, orders and instructions of this form were present in early lessons in textbooks based on oral drills. However, this may be an inappropriate form to use in some situations, for example in British English you would probably be expected to use a more indirect request form to someone more powerful, like your teacher.

This is why although teachers ask questions (see Chapter 4), pupils learning English as a second language are generally not required to produce questions in school, but to give answers. However, one structure they are asked to produce from their earliest days in an English school is *May I go to ... please?* and *Can I have ... please?*

❖ ❖ ❖ ❖ ❖

A student learning English is inevitably being positioned as a certain sort of English speaker within the social meanings of the text on offer. Learners may of course reject this positioning, but for the moment at least they must play along; as a consequence they may well (like Njoroge in the extract earlier) develop unfavourable attitudes towards the language and towards using the language. What sorts of function, then, are learners of English invited to perform through English teaching texts: what social positions may they take up in the new language?

First, an example from a general English course for beginners, published in 1978. Figure 7.2 overleaf invites learners to take part in a rather typical EFL textbook situation. The participants want to meet people in some social gathering. Frequently the role models in the textbooks have been English 'mother-tongue' speakers, as in this example. Non-English speakers have often been represented as stereotypes, like the Japanese woman in Figure 7.2. You may decide for yourself how far this has changed in the extract in Figure 7.3 from an English course written by one of the same co-authors a decade later.

Many newer textbooks have attempted to show a multilingual context similar to that found in an EFL language school or in international gatherings – where English is the common medium of communication between speakers of many different languages.

Each textbook makes assumptions about its readers' lives and what they will need to do with English. While introductions are a feature of both examples,

1 Peter Wilson   **2** Sarah Kennedy **3** Monique Lefort   **4** Yoko Suzuki   **5** Maria Jackson

6 João Medeiros **7** Pedro García   **8** Paola Bonetti   **9** Zog   **10** Eleni Dima

◇ c ◇ Conversations

Look at the pictures, and make conversations.

1	2	3
A *Is he from France?*	**A** *She's Paola Bonetti.*	**A** *Are you from England?*
B *No, he isn't.*	**B** *Where's she from?*	**B** *No, I'm not.*
A *Is he from England?*	**A** *She's from Italy.*	**A** *Where are you from?*
B *Yes, he is.*		**B** *I'm from Australia.*

Figure 7.2 (above)
Learning to socialize,
1978
(Hartley and Viney, 1978, pp. 1–2)

Figure 7.3 (left)
Learning to socialize,
1989
(Viney and Viney, 1989)

they do not feature in *High Season,* an EFL textbook for the hotel and tourist industry. The functions emphasized here are: listening carefully to others' requests, answering questions with factual information, describing rooms and facilities, understanding duties and undertaking routine procedures (reception, checking out). The workers' own personalities, wants and needs are absent. Figure 7.4 shows the learner the 'correct way' to handle complaints. Compare this

---

1 Listen to this conversation between a guest and a receptionist.
  a Make a list of the things the guest is complaining about.
  b What does she want to do?
  c What is the outcome?

2 Now listen to the second conversation. What is the outcome this time?

3 Listen to both conversations again. In what ways does the receptionist behave differently in the second conversation? What does she offer to do?

Responding to complaints

Look at this example of responding to a complaint.

Complaint	Apology	Action
▶ *This room is filthy!*	*I'm terribly sorry.*	*I'll send someone up to clean it immediately.*

Now respond to the following complaints in a similar way.

Complaint	Apology	Action
a This soup's disgusting!		
b I'm sorry to trouble you, but I don't seem to have any towels.		
c It's really noisy. Can't you do something about it?		
d The central heating's not working.		
e Look. Our sheets haven't been changed.		
f Sorry, but I ordered tea, not coffee.		
g I can't seem to get the shower to work.		

Figure 7.4 Learning to handle complaints
(Harding and Henderson, 1994, pp. 79, 80)

with the more powerful positioning of learners in *Business Opportunities* in Figure 7.5, where they are encouraged to make and justify their own choices of action among a range of alternatives. Functions emphasized in this course include making arrangements and appointments, collecting information, asking for opinions, making suggestions and giving explanations.

Extending the contrast, a functional course for immigrant learners of English as a second language, *A New Start* (Furnborough et al., 1980), offers students the

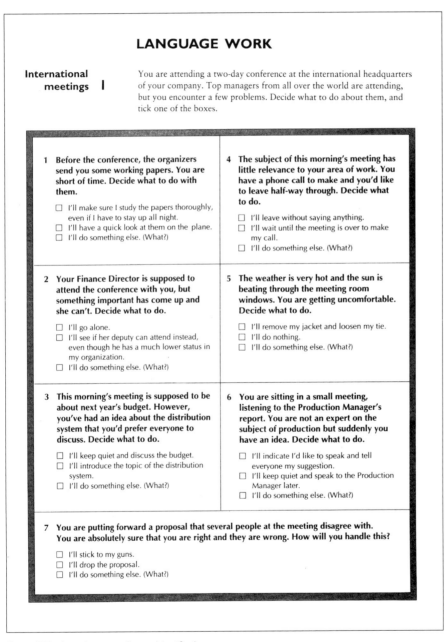

LANGUAGE WORK

International meetings I

You are attending a two-day conference at the international headquarters of your company. Top managers from all over the world are attending, but you encounter a few problems. Decide what to do about them, and tick one of the boxes.

1 Before the conference, the organizers send you some working papers. You are short of time. Decide what to do with them.

☐ I'll make sure I study the papers thoroughly, even if I have to stay up all night.
☐ I'll have a quick look at them on the plane.
☐ I'll do something else. (What?)

2 Your Finance Director is supposed to attend the conference with you, but something important has come up and she can't. Decide what to do.

☐ I'll go alone.
☐ I'll see if her deputy can attend instead, even though he has a much lower status in my organization.
☐ I'll do something else. (What?)

3 This morning's meeting is supposed to be about next year's budget. However, you've had an idea about the distribution system that you'd prefer everyone to discuss. Decide what to do.

☐ I'll keep quiet and discuss the budget.
☐ I'll introduce the topic of the distribution system.
☐ I'll do something else. (What?)

4 The subject of this morning's meeting has little relevance to your area of work. You have a phone call to make and you'd like to leave half-way through. Decide what to do.

☐ I'll leave without saying anything.
☐ I'll wait until the meeting is over to make my call.
☐ I'll do something else. (What?)

5 The weather is very hot and the sun is beating through the meeting room windows. You are getting uncomfortable. Decide what to do.

☐ I'll remove my jacket and loosen my tie.
☐ I'll do nothing.
☐ I'll do something else. (What?)

6 You are sitting in a small meeting, listening to the Production Manager's report. You are not an expert on the subject of production but suddenly you have an idea. Decide what to do.

☐ I'll indicate I'd like to speak and tell everyone my suggestion.
☐ I'll keep quiet and speak to the Production Manager later.
☐ I'll do something else. (What?)

7 You are putting forward a proposal that several people at the meeting disagree with. You are absolutely sure that you are right and they are wrong. How will you handle this?

☐ I'll stick to my guns.
☐ I'll drop the proposal.
☐ I'll do something else. (What?)

Figure 7.5 Learning to make and justify changes
(Hollett, 1994, p. 36)

following functions: saying hello and goodbye; simple transactions such as buying a ticket and paying in a supermarket; simple directions; 'insisting politely'; and making an apology. There is a great deal of emphasis on teaching the learner to follow instructions, as in Figure 7.6. In *Business Opportunities*, however, it was the learner who was expected to give instructions and make explanations.

Some of the dangers of assuming particular needs for particular groups of language learners seem immediately apparent. Are learners offered the sort of English used by the powerful or by the powerless? Do they learn about the differences between the two? Do they discuss the social consequences of making choices? How far would a certain presentation of themselves (as taught in *Business Opportunities*, for example) be seen as legitimate or appropriate by those around them in their own work context?

The extract in the box illustrates the early socialization of a young bilingual learner into the sort of English required in classroom interaction. Although all the young children here are still learning what is 'teacher discourse' and what is 'pupil discourse', Akhtar is also being socialized into certain ways of being and behaving in English.

Learning how to be a pupil and how to be a teacher

Teacher:	All right, shall we play again? Who wants to be the … holding the cards up? Right this time … you've got to ask for it. When he holds it up … you've got to say … ask Christopher for it.
Christopher:	Who got this? Akhtar you got this? What is it?
Akhtar:	Bed
Christopher: …	Good boy.
Christopher:	Who got that?
Akhtar:	Um … apple an orange an a banana
Christopher:	Good boy. Put it on the card.
Akhtar:	Good boy.
Christopher:	Who got this?
Akhtar:	Mine car

(Wiles, 1981, p. 57)

I have suggested that as speakers of other languages enter into English different positions are constructed for them – different things are judged possible and legitimate for them to say and do depending on their perceived age and social position.

Learners may be aware of this and so resist learning the English on offer, as is evident from this quotation from a community activist, Balraj Purewal, addressing an audience of teachers of ESL in Britain:

The National Front is a racist political movement in Britain.

> You made us believe that we were learning a language. Frankly, you were only teaching us how to obey orders … ESL in the classroom was like the National Front on the street. You either fought against it or ran from it.

(Quoted in Mukherjee, 1985, p. 14)

Figure 7.6 *Learning to follow instructions*
(Furnborough et al., 1980, p. 34)

Other learners may welcome new positions offered to them by the new language – for example it may offer a new gender positioning which legitimates ways of speaking and acting that would have seemed impossible in the first language. For some, English may offer a vehicle for developing a new sort of identity.

These language choices, however, are usually not free but are socially conditioned, for to be effective they are dependent on whether or not the new English-speaking society the learner is attempting to enter will accept the sort of identity he or she offers.

Tomic and Trumper (1992) have described their experiences as Chilean professionals (economists) who fled to Canada as refugees (in a similar way to Leila, the journalist referred to in Activity 7.1). Tomic and Trumper felt they were repositioned by the Canadian immigration process as 'Third World working class', and not given opportunities to receive the English teaching they required to continue their professional lives and re-establish their identity as professionals. They write:

> Although race, colour, size, gender or age cannot be taken officially into account in a hiring process, it is accepted that a certain level of fluency is essential to work in certain jobs. Denying us access to language training made us ineligible for other than unskilled and poorly paid work.
>
> (Tomic and Trumper, 1992, p. 176)

The situation Tomic and Trumper outline is not confined to Canada. Pennycook (1989) suggests that in the English programmes run by the USA for refugees in camps in south Asia there is a:

> covert policy to ensure that immigrants will have enough English to perform adequately in minimum-wage jobs while avoiding any welfare dependency, yet not enough to move beyond these levels of employment
>
> (Pennycook, 1989, p. 593)

In the UK this sort of challenge to ESL teaching has led some teachers to transfer their focus from the ESL learners themselves to the wider context within which learners must operate. Thus the National Centre for Industrial Language Training (NCILT) in the 1970s ran programmes aimed at restructuring workplace attitudes in multilingual contexts; and school-based projects like the Partnership Teaching Project (Bourne and McPake, 1991) focused on ways of changing school structures and routine ways of working to make them more receptive to a diversity of needs, including those of ESL learners.

Teachers have also sought to address the content of the English curriculum. For instance, Mukherjee (1985) recommends a language syllabus for minorities in English-dominant nations which is based around key concepts, such as power and powerlessness, identity and rootlessness, equality and justice.

The question of developing serious content has become important in English teaching outside English-dominant countries and is not an issue for oppressed minorities alone. Neville Grant, in the next reading, believes in introducing serious issues in real discussion as stimulus to a deeper engagement with the language, whatever the context for English teaching. However, in writing for countries other than his own, Grant is aware of the difficulties of providing serious stimulus material for an unknown audience 'within a vocabulary of 1,400 words' which also satisfies the political and cultural constraints imposed by government sponsors. The reading is an interesting insight into the way a textbook writer works.

❖ ❖ ❖ ❖ ❖

Activity 7.6 *(Reading B)*

1   Make a short list of the cultural and moral issues you think you would need to consider in writing English teaching materials for use in a country other than your own, and then read 'Dilemmas of a textbook writer' by Neville Grant (Reading B).

As you read, note down the ways in which Neville Grant addresses these issues. Does he identify any issues you had not thought of?

2   Why does Grant want 'to reflect national social and cultural aspirations' in his materials rather than teach about British or US culture? How successful do you think he is in this aim in the examples of material he gives?

Comment

As an educational writer specializing in syllabus design and materials development, some of the difficult questions on which Grant finds he has to take a personal stand include:

- the extent to which it is possible to teach and practise English without raising cultural and moral issues;

- whether or not EFL materials are the right place to discuss such issues with learners;

- whether there are some issues too sensitive to be touched on for cultural or other reasons (e.g. bride-wealth, arranged marriages, contraception, female circumcision);

- the extent to which authors can remain 'neutral' in introducing sensitive issues without compromising themselves.

The reading illustrates the tightrope that textbook writers walk in producing acceptable English materials for different countries. At its most basic this can mean appreciating that, for example, while a dog may be taken generally to be a positive image, a pet, in Britain, it may more frequently be interpreted as something potentially dangerous in the Middle East (Alptekin, 1993). Even the illustrations used to give clues to meanings in materials need to be carefully examined.

Grant shows that the EFL writer is not usually the sole decision maker in terms of content. Local political control is maintained over the sorts of social, cultural and political meanings conveyed through teaching materials. EFL textbooks appear to be as much part of local control mechanisms (syllabuses, classroom methods, examinations) as they are western exports.

Grant says that in China he was asked to provide a 'window on the world outside' through his materials, and to consider 'cultural differences'. In northern Europe it is generally seen as an important part of English classes for students to gain an awareness of life in English-speaking countries. The idea is that students need to learn how to operate with English speakers or in English-speaking countries – to become 'culturally competent' as well as communicatively competent. In contrast, in the African examples, where English has a local presence through a colonial history, the situation is more complicated. Grant uses English as a stimulus to get students talking about local issues. In his introduction he shows that he is anxious to avoid any charge of 'cultural imperialism and an unpleasant ethnocentrism', and to support 'native culture'. But in learning any language how far can or should issues of cultural differences be avoided? For example, Grant's choice of certain topics as 'controversial' itself indicates something of his own cultural perspective.

❖   ❖   ❖   ❖   ❖

Grant himself asks whether the author is 'downloading cultural values or raising international issues in a relatively uncontroversial manner'. In addition to the text itself, it is worth considering the sorts of activity the textbook sets up. How far is the classroom in which students sit expressing and discussing their different opinions a product of a particular culture? Consider English teaching in China, where the practice of 'intensive reading', the careful analysis of written texts in English, is a valued method of study. What does Neville Grant's invitation to students to 'form their own views' mean in this context? Pennycook (1994b) argues that teaching methods as well as content carry cultural messages. A further problem is the trivializing of issues through the holding of discussions apparently without purpose – this week freedom of the press, next week abortion.

Sociopolitical concerns such as those raised by Reading B have been high on the ESOL professional agenda in the 1990s. The next section explores ESOL in its broader sociopolitical context.

7.5   THE SPREAD OF ENGLISH LANGUAGE TEACHING

The previous section dealt with the issue of values in English teaching in terms of the methods and materials used. In this section I consider whether, and under what conditions, ESOL should be taught at all. It has been argued that ESOL is not a neutral activity, and that it necessarily serves certain interests at the expense of others.

Anthea Fraser Gupta in Chapter 5, Reading A, described the development of English teaching in India in the nineteenth century. Where earlier advantages were gained for English by British colonial activity, political pressure was renewed during the twentieth century to enhance the pace of the spread of English. In the mid twentieth century the UK and USA attempted to increase the global dominance of English as part of an effort to resist the threat of Hitler and any that might follow him. A new cultural body, the British Council, was set up by the British government in 1935 to promote Britain and the English language abroad. Routh (1941), an adviser to the British Council, wrote:

> Every nation now being educated is also possessed by ideas, opinions, doctrines, and these have to be canalised, no less than economic resources … We have to capitalise brains even more consistently than national debts.
>
> (Routh, 1941, pp. 15–16)

Routh argues that there is an untapped desire to learn English around the world, and a need to create a new 'army of linguistic missionaries' to meet that demand. However, he warns that other nations 'will not want to be anglicised', nor to 'merge their national identity in an imported civilisation'. Britain in the world peace-keeping role he envisages for it may not always be popular with those it intends to manage. The solution, he argues, is to present English as an **international language**. In the postwar settlement:

> They may have to recognise the British Empire as a disciplinarian in disguise, but not as an instructor undisguised. So if they need our language it will not be as a cultured alternative to their own, but as a business-like amplification, a *lingua franca* ... our instructor must begin by learning submergence in the comity of nations. He is to diffuse not so much English but the language which the English originated.
>
> (Routh, 1941, pp. 31–2)

In arguments like this we can see the emergence of a concept of English as neutral and as an international possession, not 'ours' but 'all of ours'.

Nor is Britain alone in the promotion of English around the world. There is increasing competition from other English-dominant nations to provide English language teaching overseas. The USA, Australia and the Republic of Ireland are all competitors with Britain for the export of English.

The promotion of English as an international language ('not ours but all of ours') is having a side-effect. There is a growing confidence in local English-teaching expertise on the part of many countries who no longer see themselves as needing outside 'experts', or, indeed, 'native speakers' of English as teachers. For what use is the concept of 'native speaker' when English is conceived of as an international language? There is a new twist in the story as other non-English-dominant countries begin to export their own English-teaching expertise; the Scandinavian countries and Austria, for example, have well-established teacher-training departments and developed methodologies, and are increasingly involved in teaching English to overseas students; and Singapore provides English language teaching for students from China and other parts of the Far East.

How are English-dominant countries responding to this competition in the market for teaching English? To take Britain as an example, there is now a counter trend to begin to play down the 'international' status of English. British providers have become interested in developing 'British Cultural Studies' (Storey, 1994; Walker, 1994); there is a new emphasis on the importance of having native-speaker English teachers, establishing Standard (British) English norms for non-native learners (Quirk, 1989), and on test materials that grade English users overseas against Standard English norms.

The validity of the concepts of 'native' and 'non-native' speaker has been questioned in relation to expertise in using English, as has the validity of assessing English in relation to a British or American norm rather than a local norm (for example, Rampton, 1990). See also the first book in this series, *English: history, diversity and change* (Graddol et al. (eds), 1996), for a discussion of native and non-native speakers.

The political and economic importance of English language teaching to Britain has been explicitly addressed in the policy statements of the British Council. Two of the main aims of the British Council project *English 2000* (Bowers, 1994), are: 'to assist in ensuring that English remains the preferred language for international communication' and 'to sustain and develop the global market for English goods and services'. Similar trends to those I've discussed in Britain can be traced in other English-exporting countries, such as the USA and Australia, as they try to carve out a niche in the global market.

There have been several responses to the global promotion of English language teaching. Phillipson (1992) sees this as an example of **linguistic imperialism**, in which the exertion of power in favour of English has led to the neglect of other languages in national language policies and education systems. In summary, he claims that arguments have been used to:

- attempt to persuade people of the superior merits of English (as the language of modernization, social mobility, liberalism, international communication, science and technology, etc.) in comparison to what are presented as the failings of other languages (divisive, parochial, community, heritage, backward-looking);

- promise goods and services to those who use English: (e.g. education, science, technology, progress, access to world markets);

- support covert threats against maintaining local languages: (e.g. internal divisions and conflicts over languages, resource costs, difficulties in learning English, problems in world markets).

Phillipson is not *against* the teaching of English, but argues that English should be in a position of equality with other languages in multilingual countries: it should be part of the available linguistic competence on which people may draw for their own purposes.

Bisong (1995) writes that in Nigeria, as in other countries, parents wish their children to learn English to open up new opportunities. But, he claims, the aim is multilingualism: 'Why settle for monolingualism in a society that is constantly in a state of flux, when you can be multilingual and more at ease with a richer linguistic repertoire and an expanding consciousness?' (Bisong, 1995, p. 125). Bisong argues that rather than replacing the first language, parents see the school as adding English to the child's language repertoire. The parent simply wants 'to ensure a good future for the child, to make certain that the child does not lose out on anything good that is going'.

A somewhat different position is taken by Annamalai (1986), who claims that English helps maintain divisions and hierarchies within a country: it is used for 'elite formation and preservation, intranational and international links between elites, and international identity' (Annamalai, 1986, p. 9). The introduction of English into schools works to exclude rather than include; it is yet another hurdle for children to jump in order to increase their life chances, providing a sorting and classifying mechanism for access to higher education. It legitimates differences in economic wealth through an appearance of providing equal opportunities, where in fact one class stands to gain from possessing the 'cultural capital' of easy access to English in the home and access to expensive extra English classes.

Rogers (1990) argues that whatever the multilingual ideal, teaching English in 'third world' contexts simply does not work for the majority. Despite the enormous resources it diverts from other educational development possibilities, it actually achieves very little. For most children (outside English-dominant countries) it is not a passport to a better job; few jobs exist at the managerial, academic and technical levels for which fluency in English is required. Few will be required to communicate with English speakers or to use English as an international language or for higher education. Rogers claims that if the aim really is access to educational opportunity, progress is more likely to be achieved by education in local languages.

Multilingual language policies

Several national language policies have attempted to recognize the needs of bi- and multilingual communities. For instance, 'the new South African Constitution recognizes the principle of multilingualism and gives equal status to eleven official languages. The extent to which this will simply remain at the level of rhetoric, however, is still an area of contention' (Desai, 1995).

The national language policy for Australia (Lo Bianco, 1987) provided a new model for language planning by integrating proposals for: English for speakers of other languages; English as a first language; Aboriginal languages; and the 'other languages for, and of Australians'. These other languages include, for example: Italian as a 'heritage language' spoken by a large Australian community; Vietnamese, spoken in local communities as well as the language of an increasingly important trade partner in the region; and Chinese, the language of a nation of geopolitical and economic importance to Australia. The aim of the Lo Bianco policy is to make every child bilingual, if not multilingual. However, the policy has not been fully implemented in Australia, and later government papers have given English renewed emphasis.

Struggles concerning the dominance of English continue in other parts of the world, too. The 'English only' movement, which aims to make English the official language in the USA, poses a threat to bilingual provision in schools. In contrast, in Hong Kong there has been ongoing debate about whether English should be taught to all children or dropped from the curriculum for most.

Countries that depend on aid will continue to be heavily influenced by the decisions of international agencies such as the World Bank, and national agencies such as the UK Overseas Development Agency (ODA), who will decide what sort of educational initiatives to fund and the priority that should be given to English teaching in them.

Generally, among the aid agencies there seems to have been a perceptible switch of resources away from English language teaching and towards wider educational projects, with higher priority being given to the use of the medium of the first language to raise attainment in learning. As the director of Britain's aid agency, the ODA, asked English language teaching experts at a British Council seminar:

> What is the economic value of English teaching? ... Increasingly we see projects that aim to develop a range of key subjects and techniques ... it will be ever more important to be able to justify educational projects with an ELT element in them in terms of their economic productivity. In aid terms the teaching of English is simply not an end in itself.
> (Iredale, 1991, pp. 8–9)

I began this chapter by discussing the range of contexts in which English is taught, and the range of methods that have been used to teach it. I then moved from questions of pedagogy in a fairly narrow sense to cultural and political dimensions of English teaching: to the values that seem necessarily to be associated with teaching materials and methods, and to broader political debates about the teaching of English in different parts of the world. (These dimensions have also run through the previous two chapters.)

❖ ❖ ❖ ❖ ❖

Activity 7.7 *(Allow 30 minutes)*

Many of the researchers and commentators I have referred to in the last two sections have seen English teaching as a threat: English teaching has been seen by some as positioning individual learners in such a way as to disempower them and, at an international level, as bound up with 'linguistic imperialism'.

Look back carefully at the examples and arguments discussed in sections 7.4 and 7.5. Try to evaluate the different arguments. Which do you agree with? How far and in what ways do you think it is possible, in Pennycook's words, to 'establish some way of teaching English that is not automatically an imperialist project' (Pennycook, 1994b, p. 69)?

❖ ❖ ❖ ❖ ❖

The teaching of English to speakers of other languages is by no means a settled area; it continues to change in response both to changing social and political imperatives and to its practitioners' attempts to come to grips with some of the issues discussed in this chapter. Current developments within TESOL include the following.

- **Diversification in English teaching**

  Douglas Brown, then president of the US-based international Teaching of English to Speakers of Other Languages (TESOL) Association, identified diversification as one of the major challenges of the future for the profession (Brown, 1991). There are calls for diverse approaches both within and between countries, for example: English as a foreign language arts subject with cultural studies or 'international' English for specific purposes (ESP) linked to the training of engineers, doctors and tour guides; English for academic purposes (EAP) for people entering higher education or intending to study abroad; and balancing a focus on literacy skills or communicative oral skills for schoolchildren, depending on national educational goals.

- **A broader focus for English**

  Increasingly, TESOL is being seen as part of wider educational programmes. For instance, in Australia there has been a focus on providing children with access to the full school curriculum – on literacy development, on the development of study skills in English and, especially, on coming to understand the different sorts of text required for science, literature, history, etc.

  Figure 7.7, from an Australian handbook for teachers, illustrates how a teacher might support an ESL learner in gaining access to a history text.

  Teaching materials may involve students in a range of activities linked to a curriculum topic: for example, working on the digestive system in science might involve preparatory activities such as labelling diagrams, sorting and matching sentences, matching pictures and sentences, constructing simple sentences using given models, etc., before students are led into constructing a carefully framed text appropriate for the subject area. At issue here is whether students are given access to powerful ways of writing, or simply coached to produce set forms or genres.

  Such approaches require students to use grammatical terminology to talk about texts. The principles are similar to those underlying approaches to teaching academic writing at university level, discussed in Chapter 8. See also the discussion about the 'genre approach' to teaching writing in Chapters 4 and 6.

- **Critical approaches**

  Pennycook (1994a) argues that, even in classes that attempt to deal with serious topics, teachers 'have often failed to link the focus of these classes either to the language being learnt or to the lives of the students' (1994a, p. 132). He argues that there is a difference between 'dealing with "serious issues"' and 'dealing with issues seriously'.

  Figure 7.8 is an extract from a South African textbook that aims not only to teach English but also to explore what being a speaker of English might mean to the students. In order to complete the activity, students need to draw on their own understanding of apartheid South Africa. The example uses little English and could be discussed with beginners using bilingual methods.

  Another example comes from Greece, where Prodromou (1990), an English teacher, suggested taking as a topic 'Grainglais': 'the English that

The Declaration of Independence

Revolution became official with the signing of the Declaration of Independence on 4 July 1776. The Declaration of Independence was made up of three parts:

- the reasons for the decision to break with Britain
- the list of British wrongs against the colonies
- the declaration that all ties with Britain were cut and that the independent nation of the United States had come into being.

Over the next six years, colonists were inspired by the Declaration of Independence to fight against Britain.

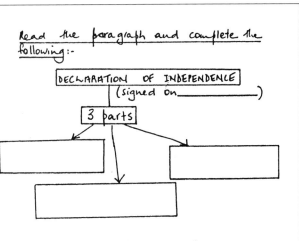

Read the paragraph and complete the following:-

DECLARATION OF INDEPENDENCE
(signed on_____)

3 parts

The Struggle Continues

There were bitter struggles in New England, Canada, South Carolina, New York and New Jersey. The Americans suffered many setbacks until, in 1777, the British were defeated at the village of Saratoga. This American victory was a turning point in the war.

French help to the colonies up to this time was secret. On 7 February 1778 the French signed a treaty of alliance with the new American nation and supplied it with vital financial, military and naval assistance. The war continued until, with the help of the French fleet, the revolutionaries under the command of Washington forced the British General Cornwallis to surrender at Yorktown, Virginia, in 1781. Soon after this victory, the war came to an end when the British and Americans signed the Treaty of Paris in 1783 and the independence of the United States was recognized.

Look at the words/phrases underlined above.

1. What does 'This American victory' refer to?_____

_____

2. What does 'it' refer to?_____

- -

3. What does 'this victory' refer to?_____

Check the meanings of the following:-

| setbacks | treaty | financial | surrender |
| turning point | alliance | revolutionaries | |

Complete the following notes:-

TURNING POINT ?_____

FINAL VICTORY
  YEAR _____
  PLACE _____
  COMMANDER _____

REASON _____
_____

END OF WAR
  YEAR _____
  TREATY _____

SIGNIFICANCE _____
_____

- In the first paragraph an "emotive" adjective and an "emotive" verb are used. Name them:- (adj.)_____
  (verb)_____

- Another word is used in the second paragraph to mean "Americans". What is it ?_____

Figure 7.7 Supporting ESL learners in history
(Houston, 1989, p. 74)

Greeks see and hear all around them' (1990, p. 37). He has two major aims: to improve students' competence in English and to increase their awareness of what happens when cultures come into contact. Students collect examples of graffiti, shop names or brand names and then consider where different words

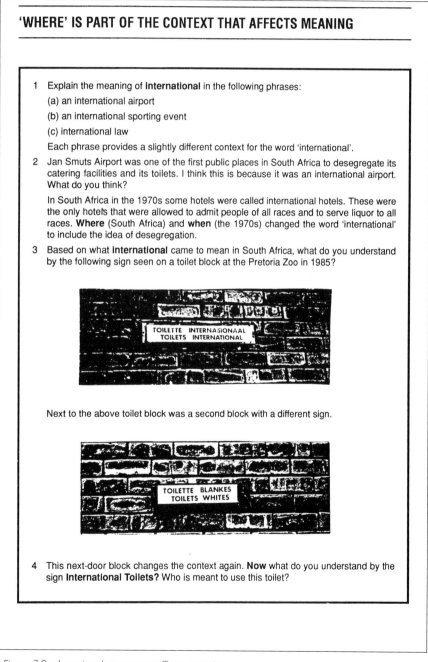

'WHERE' IS PART OF THE CONTEXT THAT AFFECTS MEANING

1   Explain the meaning of **international** in the following phrases:

(a) an international airport

(b) an international sporting event

(c) international law

Each phrase provides a slightly different context for the word 'international'.

2   Jan Smuts Airport was one of the first public places in South Africa to desegregate its catering facilities and its toilets. I think this is because it was an international airport. What do you think?

In South Africa in the 1970s some hotels were called international hotels. These were the only hotels that were allowed to admit people of all races and to serve liquor to all races. **Where** (South Africa) and **when** (the 1970s) changed the word 'international' to include the idea of desegregation.

3   Based on what **international** came to mean in South Africa, what do you understand by the following sign seen on a toilet block at the Pretoria Zoo in 1985?

TOILETTE   INTERNASIONAAL
TOILETS   INTERNATIONAL

Next to the above toilet block was a second block with a different sign.

TOILETTE   BLANKES
TOILETS   WHITES

4   This next-door block changes the context again. **Now** what do you understand by the sign **International Toilets?** Who is meant to use this toilet?

Figure 7.8   Learning that content affects meaning
(Janks, 1993, p. 17)

were found and who wrote them. They also examine local English language newspapers, looking at small ads, weather forecasts, advertisements and cultural listings. In this way they explore what it means to be a (bilingual) Greek user of English.

- **Bilingual approaches to ESOL**

  Another kind of focus on the structure of English is made possible by bilingual linguists. It is once again becoming acceptable to focus on the *forms* of language in the classroom as well as on communicative activities *using* the language. In this context, work on the contrastive analysis of English and other languages seems to offer considerable potential for learners. For example, Tony Hung (1993) suggests the examination of comparative phonology in English and Chinese to raise awareness of pronunciation patterns and avoid some of the communicative difficulties a Chinese learner of English can face.

Contrastive analysis may in time lead to experimentation and the development of more truly bilingual approaches to English teaching, including work on codeswitching and other forms of bilingual language behaviour relevant to many learners. Such approaches would also tend to recognize the expertise of local bilingual teachers.

Critical studies of how language works in society, including comparative analysis across languages and cultures, may offer a way into developing an understanding of the kind of English that Michael Christie reports an Australian Aboriginal community as demanding for their children:

> We want them to learn English. Not the kind of English you teach them in class, but your secret English. We don't understand that English but you do. To us you seem to say one thing and then do another. That's the English we want our children to learn.
>
> (Quoted in Christie, 1985, p. 50)

7.6   CONCLUSION

This chapter has emphasized the different contexts in which English is taught as a second or additional language, and the varying needs of different learners. I have also tried to give a sense of the debates that surround the teaching of English in different contexts, and to encourage you to take part in these debates. There has been considerable discussion about the particular variety of English that should serve as a model for learners; about the methods that should be used to teach English; about the content of English (the styles and functions that are made available to learners, and the topics covered in teaching materials); and about the extent to which English should be taught at all. Underlying such debates have been concerns about the social and cultural values that are bound up with English teaching, and the sorts of identities learners are invited to construct for themselves as English speakers. Many of these ideas are also relevant to the use and teaching of English in higher education, which is the topic of the next chapter.

Reading A

ENGLISH FOR SPEAKERS OF OTHER LANGUAGES: WHICH VARIETIES OF ENGLISH FOR WHICH GROUPS OF LEARNERS?

Christopher Brumfit

The term ESOL (English for speakers of other languages) is a general term borrowed from the USA to cover all types of English teaching except English as a mother tongue; the field is sometimes also referred to as English language teaching (ELT), but this falsely implies that English mother-tongue teachers have no responsibility for language development! The first section of this reading will try to make sense of the major classifications conventionally applied to English language teaching.

English, like many other ex-imperial languages, is both a 'mother tongue' and a 'second' or 'foreign' language. As with Spanish, Arabic and other languages, speakers in countries throughout the world grow up to acquire their own regional variety of the language, so that we speak of American, Australian or Canadian English (or French in Quebec), Latin-American Spanish, Egyptian Arabic, and so on. For these people it is a mother tongue, also called 'native language', 'first language' or, more technically, 'L1'. However, as with Spanish, Arabic and French (and also Russian, Chinese, Japanese and other languages), economic and political power creates international demands to learn the powerful languages. Learners (or their parents) believe that such knowledge will increase their life opportunities by giving them access to better jobs or to the levers of political power. This demand shows itself in two ways. First, throughout the world, schools, both public and private, offer learners the chance to add a language of economic power to their repertoire; second, individuals move, legally or sometimes illegally, to places where they have better economic opportunities – and these are usually places where the 'powerful' languages are used.

The outline above is a neutral account of what the situation is, but it is a partial story only, for every element in that account is bound up with issues of power and opportunity for users of English. Behind the notions of 'language' and 'education' lie crucial concerns for individuals – concerns of personal identity, cultural and economic opportunities, and control of their own lives, which language and language education are unavoidably bound up with. Imposing categories on any complex situation inevitably oversimplifies, but it will be helpful nonetheless to begin by considering the traditional ways of addressing this complex situation.

We have already offered a definition of English as an L1: this is the language learned by those who grow up in an English-speaking environment both at home and in the wider community. In schools such people are offered the subject 'English', sometimes referred to as EMT (English as a mother tongue) to distinguish it from the other types referred to below.

Conventionally, English as an L2 refers to English-using situations in which English is the language of public life for speakers of other languages at home. The term thus embraces at least two very different traditions: first, those who have moved to an English-speaking country but continue to use their own L1 at home (e.g. Panjabi speakers in the UK, Vietnamese speakers in Australia, or Ukrainian speakers in Canada); secondly, those who live in a multilingual society which (usually because it was once part of the British empire) uses English as a language of mass communication, while nearly all inhabitants have other languages as L1 (e.g. Nigeria, India, Singapore or Guyana). In principle, English speakers in both these contexts may have English indistinguishable from L1 users who have grown up in the same country, but those in the multilingual society will have developed dialectal differences from the English of the UK, just as American or New Zealand L1 speakers have. Teachers will often refer to all these speakers as 'second language learners', learning ESL (sometimes E2L) – English as a second language.

A third category of learner comes from countries where most inhabitants speak a powerful national language which performs all major functions in the community. Here they learn foreign languages (FLs) for international communication only. They are the learners of EFL (English as a foreign language). Examples include Japan, Brazil, Hungary, Germany, and indeed most countries of the world.

Two important points may be made about this classification. First, each of these categories implies very different motivations for learning English in school.

EMT learners cannot help or choose their language: it is part of their primary socialization, the means by which they learn about language in general from birth onwards. Consequently it is tied closely to their identity, and sometimes inspires deep and unthinking loyalty. Also, because English (like French and several other languages) helped to create a strong sense of nationhood in many countries, EMT learners grow up with strong single-language (or monolingual) traditions behind them. Thus they frequently assume (quite wrongly) that monolingualism in society is normal, and may find the rest of the world's expectations of bilingualism or multilingualism somewhat threatening. Primarily, English teaching is an extension of being themselves because it is difficult for them to perceive themselves independently of their own language.

ESL learners will also have strong senses of linguistic identity, but of more varied kinds. English will be both the language of the future and of public life, but it may also threaten the past, and private identity, because these were (and are) expressed in a language other than English. Individuals will differ in the extent to which they find such tensions threatening, challenging or irrelevant. Nonetheless, there will be a sense in which ESL learners need English and work in conditions where they or their society have opted for it, where EMT learners take it for granted, with choice as an irrelevant concept. ESL learning is therefore about being themselves, but not the whole of themselves, and is bound up with perceptions of future identity.

EFL learners, in principle, have prime loyalty to their mother tongue, and may, indeed, be learning English as a third or fourth language. Self-realization may be a role for some individuals, but the prime purpose of learning English is to participate in an international community, expressing what it is to be Finnish, or Chinese, or Zairean in an international context. The international role of English has extended to such an extent that it is the primary language of such diverse activities as information technology, aviation, scientific research and pop music. Only countries which choose to opt out of these can isolate themselves from English.

The second point about the classifications must be already emerging from our discussion: the categories are not watertight. Because people are so infinitely varied in the choices they make and the activities they perform, they cannot be constrained by such crude characterizations as those offered above.

EMT, for instance, embraces a wide range of spoken speech styles. Some accents may make it difficult for some other speakers of English to understand – though in practice such difficulties are rapidly overcome given goodwill and contact. Some varieties (though very few, if any, in the UK) may differ substantially from standard varieties of English in grammar and vocabulary, so that even when written down they will be scarcely intelligible to speakers of some other dialects. But of course as soon as we acknowledge variations, either in pronunciation or grammar, we raise some of the issues for EMT that were outlined above in the discussion of ESL. If we come to school to learn a variety of English different from the one we use at home, we are being expected to modify some aspects of our identity. This is something built in to all education, not just to language education, so it need be neither threatening nor exceptional – but it nonetheless undermines the oversimple distinction outlined at the beginning of this chapter.

ESL work poses similar problems of clear definition. First, the variation issue raised under EMT above poses similar problems in multilingual contexts. In British schools, for instance, there has been a major debate about who should have substantial language support: should it mainly go to 'obvious' bilingual learners who speak (for example) Panjabi, Greek or Cantonese as a first language, or will this disadvantage speakers of English dialects such as Jamaican, or indeed speakers of Scots, who equally deserve special consideration with school English? Further, ESL learners were not at all satisfied with a classification which distinguished them from EMT learners. Their parents and community leaders understandably perceived risks of being marginalized in the education system, by being offered lower expectations of achievement in such important areas for economic advancement as literacy. The classification, by leading to different administrative provision of educational facilities, raised general questions of individual need and group expectations.

Finally, the changing international scene forces us to reconsider the category 'foreign language' also. In practice, English is widely used in the European Community. But how does this EFL differ from the ESL defined in our original list? In the second half of the twentieth century traditional ESL countries have either developed a mixed local/international language means of national communication (as India has with Hindi and English), or have moved heavily towards a major local means (as Tanzania or Malaysia have). Thus the old FL countries are gradually becoming more SL and the old SL more FL. The situation is constantly changing.

One reason for the instability of these categories is that they perform three functions simultaneously: they describe social factors, they describe psychological factors, and they define administrative functions in education. Individuals and groups are constantly making choices in relation to the social factors, and institutions are adjusted by politicians to respond to (or to resist) these choices. So, although they are helpful in clarifying some of the tensions in thinking about language, we must not believe that these distinctions reflect something that is fixed or permanent. Particularly, we must not assume that in any sense there is a hierarchy of competence implicit in these classifications. A Nigerian writer of English as an L2, Wole Soyinka, won the Nobel prize for literature in 1986; two of the greatest English novelists of the past century, Conrad and Nabokov, were originally EFL learners.

The diversity of contexts in which English is learned raises the important question of what variety of English should serve as a model in the classroom. Until recently, the general consensus for mother-tongue learners was that the written language for education was the standard language of public print, adapted of course to specific communication purposes. Spoken language was expected to take care of itself, on the grounds that it was unnecessary to attack or criticize the spoken language of home since the school's business was to develop competent writing and confident speech. This position has begun to change in some countries. For instance, in England, since the introduction of the English National Curriculum (following the 1988 Education Act), there have been several attempts to introduce the notion of spoken Standard English as a goal for all learners.

For EFL learners, this was the assumed goal for many years. It was argued that without access to a native speaker model, the best described variety of English (illustrated in thousands of audiocassettes and described in thousands of textbooks) was the most economical to provide. Further, the claim was made that a 'neutral' educated variety offered the widest access to English throughout the world, while a model based in a particular locality (rather than a general British or American one) would be unpopular for learners because it was too restrictive. Only in the past 20 years, following analyses of what communicative competence demands for comprehension, has there been increasing exposure of learners to a range of different models of pronunciation and different styles of speaking.

ESL learners in multilingual countries have had more varied diets with achieving the best local usage being seen as the prime goal. But at the same time there has been a considerable debate over the extent to which acceptance of local varieties will result in the English language splitting even further into a range of mutually unintelligible dialects. The most sensible view is to recognize the limits of planning in education. Where large numbers of speakers use non-native English for many purposes, there is little that teachers can do to combat the effect of constant use of the local dialect. Consequently, if the goal is English for local communication, contact with international English will need to be maintained through reading matter, backed up perhaps by audio material for comprehension purposes. The extent to which people want to encourage local or international varieties will then be a matter of local negotiation. On the other hand, if the goals include significant international communication, means will have to be found to introduce international English as an extension language. Such decisions cannot be legislated for from outside.

Within countries in which English is the dominant language, such as the UK, the situation is different and ESL work has often been interfered with by inappropriate principles introduced from outside contexts. Here, the language of immediate need for beginners (young learners in school, adults in further education or recent arrivals in the workplace) may well be the English that is used locally. But that will vary in pronunciation from locality to locality. To stop with this local variety is, however, potentially repressive, particularly in schools. The variety of language appropriate for education, public life and employment of any kind will be a necessary goal if teachers are not to ghettoize bilingual learners by limiting their access to all those language varieties available to mother-tongue learners.

Thus the appropriate variety to offer must depend on a more refined analysis than that provided by the crude classification offered at the beginning of this chapter. Factors like age, previous learning experience, region, educational ambitions and employment opportunities all contribute to a specification of possible target language varieties – whether or not the learners are mother-tongue, second language or foreign language users of English. Above all, though, the issue has to be seen as one of freedom. Ultimately learners are entitled to the English that most effectively gives them freedom to choose who to communicate with, for whatever purposes they wish.

This reading was specially commissioned for this book.

Reading B

DILEMMAS OF A TEXTBOOK WRITER

Neville Grant

I have been a writer of English language teaching/learning materials for over 20 years. I do this as a full-time occupation, although I also undertake some consultancy work and a certain amount of teacher training.

Members of my subgroup within the English language teaching (ELT) profession fall broadly into two categories. There are those writers who develop materials for 'global' markets. These are the writers who try to satisfy the inexhaustible demands of language schools from Montevideo to Mexico City to Madrid and Milan – as well as, these days, Moscow: they tend to produce materials for a kind of international middle class. Secondly, there are those who write for the school systems of particular countries – Italy, Mexico, Nigeria or Japan. These fall into two further subcategories – those who write English as a foreign language (EFL) materials and those who write English as a second language (ESL) materials. Much of the work I have done comes into this second category. I started off writing materials for countries where I had lived and which I knew fairly well – in East and West Africa. Later I was commissioned to write for other parts of the world where it was necessary for me to get to know the countries as well as I possibly could in as short a time as I possibly could. In all cases, I worked as a member of a team with local participants. Usually, I was the only full-time professional author.

It is widely thought that it is almost impossible to learn a language without undergoing some cultural change. But language teaching/learning programmes that are 'designed to encourage learners to "become American" for example, to adopt certain values and attitudes considered appropriate for immigrants, and to shift allegiance from their native culture to the dominant American culture' (Tollefson, 1991) are, to this writer at least, anathema. It is difficult to avoid the view that such programmes smack of cultural imperialism and an unpleasant ethnocentrism. Syllabus designers and curriculum workers in the countries in which English is learned as a second language, such as Nigeria, Ghana, Kenya, South Africa or Botswana, would be aghast at suggestions that their language-learning syllabuses should in any way follow the 'integrative' line. It is hoped that the case studies below will give some insight into some of the cross-cultural issues raised in ELT.

All the work I have been involved in has been done against the background of education systems – the education systems of the target countries, including their teaching syllabuses and examination syllabuses. Materials that do not conform in detail to a national syllabus may not receive approval, and may therefore never be used within the education system for which they were devised, no matter how 'good' the materials. Similarly, materials that are not tailored to national examinations will also fail to be adopted. Such examinations are these days almost always set by national or regional examination boards. It is one of the professional hazards that such examinations may be overly influenced by educational considerations that are now considered out of date (updating examinations and/or education systems is extremely expensive). Such examinations may not be as closely tailored to economic strategies of development as may be thought desirable. Thus some examinations may unduly reward accuracy in manipulating the forms of language at the expense of functions of language, which is a criticism that has been levelled at West African examinations; or they may seem unduly literary and elitist, a criticism that has been levelled at Caribbean examinations.

In all the material development projects that I have been involved in a priority has been to reflect national social and cultural aspirations. Thus a course written for Kenya will give prominence to writing by Kenyan writers, of whom Ngũgĩ wa Thiong'o is the best known, whereas a course for Nigeria will contain a great deal of writing by such writers as Chinua Achebe, Buchi Emecheta or Wole Soyinka.

Case study 1: Nigeria

In order to accommodate syllabus changes I have recently been involved with rewriting and updating materials that I developed for Nigeria some years ago. (For an early account of this project see Grant, 1983.) The new syllabus highlights a number of lexical items that need to be taught, typically in the context of meaningful and relevant reading materials. Among these are terms concerned with marriage and weddings, including the term 'bride-price'.

It was decided to treat this topic in a four-pronged manner: (1) reading material; (2) vocabulary exercise; (3) debate; and (4) poem.

1   Reading material

A reading text, adapted for level and length, from Chinua Achebe's famous novel *Things Fall Apart*. The text includes a description of some negotiations over a 'bride-price' between two families.

Bride-price

Just then, Akueke came in carrying a wooden dish with three kola nuts and pepper. She gave the dish to Machi, her father's eldest brother, and she stretched out her hand, very shyly, to her suitor and his relatives. She was about sixteen and just ripe for marriage. Her suitor and his relatives looked her over to make sure that she was beautiful and ready for marriage.

Akueke's hair was combed up into a crest along the middle of her head. Her skin smelt of scented wood. She wore a string of black beads around her neck. On her arms were red and yellow bracelets, and on her waist four or five rows of waist-beads.

After she had held out her hand to be shaken, she returned to her mother's hut to help with the cooking.

The men in the hut were preparing to drink palm wine which Akueke's suitor had brought. Okonkwo could see that it was very good wine, for white bubbles rose and spilled over the edge of the pot.

'That wine comes from a good tree,' said Okonkwo, Obierika's friend.

The young suitor, whose name was Ibe, smiled broadly. He filled the first horn and gave it to his father, Ukegbu. Then he poured wine out for the others, starting with Akueke's father, Obierika. Okonkwo brought out his big horn from the goatskin bag, blew into it to remove any dust that might be there, and gave it to Ibe to fill.

As the men drank, they talked about everything except the thing for which they had gathered. After the pot had been emptied, the suitor's father cleared his voice and explained the reason for their visit.

(Grant et al., 1995, p. 104)

The questions include the usual mandatory comprehension questions, plus 'Discussion and opinion' questions designed to encourage learners to give their own views. Included among these were the following questions:

- In this extract, women seem to take no part in the negotiations – and no one asked Akueke's [the bride's] opinion. Do you think that this is right?

- Some people say that paying bride-price is an out-of-date custom. What do you think?

- Chinua Achebe's book *Things Fall Apart* is set in the old days in Nigeria. Could the negotiations described in this extract still take place in a similar way today, do you think?

2   Vocabulary exercise

A follow-up vocabulary exercise is provided which mentions that 'bride-wealth' is in many ways a better term to use than bride-price. The exercise consists of a cloze (blank-filling) text which first briefly describes western-style courtship patterns, and then proceeds:

However, in many cases, marriage (in Nigeria) is definitely a family affair: it is seen as the joining together of two families rather than just two people, and an engagement is preceded by a period of ... (4) ... rather than courtship. In such situations ... (5) ... must be paid by the kin of the man to that of the woman. Once this has been given and received, it is seen as a sign that the ... (6) ... is taken very seriously.

3 Debate

A debate is suggested, with these motions:

1 Bride-wealth should be abolished.
2 Polygamy should not be encouraged.

4 Poem

At the end of the unit there is a poem by the Guyanese poet Grace Nichols, followed by a wide-ranging discussion which includes the interesting question 'What do you suppose Grace Nichols would think of the institution of bride-wealth?'

Holding my Beads

Unforgiving as the course of justice
Inerasable as my scars and fate
I am here
A woman ... with all my lives
strung out like beads before me.

It isn't privilege or pity
that I seek
It isn't reverence or safety
quick happiness or purity but
the power to be what I am/a woman
charting my own futures/a woman
holding my beads in my hand.

(Nichols, 1988)

Figure 1   A Nigerian bride
From Grant et al., 1995, p. 113

Discussion

In this unit an attempt is made to treat the subject of weddings and a very common Nigerian custom in a culturally sensitive and well-informed manner. No attempt is made to 'preach' to students; every attempt is made to encourage them to use English to think about the issue. An assimilationist model in the Nigerian context is clearly unthinkable. It is not for the writer of ELT materials to make value judgements, but merely to present ideas and activities that encourage learners to think, to learn, and to make up their own minds on the issues raised.

While on one hand it would appear that the writer of ELT materials adopts a neutral stance on issues such as the custom of bride-price, it might be argued that in opening a debate and possibly encouraging dissent, the writer is 'smuggling in' western notions of self-expression associated with bourgeois liberal humanism. However anyone who has worked in Nigeria, at least in the south, would acknowledge that enthusiastic controversy and argument, far from being a feature solely of western democracy, is a prominent feature in Nigerian culture.

Case study 2: China

Between 1988 and 1992 I was involved in helping to develop a new course for the People's Republic of China, working for a project funded by UNDP, and implemented by two publishers working together – the People's Education Press in Beijing, and Longman Group from the UK. This involved extended visits to Beijing and other cities, during which I worked closely with Chinese colleagues in the People's Education Press.

English was and is seen as an essential part of China's 'modernization' programme. The development of the new course *Junior English for China* (Grant et al., 1991) was seen as a major curriculum development initiative, involving trialling in pilot schools in many parts of China, collecting feedback, and revising the materials accordingly. A detailed draft syllabus had been developed by the Chinese, but wisely remained in draft form until after the materials interpreting it had been developed, so that the syllabus itself could be fine-tuned in the light of the trialling of the materials. This might seem to be an odd way to approach curriculum development; in fact, it makes very good sense to combine top-down approaches in which working parties hammer out a draft syllabus with bottom-up approaches in which teachers in the classroom give feedback that can fine-tune, or even radically alter, the syllabus. (Curriculum development in the UK could have benefited from such a combined approach in recent years.)

From the outset it was made clear that the Chinese wanted to improve the students' ability to use the language communicatively, and at the same time provide learners with a window on the world outside China. They were and are particularly interested in studying 'cultural differences'. This was all the more remarkable given that the project developed at a particularly difficult and sensitive period in China's history. However, 'knowing about' the world outside definitely did not mean 'identifying with' it, and reading passages used in the course were, not surprisingly, closely checked to ensure that what appeared conformed to the syllabus – that is, included the lexis and grammar specified in the syllabus – and contained nothing that was 'unsuitable' or politically controversial.

It is of course quite difficult to be controversial within a limit of some 1,400 words (the number of words targeted by the syllabus). In the event, it is surprising what was included: the texts included fragments of British and American history (Abraham Lincoln is a firm favourite), and some references to modern culture (great interest evinced in fast food and fish and chips). Modern mores also played their part: the Chinese were interested in texts that highlighted cultural differences, for example the different way in which Europeans respond to compliments.

It may be imagined that it is not easy to generate interesting reading texts that have some intrinsic educational value within a very small vocabulary. No great claims are made on behalf of the text illustrated in the box other than to say that it was an attempt to break the cultural stereotype common in China that all British (English) are Caucasian and middle class, with 2.4 children, a Ford and a bowler hat. The text seeks to amuse, to treat certain target items of vocabulary, to indicate that the UK is a multicultural society and, last but not least, to address the issue of racism – which, by the way, European societies do not have a monopoly on.

The queue jumper

It was a cold spring morning in the city of London in England. The weather was very cold, and many people were ill. So there were many people in the doctor's waiting room. At the head of the queue was an old woman. The woman was a visitor. She did not live in London. She lived in the country. She was in the city to visit her daughter. She wanted to see the doctor because her back hurt.

'If I get there early, I can see the doctor quickly,' she thought. So she was first in the queue. She sat nearest to the doctor's door.

An Indian came into the waiting-room, and walked quickly to the doctor's door. The old woman thought he was a queue jumper. She stood up and took his arm. Slowly, she said, 'We were all here before you. You must wait for your turn. Do … you … understand?'

The Indian answered: 'No, madam. *You* don't understand! You're all after me! I'm the doctor!'

Everyone laughed at the woman's mistake.

(Grant et al., 1991, p. 91)

When I first presented this text in draft form to my colleagues they were pleased to see material about queuing – an important cultural feature. But they were also puzzled. 'Why is the doctor an Indian?' they asked. I explained about Britain being a multicultural society. 'Our teachers will find it difficult to understand what an Indian is doing in London. Why don't we make the doctor an Englishman?' (sic). I agreed that this would be possible, but that it would rather destroy the point of the story. I indicated that there was a gentle anti-racist lesson in the story. This gave my colleagues some pause for thought. In the end, somewhat reluctantly, the story was included in the text.

Discussion

It might be thought that I had some hidden anti-racist agenda and was persuading my Chinese colleagues, perhaps against their better judgement, to include material which they would not ordinarily have chosen. Since my Chinese colleagues had veto powers, however, the question is rather whether or not a professional author is going beyond the call of duty to try to include educational values in the text. Would I have been failing in my duty not to present materials that might not ordinarily have been selected? In so doing was I downloading cultural values or raising international issues in a relatively uncontroversial manner? Should I instead have addressed the issue of racism in a much more controversial way and included (within a vocabulary of 1,400 words) an account of race riots in Bristol or wherever? I have to confess that I avoided the latter, partly because of the technical problems of doing so within a restricted vocabulary, but partly also because my Chinese cultural antennae indicated that to describe a riot in a manner sympathetic to the victims might easily have been interpreted as a coded support for those who demonstrated in Tiananmen Square in 1989. Such interpretations could, conceivably, have ugly consequences for one's Chinese colleagues, and even for the whole project.

Case study 3: Tanzania

One of the most interesting problems arises in relation to the press. Not all the countries that one has to write for has a free press. The newspaper is the one publication most likely to be read by students in countries such as Nigeria or Tanzania where there is little tradition of reading more widely. I think it is important that the students are taught to read newspapers, and not necessarily to believe everything they contain!

Some years ago the magazine *Index on Censorship* carried an article by Graham Mitten on newspapers in the third world.

> At a party in Dar es Salaam a few years ago three Tanzanian journalists argued fiercely about an important issue ... Reports were coming in of a village settlement scheme that had failed badly. Large sums of money had been lost ...
>
> The first journalist argued that they should ignore the story. The government ... had only just launched the policy of *ujamaa* villages, involving peasants in communal agriculture. It was a difficult policy to put over and [an unfavourable report now] would reinforce existing doubts and might well sway the undecided against the policy ...
>
> The second journalist disagreed ... the press was performing a public duty if it investigated and prevented the government from 'sweeping the whole story under the rug' ... The only way to be sure that government had sensible policies was to report everything connected with those policies ...
>
> The third journalist ... agreed that the press had to say something about the story ... [Not to report it would damage] the credibility of the press ... But everything should be written with great care. The Tanzanian journalist had to be conscious of the effects of what he wrote. Journalists had no business campaigning against elected governments [particularly in Third World countries where resources of all kinds were very limited] ... It was legitimate for the government of Tanzania to expect cooperation from the press.
>
> (Mitten, 1977, p. 35)

This article (presented in a simplified form in Grant et al., 1980) generates great interest in all the classrooms where it has been tried. The book itself remains neutral on the issues raised – and leaves it to the students to be partisan, which, joyfully, they are.

Later in the unit there are two contrasting news reports, one attacking the Tanzanian government for the failure of the village settlement scheme, and one seeking to present the government's efforts in the best possible light. These news reports again generate great interest, and the students enjoy picking out examples of bias, misrepresentation and so forth.

However, the issue – for writer and publisher – arose: how would this article be received in Tanzania? Was the issue so politically sensitive that it might lead to the books not being ordered and used in Tanzania? Was this a good reason to impose self-censorship – a procedure far more common in the world than many of us realize? The material was sent to Tanzania for advice – and the message was relayed back that there was no problem. The then president of Tanzania, Julius Nyerere, welcomed frank discussions of important sensitive issues, and there was nothing in the materials that would be taken in any way amiss.

Conclusion

In all the case studies mentioned here there has been a common thread: materials that in some way or other seem to go against the grain – or at least someone's grain – are vetted for content, for cultural acceptability. Doubts are expressed about them and in each case co-authors or report writers are asked for their views, then either the doubts are allayed, or at last declared invalid, or the material is amended or discarded.

References

ACHEBE, C. (1958) *Things Fall Apart*, London, Heinemann.

GRANT, N.J.H. (1983) 'Materials design for Nigerian secondary schools' in BRUMFIT, C.J. (ed.) *Language Teaching Projects for the Third World*, Oxford, Pergamon/British Council.

GRANT, N.J.H., OLAGOKE, D.O. and SOUTHERN, K. (1980) *Secondary English Project*, Harlow, Longman.

GRANT, N.J.H. et al. (1991) *Junior English for China: students' book 2*, Beijing, People's Education Press.

GRANT, N.J.H. OLAGOKE, D.O., NNAMONU, S. and JOWITT, D. (1995) *Junior English Project (for Nigerian Secondary Schools)*, Harlow, Longman.

MITTEN, G. (1977) 'Tanzania – a case study', *Index on Censorship*, vol. 6, no. 5, p. 35.

NICHOLS, G. (1988) *I is a Long Memoried Woman*, London, Karnak House.

TOLLEFSON, J.W. (1991) *Planning Language, Planning Inequality*, London, Longman.

This reading was specially commissioned for this book.

ENGLISH IN THE ACADEMIC WORLD

Elizabeth Hoadley-Maidment and Neil Mercer

8.1 INTRODUCTION

In this chapter we look at English as an academic language as it is used by lecturers, students and researchers in universities and colleges in many parts of the world. We look at what constitutes 'academic' English and consider the expectations that people have about its correct use. Some of the issues raised in earlier chapters of the book, for example, the demands made on students by being educated in English, will reappear here as they are relevant to higher education. The main questions which we will address are as follows:

- What is 'academic' English and how is its nature related to its functions?

- How are students in higher education expected to use English?

- What kinds of problems do students encounter with 'academic' English?

- What kinds of help are students offered?

As we deal with these questions, it will become apparent that there is considerable uncertainty and dispute about how academic English should be defined and taught.

8.2 ENGLISH IN ACADEMIC LIFE

The spread of English

The use of English as a medium for communication in higher education – among researchers as well as in teaching activities – has increased dramatically through-out the world in recent years. For example, though before World War Two mathematics research was commonly published in international German-language journals, English language journals now predominate. The importance of the language in higher education is demonstrated by the fact that in 1994 the government of the Netherlands seriously considered a proposal that all Dutch higher education should in future be conducted in English. In the event, this proposal was not accepted; but in other parts of the world – in many African countries, India and Singapore, for instance – English has long been established as a medium of university education.

In countries such as India and Singapore, English was introduced as a language of education in the time of the British empire. Although in postcolonial times there have been some powerful political campaigns to encourage the greater use of other languages in academic settings (such as the pro-Mandarin campaign in Singapore in the 1980s, described in Pennycook, 1994b), many such countries continue to use English in their higher education systems and so effectively encourage the use of English as an international academic language.

See the discussion of English in India in Chapter 5, Reading A.

Support for the academic use of English throughout the world has been a part of the foreign policy of British governments, as Phillipson (1992) and Pennycook (1994b) have shown. And in the latter part of the twentieth century the USA has taken a leading role in many academic fields of research, thus increasing academic publishing in English at the expense of other languages. Another reason for the increased use of English in higher education is that, having become a commonly learned modern language, English may function as a lingua franca for scholars of different language backgrounds. Thus the official language of the European Association for Research in Learning and Instruction is English, even though the vast majority of its members have some other language as a mother tongue.

The spread of English in higher education has been at the expense of other languages, whose role in academic life is inevitably diminished. Phillipson (1992) describes as **linguistic imperialism** the process whereby a powerful language displaces others in some social functions, and in so doing assists the cultural influence of the nations which speak it. Consider, for example, the situation in Singapore, where, because the use of English in higher education has official government support, an increasing number of students pursue their education through a language which is not their traditional mother tongue. From a similar standpoint to that adopted by Phillipson, the language researcher Chua Beng-Huat (1983) has questioned the official view that the use of English in Singaporean higher education has only practical, rather than political or cultural implications. However, because English now has a status as a 'world language', its link with specific national cultures (such as those of the USA or UK) may be becoming less strong. In some multilingual academic settings, English may be attractive because it is distinct from local or regional languages and cultures. The sociolinguist David Corson illustrates this with his experience as an external examiner for a Norwegian PhD student:

> I am seated next to the candidate … I say her thesis is as good as the better theses I have examined in English-speaking countries. We talk about why she chose to be examined in English. Her reason is simple. She speaks a Nord-Trondelag rural dialect of Norwegian. If she used Norwegian, she would be examined probably by a Swede and someone from Oslo. So she would have to use 'their' language. I had never thought of English as a 'neutral' language.
>
> (Corson, 1994, p. 14)

The causes and effects of the global spread of English in higher education are complex and many. While we cannot deal with them comprehensively in this chapter, we can point to some interesting aspects of how and why English is used. But first we consider what has to be learned in order to use English as an academic language. At this point, we do not distinguish between 'native speakers' and those for whom English is a second language.

The nature of academic English

The concept of discourse community is discussed in more detail in the second book in this series, *Using English: from conversation to canon* (Maybin and Mercer (eds), 1996).

The linguist John Swales (1990) has described academic life in terms of the activities of various **discourse communities**, each focused on a particular academic subject or area of research. Such communities are often spread world-wide and depend heavily on written communications. Latin was the lingua franca of such academic communities in the Europe of the Middle Ages; and as mentioned above, international academic communications are now commonly conducted in English.

Academic English has a number of varieties which are associated with par-ticular academic subjects or disciplines in the arts, sciences and social sciences. It is common for scholars in each discipline to establish their own language conven-tions and practices, which new members have to acquire. The educational researcher Gordon Wells explains:

> Each subject discipline constitutes a way of making sense of human experience that has evolved over generations and each is dependent on its own particular practices: its instrumental procedures, its criteria for judging relevance and validity, and its conventions of acceptable forms of argument. In a word, each has developed its own modes of discourse. To work in a discipline, therefore, it is necessary to be able to engage in these practices and, in particular, to participate in the discourse of that com-munity.
>
> (Wells, 1992, p. 290)

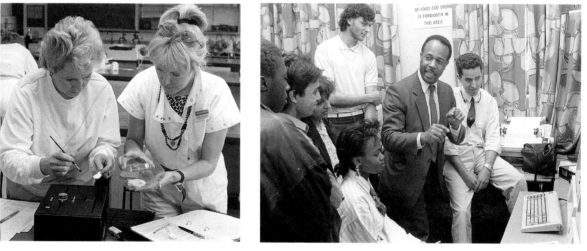

Scholars in different disciplines establish their own language conventions and practices which new members have to acquire

Halliday (1978) has suggested that one common feature of the creation of a suitable functional variety of language for a field of study is the creation of new 'thing-names' – words for referring to newly discovered or specially defined objects, processes, relationships and so on. He suggests that this kind of lexical development is achieved in various ways:

(i) Reinterpreting existing words. Examples from mathematical English are: *set, point, field, row, column, weight, stand for, sum, move through, even* (number), *random.*

(ii) Creating new words out of native word stock. This process has not played a very great part in the creation of technical registers in

English (an early example of it is *clockwise*), but recently it has come back into favour with words like *shortfall, feedback, output.*

(iii)   Borrowing words from another language. This has been the method most favoured in technical English. Mathematics examples include *degree, series, exceed, subtract, multiply, invert, infinite, probable.*

(iv)   'Calquing': creating new words in imitation of another language. This is rare in modern English, though it is a regular feature of many languages; it was used in old English to render Christian terms from Latin, e.g. *almighty* calqued on *omnipotens.* (Latin *omnipotens* is made up of *omni* meaning 'all' and *potens* meaning 'mighty' …)

(v)   Inventing totally new words. This hardly ever happens. About the only English example is *gas*, a word coined out of nowhere by a Dutch chemist in the eighteenth century.

(vi)   Creating 'locutions'. There is no clear line between locutions, in the sense of phrases or larger structures, and compound words. Expressions like *right-angled triangle, square on the hypotenuse, lowest common multiple* are examples of technical terms in mathematics English that are to be classed as locutions rather than compound words.

(vii)   Creating new words out of non-native word stock. This is now the most typical procedure in contemporary European languages for the creation of new technical terms. Words like *parabola, denominator, binomial, coefficient, thermodynamic, permutation, approximation, denumerable, asymptotic, figurate,* are not borrowed from Greek and Latin – they did not exist in these languages. They are made up in English (and in French, Russian and other languages) out of elements of the Greek and Latin word stock.

(Halliday, 1978, p. 195–6)

❖ ❖ ❖ ❖ ❖

Activity 8.1   *(Allow about 5 minutes)*

If Halliday had been compiling his list more recently, he would probably have included some computer-related examples. In which of Halliday's categories would you include the following words?

1   Interface

2   Boot

3   Disk

4   Download

5   Hypertext

6   Read Only Memory (ROM)

Comment

We would place examples 1 and 4 in Halliday's category (ii), examples 2 and 3 in category (i) and 6 in category (vi). Example 5 would qualify for category (vii) as it was created from Greek ('hyper') and Latin ('text') elements.

❖ ❖ ❖ ❖ ❖

Of course, academic discourse communities are not entirely distinct, and in practice they are hard to define. Discourse communities can overlap, and members of some may use English in ways that are quite similar to others. The discourses of sociologists and historians, for instance, are more similar to each other than they are to the discourse of biologists, but historians of science use English in ways that are similar to both historians and biologists. Should science historians be considered a separate academic discourse community? Swales (1990) offers a very narrow definition of a discourse community, which includes the requirement that its members have a publicly stated set of common aims. This then excludes all but the most formal kinds of communicative groups and so it greatly reduces the applicability of a useful concept. While we would favour a looser definition, we certainly agree with Swales that students studying any subject or discipline have to learn to understand, and eventually to speak and write, a specialized English discourse. There is a well-established field of educational research and English language teaching concerned with **English for academic purposes** or **academic English** which has developed to help students (not only those for whom English is a second language) achieve this. We consider some approaches to this later in the chapter.

❖ ❖ ❖ ❖ ❖

Activity 8.2   *(Allow about 20 minutes)*

Read the following examples of specialized academic discourse. All three are extracts from the introductory sections of articles in research journals. As you read, focus on the following linguistic features: *lexis* (the particular words used; any specialized terminology) and overall *style* (e.g. whether they represent *formal* or *informal, personal* or *impersonal* ways of using language). Then consider:

- Which text is easiest for you to understand?
- What does reading them reveal about your own relationship to academic discourse communities?
- How do the texts differ?
- What, if anything, do the texts have in common in terms of style?

---

1   Written language like spoken language achieves communicative and conceptual goals by using a complex system of arbitrary symbols and conventional rules … Writing however is a visible language, a graphic symbolic system whose roots we suggest lie in pictographic representation before links are established with spoken language. In this respect, development reflects evolution in that all writing systems which represent sounds of language evolved from pictorial representations rather than from spoken language. In literate societies, a developed writing system is pervasive in children's environment and it is likely that each individual child constructs, or re-invents, their own approach to writing from whatever salient experience the environment offers which they can utilize at different levels of development.

(Martlew and Sorsby, 1995, p. 1)

2   The attempt to give a comprehensive account of the many hundreds of differences between the 1608 (Pied Bull) Quarto of *King Lear* (Q) and the1623 First Folio version (F), has occasioned a daunting

amount of scholarly study, and the three hundred lines that appear in Q but not in F, and the hundred or so that are in F but not in Q, are an obvious focus for analysis and debate. Of these, W.W. Greg said in 1955 that 'The explanation of the deficiencies need not be the same in all cases, but for the most part omission can be assumed.' It is with F's 'omissions' that I shall mainly concern myself, in taking issue with the 'new revisionists' of the last fifteen years or so, who argue that F is the product of systematic authorial revision of *King Lear*, with Q (however imperfectly) representative of its unrevised state. My own observations will be made from the perspective of the theatre practitioner.

(Clare, 1995, p. 1)

3   In earlier papers we have reported the excess volumes and viscosities of different binary mixtures containing N-methylmethane-sulfonamide as one component. In view of the importance of alcohols as solvents, it was of interest to continue this work with an investigation of the properties of the (methanesulfonamide + an aliphatic alcohol). In this study we report the excess volumes for NMMSA + methanol, + propan-1-ol, + propan-2-ol, + butan-1-ol, and + 2-methylpropan-2-ol.

(Pikkarainen, cited in Bhatia, 1993, p. 89)

Comment

Our guess is that most readers of this book found example 1 or example 2 the easiest to comprehend, and example 3 the hardest. Possible reasons for this are:

1   The first example (which comes from the European educational research journal *Learning and Instruction*) and the second (from *The Library: the transactions of the Bibliographical Society*) include not only fewer specialized lexical items than the third (which is from the *Journal of Chemical Thermodynamics*) but also fewer whose meaning is completely impenetrable to any reader who is 'outside' the specialized academic community of discourse. The meaning of technical terms such as 'graphic notation' and 'metalinguistic' (in example 1), could perhaps be guessed at by educated 'outsiders' to the discourse of language study, if they drew on their general knowledge of English. This might also be the case for terms like 'Quarto' and 'Folio' in example 2; but it is not possible for many of the terms in example 3. The third example even uses a specialized English morphology (for example, the numbers and dashes in 'propan-2-ol') and syntax (e.g. the use of plus signs in '+ methanol, + propan-1-ol') which render it even more code-like and incomprehensible to the uninitiated.

2   Compared with the third example, the first and second, while coming from two distinct fields of study (research into children's literacy development and the study of published literary texts), are both from fields which are relatively close to the subject matter of this chapter and this book. Even if one is not a 'full' member of an educational or language studies research community, a reader of a book on the English language is more likely to have interests which provide the kind of background knowledge required for making sense

of an article on literacy in *Learning and Instruction* or *The Library* than for understanding the contents of the *Journal of Chemical Thermodynamics*.

3   In terms of the differences between these abstracts, the most obvious relate to their subject matter and the use in each of a different *specialized lexis*, or vocabulary of technical terms associated with a specific field of study. Also, the author of example 2 refers to himself ('I').

4   In terms of their similarities, the use in all three texts of a specialized lexis is a kind of similarity. But academic discourses are made up of more than specialized vocabulary: they have other characteristic features of style. One stylistic feature that both examples 1 and 3 illustrate which is typical of most writing in scientific research journals is the lack of any sense of the personal presence of their authors. The authors make no reference to themselves (as 'I' or 'we') and there is no reference to personal emotions or attitudes; they offer what appears to be a detached, objective account of their research.

The three abstracts have an obvious functional similarity – each is meant to introduce and summarize a report of a research study to a very specific audience. Swales (1990) has suggested that the conventional sections of academic articles – 'abstract', 'introduction', 'method', 'results' and 'conclusion' – may also commonly serve other rhetorical purposes. So the introductions to scientific research articles often have a common basic structure, one which reflects the aim of authors to claim a niche for themselves in the contested territory of the research field they are involved in. Swales has proposed a structural model for the 'introduction' sections to journal articles, made up of four consecutive 'moves' through the text, as follows:

Move 1:   establishing the field of study
Move 2:   summarizing previous research
Move 3:   preparing for present research (including indicating a 'gap' in the findings of existing research)
Move 4:   introducing the present research

❖   ❖   ❖   ❖   ❖

Academic English and academic cultures

Two features mentioned above – a *specialized lexis* and an *impersonal style* – are typical of many varieties of academic English. To the best of our knowledge, they are also a common feature of academic writing in most other languages besides English. However, some interesting variations in academic style exist. For example, the accepted French style of academic writing, at least in the social sciences and humanities, is more self-consciously eloquent and personally expressive than that used by British scholars writing in English. The linguists Bloor and Bloor (1991) comment on how academic writing in French is also noticeably influenced by the ideal model for essay writing that is taught in French schools, in which argument is constructed through the repeated consideration of a 'thesis' (one side of the argument) and an 'antithesis' (the other side of the argument), leading finally to a 'synthesis' (resolution). Bloor and Bloor also note that when personal opinions or disagreements are expressed in formal academic English, authors tend to use a polite, self-effacing style, with many 'hedged propositions' (such as 'it would seem that ...' and 'one possible interpretation of this finding might be …'). They contrast this with a more direct, personal 'unhedged' style found in academic journals written in the Czech language. Clyne (1987) has described differences between German and English styles of writing on linguistics and sociology, concluding that 'texts by Germans are less designed to be easy to read' (p. 238). It is of course very difficult to distinguish between an author's use of a style associated with a particular *academic culture* (e.g. a French style of sociological research, rather than a British one) and his or her use of a particular *language*. However, we can consider whether there is much variation between academics working in different cultural settings but writing in the same language, that is English.

❖　❖　❖　❖　❖

Activity 8.3　*(Reading A)*

Read 'Culture in rhetorical styles: contrastive rhetoric and world Englishes', by Yamuna Kachru (Reading A). Use the following points and questions to guide your reading.

- 'Contrastive rhetoric' (CR) is a kind of research which examines how language use varies in style across different cultures. In recent years it has been used particularly to study variations in styles of writing. What does Kachru identify as the 'major assumptions' underlying this approach? What does she see as some of the (undesirable) consequences of its influence on research and teaching?

- Kachru uses the terms 'inner circle' and 'outer circle' to define two groups of English speakers in the world today (the terms are defined in note 1 to the reading). How does she see CR research as discriminating against academic writers in the outer circle?

- What are some of the differences she identifies, in the ways texts are organized and arguments are presented, between inner circle academic writers and those of some outer circle countries (for example, India)?

- What changes do you think that Kachru would like to see in the way academic English is defined and taught?

❖　❖　❖　❖　❖

The style of academic English

In Reading A, Kachru argues that contrastive rhetoric research has implicitly incorporated some questionable ideas about what constitutes 'good' academic writing, ideas which are essentially those of the academic cultures of countries in the 'inner circle' of English speakers. The consequence is that CR research treats as problematic any deviation in the academic use of English away from 'inner circle' conventional styles. On the basis of this argument, she attempts to do two things: (1) to show that some culturally established styles of English academic writing other than those conventionally used in 'inner circle' countries are legitimate and valuable, because they represent rather different but not inferior ways of thinking and presenting knowledge; and (2) to propose some ways in which contrastive rhetoric research should become more sensitive to cultural diversity in academic English.

The nature of academic English, in any of its varieties, is shaped by its various social and cultural functions as the language of academic communities of discourse. In Reading A, Kachru draws special attention to the diversity of cultures within which academic activity is pursued in English. We have suggested, however, that although there are many varieties of academic English, some of these varieties share common stylistic features. Take, for instance, the English used in science research journals. According to the linguist Bhatia (1993), there is a common expectation in academic discourses across the world that writers should make their *reasoning explicit* in the text, so that other researchers can evaluate that reasoning. Although Kachru is arguing for more cultural flexibility in upholding the conventions of academic 'Englishes', she is not necessarily arguing against the desirability of maintaining that expectation. Rather, she is suggesting that there is more than one valid, culturally based way of making such reasoning explicit in English.

The analysis of academic varieties of English – their nature and function, the styles to which students are meant to conform and the justifications for upholding and enforcing those style conventions – is bound eventually to bring us up against some profound and difficult questions. Is the 'truth' or validity of a piece of academic work affected by the style of most academic English a necessary counterpart of 'rigorous thinking', or merely a conventional, superficial aspect of linguistic style?

The concept of genre is discussed in more detail in Chapter 4, especially Reading C.

There are no firm answers to these questions. Many people involved in academic work are aware of them, and some of the accepted conventions or 'ground rules' of academic writing have been brought under critical scrutiny (Sheeran and Barnes, 1991; Bhatia, 1993). Genres also change over time, as can be seen by comparing styles of writing in academic journals of, say, the early, middle and late parts of the twentieth century.

But for any student the plain truth remains that academic success usually depends on following the conventions for academic English in the relevant field of study. An important aim of higher education is to enable students to become fluent 'speakers' of the discourse of relevant academic communities. Lecturers and tutors present students with texts written in one or more varieties of academic English, and they expect students to write assignments in English which approaches these models and so is appropriately 'academic'. Much of the work by language researchers on communities of discourse (for example, Lemke, 1990, and Swales, 1990) and contrastive rhetoric ('CR', as mentioned by Kachru in Reading A) has in fact been motivated by the practical, educational issue of helping students cope with the demands of academic English. We now go on to look more closely at what is expected of students in their use of English.

Standards and expectations in higher education

Let us first of all consider students who are native speakers of English, such as the great majority of those who enter higher education in the UK, the USA and Australasia. The majority of those who do enter universities and colleges in those countries will have gained better-than-average qualifications in school and may well have begun to study in school the subject that they are studying at university. One might expect that the task for such people would be relatively easy – to use the basis of their educational experience and strong competence in English to make sense of the structure and lexis of the more advanced academic Englishes they encounter. It seems, however, that many such students fail to meet the standards expected of them by their tutors and examiners.

❖   ❖   ❖   ❖   ❖

Activity 8.4   *(Allow about 10 minutes)*

Read the following extracts from articles in the British weekly *The Times Higher Education Supplement* about standards of English in use. As you do, consider what aspects of students' English usage are claimed to be inadequate and what kind of evidence is being used to make these claims.

Teach yourself answer to poor English

More than 100 departments in universities have expressed interest in using a diagnostic English test aimed at improving the spelling, grammar and punctuation of new students, following a survey revealing that 'poor English' is widespread across all subjects.

(Sian Griffiths in *The Times Higher Education Supplement*, 25 September 1992, p. 2)

NZ home students 'lack literacy'

Questions about the literacy of immigrant students in New Zealand have spread to students who have come through the country's school system.

Albert Brownlie, vice chancellor of Canterbury University, said the native students were a greater concern than immigrants and their children.

The literacy issue has gained wide publicity in New Zealand following a review of Canterbury University's English department which highlighted a significant number of students, undergraduate and postgraduates, enrolled in a writing skills course or receiving individual help.

'At least 15 per cent of the university's enrolments are in need of some remedial work or guidance with their written work; such as composing sentences, writing essays and punctuation,' Professor Brownlie said.

(Janet Rivers in *The Times Higher Education Supplement*, 28 October 1994, p. 9)

Comment

You may have noticed that the criticisms of students' writing, as they are reported, vary slightly in each of the extracts. The first focuses on the 'surface features' of spelling, grammar and punctuation, while the second mentions the more stylistic issues of 'composing sentences' and 'writing essays'. But both claim that an unacceptably high proportion of students in higher education institutions in a country where English is the first language of the great majority (Britain and New Zealand) have problems in using English, and so cannot cope with the language demands of their higher education studies. This has been a regular topic of concern in recent years in the British press, where it is sometimes also linked to claims that graduates disappoint their eventual employers by being unable to cope with the English language demands of the workplace.

The kind of evidence that would be most helpful in pursuing this issue would come from large-scale surveys of the actual performance in English by students 'in context' in academic settings, and a set of criteria for judging that performance against explicit standards. Unfortunately, no such substantial body of evidence of that kind has been collected. However, it seems that there is some significant level of concern among students who are native speakers of English, and their lecturers, about levels of competence in English. This in itself makes the topic worthy of close examination. And of course we have not yet mentioned the many students in higher education throughout the world who are studying in English but who have learned it as a second or other language. Such students may have more obvious difficulties with using English as required in their studies.

❖   ❖   ❖   ❖   ❖

Students for whom English is a second language

Every year, more and more students pursue university-level education through English, not only in the universities of what Kachru in Reading A calls the 'inner circle' of English-speaking countries, but in many other countries worldwide. For most of those students, the task is one of learning how to talk and write 'academically' in a language which is not their mother tongue. What kinds of problems do they encounter?

❖   ❖   ❖   ❖   ❖

Activity 8.5   *(Reading B)*

Read 'Some language problems faced by overseas students in British universities' by Tony Bex (Reading B). On the basis of his experience as a university tutor, Bex discusses the problems faced by overseas students as they encounter the academic language demands of studying in a British university.

Comment

You will have seen that Bex suggests that students who enter the UK to study in universities, and whose first language is not English, encounter problems with academic writing because their experience of the use of English is (compared with that of a native speaker, living in an English-dominant country) limited to a relatively few social contexts. (Bex uses Hymes's concept of 'communicative competence' to discuss this.) The students in question are expected to cope not only with writing in a second language, but also with the particular 'ground rules' of English language use in British academic life. That is, they are being expected to follow sociolinguistic rules (concerned with appropriateness) as well as linguistic ones (to do with correct use of Standard English grammar, spelling and punctuation).

❖   ❖   ❖   ❖   ❖

Bex thus offers a useful account of the special language demands which overseas students in the UK may encounter. But we should remember that many students who are native speakers seem to have problems with both kinds of rules for academic writing too (for instance, it was such students who were referred to in the newspaper reports in Activity 8.4). We go on to consider these matters further in the next section.

8.3 ACQUIRING ACADEMIC ENGLISH

Now that you have an idea of the range of demands academic English makes on students, we would like to examine how students acquire skills in using it.

When students enter university, they have to learn appropriate ways of behaving and a set of rules for using English, many of which are unwritten

Access to the culture of academic English

When students enter university, they have to learn appropriate ways of behaving and a set of rules for using English, many of which are unwritten. Students are, in effect, taking on a new identity as they enter the culture of higher education and language use is part of this culture. To see what this means, take the example of the 'seminar' or 'group tutorial' as a teaching method. Although small group work is increasingly found in the final years of secondary schooling, students are unlikely previously to have experienced seminars where a topic is discussed with several other students under the guidance of a tutor, often using a piece of written work by one of the students as a starting point. In order to participate fully in the seminar, a student needs to learn rules about turn-taking and how far it is appropriate to criticize another student's work, as well as knowing the appropriate register in which to make comments. In addition, the 'language' of the seminar will be the discourse of the academic subject. In other words, the sociolinguistic framework of the seminar makes particular demands on the participants. A similar situation occurs with written work. Students are expected to use the technical discourse of a subject (although not necessarily to be sophisticated users of it initially), to write in an academic style and to follow the conventions of essays, laboratory reports or research papers. All this can be quite confusing to new students.

There have been a number of research studies looking into students' experiences as they begin university study. The majority have focused on the development of academic writing skills rather than academic English as a whole. Ballard (1984) was particularly interested in comparing the experience of Australian-born and overseas students in Australian universities. Her study examined the writing of students who had been referred for extra help with writing and study skills. She concluded that all students had to go through a linguistic and cultural learning process, as there was a disjunction between school learning and university study. Overseas students, however, faced an added dimension: they also had to learn the intellectual traditions of Australia which were sometimes very different from those of their own education systems. Ballard uses the term 'cultural shift' to describe the learning demands made on students and 'double cultural shift' to refer to the experience of the overseas students.

Identity and academic writing

The concept of 'cultural shift' is a useful one which can be applied elsewhere. We would like to discuss it in relation to the students with whom we are most familiar: Open University students in the UK. Open University students are adults who may have been out of the formal education system for a long time. Many of these students lack recent experience in using language appropriately in academic ways. This is particularly true of written language. Though many higher education students of all ages experience some problems in producing appropriately 'academic' writing, Ivanič and Simpson (1992) found that the written language used by adult students was further from the academic 'norm' (the language used by the academic community) than was the language used by younger students. Some students also have to shift across linguistic and/or cultural systems because of their ethnic and/or class background. Such cultural shifts can have implications which go beyond changes in language practices, affecting students' sense of personal identity.

Ivanič (1992) describes what happens to students' identities as they learn academic English. She cites the case of Donna, a mature black student. Donna's writing showed some discourse features that identified her as an apprentice member of the academic community, someone who had begun to adopt some academic ways of writing. For example, she tended to use a detached third-person presentation rather than using the first person ('It can be argued …' rather than 'I think …'). At the same time she indicated other identities which she wished to retain by using language associated with her existing beliefs and values. These included expressions by which 'she is reaffirming herself as a Black person in her own mind, and showing her reader that she is Black' (Ivanič, 1992, p. 7), such as the use of capital 'B' in the word 'Black' when used to describe an ethnic group, and the use of some dialect expressions common in black English. Moreover, she identified herself as a feminist when she chose the term 'her stories' rather than 'history'. Ivanič concludes that university culture puts students under considerable pressure to change their identities, but that the way they ultimately choose to write also reflects values and beliefs that are central to other parts of their lives.

In order to become a writer of 'academic English' a student has to become sensitive to a sociocultural context, that of an academic community with its own discourse, and then create an identity for herself or himself which maintains some kind of equilibrium between this and their 'non-student' persona. Some students find this very easy: they learn the ground rules quickly and write competently and confidently from their first assignment. For others it is a slower process. As we saw in the previous section, academic discourse includes specific lexical, and grammatical features. It is also marked by distinctive textual and stylistic features. Learning to write academic English means learning a set of skills which gives you command of all these features. People do this in different ways. To show how this happens, the next activity looks at two examples of student writing taken from a first-year course.

❖   ❖   ❖   ❖   ❖

Activity 8.6   *(Allow about 30 minutes)*

The following extracts are taken from a first-year Open University essay on art history. As you work through the activity, you need to remember that these are native-speaking British students who are learning the academic English of the 'inner circle'. The original essay question asked students to compare two paintings, 'commenting on generic category, subject-matter, mode of representation, and meaning'.

When you have read each extract, consider the following questions:

1   Is this what you think a university essay should be like? What strikes you when you first read it?

2   Is the content relevant to the assignment? If not, what do you think is the problem?

3   What is your reaction to the students' use of English, including grammar and vocabulary, as well as features such as spelling?

Extract 1

In John Constable's Wivenhoe Park, there is a wide view of the countryside. It stretches fourth vastly. There is a feeling of peace, almost tranquility, and lazyness like a Sunday afternoon, non activity.

The light and dark green which is throughout the picture contrasts very well, and the water appears to reflect more green and grey then blue. The sky is a contrast of light blue, with grey clouds building up as it a storm is coming. We see a strong contrast of light from the sun and shade from the trees. Wivenhoe park could be depicted any time of the day.

There is a feeling of richness, vastness, expansiveness about the park, and also although two figures can be seen there is solitude.

There is also self sufficiency with the cows producing milk and possibly meat.

One feels like looking from side to side at this painting. The view is horizontal, and one must turn the head from side to side to take in the vastness.

The brush strokes in the painting are very light, fine and subtle with heavier strokes in the clouds.

There were not a lot of sports as such in 1816, however water sports were enjoyed such as fishing and boating, thus depicted in the picture.

The genre of Wivenhoe park is an everyday life scene, a landscape. Wivenhoe park would probably have been used mostly by local people from the surrounding area.

Extract 2

In comparing and contrasting John Constable's Wivenhoe Park, Essex, 1816 and William Dyce's Pegwell Bay, A recollection of October 5th 1858, 1860, I shall be looking at genre (classification by subject matter) and technique including the way artists use colour, line, texture, light, shape and space. I shall also comment on the context of, and meaning behind, these two pictures.

Both pictures are oil on canvas. Pegwell Bay (64 × 89 cm) occupies slightly more canvas space then Wivenhoe Park (55 × 100 cm). Both pictures belong to the landscape genre, although Pegwell Bay also has a conflation of genre and narrative, in that it depicts a scene in everyday life, and also includes visual references to the Victorian interests of Geology and Astronomy.

Wivenhoe Park is a peaceful view of the house and park which occupy horizontally slightly more than half the picture. The artist is looking across the lake to the parkland surrounding the house, which is placed centrally and occupies the highest point on the horizon. There are cattle grazing in the foreground and duck, swans and a boat on the lake in the mid-ground. Above is a lovely cloudscape, showing Constable's keen observation of cloudform, not only from nature but also from drawings by Alexander Cozen, the eighteenth century landscape painter (page 150 Art and Illusion). On the same page, Gombrich tells us that Constable acknowledged that art had its 'traditional schemata', but that he sought to portray nature as accurately as possible and experimented with colour and form.

Comment

One of the chapter authors (Elizabeth) read not only the extracts but the complete essays written by the students. Her answers to the above questions are given below. You may like to compare your answers with hers.

> In analysing the extracts I took into account the fact that this was only the fourth essay the students had written. I expected them to use some features of academic discourse, but not all, and I was interested to see which ones each student had grasped and what similarities and differences they showed at this stage of their studies.

Question 1

At first glance both extracts looked to me like academic essays: the students appeared to have grasped some features of the academic English discussed earlier in Activity 8.2, such as the use of formal and impersonal language. However, while I found the second extract a perfectly acceptable piece of academic writing, I did not consider the first extract to be such.

The second essay is better organized. It has a strong introductory paragraph and each of the subsequent paragraphs takes one idea and expands on it. The first student appears to be less aware of *how* to use paragraphs, although the essay is laid out in paragraph form. Most of the paragraphs, however, consist of only one sentence. Ideas are not developed and the essay lacks cohesion. The overall impression is that the essay – and by implication, the student's understanding of the topic – is somewhat disjointed. This underlines how linguistic style can influence a tutor's impression of a student's understanding.

Question 2

The first extract addresses some of the question, but it does not develop its argument in any detail. The student identifies relevant information in the teaching materials but seems unsure of how to use it. Sentences such as 'There is also self sufficiency with the cows producing milk and possibly meat' do not relate to the general thread of the essay. Another normal requirement of academic discourse is that the points being argued must be supported by *evidence*: properly referenced examples taken from academic reading or research findings. Students have to learn that personal opinion should only be included where it relates to agreed academic findings. There were several places in the first essay where I was tempted to write 'Who says so?' beside an example such as 'There were not a lot of sports as such in 1816'.

Few technical terms are used in the first extract, and where they are used, as in the sentence 'The genra of Wivenhoe park is an everyday life scene, a landscape', it is difficult to know if the student understands what they mean, as no subsequent explanations of what is meant by the terms are given. In the example of 'genra', the spelling mistake may also indicate uncertainty about the term.

The second writer is better at relating what has been learned from the university course to the text (painting) she is describing. Although we only have an extract here, I also thought the student knew how to organize the essay. The first paragraph begins by acknowledging the essay question. This is an important rule in the game of 'essay writing' and signals to readers that students know what is expected of them. Each paragraph appears to be clearly related to one aspect of the question and there is some indication that the student wrote an essay plan. The student also handles the subject-specific lexis with some confidence. The third sentence of the second paragraph reproduced above, for example, has a very academic style which I think is created partly by the use of terms such as 'landscape genre', 'conflation of genre and narrative' and 'visual references'.

Question 3

I had no difficulty in understanding either of the essays. The first one contains several spelling mistakes and I personally would have used more commas, but otherwise I did not have any serious concerns about the student's use of English. However, the second student is obviously a more competent academic writer. This more favourable impression is created by correct spelling and a better use of punctuation but also by some lexical and syntactic features which are well illustrated in the sentence below.

> Both pictures belong to the landscape genre, although *Pegwell Bay* also has a conflation of genre and narrative, in that it depicts a scene in everyday life and also includes visual references to the Victorian interests of Geology and Astronomy.

Here we have examples of specialized lexis (*genre, narrative, visual references*). The sentence contains four clauses which are organized in a hierarchical manner so that the relationships between the ideas are clearly indicated. The ideas are presented in a detached way with no personal reference.

In contrast, the first essay has some stylistic features that I would expect to see in other, more informal genres (such as notes or personal letters) and fewer of the characteristic features of formal academic English. The things I noticed were:

- Sentence structure is simple and invariable. Most of the sentences consisted of a main clause plus one phrase or dependent clause.

- There are few cohesive devices – for instance the student does not use pronouns or relative clauses to link ideas between sentences or paragraphs.

- The style is repetitive. I counted the phrase 'there is' four times.

- There is a stylistic inelegance and awkwardness to: 'One feels like looking from side to side at this painting'.

The errors of spelling and punctuation in the first extract are worthy of further comment. I mentioned that I could make sense of the essay despite those errors, so if they are a problem it is not because they affect the intelligibility of the essay. The question of whether errors of spelling and punctuation should be corrected (and if they should be taken into account in grading assignments) is frequently debated among academics; there are many different responses to it. In UK universities tutors frequently have considerable freedom to decide how much weight to put on such matters. Most tutors would probably comment on features that they consider impede communication, such as sentence fragments without a complete verb, sentences joined by commas rather than full stops and misplaced clauses. But there is considerable variation relating to items such as spelling, punctuation within sentences and other matters of style. When asked about their practice, Open University tutors have replied with statements as diverse as 'I do not correct spelling because it destroys students' confidence', and 'I correct most spelling. Employers and others expect graduates to be able to write correct English and ensuring that they can do this is therefore part of a university education'.

In English-medium education systems outside the UK there may be greater emphasis on 'correct' English. In many higher education institutions, in the UK and elsewhere, marks are deducted in examinations and essays for poor spelling, punctuation and grammar, no matter what the subject.

❖ ❖ ❖ ❖ ❖

Academic writing as argument

As well as writing in an appropriate kind of English, in most academic subjects students are expected to plan their essays so that they present a clear argument. The exact nature of the argument varies from one discipline to another. Art history, like literature and music, is a form of critical textual analysis in which students must relate the ideas they have learned to examples of text, in this case paintings. So there is a level at which developing an argument is a *conceptual* process concerned with linking ideas. But these ideas can only be expressed in language, and it is this combination of conceptual thinking and linguistic expression that, among other features, contribute to an impression of a piece of stduent writing being 'good' or 'weak'. At an early stage students may recognize that the ways they are writing are inappropriate – for example, that they are writing 'narrative' rather than 'argument' – but they do not necessarily know how to change their way of writing. As an Open University student remarked to one of us about her first social sciences essay:

> I understood what was being asked and I understood the reading but had difficulty in getting it down in the 'proper' way. Maybe I was inhibited in the use of the 'new language' and 'new words'. I didn't feel confident in using them. I know I wrote a 'story', not 'academic' writing, but I couldn't find a way round it. I didn't know how to change.

Students are expected to write in an appropriately academic way, but also to present in their essays an effective and rational argument

8.4   TEACHING ACADEMIC ENGLISH

We have suggested that all students entering university in English-speaking countries have to learn academic English. When we come to consider teaching approaches, however, we find that distinctions have traditionally been made between students whose first or only language is English and those for whom it is a second or foreign language. Historically these groups were often seen as distinct and offered different types of English course. Today there is an increasing recognition of the common linguistic analysis that underpins the teaching of academic English and this is reflected in current approaches and methodologies. In this section we outline ways in which the teaching of academic English has developed over the last 30 years or so. The approaches we consider are of three kinds:

- the study skills approach;
- English for academic purposes (EAP); and
- the genre analysis approach.

We conclude with a brief consideration of current developments in this field.

The study skills approach

The teaching of **study skills** has a long history. The concept is well understood by academics and by students. Even students who feel confident about their English writing skills may recognize that they need help with such matters as planning and preparing essays, time management and preparing for examinations. Study skills courses which focus on these areas have existed for many years. They may be

Even students who feel confident about their English writing skills may need help with other study skills

offered as optional preparatory or 'pre-sessional' courses, or as study skills support during the academic year. In some cases study skills are an integral part of first-year university study, either as free-standing modules or built into the teaching of mainstream courses. But how much English do study skills courses include? Most deal with English grammar, but this is frequently seen as 'remedial' rather than as an introduction to specific academic discourse of the kind described in section 8.2. The focus is often on common errors of usage, spelling and punctuation. Textual organization is not considered in a linguistic framework but in terms of the processes involved in essay writing such as note taking and writing introductions and conclusions. Features of academic genres such as the use of other writers' work are covered by material on 'avoiding plagiarism' and how to record references and bibliographies correctly.

Many books for students on developing study skills are now available – including, for example, the Open University's popular *The Good Study Guide* (Northedge, 1990). We concentrate here on some which deal expressly with aspects of English language use. While the advice given in such books is always practical, they vary greatly in style: some offer students 'handy tips' on language use in 'bullet point' lists while others adopt a narrative style explaining to students how and why they should use particular features of English in their assignments. Fairbairn and Winch's (1991) book *Reading, Writing and Reasoning*, for example, has six pages on 'writing impersonally'. These are headed 'First, second and third person?' with subheadings including 'Should you adopt first or third person?', 'Writing well in the first person', 'Writing well in the third person' and 'Picking and mixing'. The text is illustrated with extracts from academic texts but is essentially advice, as there are no practical exercises. Johnson's (1993) book *Writing Essays: guidance notes for students* deals with the same topic, though indirectly. In a section headed 'What makes a good essay?' under 'Appropriate style' he writes:

> For an academic essay the third person ('he', 'she' or 'it') rather than the first person ('I') is preferable – although occasional use of 'I' may be accepted if a personal opinion has been specifically requested.
>
> (Johnson, 1993, p. 6)

In a later section headed 'Tone' he writes:

> Too much use of 'I think that' and 'I feel that' has the effect of making an essay too personal and subjective in tone …
>
> You can avoid the use of 'I think' and 'I believe' by substituting impersonal expressions such as 'It seems that … Carr argues that … but there is now increasingly good evidence to show that …'
>
> (Johnson, 1993, p. 50)

Both these books are written for native English speakers. When it comes to books for students who are users of English as a second or foreign language, there is considerable overlap between books on study skills and those teaching English for academic purposes (as discussed below). Take Smith and Smith's (1990) *A Study Skills Handbook*, for example. At first glance the student may not realize that the book teaches academic English. Yet it has sections on argumentative and descriptive essays and in many ways combines the study skills approach of Fairbairn and Johnson with a more explicit concern with English usage. There are practical activities based on authentic text and practice exercises on aspects of syntax.

In linguistic terms, most study skills texts focus on the surface forms of language needed for academic study. They assume that students can learn a set of language 'tools', which when applied to their assignments, will result in writing that looks like academic English. One weakness of many such tools is that they do not encourage students to make a link between the English conventions they are expected to use when writing essays and the 'academic' ways of thinking that they are expected to demonstrate in their writing.

English for academic purposes (EAP)

English for academic purposes (EAP) has traditionally been regarded as a branch of teaching English as a foreign language (EFL). As such, EAP courses have typically focused on teaching students the correct linguistic forms for representing their knowledge in English (and assumed that students had appropriate 'study skills' and some prior knowledge of the discipline they were studying). But over the last 30 years EAP approaches have changed considerably as they have incorporated findings from research into both academic English usage and methods of teaching English as a foreign language. EAP courses were originally developed for students from the developing world who had to study in English. Most of these students were studying technical and professional subjects in areas such as science, agriculture, engineering and technology and so throughout the 1970s and early 1980s both the course content and the teaching methods often focused on the acquisition of scientific and technical discourse. The needs of such EAP students were therefore seen as very different from those of 'native speakers' (such as the Open University students whose work we looked at in section 8.3).

The genre analysis approach

The 1980s saw an increased awareness of the varieties of academic English associated with particular academic subjects. This had implications for the organization of teaching, and courses began to be planned by English and subject specialists together. In some cases self-contained EAP courses disappeared, as EAP teaching was incorporated more into subject teaching. In other EAP courses the emphasis shifted to textual organization rather than sentence grammar. For example, Jones et al. (1989) describe courses at the University of Sydney in which students were encouraged to read a wide range of authentic texts in order to become aware of the range of genres and registers they would encounter within their own subject areas. As they read both popular scientific journals and specialist newspapers they were helped to become aware of the differences between academic and non-academic genres. The rationale was that by undertaking detailed analyses of the lexical, grammatical and organizational features of the texts they read, students would be more able to develop their own writing skills. Courses similar to this, often explicitly based on Halliday's systemic linguistics, became increasingly influential during the late 1980s and 1990s (Bhatia, 1993).

Chapters 4 and 6 of this book explore in more detail the use of genre analysis in teaching writing. For more on Halliday's systemic grammar, see *Describing Language* (Graddol et al., 1994).

Such courses aim to give students a practical understanding of academic discourse through the analysis of texts and through making explicit the conventions of each genre. The analysis is often conducted at a number of levels: from the organization of a whole text (such as a journal article) or parts of it (such as introductions or conclusions), to the syntactic and lexical features of a particular genre. The tutor has an important role to play as a guide to the text analysis, although students are also commonly encouraged to learn together by analysing and discussing texts in groups. Critics of the genre approach (e.g. Lee, 1990) claim that, like most earlier approaches to teaching academic writing, it encourages students to believe that academic genres are fixed and immutable, and that they simply have to learn the rules and apply them uncritically in their own writing. The extent to which this is the case, however, is probably highly dependent upon the way that the nature and function of academic genres are introduced and discussed by tutors with students.

Current developments

Recently many courses and texts on academic English have become eclectic in their approach and teaching methods. Research of the contrastive rhetoric kind (as described in Reading A) is found in many courses which also draw on Halliday's genre theory (Clark and Ivanič, 1991; Morrison, 1994). Courses often involve students working together, analysing and redrafting their own and other students' essays. Discussion and peer teaching are also encouraged because students can then practise their spoken academic English while working on their written skills. At the same time they reflect on the skills they are learning and in this way address issues of the kind favoured by the study skills approach. There is an increasing overlap between courses for learners of English and those that are designed for students whose first language is English.

8.5   CONCLUSION

In recent years, English has become increasingly dominant as a world language in higher education. This means that students whose mother tongue is not English now often have to develop a high level of competence in the language to pursue their studies. Moreover, study in higher education requires a special kind of competence in English. 'Academic English' is a collection of genres of English, each of which is shaped by the functional requirements and social conventions of academic communities of discourse. Familiarity with the conventions or 'ground rules' which apply to any genre of academic English is an important factor in a student's progress. As Reading A showed, however, there is pressure from some academics for some of the accepted conventions of 'inner circle' English academic writing to be critically examined. Such conventions may be seen by some as necessary for intellectual rigour, but others argue that they are culturally based and unnecessarily constricting, intellectually and linguistically.

Informal evidence suggests that many students, including many for whom English is a mother tongue, appear to have problems in learning to write academic English. That is, they have difficulty in writing English in a way that meets the conventional requirements of the academic discourse community of the subject they are studying. One possible reason for this is that teachers of specific subjects in higher education rarely deal with requirements explicitly. Though a variety of approaches have been developed for helping students improve their competence in English, surprisingly little systematic research has been done on the nature and extent of the problems students encounter when attempting to become academic English users.

Reading A

CULTURE IN RHETORICAL STYLES: CONTRASTIVE RHETORIC AND WORLD ENGLISHES

Yamuna Kachru

Introduction

This reading investigates the linguistic and rhetorical conventions followed by academic writers of English across the world. Data are drawn from Indian and Nigerian varieties of English to determine the shared and variety-specific characteristics of writing in the 'inner and outer circle' (Kachru, B.B, 1985).[1] This discussion has clear implications for the theory and methodology of research into **contrastive rhetoric,** or **CR** (the study of how language is used in writing in different cultural settings).

The field of CR developed out of pedagogical concerns related to teaching English as a second language (Kaplan, [1966]1980). By now, the concern is no longer purely pedagogical; language teaching and learning, however, remain a strong motivation for such studies. Although the findings and the resultant claims of the Kaplan study have been seriously questioned in many respects, it is undeniable that CR has had a significant impact on research on writing across cultures and on the teaching of English to speakers of other language(s) (Kachru, Y., 1995b and Martin, 1992 contain extensive bibliographic references).

Secondly, any claims and assumptions made in CR studies are increasingly presented as universally valid. It is therefore quite appropriate to reflect upon the relationship of CR to writing across languages and cultures and to determine if this research area sufficiently represents the 'socially realistic' theoretical and methodological concerns of cross-cultural linguistic research. It is also timely in that several recent studies have looked critically at CR from the perspective of cultural meanings in rhetorical styles across languages and discourse communities, especially in the broader context of the use of English as an international language (Kachru, Y., 1983, 1987, 1988, 1992, 1995a, 1995b, 1995c; Reynolds, 1993; Vavrus, 1991). In this reading, I propose to look at the research area of CR in the context of the multilingual and multicultural users of world Englishes.

Assumptions of CR

The major claim of the CR hypothesis is that writers of English from the outer and expanding circles employ 'a rhetoric and a sequence of thought which violate the expectations of the native [inner circle] reader' (Kaplan, [1966]1980).[2] Hence their writing is perceived as 'out of focus', 'lacking organization', or 'lacking cohesion' (Kaplan, [1966]1980). This claim is based on the assumption that there *is* a clearly established inner circle norm of writing in English, and its effect is to devalue rhetorical patterns which do not conform to the expectations of readers from the inner circle. It also leads to rather contradictory practices in pedagogical contexts. For instance, although some differences between US and British English are well known and the different spelling and grammatical conventions practised by the British and Americans do not affect their international

Related issues on the teaching of English as a second or subsequent language are dealt with in Chapter 7.

credibility, the same conventions, we are told, if practised by international students (say, from Malaysia), would affect their credibility in a US academic setting (Mackay, 1993, p. 3). This puts the whole English-using population from Asia, Africa and other parts of the world at a disadvantage, since various regions have been and are still being differentially influenced by US or UK educational practices.

My concern in this paper, however, is with a range of more general issues raised by the CR hypothesis as currently practised. The first of these relates to the tentative nature of the findings of the CR studies and their methodologies. The second directs attention to the myth of an established inner circle English norm in academic writing. The third draws upon the findings of investigations in the acquisition of literacy. And the fourth considers the evidence from writing in English in the outer circle. The discussion takes the CR hypothesis out of the realm of English as a second language (ESL) and looks at the wider world of cross-linguistic and cross-cultural writing in general.

A critique of current practices

This discussion is restricted to studies that have implications for teaching/ learning English in the outer and expanding circles of English, and the participation of scholars from these regions in contributing to human knowledge. The studies that have investigated the interplay of culture and rhetorical mode have resulted in certain findings which may or may not be corroborated by further research. However, it is instructive to assess the current status, the methodology and the consequences of CR research for the outer and expanding circles of English.

CR hypothesis and methodology

Two sets of CR findings are relevant for our purposes: one related to inner circle writing and the other to writing across languages. Contrary to the myth of a well-established inner circle norm for academic writing, Americans, Australians, Britons and New Zealanders have been shown to differ significantly from each other in their rhetorical styles (e.g. Connor and Lauer, 1985; Vähäpässi, 1988; see also Hoey, 1983, p. 68; Smith and Liedlich, 1980, p. 21). Clear differences have been found even within one particular variety (e.g. Braddock, 1974; Meade and Ellis, 1970). It seems reasonable to conclude that writing in other languages has been and is being compared with some idealized notion of writing in English based on style manuals and textbooks for teaching rhetoric.

Cross-linguistic CR studies have shown that languages such as Arabic, Chinese, German, Hindi, Japanese, Korean, Marathi and Persian have their characteristic rhetorical organizations of expository and argumentative prose not shared by the native varieties of English (Eason, 1995; Kachru, Y., 1995b; Martin, 1992 contain extensive bibliographical references). It should, however, be noted that the findings of differences, at least in some of these studies, may be an artefact of the methodologies followed in them (Kenkel, 1991). Additionally, it is doubtful that there are well-defined text types such as 'expository' and 'argumentative prose' in English (Biber, 1989; Grabe, 1987) which form the basis of CR research. Such genre distinctions may be 'foreign' to some literate cultures at least.

Literacy

Literacy practices in English are discussed in the second book in this series, *Using English: from conversation to canon* (Maybin and Mercer (eds), 1996).

Work on the acquisition of literacy in different communities has shown that even within a developed industrial society such as the USA communities may differ in terms of the functions, domains, roles and value of literacy in their lives (Heath, 1983). That communities which belong to different societies will show greater variation in their literacy practices is therefore not surprising (Scribner and Cole, 1981). Access to a writing system, or printing, or other devices to produce and reproduce written texts can be used to support a wide variety of literacy practices.

Ancient India had an advanced writing system probably by 500 BC (Macdonell, [1900]1968, p. 17), in addition to well-developed traditions of creative literature (both prose and poetry), arithmetic, algebra, astronomy, grammar, logic and philosophy. However, there is no evidence that written texts played an important role in the transmission of this body of knowledge. Thus the claim in CR literature that western rhetoric is a result of the development of writing and, subsequently, of printing and the rapid diffusion of literacy following the industrial revolution, needs to be further examined.

Furthermore, perspectives such as Kaplan's fail to acknowledge the ideological nature of *fact* and *truth* as widely discussed in philosophical, social scientific and humanistic (including linguistic) literature. Foucault, for example, says that:

> Truth ... is produced only by virtue of multiple forms of constraint. And it induces regular effects of power. Each society has its régime of truth, its 'general politics' of truth: that is, the types of discourse which it accepts and makes function as true; the mechanisms and instances which enable one to distinguish true and false statements, the means by which each is sanctioned; the techniques and procedures accorded value in the acquisition of truth; the status of those who are charged with saying what counts as true.
>
> (Foucault, 1980, p. 131)

Truth or fact, whether transmitted orally or in writing, is always to some extent both socially constructed and mutable. One has only to consider the history of sciences and social sciences to realize that this view is legitimate.

Writing in English in the outer circle

The history of writing in English in the outer circle indicates that cultural considerations play a role in the development of linguistic structures and discourse patterns (Kachru, B.B., 1992). Some of the discourse features that occur in Indian English academic writing, for example, are the following: nonlinear macro structure; global introductions rather than just the relevant background of the topic under discussion; more than one topic in a single paragraph; cyclical sequencing of components such as initiation, problem, elaboration, solution, evaluation, etc.; and use of ornate language. The characteristics of outer circle writing can be illustrated by the following examples from the writing of undergraduate students in India and graduate students from Nigeria in the USA.

Essay 1 is written by a BA student (second year) in an Indian college. (Paragraph numbers have been added for use in analysis.)

'Dowry System' in India

1   Growing up is a discarding of dreams and a realisation of the various facts of life. A general awareness creeps in. It is a process of drinking deep the spring of knowledge and perceiving the different facets of life. Life is panorama of events, moments of joys and sorrows. The world around us is manifested by both, good and evil.

2   Dowry system is one of the prevalent evils of today. *Like a diabolic adder* it *stings* the life on many innocent people and is the burning topic of discussion. Looking down the vista of years, we find that is has permeated gradually into the fabrics of our customs and has acquired a prodigious form lately. Marriage which is supposed to be a sacred ceremony is made sour and becomes like any other business transactions. The extracting of money from the bride's family is ridiculous, attracious [sic] and above all sacrilegious.

3   It is truly said that making somebody happy is a question of give and take. Human beings by instinct show their concern and love by giving gifts. This even holds true for a bride's father. All fathers have a penchant to give something to their daughters. It is a propensity of human nature to see their daughters well settled. But this exchange of gifts should be a willing gesture and not an imposed cannon. The money and affluence becomes an asset to start a settlement in life. But is should be considered a crime if the money is taken from someone who is left financially crippled. Each one should learn to lay the bricks of her own house herself.

4   Dowry system is biting into the very vitals of the Indian society. There are many evidences of burning of the bride, and disparages in matches because of this root cause. To eradicate this will be to clear the weeds of our society. There are many laws passed on this issue but still it needs to be dealt by delving deeper. It is said that 'Eclipses stain both moon and sun'. The custom of dowry is the biggest flaw and a scar which mars the beauty of a sacred union.

5   Various endeavours are being made to eradicate this. But what is necessary, that it should be the loudest cry of each person! Someone has to take a firm stand and the first step so that it benefits mankind. Everything can be cured and all evils can be purged. After all Raja Ram Mohan Roy did succeed in abolishing Sati system, Lord William Bentick worked to elevate the position of women. *To wipe out this will be like a rise from a stagnant, putrid pool to the great height of perfection. Living will be a bliss!*

As far as linguistic competence is concerned, the writer of this essay is obviously highly competent. The grammatical and spelling errors may be attributed to the pressure of time (Kachru, Y., 1995c). As regards the conventions of language use, however, the text exhibits all the characteristics of Indian writing mentioned above. In view of limitation of space, I can comment on only some of the characteristics of the text. The CR hypothesis would suggest that the macro-structure of the text (the organization of the text as a whole and the contents of the paragraphs) will violate the expectations of inner circle readers. The sequence of problem–elaboration in paragraph 2, elaboration–solution in paragraph 4, and the occurrence of comment in paragraphs 3 and 5 ('comment' provides more historical background or expresses the writer's hopes and wishes) are worth noting. This is a perfect example of the spiral or circular rhetorical pattern that is found in Indian writing in general.[3] The first paragraph is a good example of the global introduction phenomenon mentioned above and the italicized parts throughout illustrate the use of ornate language, but such usage is not uncommon and does not make Indian English readers uncomfortable.

Essay 2 was written by a Nigerian student and published in the *African Report*, a magazine published by African students in the USA.

Academics in chains

Paul Baran in his famous article on 'The Commitment of the Intellectual' outlined on the expected role an intellectual must play particularly in the present-day society where there is the tendency towards misrule, abuse of power, corruption, tyranny, misery and mass poverty, and affluence of the few to the detriment of the rest of us. Paul Baran must have had in mind the role of the intellectual as the conscience of the nation, as the last bastion of hope, the voice of courage and reason that will speak against oppression and exploitation, against all vices that abound in the contemporary society.

However, a critical look at the expectations of our academics today and the realities in our contemporary political situation indicates that our intellectuals are in chains. Chains, though not visibly seen but are easily apprehended by the existing condition in our citadels of learning, in the increasing atomization of not only academicians but also of democratic forces in the country, in the emergence of a culture of intolerance now quickly eating deep into the embers of our national life, in the precarious state of affairs that now characterizes learning, now defined in terms of certificate acquisition instead of knowledge comprehension, and in the increasing destitution and frustration of products of our education institutions which are the mirror of future societal progress.

Nigerians do not need the services of any fortune teller for them to understand that the glamour of learning is no longer there, that those days when people dreamt of making it through their degrees acquired from the universities are over; when it was a pride to be a graduate, when learning was characterized by excellence, flexibility and dedication.

Today, the story is different. It is no longer fun to be a graduate; no longer news to make a first class, it is no longer a joy to read, write, study and research into knowledge. Gone are the days when lecturers were respected. Their rewards are in 'heaven' even though they have responsibilities on earth.

Our universities had always been hot-beds of radicalism. Hence they must be cowed, and harassed. Their basic freedom to associate is trampled upon as the nation increasingly moves towards intolerance. Something informs me that our educational system which is a product of the economic condition in our society would witness increasing retardation, regression, malfunctioning and depression in the near future. The realities of the moment have shown that there is no way Africans can sustain a high degree of excellence when our educational institutions are under-funded and under-staffed. Worse, the few available manpower are treated shabbily.

The culture of learning is slowly being killed by those who run our educational systems as Emirate-systems, dividing our countries into council and district headquarteres serving local champions and prejudiced warlords. What we need is greater tolerance, flexibility, consensus, fairness and justice in the running of African education systems.

(Cited in Vavrus, 1991, pp. 194–5)

Nigerian readers found this text well written. However, the reactions of US students studying for an MA in teaching English as a second language (TESL) at a Midwestern university were quite different. They were asked to evaluate the text from two perspectives: one group was asked to consider it as something intended for a US audience, and the other was asked to judge it as something intended for an African audience. Both groups made comments such as the following:

> Though the topic is eloquently discussed, there are omissions in terms of logic – who? how? why? Also the style is rather grandiose and editorial for a magazine article.
>
> I really didn't understand what the person was trying to say. What was the point of the essay? The vocabulary was flowery. The sentences were too long – almost continuous.
>
> The lack of development was difficult for me. I'm not sure what the point was ... the writer seemed to feel no need to explicitly demonstrate the validity of an opinion through reasoning.
>
> These are the kinds of essays I don't like grading – at first they seem well-written and sophisticated. But on closer inspection there are bizarre expressions, logical connections that aren't, and dramatic vocabulary (see paragraph 2). In short, the writer's ideas outrun his ability to effectively express them in English.

(Vavrus, 1991, p. 190–1)

Implications for research

Research into CR has to be much more sensitive to criteria establishing comparability of data from languages and varieties under focus. As has been pointed out by Vähapässi (1988), it is not easy either to establish the congruency of writing tasks, or to determine the comparability of the genres of writing (argumentative, persuasive, narrative, etc.). A study of the traditions of writing in different cultures is necessary to establish clear criteria for comparability across genres and registers, since (1) there may be genres which are unique to a language and culture, and (2) there may be different rhetorical patterns associated with different genres. For instance, the genre of writing horoscopes (*patra* in Hindi) in the Indian tradition has no parallel in many other cultures, including the European experience. Similarly, the Anglo-American genre of written invitations (for weddings, parties, etc.) has no parallel in the traditional Indian context. In academic writing, there is a text type in Hindi that is labelled 'deliberative' (*vicaratmak* in Hindi), which is not necessarily equivalent to the Anglo-American 'argumentative' essay. In an argumentative text the goal is to prove that the view put forward in the text is right and that all competing opinions are wrong. In the deliberative text, however, the points in favour as well as those opposed to a particular position are put forward so that readers are informed on all facets of an issue, and the decision as to which one of the positions presented is right or wrong is left to the reader. The writer, however, is free to indicate his/her preference, if (s)he so desires.

An example of specific rhetorical patterns associated with particular genres is the circular or spiral rhetorical pattern of expository prose in Hindi (Kachru, Y., 1983, 1988). Such non-linear patterns may have a social meaning. Hinds (1987) suggests that the non-linear pattern of Japanese expository prose is in harmony with the expectation that the listener/reader has the primary responsibility for effective communication. This contrasts sharply with the expectation in

US English that the primary responsibility for effective communication lies with the speaker/writer. Hinds then goes on to suggest a typology of listener/reader versus speaker/writer responsibility in different languages. CR could explore this typology further to determine its value as a theoretical construct.

The framework of CR must take into account one important component of sociocultural meaning, that of the intertextuality of texts, since all texts derive their meaning from others in the tradition too. For instance, the texts in the Indian tradition derive their meaning from the classical Sanskrit or Perso-Arabic tradition, in addition to the (partially, via English) shared Graeco-Roman tradition. In the genres of literary criticism, philosophy and grammar, for instance, a Hindi text may refer to the works of Panini (seventh century BC) and Bhartrihari (early sixth century AD) just as easily as to Aristotle, Humboldt or de Saussure.

Coming back to the social context, it has been observed that writers from several parts of the world, including China and India, give too much background information without relating it directly to the topic under discussion. The social meaning behind what appears to be a redundant amount of background information is related to the notion of politeness in these cultures. In most interactional contexts, directness is not as polite as indirectness. Instead of coming directly to the point, giving a great deal of background information allows readers to draw their own conclusions with regard to the topic being discussed. The reader responsibility phenomenon that Hinds (1987) mentions may be related to the East Asian notions of politeness too, in that the texts in these traditions give readers choices, instead of attempting to bring them round to the writer's point of view.

Conclusion

The teaching and evaluation of academic writing seem to involve an idealized notion of what an English paragraph or composition is, while most real texts, even within the inner circle, exhibit variation from the idealized pattern(s). If academic writing in general is not to become a sterile, formula-oriented activity, we have to encourage individual creativity in writing. It is the tension between received conventions and the innovative spirit of the individual that produces good writing in academic disciplines as well as in creative literature. Moreover, a narrow view of what constitutes good writing may bar a large number of original studies from publication and dissemination, since most of the information technology is under the control of the inner circle English-speaking world.[4] Any view of rhetoric that shuts out a majority of people from contributing to the world's knowledge base, and legitimizes such exclusion on the basis of writing conventions, hurts not only those who are excluded but also those who would benefit from such contributions.

Communication between interlocutors is a mutually shared responsibility. Users of world Englishes may well appreciate the conventions of US, Australian, British, Canadian and New Zealand Englishes. Instead of putting all responsibility on the writers from the wider English-using world, it is desirable for the readers from the inner circle to share the responsibility of making meaning. In order to achieve this goal, it is necessary to educate the readers who, for whatever reason, come across texts produced by international users of English so that they are able to appreciate writing conventions different from their own. This will enrich the available and acceptable range of linguistic structures and rhetorical modes, and serve the cultural diversity of which we are becoming increasingly aware. The sharing of responsibility is already happening in creative literature, as is evident from the awarding of several major literary prizes in recent years to multilingual, multicultural authors writing in English (Kachru, Y, 1995a).

CR research, as presently conceived and practised, is not compatible with either the aims of cross-linguistic and cross-cultural research, or with the demonstrated pluricentricity of English. Contrasting rhetorical patterns is as legitimate an activity as contrasting linguistic structures and should aim at arriving at a typology and, ultimately, a set of universals of rhetorical patterns. That is to say, it is reasonable to conceptualize a set of universal rhetorical patterns, analogous to the substantive universals in linguistics, out of which different languages may be shown to select different subsets for different genres. This goal can only be achieved if CR studies are based on a theoretical framework that takes into account the total social meaning of texts, and not based exclusively on a theory of text as suggested in Martin (1992). Currently, not only CR, but all research into English as a second or foreign language is guided by the narrow concerns of the perceived needs of the students enrolled in the educational institutions in the UK and USA and their teachers. The blinkers the profession has put on prevents it from seeing the wider context of English in the world. It is time we respond to these worldwide concerns and accord respect to all institutionalized varieties of English.

Notes

1   B.B. Kachru (1985) divides the English-using world into three concentric circles. The *inner circle* consists of the native English-speaking countries (e.g. Australia, Canada, New Zealand, the UK and the USA). The *outer circle* comprises the former colonies or spheres of influence of the UK and USA (e.g. India, Kenya, Nigeria, the Philippines, Singapore). In these countries, nativized varieties of English have achieved the status of either an official language or of a language widely used in education, administration, the legal system, etc. The *expanding circle* consists of countries where English is fast becoming a dominant second language in the domains of education, science and technology (e.g. China, Japan, Taiwan, Thailand and the countries of Europe).

2   This 'finding' of Kaplan's 1966 study has been repeated in a large number of MA and PhD theses and research papers (Kachru, Y., 1995b; Vavrus, 1991).

3   I am using 'circular' and 'spiral' as purely descriptive terms, with no implication that they are either 'illogical' or unfit for scientific/technical discussions.

4   This is not an emotional reaction. Although most learners and users of English are in the outer and expanding circles, most publications on topics crucial to the learners and teachers of English as a second/foreign language are concerned mainly with the problems of much smaller numbers of learners and teachers of English in the inner circle contexts. A survey of journals of applied linguistics, second language acquisition and ESL/EFL will confirm this easily. It is also interesting to note that most of these publications seem to be unaware of the research and publication efforts of even well-established institutions such as RELC, CIEFL and other educational and research facilities in the outer and expanding circles.

References

BIBER, D. (1989) A typology of English texts, *Linguistic* 27, pp. 3–43.

BRADDOCK, R. (1974) 'The frequency and placement of topic sentences in expository prose', *Research in the Teaching of English* 8, pp. 287–302.

CONNOR, U. and LAUER, J. (1985) 'Understanding persuasive essay writing: linguistic/rhetoric approach', *Text*, vol. 5, no. 4, pp. 309–26.

EASON, C. (1995) 'Argumentative essay written by native speakers of Chinese and English: a study in contrastive rhetoric', PhD dissertation, University of Illinois at Urbana-Champaign.

FOUCAULT, M. (1980) *Power/Knowledge: selected interviews and other writings 1972–1977*, edited Colin Gordon, New York, Pantheon.

GRABE, W. (1987) 'Contrastive rhetoric and text type research' in CONNOR, U. and KAPLAN, R.(eds) *Writing across Languages: analysis of L2 Text*, Reading, Mass., Addison-Wesley.

HEATH, S.B. (1983) *Ways with Words: language, life and work in communities and classroom*, Cambridge, Cambridge University Press.

HINDS, J. (1987) 'Reader versus writer responsibility: a new typology', in CONNOR, U. and KAPLAN, R. (eds) *Writing across Languages: analysis of L2 Text*, Reading, Mass., Addison-Wesley.

HOEY, M. (1983) *On the Surface of Discourse*, London, Allen & Unwin.

KACHRU, B.B. (1985) 'Standards, codification and sociolinguistic realism: the English language in the outer circle' in QUIRK, R. and WIDDOWSON, H. (eds) *English in the World*, Cambridge, Cambridge University Press.

KACHRU, B.B. (ed.) (1992) *The Other Tongue: English across cultures*, 2nd edn, Urbana, Ill., University of Illinois Press.

KACHRU, Y. (1983) 'Linguistics and written discourse in particular languages: contrastive studies: English and Hindi', *Annual Review of Applied Linguistics*, vol. 3, pp. 50–77.

KACHRU, Y. (1987) 'Cross-cultural texts, discourse strategies and discourse interpretation' in SMITH, L. (ed.) *Discourse across Cultures: strategies in world Englishes*, London, Prentice Hall.

KACHRU, Y. (1988) 'Writers in Hindi and English' in PURVIS, A. (ed.) *Writing across Languages and Cultures: issues in contrastive rhetoric*, Newbury Park, Calif., Sage.

KACHRU, Y. (1992) 'Culture, style and discourse: expanding noetics of English' in KACHRU, B.B. (ed.) *The Other Tongue: English across cultures*, 2nd edn, Urbana, Ill., University of Illinois Press.

KACHRU, Y. (1995a) 'Contrastive rhetoric in world Englishes', *English Today*, vol. 11, no. 1, January, pp. 21–31.

KACHRU, Y. (1995b) 'Cultural meaning and rhetorical styles: toward a framework for contrastive rhetoric' in SEIDLHOFER, B. and COOK, G., *Principle and Practice in Applied Linguistics: studies in honour of H.G. Widdowson*, London, Oxford University Press.

KACHRU, Y. (1995c) 'Language and cultural meaning: expository writing in South Asian English' in BAUMGARDNER, R. (ed.) *South Asian English: structure, use and users*, Urbana, Ill., University of Illinois Press.

KAPLAN, R.B. ([1966]1980) 'Cultural thought patterns in inter-cultural education', *Language Learning*, vol. 16, pp. 1–20. Reprinted in CROFT, K. (ed.) *Readings
on English as a Second Language for Teachers and Teacher Trainees*, Cambridge, Mass.,
Winthrop.

KENKEL, J. (1991) 'Argumentation pragmatics, text analysis and contrastive rhetoric', PhD dissertation, University of Illinois at Urbana-Champaign.

MACDONELL, A.A. ([1900]1968) *A History of Sanskrit Literature*, New York, Haskell
House.

MACKAY, S. (1993) 'Sociocultural factors in teaching composition to Pacific Rim
writers: an overview' in BROCK, M.N. and WALTERS, L. (eds) *Teaching Composition
around the Pacific Rim: politics and pedagogy*, Philadelphia, Pa., Multilingual Matters.

MARTIN, J.E. (1992) *Towards a Theory of Text for Contrastive Rhetoric: an introduction to
issues of text for students and practitioners of contrastive rhetoric*, New York, Peter Lang.

MEADE, R. and ELLIS, W.G. (1970) 'Paragraph development in the modern age of
rhetoric', *English Journal*, vol. 59, pp. 219–26.

REYNOLDS, D.W. (1993) 'Illocutionary acts across languages: editorializing in
Egyptian English', *World Englishes*, vol. 12, no. 1, pp. 35–46.

SCRIBNER, S. and COLE, M. (1981) *The Psychology of Literacy*, Cambridge, Mass.,
Harvard University Press.

SMITH, W.F. and LIEDLICH, D. (1980) *Rhetoric for Today*, New York, Harcourt Brace
Jovanovich.

VÄHAPÄSSI, A. (1988) 'The problem of selection of writing tasks in cross-cultural
study' in PURVES, A. (ed.) *Writing across Languages and Cultures: issues in contrastive
rhetoric*, Newbury Park, Calif., Sage.

VAVRUS, F.K. (1991) 'When paradigms clash: the role of internationalized varieties
in language teacher education', *World Englishes*, vol. 10, no. 2, pp. 181–95.

This reading was specially commissioned for this book.

Reading B

SOME LANGUAGE PROBLEMS FACED BY OVERSEAS STUDENTS IN BRITISH UNIVERSITIES

Tony Bex

Exactly how many speakers of English there are in the world is open to dispute.
Estimates range from 400 million to over 700 million (Bex, 1993, pp. 249–50). Raw
figures such as these, however, give us very little information about the ways in
which the language has been learned, or is used, by such speakers.

For mother-tongue speakers, English is first learned in the home and, as the
medium for the first personal relationships, carries many emotional resonances.
Subsequently, it is expanded at school and used to forge a wider range of social
relationships. However, it continues to be the language of intimacy between
friends, although often expressed in a different dialect and/or accent from that

used in school. Later, it also becomes the primary means for expressing certain aspects of abstract thought.

For second language speakers, however, English may not be used in the home, and is often first learned at school. It may not have been used across a wide range of social settings, and so may not have the same emotional resonances as is the case for first language speakers. For people who live in a society where English is not generally spoken and who have learned it in school, the language has very few functions outside the educational sphere (although it may be perceived as an important language in terms of an eventual career).

These distinctions are not absolute, but they indicate important differences in how English is learned and used in different societies around the world. They also suggest that *all* learners of English are likely to develop different linguistic repertoires appropriate to their particular situations, and that these repertoires may differ from each other in quite significant ways.

This is important because all too often when non-native speakers arrive in Britain they face a number of language problems of which neither they nor their hosts may be immediately aware. Although such problems may be perceived initially as cultural, they tend to manifest themselves through subtle misunderstandings of language. However, it would be a mistake to assume that these difficulties are simply a manifestation of limited proficiency in English. More often, they are the result of linguistic choices which have slightly different meanings in different cultures.

Before discussing this we need to deal with an apparent paradox. If second- and other language speakers learn English at school (and later at university), then for them it is obviously and intimately related to academic achievement. The transition to higher education where they are studying the same subjects (albeit at a higher level) in that language should be problem-free and it would seem that such problems as remain would only attach to their lives outside the college or the university. This, though, is all too frequently not the case. To appreciate more clearly the problems of such students, one must recognize how attitudes to language operate in British society as a whole, and also how language choices are deeply influenced by the particular contexts of use (in this case, the educational setting).

We can usefully draw on the concept of communicative competence which was first proposed by the linguist Dell Hymes (1979). Hymes broke this down into four components:

- the extent to which something is possible;
- the extent to which something is feasible;
- the extent to which something is appropriate;
- the extent to which something is done.

The first of these refers to the grammaticality of sentences. Native speakers of English would regard the following sentence as (grammatically) *possible*:

(1) The cat that the dog bit ran away

But they would probably treat sentence 2 as both ill-formed and uninterpretable:

(2) Cat dog bit the the away ran that

Sentence (1) indicates that there is a grammatical rule in English which allows clauses to be embedded as relatives within the subject–noun phrase. In principle therefore sentence 3 should be treated as grammatical:

(3) The mouse that the cat that the dog bit chased squeaked

Chapter 1 discusses how children acquire and use English as a mother tongue, and Chapter 2 discusses the acquisition of English in bilingual and multilingual settings.

Communicative competence is discussed in Chapter 2 (in relation to language acquisition) and in Chapter 7 (in relation to the teaching of English as an additional language).

Most readers, though, would find this difficult to interpret because the processing effort required to establish the grammatical relationships between the noun phrases and their associated verb phrases would be too overwhelming. Thus, although the sentence is grammatical at the formal level, it is *unfeasible*.

Appropriateness is a rather more problematic notion since it is concerned with matters of linguistic etiquette. Broadly speaking, it acknowledges that there are three degrees of linguistic formality which we typically adopt in given social circumstances. Thus, although I may address my professor by her first name and speak casually to her when we meet over a drink, when I write to her in her official capacity, not only do I address her by her title, I also choose my vocabulary carefully, check my spelling and screen out what I consider to be grammatical solecisms.

Linked to this is what native speakers actually *do*. Take the phrase 'to be in a quandary'. (The *Collins COBUILD Dictionary* defines *quandary* as a count noun meaning 'the state of not being able to decide or think what to do about a situation you are involved in'.) A search through a corpus of two million words only found two instances of use. Both of these were in the singular. One was in a title and the other an appositional noun phrase within a subject group. The grammatical rules of Standard English allow us to construct the sentence 'The quandaries I was in have been resolved.' Yet most native speakers would find this an odd sentence and one they would not normally construct themselves, although they would have little difficulty in understanding it. To that extent, some 'correct' usages are simply not used.

The theory of communicative competence was an important influence in the development of language teaching that took place in the 1970s. Language teachers became increasingly aware of the distinction between 'usage' and 'use' and recognized that simply teaching the grammar of the foreign language was not likely to encourage communicative competence in their pupils. However, the development of communicative skills in the language classroom does not guarantee that such skills will transfer successfully when the pupils come into contact with native speakers in the target culture.

If we reconsider our putative native speakers, it will be apparent that they are familiar with a great number of different varieties of language. These varieties have been described by Halliday (in Halliday and Hasan, 1989, p. 43) as consisting of **dialects** and **registers**. He considers that dialects represent regional and class differences but that such differences are not semantically significant. Registers, on the other hand, develop to express different meanings and are semantically significant. McCarthy and Carter (1994, p. 22; see also Bex, 1993) have pointed out that the distinction is perhaps not as clear-cut as Halliday suggests. Meanings are developed as part of an interchange between writers/readers or speakers/hearers and the perceived meaning of an utterance will be deeply influenced by the variety (register or dialect) in which it is produced.

When they arrive at university, then, native speakers are sensitive to a wide range of language uses and the social attitudes to such uses in ways which cannot easily be recreated in the foreign language classroom and which may therefore be deeply puzzling to foreign speakers. Perhaps more importantly, native speakers are able to exploit these varieties in a number of different ways. One way of expressing this insight is to claim that language does not merely reflect the social relationships between speakers but is also constitutive of such relations. In an educational context we can go further and argue that appropriate generic choices are also (partly) constitutive of the academic discipline that is being studied.

To illustrate the first point, consider the following note I received from a Japanese student: 'I wish you a nice Christmas and vacation (I do not know whether I am supposed to say this to teachers, but anyway)'. This indicates a clear recognition of the appropriate greeting for the time of the year and an adequate grasp of linguistic forms, but the disclaimer suggests that the student is not quite sure how to make the linguistic shift between the formalities appropriate to a teacher–student relationship and the more relaxed relationship that can occur outside the classroom.

Of course, this is a very simple example, and a moment's reflection would indicate that the choice of language is likely to be affected by the relative status of the interlocutors in more subtle ways than I have suggested. Nevertheless, the essential point that language can be seen as a form of behaviour, and that the choice of linguistic forms may be considered to be analogous to social manners, should be clear. To the extent that foreign students are unfamiliar with the sets of behaviours that occur within a particular culture, so they will be unaware of the linguistic choices which realize such behaviours. Even though some students may have been taught English through a fully communicative syllabus, and may be familiar with a wide range of linguistic 'behaviours' in their home country, it is extremely unlikely that they will have been exposed to the full range of cultural variation that occurs within the British Isles.

Moreover these students are also unlikely to be entirely familiar with the varieties of English which realize the genres appropriate to university study. Most syllabuses do not explore the functional varieties of English. Even where the syllabus is adventurous and includes the use of English across a range of social contexts, it rarely introduces students to the specifics of academic English.

It might be argued that these students will already have been exposed to the generic conventions of the particular academic discipline in their own language and that all that is required of them is a simple transfer of skills. Unfortunately, it is not quite that simple. Although it may be true that some academic disciplines have developed standardized, international forms of discourse (the physical sciences are often taken as typical examples of such discourses), the majority are constructed in subtly different ways within different cultures. Michael Clyne (1987), for example, has conducted a number of cross-cultural studies of rhetorical organization and concluded that German students construct their arguments in subtly different ways from Australian students.

If we consider the tasks that students typically engage in and investigate the kinds of language that are appropriate to such tasks, other differences begin to appear. Essay writing is an activity that is common to many disciplines, particularly within the humanities and the social sciences. However, 'essay writing' differs quite considerably across different subjects. Broadly, we may anticipate that most essays should state, in an introduction, what the topic is. Even here, there is room for confusion. I once received an essay on 'The acquisition of language' from a Malaysian student which opened:

> Language, which is the system of human expression by means of words, is an essential tool to communicate with each other in our everyday life. Have you supposed whether you can think of anything without language? Since it is a very normal activity for human beings to speak or write language, they tend to think there is no mystery about it. How language is acquired is examined.

Although not deficient grammatically, this is unsatisfactory as an opening. The rhetorical search for a subject matter may be quite appropriate within Malaysian writing styles, yet is at odds with conventional British academic styles of writing.

(I should make it very clear here that I am not claiming any superiority for the British style, but that style is a conventional requirement for success in British higher education.)

Typically, an essay continues by discussing this topic in an informative way with references and appropriate readings. The arguments are then drawn together in a conclusion. However, in the two disciplines with which I am most familiar, English language and literature, there are marked differences in the ways in which the arguments are constructed. Although specific titles will lead to different kinds of essays, it would be broadly true to say that essays on literature tend to be more discursive, to contain more evaluation and to allow more personal responses to the material than essays in other disciplines.

But essays on language topics are not like essays on literary topics. They involve different ways of dealing with data and stand in a subtly different relationship to the judgements made in the textbooks. Such essays are more like reports on the students' reading in which they demonstrate that they have understood and can apply the relevant theories. Only rarely (and then at postgraduate level) are they expected to offer personal, evaluative responses to such theories. By and large, native speakers can switch between these two different essay-writing techniques reasonably successfully, since they are already familiar with the different discourse styles which realize such different approaches. Overseas students, however, from heterogeneous backgrounds, are faced with problems which often derive from their previous educational experience. I recently received an essay which mixed material from the textbooks with extraneous, and often irrelevant, material derived from lecture notes. This material was offered in the form of statements with little indication as to how the different elements were related to each other, or how the material in general was part of a developing argument. It transpired that the student had (mistakenly) assumed that everything said in lectures had to be repeated as a way of showing that she had been paying attention. It seemed that her educational experience in Singapore had encouraged a style in which knowledge supplied by the teacher needed to be 'displayed'.

Other students face different problems. For example, the essays German students are usually expected to write are typically 'term papers' and are considerably longer and more formal than those produced by British students. One German student, in attempting to adapt to the British discourse style, assumed it was necessarily much more informal and produced an essay which used the terms 'the child', 'the little one' and 'kid' in the same paragraph, leading to stylistic inconsistency. An essay which does not conform to the genre that is considered appropriate to the particular academic discipline in any country's higher education system is likely to be a failed essay.

I have concentrated on essay writing because it is an area that creates major problems for students, since it is usually conducted in private. However, there are other activities which also require specific skills. For example, the presentation of seminar papers is often a major source of anxiety for foreign language students. Not only do they worry about their accents, they are also unclear about the levels of formality that are appropriate to such occasions. Native speakers are able to slide naturally between different modes of presentation, to introduce idioms, to utter asides, or to switch between personal recollection and mention of a technical book. One of my more adventurous (mother-tongue) groups once presented a very successful seminar in the form of a Christmas pantomime. Such options are simply not available to the majority of non-native speakers because they are at the interface of study skills and communicative competence.

The same point could be made about the listening skills necessary for note taking in lectures. Instructions to listen for what is important by noticing such features as a reduction in speech rate or increased emphasis are very helpful, but they may not apply to all lectures. It is not uncommon for lecturers to reduce the formality of the occasion by presenting a lecture as though it were a one-sided conversation. Examples, which may be essential to the development of an argument, can be thrown in as an aside. Without denying that this gives British students problems, it is likely to give foreign students even greater ones.

Inevitably, in such a brief discussion, I have only been able to hint at the kinds of linguistic problems that face non-native speakers of English studying in the United Kingdom. Although it is important to recognize that different students are likely to face specific problems related to their individual (linguistic) experiences, it is worth trying to generalize. I have claimed that much EFL/ESL teaching is based on approaches designed to improve communicative competence. However, even the most communicative classroom is unable to present the full variety of language that is available to the native speaker. Further, this teaching is often centred on a narrow range of English which can be broadly referred to as 'core' English. For many students this variety is taken to be representative of the language as a whole, whereas in Britain it is typically used between strangers in non-threatening service encounters. On entering university, many foreign and second language students discover that it fails to meet all their linguistic needs. Not only do they need to learn an enlarged (or, in the case of second language students, different) repertoire which will enable them to socialize with such diverse social groups as their landlords/ladies, fellow students and lecturers, they also need to learn the specific discourse skills appropriate to carrying out a range of different linguistic tasks within a number of different academic disciplines. Although these difficulties are also faced by native speakers of English, native speakers are already sensitive to such differences. Hasan (1984) has stated that 'how we say is how we mean'. Where students have been exposed to different ways of 'saying', then they will have different ways of 'meaning'. These ways of meaning may not be 'wrong', but they may prove to be inappropriate for the new situations in which students find themselves.

References

BEX, A.R. (1993) 'Standards of English in Europe', *Multilingual,* vol. 12, no. 3, pp. 249–64.

CLYNE, M. (1987) 'Discourse structures and discourse expectations: implications for Anglo-German academic communication in English' in SMITH, L.E. (ed.) *Discourse across Cultures,* London, Prentice Hall.

HALLIDAY, M.A.K. and HASAN, R. (1989) *Language, Context and Text,* Oxford, Oxford University Press.

HASAN, R. (1984) 'Ways of saying; ways of meaning' in FAWCETT, R.P., HALLIDAY, M.A.K., LAMB, S.M. and MAKKAI, A. (eds) *The Semiotics of Culture and Language, vol. 1, Language as Social Semiotic,* London, Pinter.

HYMES, D.H. (1979) 'On communicative competence', reprinted in BRUMFITT, C and JOHNSON, K. (eds) *The Communicative Approach to Language Teaching,* Oxford, Oxford University Press.

MCCARTHY, M. and CARTER, R. (1994) *Language as Discourse,* London, Longman.

This reading was specially commissioned for this book.

REFERENCES

ALDRIDGE, M. (1991) 'How language grows up', *English Today*, no. 25, pp. 14–20.

ALPTEKIN, C. (1993) 'Target-language culture in EFL materials', *ELT Journal*, vol. 47, no. 2, pp. 136–43.

ANDERSON, A. and STOKES, S. (1984) 'Social and institutional influences on the development and practice of literacy' in GOELMAN, H., OBERG, A. and SMITH, F. (eds) *Awakening to Literacy*, London, Heinemann Educational.

ANDERSON, A.H., CLARK, A. and MULLIN, J. (1991) 'Introducing information in dialogues: forms of introducing chosen by young speakers and the responses elicited from young listeners', *Journal of Child Language*, no. 18, pp. 663–87.

ANNAMALAI, E. (1986) 'A typology of language movements and their relation to language planning' in ANNAMALAI, E. and RUBIN, J. (eds) *Language Planning*, Mysore, Central Institute of Indian Languages.

APPLEBEE, A. (1974) *Tradition and Reform in the Teaching of English*, Urbana, Ill., National Council of Teachers of English.

ARTHUR, J. (1992) *Talking Like Teachers: teacher and pupil discourse in standard six Botswana classrooms*, Working Paper no. 25, Centre for Language in Social Life, University of Lancaster.

ATKINSEN, K., McWHINNEY, B. and STOEL, C. (1970) 'An experiment on the recognition of babbling', *Papers and Reports on Child Language Development*, Committee on Linguistics, Stanford, Ca., Stanford University.

AUSTRALIAN EDUCATION COUNCIL (1994a) *A Statement on English for Australian Schools*, Carlton, Vic., Curriculum Corporation.

AUSTRALIAN EDUCATION COUNCIL (1994b) *English – a Curriculum Profile for Australian Schools*, Carlton, Vic., Curriculum Corporation.

BALDAUF, R. (1990) 'Education and language planning in the Samoas' in BALDAUF, R. and LUKE, A. (eds) *Language Planning and Education in Australasia*, Clevedon, Multilingual Matters.

BALLARD, B. (1984) 'Improving student writing: an integrated approach to cultural adjustment' in WILLIAMS, R. and SWALES, J. (eds) *Common Ground: shared interests in ESP and communication skills*, ELT Documents no. 117, British Council/Pergamon.

BANCROFT, D.M.R. (1985) 'The development of temporal reference', unpublished PhD thesis, University of Nottingham.

BARNES, D. and TODD, F. (1995) *Discussion and Learnings Revisited: making meaning through talk*, Portsmouth, N.H., Heinemann.

BARRETT, M., HARRIS, M. and CHASIN, J. (1991) 'Early lexical development and maternal speech: a comparison of children's initial and subsequent use of words', *Journal of Child Language*, no. 18, pp. 21–40.

BARTON, D. (1994) *Literacy*, Oxford, Blackwell.

BARTON, M.E. and TOMASELLO, M. (1994) 'The rest of the family: the role of fathers and siblings in early language development' in GALLAWAY, C. and RICHARDS, B.J. (eds) *Input and Interaction in Language Acquisition,* Cambridge, Cambridge University Press.

BENEDICT, H. (1979) 'Early lexical development: comprehension and production', *Journal of Child Language,* no. 6, pp. 183–200.

BENG-HUAT, C. (1983) 'Re-opening ideological discussion in Singapore: a new theoretical direction', *Southeast Asian Journal of Social Science,* vol. 2, no. 2, pp. 31–45.

BERKO GLEASON, J. (1973) 'Code switching in children's language' in MOORE, T.E. (ed.) *Cognitive Development and the Acquisition of Language,* London, Academic Press.

BHATIA, V. (1993) *Analysing Genre: language use in professional settings,* London, Longman.

BIBER, D. (1988) *Variation across Speech and Writing,* Cambridge, Cambridge University Press.

BISONG, J. (1995) 'Language choice and cultural imperialism: a Nigerian perspective', *English Language Teaching Journal,* vol. 49, no. 2, pp. 122–32.

BISSEX, G. (1984) 'The child as teacher' in GOELMAN, H., OBERG, A. and SMITH, F. (eds) *Awakening to Literacy,* London, Heinemann Educational.

BLOOM, L. (1973) *One Word at a Time,* The Hague, Mouton.

BLOOR, M. and BLOOR, T. (1991) 'Cultural expectations and socio-pragmatic failure in academic writing' in ADAMS, P., HEATON, B. and HOWARTH, P. (eds) *Socio-cultural Issues in English for Academic Purposes* (British Association of Lecturers in English for Academic Purposes conference papers), London, Modern English Publications in association with the British Council.

BOARD OF EDUCATION (1921) *The Teaching of English in England* (Newbolt Report), London, HMSO.

BOGGS, S. (1985) *Speaking, Relating and Learning: a study of Hawaiian children at home and in school,* Norwood, N.J., Ablex.

BOURNE, J. (1989) *Moving into the Mainstream: LEA provision for bilingual pupils,* Windsor, NFER-Nelson.

BOURNE, J. and McPAKE, J. (1991) *Partnership Teaching: co-operative teaching strategies for multilingual schools,* London, HMSO.

BOWERS, R. (1994) *English 2000,* Manchester, British Council.

BRITISH COUNCIL (1993) *English Teaching Profiles,* Manchester, British Council.

BRITTON, J., SHAFER. R.E. and WATSON, K. (eds) (1990) *Teaching and Learning English Worldwide,* Clevedon, Multilingual Matters.

BROWN, H.D. (1991) 'TESOL at twenty-five: what are the issues?', *TESOL Quarterly,* vol. 25, no. 2, pp. 245–60.

BRUMFIT, C. (ed.) (1991) *Literature on Language: an anthology,* London, Macmillan.

BRUNER, J. (1978) 'Learning how to do things with words' (Wolfson College Lectures 1976) in BRUNER, J. and GARTON, A. (eds) *Human Growth and Development,* Oxford, Clarendon.

BRUNER, J. (1986) *Actual Minds, Possible Worlds*, Harvard, Mass., Harvard University Press.

BRYANT, P. (1994) 'Literacy and phonological awareness', *The Encyclopedia of Language and Linguistics*, vol. 4, pp. 2246–7, Oxford, Pergamon.

BRYANT, P.E. and BRADLEY, L. (1985) *Children's Reading Problems*, Oxford, Blackwell.

BRYANT, P., BRADLEY, L., MACLEAN, M. and CROSSLAND, J. (1989) 'Nursery rhymes, phonological skills and reading', *Journal of Child Language*, vol. 16, pp. 407–28.

BULLOKAR, W. ([1580] 1966) 'A Short Introduction or Guiding' (facsimile reprint) in DANIELSSON, B. and ALSTON, R.C. (eds) *The Works of William Bullokar*, vol. 1, School of English, University of Leeds.

BURKE, R.A. (1993) 'Reading in early Britain' in BROOKS, G., PUGH, A.K. and HALL, N. (eds) *Further Studies in the History of Reading*, Widnes, UK Reading Association.

BURLING, (1978) 'Language development of a Garo and English-speaking child' in HATCH, E.M. (ed.) *Second Language Acquisition*, Rowley, Mass., Newbury House.

CAMBOURNE, B. and TURBILL, J. (1987) *Coping with Chaos*, Rozelle, NSW, Primary English Teaching Association.

CAMILLERI, A. (1994) 'Talking bilingually, writing monolingually', paper presented at the Sociolinguistics Symposium, University of Lancaster, March.

CARTER, R. (1989) *The National Curriculum in English*, London, British Council.

CARTER, R. (ed.) (1990) *Knowledge about Language and the Curriculum*, Sevenoaks, Hodder & Stoughton.

CELCE-MURCIA, M. (1978) 'The simultaneous acquisition of English and French in a two-year-old child' in HATCH, E.M. (ed.) *Second Language Acquisition*, Rowley, Mass., Newbury House.

CENTRAL ADVISORY COUNCIL FOR EDUCATION (CACE) (1963) *Half our Future* (Newson Report), London, HMSO.

CHESHIRE, J. (1982) 'Linguistic variation and social function' in ROMAINE, S. (ed.) *Sociolinguistic Variation in Speech Communities*, London, Edward Arnold.

CHOMSKY, N. (1965) *Aspects of the Theory of Syntax*, Cambridge, Mass., MIT Press.

CHRISTIE, M. (1985) *Aboriginal Perspectives on Experience and Learning: the role of language in Aboriginal education*, Deakin, Vic., Deakin University Press.

CHRISTOPHERSON, P. (1973) *Second Language Learning: myth and reality*, Harmondsworth, Penguin.

CIPOLLA, C.M. (1969) *Literacy and Development in the West*, Harmondsworth, Penguin.

CLANCHY, M.T. (1984) 'Learning to read in the middle ages and the role of mothers' in BROOKS, G. and PUGH, A.K. (eds) *Studies in the History of Reading*, Reading, University of Reading Centre for the Teaching of Reading and UK Reading Association.

CLANCHY, M.T. (1993) *From Memory to Written Record*, 2nd edn, Oxford, Blackwell.

CLARE, R. (1995) '"Who is it that can tell me who I am?" The theory of authorial revision between the quarto and folio texts of King Lear', *The Library: the transactions of the Bibliographical Society*, Oxford, Oxford University Press.

CLARK, M. (1976) *Young Fluent Readers*, London, Heinemann Educational.

CLARK, R. and IVANIČ, R. (1991) 'Consciousness about the writing process' in JAMES, C. and GARRETT, P. (eds) *Language Awareness in the Classroom*, London, Longman.

CLAY, M.M. (1975) *What Did I Write?* Auckland, New Zealand, Heinemann.

CLAY, M.M. (1983) 'Getting a theory of writing' in KROLL, B. and WELLS, G. (eds) *Explorations in the Development of Writing*, Chichester, John Wiley.

CLEGHORN, A., MERRIT, M. and OBAGI, J.O. (1989) 'Language policy and science instruction in Kenyan primary schools', *Comparative Education Review*, vol. 33, no. 1, pp. 2–39.

CLYNE, M. (1987) 'Cultural differences in the organisation of academic texts: English and German', *Journal of Pragmatics*, no. 11, pp. 211–47.

COMMISSION ON ENGLISH OF THE COLLEGE ENTRANCE EXAMINATION BOARD (1965) *Freedom and Discipline*, Princetown, N.J., College Entrance Examination Board.

CORDER, S. (1974) 'The significance of learners' errors' in RICHARDS, J. (ed.) *Error Analysis: perspectives on second language acquisition*, London, Longman.

CORDER, S.P. (1978) 'Language-learner language' in RICHARDS, J.C. (ed.) *Understanding Second and Foreign Language Learning: issues and approaches*, Rowley, Mass., Newbury House.

CORSON, D. (1994) 'Don's diary', *Times Higher Education Supplement*, 9 December, p. 14.

COX, B. (1995) *Cox on the Battle for the English Curriculum*, London, Hodder & Stoughton.

CRESSY, D. (1980) *Literacy and the Social Order: reading and writing in Tudor and Stuart England*, Cambridge, Cambridge University Press.

CRYSTAL, D. (1975) 'Linguistic perspectives', *Reading*, vol. 9, no. 2, pp. 39–50.

CRYSTAL, D. (1986) *Listen to your Child: a parent's guide to children's language*, Harmondsworth, Penguin.

CRYSTAL, D. (1995) *The Cambridge Encyclopedia of the English Language*, Cambridge, Cambridge University Press.

CUMMINS, J. (1979) 'Cognitive/academic language proficiency: implications for bilingual education and the optimal age issue', *TESOL Quarterly*, vol. 14, pp. 175–87.

CURTIS, E. (1950) *A History of Ireland*, London, Methuen.

DAVIS, D. and WATSON, K. (1990) 'Teaching English in Australia: a personal view' in BRITTON, J., SHAFER, R.E. and WATSON, K. (eds) *Teaching and Learning English Worldwide*, Clevedon, Multilingual Matters.

DE VILLIERS, P.A. and DE VILLIERS, J.G. (1979) *Early Language*, London, Open Books.

DENDRINOS, B. (1992) *The EFL Textbook and Ideology*, Athens, Grivas.

DEPARTMENT OF EDUCATION AND SCIENCE (DES) (1975) *A Language for Life: report of the committee of inquiry into reading and the use of English* (Bullock Report), London, HMSO.

DEPARTMENT FOR EDUCATION AND WELSH OFFICE (DFEWO) (1995) *English in the National Curriculum*, London, HMSO.

DESAI, A. (1995) 'The evolution of a post-apartheid language policy in South Africa: an ongoing site of struggle', *European Journal of Intercultural Studies*, vol. 5, no. 3, pp. 18–25.

DETERDING, D.H. (1984) *A Study of the Ways in which a Two-year-old Bilingual Child Differentiates between his Two Languages*, MPhil dissertation, University of Cambridge Department of Linguistics.

DEUCHAR, M. and QUAY, S. (1994) 'Language choice and code switching in bilingual children', paper delivered to annual meeting of British Association of Applied Linguistics.

DILLON, J.J. (ed.) (1988) *Questioning and Discussion: a multidisciplinary study*, London, Croom Helm.

DIXON, J. (1967) *Growth Through English*, Oxford, Oxford University Press for National Association for the Teaching of English (NATE).

DOBSON, J.L. (1984) 'The interpretation of statistical data on the levels of literacy in nineteenth-century England and Wales' in BROOKS, G. and PUGH, A.K. (eds) *Studies in the History of Reading*, Reading, University of Reading Centre for the Teaching of Reading and UK Reading Association.

DOMBEY, H. (1992) 'Lessons learnt at bedtime' in KIMBERLEY, K., MEEK, M. and MILLER, J. (eds) *New Readings: contributions to an understanding of literacy*, London, A & C Black.

DONALDSON, M. (1984) 'Speech and writing and modes of learning' in GOELMAN, H., OBERG, A. and SMITH, F. (eds) *Awakening to Literacy*, London, Heinemann Educational.

DOUGHTY, A. and DOUGHTY, P. (1974) *Using Language in Use*, London, Edward Arnold.

DOUGHTY, P., PEARCE, J. and THORNTON, G. (1971) *Language in Use* (Schools Council Programme in Linguistics and English Teaching), London, Edward Arnold.

DOWNING, J. (1973) *Comparative Reading*, New York, Macmillan.

DOWNING, J. and LEONG, C. K. (1982) *Psychology of Reading*, New York, Macmillan.

DULAY, H.C. and BURT, M.K. (1976) 'Creative construction in second language learning and teaching' in BROWN, H.D. (ed.) *Language and Learning* (papers in second language acquisition, proceedings of the Sixth Annual Conference on Applied Linguistics), University of Michigan, Special Issue no. 4, January.

EAGLETON, T. (1976) Criticism and Ideology, London, New Left Books.

EDELSKY, C. (1977) 'Acquisition of an aspect of communicative competence: learning what it means to talk like a lady' in ERVIN-TRIPP, S. and MITCHELL-KERNAN, C. (eds) *Child Discourse*, New York, Academic Press.

EDGE, J. (1993) *Essentials of English Language Teaching*, London, Longman.

EDWARDS, A.D. (1976) *Language in Culture and Class*, London, Heinemann.

EDWARDS, A.D. (1992) 'Teacher talk and pupil competence' in NORMAN, K. (ed.) *Thinking Voices: the work of the National Oracy Project*, London, Hodder & Stoughton.

EDWARDS, J.R. (1979) 'Social class differences and the identification of sex in children's speech', *Journal of Child Language*, vol. 6, pp. 121–7.

EDWARDS, V. and SIENKEWICZ, T. (1990) *Oral Cultures Past and Present: rappin' and Homer*, Oxford, Blackwell.

EISIKOVITS, E. (1989) 'Girl-talk/boy-talk: sex differences in adolescent speech' in COLLINS, P. and BLAIR, D. (eds) *Australian English: the language of a new society*, Queensland, University of Queensland Press.

ELLIS, A. (1984) *Reading, Writing and Dyslexia*, London, Lawrence Erlbaum.

ENGLISH AND MEDIA CENTRE (1995) *Key Stage 3 English Units*, London, English and Media Centre.

ERVIN-TRIPP, S. (1971) 'Social backgrounds and verbal skills' in HUXLEY, R. and INGRAM, E. (eds) *Language Acquisition: models and methods*, New York, Academic Press.

ERVIN-TRIPP, S. (1977) 'Wait for me, roller skate!' in ERVIN-TRIPP, S. and MITCHELL-KERNAN, C. (eds) *Child Discourse*, New York, Academic Press.

FAIRBAIRN, G.J. and WINCH, C. (1991) *Reading, Writing and Reasoning: a guide for students*, Buckingham, Society for Research in Higher Education/Open University Press.

FAIRCLOUGH, N. (1989) *Language and Power*, London, Longman.

FANTINI, A. (1985) *Language Acquisition of a Bilingual Child: a sociolinguistic perspective*, San Diego, College Hill.

FARMER, M. (ed.) (1986) *Consensus and Dissent*, Urbana, Ill., National Council of Teachers of English.

FILLMORE, L.W. (1979) 'Individual differences in second language acquisition' in FILLMORE, C., KEMPLER, D. and WANG, W. (eds), *Individual Differences in Language Ability and Language Behaviour*, New York, Academic Press.

FOX, C. (1989) 'Children thinking through story', *English in Education*, vol. 23, no. 2, pp. 25–36, National Association of Teachers of English (NATE).

FREEDMAN, A. (1995) 'Show and tell? The role of explicit teaching in the learning of new genres' in SAWYER, W. (ed.) *Teaching Writing: is genre the answer?*, Canberra, Australian Education Network.

FURNBOROUGH, P., COWGILL, S., GREAVES, H. and SAPIN, K. (1980) *A New Start: a functional course in basic spoken English*, London, Heineman Educational.

GAIK, S.C. (1992) 'Home and away: raising awareness of mother tongue in the classroom' in BAIN, R., FITZGERALD, B. and TAYLOR, M. (eds) *Looking into Language: classroom approaches to knowledge about language*, London, Hodder & Stoughton.

GILLIGAN, C. (1995) 'The centrality of relationship in psychological development: a puzzle, some evidence, and a theory 'in HOLLAND, J. and BLAIR, M. (eds) *Research and feminist pedagogy*, Clevedon, Multilingual Matters.

GOELMAN, H., OBERG, A. and SMITH, F. (eds) (1984) *Awakening to Literacy*, London, Heinemann Educational.

GOFFMANN, E. (1981) *Forms of Talk*, Oxford, Blackwell.

GOLDSTROM, J.M. (1972) *The Social Context of Education 1808–1860: a study of the working-class school reader in England and Ireland*, Shannon, Irish University Press.

GOODMAN, Y. (1984) 'The development of initial literacy' in GOELMAN, H., OBERG, A. and SMITH, F. (eds) *Awakening to Literacy*, London, Heinemann Educational.

GOODMAN, K., GOODMAN, Y. and BURKE, C. (1978) 'Reading for life: the psycholinguistic basis' in HUNTER-GRUNDIN, E. and GRUNDIN, H. (eds) *Reading: implementing the Bullock report,* London, Ward Lock Educational.

GOODMAN, S. and GRADDOL, D. (eds) (1996) *Redesigning English: new texts, new identities,* London, Routledge/The Open University.

GORDON, P. and LAWTON, D. (1978) *Curriculum Change in the Nineteenth and Twentieth Centuries,* London, Hodder & Stoughton.

GOSWAMI, U. and BRYANT, P. (1990) *Phonological Skills and Learning to Read,* London, Lawrence Erlbaum.

GRADDOL, D., CHESHIRE, J. and SWANN, J. (1994) *Describing Language,* 2nd edn, Buckingham, Open University Press.

GRADDOL, D., LEITH, D. and SWANN, J. (eds) (1996) *English: history, diversity and change,* London, Routledge/The Open University.

GRAFF, H.J. (1979) *The Literacy Myth: literacy and social structure in the nineteenth century city,* New York, Academic Press.

GRANT, N. (1987) *Making the Most of Your Textbook,* London, Longman.

GREGORY, E. (1992) 'Learning codes and contexts: a psychosemiotic approach to beginning reading in school' in KIMBERLEY, K., MEEK, M. and MILLER, J. (eds) *New Readings: contributions to an understanding of literacy,* London, A & C Black.

GUPTA, A.F. (1994) *The Step Tongue: children's English in Singapore,* Clevedon, Multilingual Matters.

HAKUTA, K. (1986) *Mirror of Language: the debate on bilingualism,* New York, Basic Books.

HALL, N. (1987) *The Emergence of Literacy,* Sevenoaks, Hodder & Stoughton.

HALL, N. (ed.) (1989) *Writing with Reason: the emergence of authorship in young children,* Sevenoaks, Hodder & Stoughton.

HALLIDAY, M.A.K. (1973) 'A sociosemiotic perspective on language development', paper presented to the Fifth Child Language Research Forum, Stanford, Ca. Stanford University.

HALLIDAY, M.A.K. (1978) *Language as Social Semiotic: the social interpretation of language and meaning,* London, Edward Arnold.

HALLIDAY, M.A.K. (1985) *Spoken and Written Language,* Deakin, Vic., Deakin University Press.

HAMPSON, J. and NELSON, K. (1993) 'The relation of maternal language to variation in rate and style of language acquisition', *Journal of Child Language,* no. 20, pp. 313–42.

HARDING, K. and HENDERSON, P. (1994) *High Season: English for the hotel and tourist industry,* Oxford, Oxford University Press.

HARNESS-GOODWIN, M. (1990) *He-Said-She-Said: talk as social organization among black children,* Bloomington and Indianapolis, Indiana University Press.

HARRISON, G.J. and PIETTE, A.B. (1980) 'Young bilingual children's language selection', *Journal of Multilingual and Multicultural Development,* vol. 1, no. 3, p. 200.

HARSTE, J., BURKE, C. and WOODWARD, V. (1981) *Children, their Language and World: initial encounters with print,* National Institute of Education, Bloomington, Indiana University Press.

HARTLEY, B. and VINEY, P. (1978) *Streamline English: departures*, Oxford, Oxford University Press.

HATCH, E.M. (ed.) (1978) *Second Language Acquisition*, Rowley, Mass., Newbury House.

HAUGEN, E. (1956) *Bilingualism in the Americas: a bibliography and research guide*, Alabama, University of Alabama Press.

HEATH, S.B. (1982a) 'Protean shapes in literacy events: ever-shifting oral and literate traditions' in TANNEN, D. (ed.) *Spoken and Written Language*, Norwood, N.J., Ablex.

HEATH, S.B. (1982b) 'Questioning at home and at school: a comparative study' in SPINDLER, G. (ed.) *Doing the Ethnography of Schooling*, New York, Holt, Rinehart & Winston.

HEATH, S.B. (1983) *Ways with Words: language, life and work in communities and classrooms*, Cambridge, Cambridge University Press.

HÉBRARD, J. and CHARTIER, A-M. (1990) 'La préhistoire d'une discipline scolaire: l'écriture' in FIJALKOW, J. (ed.) *Décrire l'écrire*, Toulouse, Presses Universitaires du Mirail et CRDP de Toulouse, pp. 17–32.

HELLER, M. (1992) 'The politics of code-switching and language choice', *Journal of Multilingual and Multicultural Development*, vol. 13, no. 1, pp. 123–42.

HMSO (1959) *Primary Education: suggestions for the consideration of teachers and others concerned with the work of primary schools*, London, HMSO.

HOLLETT, V. (1994) *Business Opportunities*, Oxford, Oxford University Press.

HOLLINGWORTH, B. (1974) 'The mother tongue and the public schools in the 1860s', *British Journal of Education Studies*, vol. 22, no. 3, pp. 312–24.

HOLMES, J. (1992) *An Introduction to Sociolinguistics*, London, Longman.

HORGAN, D. (1981) 'Learning to make jokes: a study of metalinguistic abilities', *Journal of Child Language*, no. 8, pp. 217–24; reprinted in FRANKLIN, M.B. and BARTEN, S.S. (eds) (1988) *Child Language: a reader*, Oxford, Oxford University Press.

HOUSTON, C. (1989) *English Language Development Across the Curriculum (ELDAC)*, Qld, Immigrant Education Services, Division of Special Services, Queensland Department of Education

HUANG, J. and HATCH, E.M. (1978) 'A Chinese child's acquisition of English' in HATCH, E.M. (ed.) *Second Language Acquisition*, Rowley, Mass., Newbury House.

HUEY, E.B. (1908) *The Psychology and Pedagogy of Reading*, New York, Macmillan.

HULL, R. (1985) *The Language Gap*, London, Methuen.

HUNG, T. (1993) 'The role of phonology in the teaching of pronunciation to bilingual students', *Language, Culture and Curriculum*, vol. 6, no. 3, pp. 249–56.

HUTCHISON and TORRES (1994) 'The textbook as agent of change', *English Language Teaching Journal*, vol. 48, no. 4, pp. 315–28.

HYDE, K. (1993) 'Reading and writing in relation to work in later medieval Italy' in BROOKS, G., PUGH, A.K. and HALL, N. (eds) *Further Studies in the History of Reading*, Widnes, UK Reading Association.

HYMES, D.H. (1979) 'On communicative competence' in BRUMFIT, C. and JOHNSON, K. (eds) *The Communicative Approach to Language Teaching*, Oxford, Oxford University Press.

IMEDADZE, N.V. (1978) 'On the psychological nature of child speech formation under condition of exposure to two languages' in HATCH, E.M. (ed.) *Second Language Acquisition*, Rowley, Mass., Newbury House.

INGLIS, F. (1977) 'The Use of English and the use of English', *Use of English*, vol. 28, no. 39, pp. 39–48.

INGRAM, D. (1989) *First Language Acquisition: method, description, and explanation*, Cambridge, Cambridge University Press.

IREDALE, R. (1991) 'The economic benefits of English language teaching', *Dunford Seminar Report: the social and economic impact of ELT in development*, Manchester, British Council, pp. 8–9.

IVANIČ, R. (1992) *I is for Interpersonal: the discoursal construction of writer identities and the teaching of writing*, Working Paper no. 43, Centre for Language in Social Life, University of Lancaster.

IVANIČ, R. and SIMPSON, J. (1992) 'Putting the people back into academic writing' in DOMBEY, H. and ROBINSON, M. (eds) *Literacy for the Twenty-first Century* (proceedings of the conference Literacy for the Twenty-first Century), Brighton, Literacy Centre, Brighton Polytechnic.

JACOBSON, R. (1990) 'Allocating two languages as a key feature of a bilingual methodology' in JACOBSON, R. and FALTIS, C. (eds) *Language Distribution Issues in Bilingual Schooling*, Clevedon, Multilingual Matters.

JAGER ADAMS, M. (1994) *Beginning to Read: thinking and learning about print*, Cambridge, Mass., MIT Press.

JANKS, H. (1993) *Language and Position*, Johannesburg, Hodder & Stoughton.

JOHNSON, R. (1993) *Writing Essays: guidance notes for students*, 4th edn, Manchester, Clifton.

JOHNSON, R.K. and LEE, P.L.M. (1987) 'Modes of instruction: teaching strategies and students' responses' in LORD, R. and CHENG, H. (eds) *Language Education in Hong Kong*, Hong Kong, Chinese University Press.

JONES, J., GOLLIN, S., DRURY, H. and ECONOMOU, D. (1989) 'Systemic-functional linguistics and its application to the TESOL curriculum' in HASAN, R. and MARTIN, J.R. (eds) *Language Development: learning language, learning culture (Meaning and choice in language: studies for Michael Halliday, vol. 1)*, Norwood, N.J., Ablex.

JORDAN, J. (1992) *An Introduction to ESOL Teaching*, London, Adult Learning and Basic Skills Unit (ALBSU).

KAMWANGAMALU, N.M. (1992) 'Multilingualism and social identity in Singapore', *Journal of Asian Pacific Communication*, vol. 3, no. 1, p. 33.

KEEN, J. (1994) 'Standard English, economic advantage and cultural values: a discussion of recent National Curriculum proposals for English', *Economic Awareness*, September, pp. 26–8.

KHLEIF, B.D. (1980) *Language and Ethnicity in Wales*, The Hague, Mouton.

KIMBERLEY, K., MEEK, M. and MILLER, J. (eds) (1992) *New Readings: contributions to an understanding of literacy*, London, A & C Black.

KNAPP, P. and WATKINS, M. (1994) *Context – Text – Grammar: teaching the genres and grammar of school writing in infants and primary classrooms*, Broadway, NSW, Text Productions.

KRASHEN, S. (1981) *Second Language Acquisition and Second Language Learning*, Oxford, Pergamon.

LABOV, W. (1964) 'Stages in the acquisition of Standard English' in SHUY, R.W. (ed.) *Social Dialects and Language Learning* (proceedings of the Bloomington, Indiana Conference), Champaign, Ill., NCTE.

LABOV, W. (1977) *Language in the Inner City: studies in the black English vernacular*, Oxford, Blackwell.

LACQUEUR, T.W. (1983) Towards a cultural ecology of literacy in England, 1600–1850' in RESNICK, D.P. (ed.) *Literacy in Historical Perspective*, Washington, Library of Congress.

LAKOFF, R. (1973) 'Language and woman's place', *Language in Society*, no. 2, pp. 45–80.

LANGUAGE IN THE NATIONAL CURRICULUM (LINC) (1991) *Language in the National Curriculum: materials for professional development*, Department of English, University of Nottingham.

LANKSHEAR, C. and LAWLER, M. (1987) *Literacy, Schooling and Revolution*, Lewes, Falmer.

LATHEY, G. (1992) 'Talking in your head: young children's developing understanding of the reading process', *English in Education* (National Association of Teachers of English (NATE)), vol. 26, no. 2, pp. 71–82, .

LE PAGE, R.B. and TABOURET-KELLER, A. (1985) *Acts of Identity: creole-based approaches to language and ethnicity*, Cambridge, Cambridge University Press.

LEAVIS, F.R. (1930) *Civilization and Minority Culture*, Cambridge, Cambridge University Press.

LEAVIS, F.R. (1943) *Education and the University*, London, Chatto & Windus.

LEAVIS, F.R. AND THOMPSON, D. (1933) *Culture and Environment*, London, Chatto & Windus.

LEE, A. (1990) 'The genre debate and tertiary writing' in MARSHALL, L. (ed.) *Learning from Each Other*, Proceedings of the 7th Language and Learning Skills Conference, Murdoch Educational Services and Teaching Resources Unit, Murdoch University, WA, pp. 73–84.

LEMKE, J.L. (1990) *Talking Science: language, learning and values*, Norwood, N.J., Albex.

LEOPOLD, W.F. (1978) 'A child's learning of two languages', reproduced in HATCH, E.M. (ed.) *Second Language Acquisition*, Rowley, Mass., Newbury House.

LEVITT, A.G. and UTMAN, J.G.A. (1992) 'From babbling towards the sound systems of English and French: a longitudinal two-case study', *Journal of Child Language*, no. 19, pp. 19–49.

LIEVEN, E.V.M. (1994) 'Crosslinguistic and crosscultural aspects of language addressed to children' in GALLOWAY, C. and RICHARDS, B.J. (eds) *Input and Interaction in Language Acquisition*, Cambridge, Cambridge University Press.

LI WEI, (1994) *Three Generations, Two Languages, One Family*, Clevedon, Multilingual Matters.

LI WEI and MILROY, L. (1994) 'Conversational code-switching in a Chinese community in Britain: a sequential analysis', paper presented to annual meeting of British Association of Applied Linguistics.

LIN, A. (1988) 'Pedagogical and para-pedagogical levels of interaction in the classroom: a social interactional approach to the analysis of the code-switching behaviour of a bilingual teacher in an English language lesson', *Working Papers in Linguistics and Language Teaching*, no. 11, University of Hong Kong Language Centre.

LO BIANCO, J. (1987) *National Policy on Languages*, Canberra, Commonwealth Department of Education.

LONGMAN'S 'SHIP' LITERARY READERS (1989) *The Fourth Reader*, London, Longman, Green & Co.

MACAULAY, R.K.S. (1978) 'Variation and consistency in Glaswegian English' in TRUDGILL, P. (ed.) *Sociolinguistic Patterns in British English*, London, Edward Arnold.

MAGALHAES, M.C.C. (1994) 'An understanding of classroom interactions for literacy development' in MERCER, N. and COLL, C. (eds) *Teaching, Learning and Interaction*, Explorations in Socio-cultural Studies, vol. 4, Madrid, Infancia y Aprendizaje.

MALCOLM, I. (1982) 'Speech events of the Aboriginal classroom', *International Journal of the Sociology of Language*, no. 36, pp. 115–34.

MARTIN, J.A., CHRISTIE, F. and ROTHERY, J. (1987) 'Social processes in education: a reply to Sawyer and Watson (and others)' in REID, I. (ed.) *The Place of Genre in Learning: current debates*, Deakin, Vic., Deakin University, Centre for Studies in Literary Education.

MARTLEW, M. and SORSBY, A. (1995) 'The precursors of writing: graphic representation in preschool children', *Learning and Instruction*, vol. 5, no. 1, pp. 1–19.

MARTYN-JONES, M. (1995) 'Code-switching in the classroom' in MILROY, L. and MUYSKEN, P. (eds) *One Speaker, Two Languages: cross disciplinary perspectives on code-switching*, Cambridge, Cambridge University Press.

MAYBIN, J. (1994a) 'Children's voices: talk, knowledge and identity' in GRADDOL, D., MAYBIN, J. and STIERER, B. (eds) *Researching Language and Literacy in Social Context*, Clevedon, Multilingual Matters.

MAYBIN, J. (1994b) 'Teaching writing: process or genre?' in BRINDLEY, S. (ed.) *Teaching English*, London, Routledge/The Open University.

MAYBIN, J. and MERCER, N. (eds) (1996) *Using English: from conversation to canon*, London, Routledge/The Open University.

MAZRUI, A.M. and MAZRUI, A.A. (1992) 'Language in a multicultural context: the African experience', *Language and Education*, vol. 6, nos. 2–4, pp. 83–98.

MCCALDON, S. and JONES, L. (1989) 'An author is a rat' in HALL, N. (ed.) *Writing with Reason: the emergence of authorship in young children*, Sevenoaks, Hodder & Stoughton.

McCLURE, E. (1977) 'Aspects of code-switching in the discourse of Mexican-American children' in SAVILLE-TROIKE, M. (ed.) *Linguistics and Anthropology*, GURT, Wash., Georgetown University Press.

MEEK, M. (1988) *How Texts Teach What Readers Learn*, Stroud, Thimble.

MEEK, M. (1990) 'What do we know about reading that helps us teach?' in CARTER, R. (ed.) *Knowledge about Language and the Curriculum*, Sevenoaks, Hodder & Stoughton.

MEHAN, H. (1979) *Learning Lessons: social organization in the classroom*, Cambridge, Mass., Harvard University Press.

MERCER, N. (1995) *The Guided Construction of Knowledge: talk amongst teachers and learners*, Clevedon, Multilingual Matters.

MICHAEL, I. (1987) *The Teaching of English: from the sixteenth century to 1870*, Cambridge, Cambridge University Press.

MILROY, L. (1980) *Language and Social Networks*, Oxford, Blackwell.

MINISTRY OF EDUCATION (1954) *Language: some suggestions for teacher of English and Others*, Pamphlet no. 26, London, HMSO.

MINISTRY OF EDUCATION (1993) *English in the New Zealand Curriculum (Draft)*, Wellington, New Zealand, Learning Media.

MITCHELL-KERNAN, C. and KERNAN, K.T. (1977) 'Pragmatics of directive choice amongst children' in ERVIN-TRIPP, S. and MITCHELL-KERNAN, C. (eds), *Child Discourse*, New York, Academic Press.

MOORE, A. (1995) 'The academic, linguistic and social development of bilingual pupils in secondary education: issues of diagnosis, pedagogy and culture', unpublished PhD thesis, Milton Keynes, The Open University.

MORRIS, J.M. (1988) 'Focus on phonics: Phonics 44 for initial literacy in English' in MERCER, N. (ed.) *Language and Literacy from an Educational Perspective*, vol. 2, Milton Keynes, Open University Press.

MORRIS, R.C. (1981) *Reading, 'Riting and Reconstruction: the education of freedmen in the South*, 1861–1870, Chicago, University of Chicago Press.

MORRISON, A. (1994) 'Study arts: from critical communication skills to subject specific study in a faculty of arts', *Language, Culture and Curriculum*, vol. 7, no. 3, pp. 55–78.

MUKHERJEE, T. (1985) 'ESL: an imported new empire' in NORTH LONDON COMMUNITY GROUP (eds) *Language and Power: dynamics of change and control*, London, North London Community Group.

NATIONAL WRITING PROJECT (1989a) *Audiences for Writing*, Walton-on-Thames, Thomas Nelson.

NATIONAL WRITING PROJECT (1989b) *Becoming a Writer*, Walton-on-Thames, Thomas Nelson.

NATIONAL WRITING PROJECT (1990) *A Rich Resource: writing and language diversity*, Walton-on-Thames, Thomas Nelson.

NELSON, K. (1973) 'Structure and strategy in learning to talk', *Monographs of the Society for Research in Child Development*, no. 38, pp. 1–2, serial no. 149.

NGŨGĨ WA THONG'O (1964) *Weep Not, Child*, Oxford, Heinemann.

NORMAN, K. (ed.) (1992) *Thinking Voices: the work of the National Oracy Project*, London, Hodder & Stoughton.

NORTHEDGE, A. (1990) *The Good Study Guide*, Milton Keynes, The Open University.

O'MALLEY, R. and THOMPSON, D. (1955) *English One*, London, Heinemann Educational.

ONG, W. (1982) *Orality and Literacy*, London, Methuen.

OPEN UNIVERSITY (1981) E262 *Language in Use*, Block 3 *Language Learning and Language Use*, Part II 'Literacy and the development of the teaching of English', Milton Keynes, The Open University.

OPEN UNIVERSITY (1991) *Talk and Learning 5–16: an in-service pack on oracy for teachers*, Milton Keynes, The Open University.

OPEN UNIVERSITY (1994) E880 *Learning to Teach Reading*, PGCE, Milton Keynes, The Open University.

PARADISE, R. (forthcoming) 'Passivity or tacit collaboration: Mazahua interaction in cultural context', *Learning and Instruction* (special edn on cooperation and social context in adult–child interaction, edited E. Elbers).

PAYNE, A. (1980) 'Factors controlling the acquisition of the Philadelphia dialect by out-of-state children' in LABOV, W. (ed.) *Locating Language in Time and Space*, New York, Academic Press.

PENNYCOOK, A. (1989) 'The concept of method, interested knowledge, and the politics of language teaching', *TESOL Quarterly*, vol. 23, no. 4, pp. 589–618.

PENNYCOOK, A. (1994a) 'Incommensurable discourses?', *Applied Linguistics*, vol. 15, no. 2, pp. 132.

PENNYCOOK, A. (1994b) *The Cultural Politics of English as an International Language*, London, Longman.

PERERA, K. (1994) 'Standard English: the debate', in BRINDLEY, S. (ed.) *Teaching English*, London, Routledge.

PHILIPS, S. (1972) 'Participant structures and communicative competence' in CAZDEN, C., JOHN, V. and HYMES, D. (eds) *The Functions of Language in the Classroom*, New York, Teachers College Press.

PHILLIPPS, K.C. (1984) *Language and Class in Victorian England*, Oxford, Blackwell.

PHILLIPSON, R. (1992) *Linguistic Imperialism*, Oxford, Oxford University Press.

POPLACK, S. (1980) 'Sometimes, I'll start a sentence in Spanish y termino en espanol (sic)', *Linguistics*, vol. 18, pp. 581–618.

POUND, E. (1934) *ABC of Reading*, London, Faber.

PREYER, W. (1889) *The Mind of the Child*, New York, Appleton.

PRODROMOU, L. (1990) 'English as cultural action' in ROSSNER, R. and BOLITHO, R. (eds) *Currents of Change in ELT*, Oxford, Oxford University Press.

PROTHEROUGH, R. and ATKINSON, J. (1991) *The Making of English Teachers*, Buckingham, Open University Press.

PYE, C. (1986) 'Quiché Mayan speech to children', *Journal of Child Language*, no. 13, pp. 85–100.

QUILLER-COUCH, A. (1920) *On the Art of Reading*, Cambridge, Cambridge University Press.

QUIRK, R. (1989) 'Separated by a common dilemma', *Times Higher Education Supplement*, 10 February, pp. 15, 18.

RAMPTON, B. (1995) *Crossing: language and ethnicity among adolescents*, London, Longman.

RAMPTON, B. (1996) 'Youth, race, resistance: a sociolinguistics perspective', *Linguistics and Education*, forthcoming.

RAMPTON, M. (1990) 'Displacing the "native-speaker": expertise, affiliation and inheritance', *ELT Journal*, vol. 44, no. 2, pp. 97–101.

RASHID, R. (1993) *A Malaysian Journey*, Kuala Lumpur, 15 Larong 1412C, 46100 Petaling Jaya, Selangor Darul Ehsan.

RAVEM, R. (1974) 'The development of wh-questions in first and second language learners' in RICHARDS, J. (ed.) *Error Analysis: perspectives on second language acquisition*, London, Longman.

READ, C. (1975) *Children's Categorisation of Speech Sounds in English*, Urbana, Ill., National Council of Teachers of English.

READ, C. (1985) 'The effects of phonology on beginning spelling: some cross-linguistic evidence' in OLSON, D., TORRANCE, N. and HILDYARD, A. (eds) *Literacy, Language and Learning*, Cambridge, Cambridge University Press.

REDLINGER, W.E. and PARK, T-Z. (1980) 'Language mixing in young bilinguals', *Journal of Child Language*, vol. 7, no. 2, pp. 337–52.

REEVES, N. (1983) 'Teaching convicts to read in colonial Australia', *Australian Journal of Reading*, vol. 6, no. 2, pp. 65–72.

REID, E. (1978) 'Social and stylistic variation in the speech of children: some evidence from Edinburgh' in TRUDGILL, P. (ed.) *Sociolinguistic Patterns in British English*, London, Edward Arnold.

ROBINSON, S., WALKER, L., JOHNSON, N. and GAMBELL, T. (1990) 'Teaching English language arts in Canada: 1965–1985' in BRITTON, J., SHAFER, R.E. and WATSON, K. (eds) *Teaching and Learning English Worldwide*, Clevedon, Multilingual Matters.

ROGERS, J. (1990) 'The world for sick proper' in ROSNER, R. and BOLITHO, R. (eds) *Currents of Change in English Language Teaching*, Oxford, Oxford University Press.

ROMAINE, S. (1975) *Linguistic Variability in the Speech of some Edinburgh Schoolchildren*, MLitt thesis, University of Edinburgh.

ROMAINE, S. (1984) *The Language of Children and Adolescents*, Oxford, Blackwell.

ROMAINE, S. (1989) *Bilingualism*, Oxford, Blackwell.

ROMAINE, S. (1995) *Bilingualism: second edition*, Oxford, Blackwell.

ROUTH, H. (1941) *The Diffusion of English Culture Outside England: a problem of post-war reconstruction*, Cambridge, Cambridge University Press.

SAHNI, U. (1992) 'Literacy for empowerment', paper presented at the First Conference for Socio-cultural Research: a research agenda for educational and cultural change, Universidad Complutense de Madrid, October.

SAMPSON, G. (1921) *English for the English*, Cambridge, Cambridge University Press.

SANDERS. E.K. (1961) 'When are speech sounds learned?' *Journal of Speech and Hearing Disorders*, no. 37, pp. 55–63.

SAVILLE-TROIKE, M. (1986) 'Children's dispute and negotiation strategies: a naturalistic approach' in FISHMAN, J., TABOURET-KELLER, A., CLYNE, M., KRISHMAMURTI, B.H. and ABDULAZIZ, M. (eds) *The Fergusonian impact: in honor of Charles A. Ferguson on the occasion of his 65th birthday*, Berlin, Mouton de Gruyter.

SAWYER, W. (1995) 'Writing genres, writing for learning and writing teachers' in SAWYER, W. (ed.) *Teaching Writing: is genre the answer?*, Canberra, Australian Education Network.

SAWYER, W. and WATSON, K. (1995) 'Writing in science' in SAWYER, W. (ed.) *Teaching Writing: is genre the answer?*, Canberra, Australian Education Network.

SAXENA, M. (1993) 'Literacies among the Panjabis in Southall' in HAMILTON, M., BARTON, D. and IVANIČ, R. (eds) *Worlds of Literacy*, Clevedon, Multilingual Matters.

SCHIEFFELIN, B. and COCHRAN-SMITH, M. (1984) 'Learning to read culturally: literacy before schooling' in GOELMAN, H., OBERG, A. and SMITH, F. (eds) *Awakening to Literacy*, London, Heinemann Educational.

SCHMIED, J. (1991) 'Arguments for and against English as a medium of instruction' in SCHMIED, J. *English in Africa: an introduction*, London, Longman.

SCHOOLS COUNCIL (1979) *English in the 1980s: a programme of support for teachers*, Schools Council Working Paper no. 62, London, Evans/Methuen.

SEARLE, C. (1977) *The World in a Classroom*, London, Writers and Readers Publishing Cooperative.

SHEERAN, Y. and BARNES, D. (1991) *School Writing: discovering the ground rules*, Buckingham, Open University Press.

SHERIDAN, A. (1980) *Michel Foucault: the will to truth*, London, Tavistock.

SHUY, R. (1978) 'What children's functional language can tell us about reading or how Joanna got herself invited to dinner' in BEACH, R. (ed.) *Perspectives on Literacy: proceedings of the 1977 Perspectives on Literacy conference*, Minneapolis, University of Minnesota.

SIMMONS, J.S., SHAFER, R.E. and SHADIOW, L.K. (1990) 'The swinging pendulum: teaching English in the USA, 1965–1987' in BRITTON, J., SHAFER, R.E. and WATSON, K. (eds) *Teaching and Learning English Worldwide*, Clevedon, Multilingual Matters.

SINCLAIR, J. and COULTHARD, M. (1975) *Towards an Analysis of Discourse: the English used by teachers and pupils*, Oxford, Oxford University Press.

SMITH, F. (1978) *Reading*, Cambridge, Cambridge University Press.

SMITH, F. (1985) *Reading*, 2nd edn, Cambridge, Cambridge University Press.

SMITH, M. and SMITH, G. (1990) *A Study Skills Handbook*, Melbourne, Oxford University Press.

SNOWLING, M.J. (ed.) (1985) *Children's Written Language Difficulties*, Windsor, NFER-Nelson.

SOLSKEN, S. (1993) *Literacy, Gender and Work in Families and in School*, Norwood, N.J., Ablex.

STARK, R.E. (1986) 'Prespeech segmental feature development' in FLETCHER, P. and GARMAN, M. (eds) *Language Acquisition: studies in first language development*, 2nd edn, Cambridge, Cambridge University Press.

STEPHENS, W.B. (1987) *Education, Literacy and Society, 1830–1870: the geography of diversity in provincial England*, Manchester, Manchester University Press.

STOREY, J. (1994) 'Mapping the popular: the study of popular culture within British cultural studies', *The European English Messenger*, vol. 3, no. 2, pp. 47–59.

SWAIN, M. (1972) *Bilingualism as a First Language*, PhD dissertation, Irvine, University of California.

SWALES, J.M. (1990) *Genre Analysis: English in academic and research settings*, Cambridge, Cambridge University Press.

TAYLOR, D. (1983) *Family Literacy: young children learning to read and write*, Exeter, N.H., Heinemann.

TEALE, W. and SULZBY, E. (1988) 'Emergent literacy as a perspective for examining how young children become writers and readers' in MERCER, N. (ed.) *Language and Literacy from an Educational Perspective*, vol. 1, Milton Keynes, Open University Press.

TEMPLE, C.A., NATHAN, R.G. and BURRIS, N.A. (1982) *The Beginnings of Writing*, Boston, Allyn & Bacon.

TODD, L. AND HANCOCK, I. (1990) *International English Usage*, London, Routledge.

TOMIC, P. and TRUMPER, R. (1992) 'Canada and the streaming of immigrants: a personal account of the Chilean case' in SATZEWICH, V. (ed.) *Deconstructing a Nation: immigration, multiculturalism and racism in '90s Canada*, Halifax, NS, Fernwood.

TRUDGILL, P. (1986) *Dialects in Contact*, Oxford, Blackwell.

VINEY, P. and VINEY, K. (1989) *Grapevine: students' book 1*, Oxford, Oxford University Press.

VOLTERRA, V. and TAESCHNER, T. (1978) 'The acquisition and development of language by bilingual children', *Journal of Child Language*, vol. 5, pp. 311–26.

VYGOTSKY, L. (1978) *Mind in Society: the development of higher psychological processes*, Cambridge, Mass., Harvard University Press.

WALKER, R. (1994) 'Back to basics: the revival of British studies', *International Association for Teachers of English as a Foreign Language (IATEFL) Newsletter*, no. 123, pp. 9–10.

WARD, LOCK & CO. (undated) *The Complete Letter-writer for Ladies and Gentlemen*, London, Ward Lock.

WATSON-GEGEO, K.A. and BOGGS, S.T. (1977) 'From verbal play to talk story: the role of routines in speech events among Hawaiian children' in ERVIN-TRIPP, S. and MITCHELL-KERNAN, C. (eds) *Child Discourse*, New York, Academic Press.

WELLS, G. (1986) *The Meaning Makers: children learning language and using language to learn*, London, Hodder & Stoughton.

WELLS, G. (1992) 'The centrality of talk in education' in NORMAN, K. (ed.) *Thinking Voices: the work of the National Oracy Project*, London, Hodder & Stoughton.

WILES, S. (1981) 'Language issues in the multicultural classroom' in MERCER, N. (ed.) *Language in School and Community*, London, Edward Arnold.

WILKINSON, A. (1977) *Language and Education*, Oxford, Oxford University Press.

WILLES, M. (1983) *Children into Pupils: a study of language in early schooling*, London, Routledge & Kegan Paul.

WILLIAMS, R. (1961) *The Long Revolution*, London, Chatto & Windus.

WILLINSKY, J. (1990) *The New Literacy: redefining reading and writing in the schools*, London, Routledge.

WOOD, D. (1992) 'Teaching talk' in NORMAN, K. (ed.) *Thinking Voices: the work of the National Oracy Project*, London, Hodder & Stoughton.

WRAY, D., BLOOM, W. and HALL, N. (1989) *Literacy in Action*, Lewes, Falmer.

YOSHIDA, M. (1978) 'The acquisition of English vocabulary by a Japanese-speaking child' in HATCH, E.M. (ed.) *Second language Acquisition*, Rowley, Mass., Newbury House.

YOUSSEF, V. (1991) 'The acquisition of varilingual competence', *English World-Wide*, vol. 12, no. 1, pp. 87–102.

ZENTELLA, A.C. (1981) 'Ta bien, you could answer me in cualquier idioma: Puerto Rican code-switching in bilingual classrooms' in DURAN, R. (ed.) *Latino Language and Communicative Behavior*, Norwood, N.J., Ablex.

ACKNOWLEDGEMENTS

Grateful acknowledgement is made to the following sources for permission to reproduce material in this book:

Text

Pages 21 and 28: de Villiers, P.A. and de Villiers, J.G. 1979, *3 Words 4 Rules*, HarperCollins Publishers Limited; *pages 36–8:* Lieven, E.V.M. 1994, 'Crosslinguistics and crosscultural aspects of language addressed to children' in Gallaway, C. and Richards, B.J. (eds) *Input and Interaction in Language Acquisition*, Cambridge University Press; *page 38–40:* Barton, M.E. and Tomasello, M. 1994, 'The child's expanding social world' in Gallaway, C. and Richards, B.J. (eds) *Input and Interaction in Language Acquisition*, Cambridge University Press; *pages 60–1:* Gleason, J.B. 1973, 'Code switching in children's language' in Moore, T.E. *Cognitive Development and the Acquisition of Language*, Academic Press Inc. and by permission of the author; *page 66:* Eisikovits, E. 1989, 'Girl-talk/boy-talk: sex differences in adolescent speech' in Collins, P. and Blair, D. (eds) *Australian English*, University of Queensland Press; *pages 107–13:* Dombey, H. 1992, 'Lessons learnt at bed-time' in Kimberley, K., Meek, M. and Miller, J. (eds), *New Readings*, A & C Black Ltd, © 1992 Henrietta Dombey; *pages 114–18:* Reprinted by permission of Gordon Wells, *The Meaning Makers: children learning language and using language to learn*, Heinemann, A division of Reed Elsevier Inc., Portsmouth, N.H., 1986; *pages 148–51:* Schmied, J.J. 1991, *English in Africa: an introduction*, © Longman Group UK Limited 1991, reprinted by permission of Addison Wesley Longman Ltd; *pages 151–8:* Maybin, J. 1994, 'Teaching writing: process or genre?' in Brindley, S. (ed.) *Teaching English*, Routledge; *page 162:* Clanchy, M.T. 1984 'Learning to read in the Middle Ages and the role of mothers' in *From Memory to Written Record*, 2nd edition 1993, Blackwell Publishers Ltd, Oxford; *page 171–3:* Dobson, J.L. 1984, 'The interpretation of statistical data' in Brooks, G. and Pugh, A.K. (eds) *Studies in the History of Reading*, NFER; *pages 195–8:* Lankshear, C. and Lawler, M. 1987, 'The corresponding societies: working-class literacy and political reform' in *Literacy, Schooling and Revolution*, © 1987 Colin Lankshear, The Falmer Press, by permission of Taylor and Francis; *pages 201–2:* Carter, R. 1990, *Knowledge about Language and the Curriculum*, Hodder & Stoughton Ltd; *pages 222–3: Language in the National Curriculum (LINC): Materials for professional development* are obtainable from LINC secretary, Department of English, University of Nottingham. Permission for reproducing extracts supplied by Professor R.A. Carter; *pages 238–41:* Martin, J.R., Christie, F. and Rothery, J. 'Social processes in education: a reply to Sawyer and Watson (and others)' in Reid, I. 1987, *The Place of Genre in Learning*, Centre for Research in Cultural Communication, Deakin University; *page 252:* Thiong'o, N.W. 1964, *Weep Not, Child*, Heinemann Educational Books, reprinted by permission of Heinemann Publishers (Oxford) Ltd; *page 277:* Adapted from Achebe, A. 1958, *Things Fall Apart*, Heinemann Educational Books Ltd, by permission of Reed Books; *page 278:* Permission to reprint the poem 'Holding my beads', taken from the collection *I is a long memory woman*, by Grace Nichols, © 1983/1996 Karnak House. All rights reserved; *pages 285–6:* Halliday, M.A.K. 1978, *Language as Social Semiotic*, © 1978 M.A.K. Halliday. Reproduced by permission of Hodder & Stoughton Ltd; *page 292:* Rivers, J. 1994, 'NZ home students "lack literacy"', *The Times Higher Education Supplement*, 28 October 1994, © 1994 Janet Rivers; *page 309:* Vavrus, F.K. 1993, 'When paradigms clash' in Kachru, B.B. (ed.) *Word Englishes: Journal of English as an International and Intranational Language*, Basil Blackwell Ltd.

Figures

Figure 1.1: Bruner, J.S. and Garton, A. 1978, *Human Growth and Development*, Clarendon Press, by permission of Oxford University Press; *Figure 3.1:* Central Project Team 1989, *National Writing Project 1989, Becoming a Writer*, School Curriculum and Assessment Authority; *Figures 3.6 and 3.7: A Rich Resource – writing and language diversity*, Thomas Nelson and Sons Ltd, © 1990 School Curriculum and Assessment Authority; *Figure 5.2:* Cressy, D. 1980, *Literary and Social Order*, p. 177, graph 8.1, Cambridge University Press; *Figure 6.1: KS3 English Units*, 1995, English and Media Centre; *Figure 7.1:* Ueyama, M. and Tamaki, D.C. 1984, *Chuo English Studies Book 1*, Chuotosho, Japan; *Figure 7.2:* Hartley and Viney 1978, *Streamline English – departures*, © Oxford University Press. Reprinted by permission of Oxford University Press; *Figure 7.3:* Viney and Viney 1989, *Grapevine: Students Book 1*, © Oxford University Press. Reprinted by permission of Oxford University Press; *Figure 7.4:* Harding, K. and Henderson, P. 1995, *High Season*, © Oxford University Press. Reprinted by permission of Oxford University Press; *Figure 7.5:* Hollett, V. 1994, *Business Opportunities*, © Oxford University Press. Reprinted by permission of Oxford University Press; *Figure 7.6:* Furnborough, P., Cowgill, S., Greaves, H. and Sapin, K. 1980, *A New Start*, Heinemann Educational Books, reprinted by permission of Heinemann Publishers (Oxford) Limited; *Figure 7.7:* Houston, C. 1989, *English Language Development Across the Curriculum (ELDAC)* © 1989 Immigrant Education Services, Division of Special Services, Department of Education, Queensland; *Figure 7.8:* Janks, H. 1993, *Language Position*, Witwatersrand University Press and Hodder & Stoughton Education (S.A.).

Tables

Table 1.1: Sanders, E.K. 1961, 'Where are speech sounds learned', *Journal of Speech and Hearing Disorders*, pp. 55–63, figure 1, American Speech–Language–Hearing Association; *Table 1.2:* Ingram, D. 1989, *First Language Acquisition*, p. 142, table 6.1, Cambridge University Press; *Table 5.1:* Cressy, D. 1980, *Literary and Social Order*, p. 136, table 6.8, Cambridge University Press.

Other illustrations

Front cover: Monk, J. 1992, 'The language of argument in the writing of young children' in Bain, R. et al. (eds) 1992, *Looking into Language*, Hodder Headline plc; *page 108:* Hutchins, P. 1970, *Rosie's Walk*, Penguin Books, © 1970 Patricia Hutchins; *page 114:* Lord, J.V. and Burroway, J. 1988, *The GIANT Jam Sandwich*, Random House UK Ltd; *page 161 and 172 (top):* The Mansell Collection Ltd; *page 237 Figure 1:* Taken from *1 The Magic Key: Stage 5 Reading Tree* by Roderick Hunt, by permission of Oxford University Press; *page 278:* Barnaby's Picture Library/Gerald Cubitt; *page 301:* The Learning Workshop, Centre for Higher Education and Access Development, University of North London.

Index